Analyzing Broadband Networks

Frame Relay, SMDS, & ATM

THE NETWORK TROUBLESHOOTING LIBRARY

Analyzing Broadband Networks

Frame Relay, SMDS, & ATM

Mark A. Miller, P.E.

M&T BOOKS

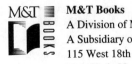

M&T Books
A Division of MIS:Press
A Subsidiary of Henry Holt and Company, Inc.
115 West 18th Street
New York, New York 10011

Limits of Liability and Disclaimer of Warranty
The Author and Publisher of this book have used their best efforts in preparing the book and the programs contained in it. These efforts include the development, research, and testing of the theories and programs to determine their effectiveness.

The Author and Publisher make no warranty of any kind, expressed or implied, with regard to these programs or the documentation contained in this book. The Author and Publisher shall not be liable in any event for incidental or consequential damages in connection with, or arising out of, the furnishing, performance, or use of these programs.

Trademarks
All products, names, and services are trademarks or registered trademarks of their respective companies. See "Trademarks" section beginning on page 509.

Library of Congress Cataloging-in-Publication Data

Miller, Mark, 1955–
    Analyzing broadband networks: frame relay, SMDS & ATM / by Mark A. Miller.
      p. cm. — (The Network troubleshooting library)
    Includes bibliographical references and index.
    ISBN 1-55851-389-2 : $44.95
    1. Broadband communication systems. I. Title. II. Series.
TK5103.2.M55   1994   94-32690
004.6'6--dc20   CIP

97 96 95 94   4 3 2 1

Development Editor: Cheryl Goldberg
Technical Editor: John Thompson
Copy Editor: Laura Moorehead

Cover Design: Gary Szczecina
Production Editor: Eileen Mullin
Associate Production Editor: Cari Geffner

To my parents,
for the good things they taught me

Contents

Table of Illustrations

Preface

Previous volumes in the *Network Troubleshooting Library* have looked at LANs and internetworks using traditional WAN technologies, such as leased lines, T1 circuits, and X.25. This seventh volume in the series considers the next generation—the broadband technologies.

Several key factors are driving the demand for the increased bandwidth of broadband technologies. The increasing popularity of LANs has lead to an increase in traffic on local LAN segments. New desktop applications, such as multimedia, further strain the capacity of the local segment. And as more LAN segments have been installed, the need to interconnect these segments has placed greater demands on WAN segments.

This book examines how three broadband technologies, frame relay, Switched Multimegabit Data Service (SMDS), and Asynchronous Transfer Mode (ATM), solve the bandwidth challenge.

Chapter 1 discusses the market requirements for broadband networks, topologies for frame relay, SMDS, and ATM networks, and uses case studies to illustrate implementations of these technologies.

The next nine chapters are devoted to frame relay, SMDS, and ATM. Each section contains three chapters. The first chapter in each section discusses architectural issues, including standards and topologies. The second details the protocols; the third presents case studies to illustrate the operation of the protocols, and how they interact with other LAN and WAN systems. The concluding chapter discusses the management of broadband networks.

As always, I am indebted to a number of companies and individuals who supported this project.

Three protocol-analyzer vendors generously loaned their equipment and resources to support this project. The frame relay section was supported by Network General Corp., Bob Berger, John Lenko, and Tim O'Neill. The SMDS section was supported by Tekelec, Josh Barinstein, Ted Butch, Eric Rosser, Jim Smith, and Steve Smith. The ATM section was supported by the Hewlett-Packard Co., Gregan Crawford, Pauline Hale, Dragos Ruiu, and Andrew Scott.

The following network managers contributed case studies that appear in Chapters 1, 4, 7, and 10: Gregan Crawford, Dan Cude, Dan Grim, Russel Hale, Ellis Hillinger, Peter Kavaler, Leslie Nelson, Dragos Ruiu, and Rudy Welter.

Several individuals, each expert in specific protocols, deserve credit for their review and comments on the manuscript: Gregan Crawford, Cedric Druce, Paul Franchois, Dick Rawson, Dave Rubal, Andrew Scott, and Carl M. Shinn, Jr.

Carol Goodwin did much of the research for the appendices, and Krystal Valdez provided word-processing support. David Hertzke of Integrated Graphics Communication took stacks of very rough drawings and turned them into legible figures.

My editors, including Brenda McLaughlin, Cheryl Goldberg, Laura Moorhead, Eileen Mullin, and John Thompson, looked after the details—from misplaced semicolons to incorrect bit patterns.

Most important, Holly, Nathan, and Nicholas provided the support that made a project of this magnitude possible. Boomer faithfully took me on 5 a.m. runs, and Brutus handled household security while we were gone.

It's good to be part of such a distinguished team.

mark@diginet.com
August 1994

Why This Book is for You

Analyzing Broadband Networks, the seventh volume of the popular Network Troubleshooting Library, has been designed to prepare network designers, managers and engineers to troubleshoot the new generation of networking services: Frame Relay, Switched Multimegabit Data Service (SMDS) and Asynchronous Transfer Mode (ATM).

These broadband transmission systems address three key networking trends: high bandwidth applications, such as CAD/CAM and multimedia, at the desktop; increased traffic on local LAN segments as a result of the growth in users; and extensive internetworking between local and remote LAN segments. And if the projections of industry analysts hold true, at least one of these three trends will surface on your network.

Two types of readers will benefit from this book. LAN administrators will learn about the WANs that their systems and hosts depend on for remote access and connectivity. WAN administrators will learn about the technologies that are quickly replacing proven analog and leased lines for network-to-network communications. This book will help both types of readers position themselves to understand the new technologies that are expected to rearchitect the networking landscape by the end of this decade.

From this book, you will:

▼ Discover which broadband technology is best suited for a particular application.

▼ Explore the architecture of frame relay, SMDS and ATM - how these networks are designed, and their functional characteristics.

▼ Understand the broadband protocols—studying their operation at the bit level.

▼ Learn from 14 case studies, which illustrate these protocols in operation, and typical failures that may occur.

▼ Identify typical protocol failures in frame relay, SMDS and ATM networks.

▼ Benefit from the nine reference appendices, packed with useful information on broadband networking vendors, standards and terminology.

Use this book as a guide to prepare yourself and your networks for the next generation in data communications.

Broadband Technologies

This book examines the analysis of the following broadband networking technologies: frame relay, Switched Multimegabit Data Service (SMDS), and Asynchronous Transfer Mode (ATM). But before I discuss these technologies in detail, you need to understand why these broadband transport systems are necessary.

1.1 Broadband Applications

High-bandwidth technologies are necessary primarily for three reasons: increased traffic on local LAN segments, internetworking between local and remote LAN segments and high-bandwidth desktop applications.

In the late 1980s, applications such as terminal-to-host communication and file sharing operated over low- to medium-speed LANs such as ARCnet, Ethernet, and token ring. As LANs became more prevalent in business environments, the number of users per LAN increased. And as users became more aware of the capabilities of LANs, the traffic per user increased as well. Both of these factors increased traffic on the local LAN segment. In many cases, network managers redistributed computing loads by segmenting a large LAN into several smaller subnetworks using bridges or routers. However, once they reached the network capacity, managers needed a high-bandwidth solution.

Distributed computing architectures, based on minicomputers, caused a second source of internetwork traffic, LAN-to-LAN communication. As this traffic increased, older solutions such as 9.6 Kbps and 56 Kbps leased lines were replaced by higher capacity T1 circuits operating at 1.544 Mbps. But such increased speed came at a price. Not only was each T1 line expensive, but distributed environments required numerous T1 lines. As a result, the cost of point-to-point circuits became a significant issue. Again, economical, high-bandwidth LAN and/or WAN channels were becoming increasingly necessary.

Desktop applications, such as computer-aided design (CAD), computer-aided manufacturing (CAM), and large database files, also stretched the limits of LANs and WANs (see Figure 1–1). Isochronous, or time-sensitive applications, such as video or multimedia, require both high bandwidth and a low end-to-end delay. As these applications grow in popularity, internetwork designs will have to support them.

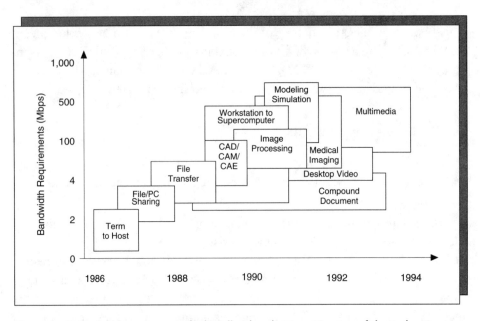

Figure 1–1. Bandwidth requirements for broadband applications (*Courtesy of the Yankee Group*)

Unfortunately, growing application requirements have not necessarily been matched by increasing resources. Studies by market researchers at Infonetics Research Inc. of San Jose, Calif., show a great disparity between the growth in LANs and internetworking devices and the systems and staff to support them [1–1]. Between 1991 and 1995, the number of installed LAN segments is projected to increase 150 percent, while internetwork devices, such as bridges and routers, will increase 140 percent (see Figure 1–2). Unfortunately, budgets are expected to increase just 50 percent during the same time period, and staff expenditures will only rise by 10 percent. So, growing applications, support requirements, and interconnection traffic, will be putting a technological squeeze on network managers. And in many cases, networking managers will have to do more with fewer resources.

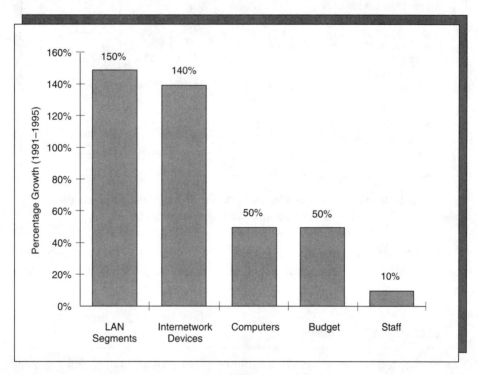

Figure 1–2. LAN and resource growth (1991 to 1995) (© 1992 Infonetics Research Inc. "Critical Network Management Tools: What Network Managers Really Need")

The high bandwidth and favorable economics of broadband technologies such as frame relay, SMDS, and ATM offer one way out of this jam. As a result, these technologies are expected to shoulder the growth in interconnection traffic, edging out the traditional solutions, such as leased lines, X.25, and multiplexer backbones (see Figure 1–3 and Reference [1–2]).

Technology	Avg. % of Traffic			Avg. % Change
	1993	1995	1997	
ATM	0%	8%	16%	16%
Frame Relay	4%	10%	10%	6%
Transparent LAN Services	2%	3%	3%	1%
SMDS	1%	1%	1%	0%
ISDN	2%	2%	2%	0%
Leased Non-Digital Line, router Backbone	2%	0%	0%	-2%
Leased Non-Digital Line, Multiplexer Backbone	5%	3%	3%	-2%
Leased Digital Line, router backbone	21%	24%	22%	-2%
Dial-up	9%	8%	7%	
X.25	10%	8%	7%	-3%
SNA	17%	13%	13%	-4%
Leased digital line, Multiplexer Backbone	21%	16%	14%	-7%

Figure 1–3. Large-site LAN interconnection traffic mix (1993 to 1997) (© 1993 Infonetics Research Inc. "The Branch Office Explosion: LAN Interconnection in the '90s")

This chapter gives you an overview of these technologies and looks at some real-world examples of how these broadband technologies have solved internetworking challenges.

1.2 Fast Packet Technologies

Fast packet technologies, which are the foundation of all broadband architectures, can be divided into two categories: frame relay and cell relay technology (see Figure 1–4). Frame relay technologies use a variable length unit for data transmission. In other words, the size of a frame transmitted on a LAN or WAN may vary, depending on the amount of information coming from the higher layer protocol process. Frames may contain thousands of octets of user information. As a result, the effects of the frame overhead, such as the frame header and trailer, which typically contain addressing, error control, and other administrative information, is usually insignificant.

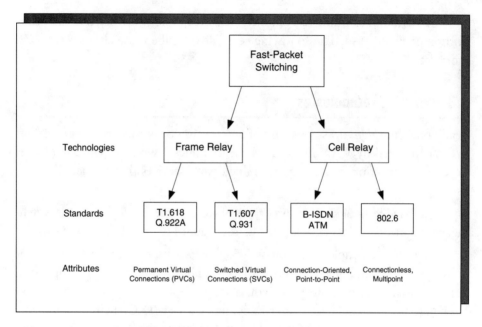

Figure 1–4. Fast packet switching technologies *(Source: Frame Relay Forum)*

Cell relay technology, on the other hand, uses fixed-length cells, usually 53 octets long. (An octet is a data unit that is 8 bits long). Cells typically have a 5-octet header (the overhead) followed by a 48-bit payload. As a result, the overhead ratio is relatively high (5/53 or about 9.4 percent). But because cells have a fixed length, they may be transmitted (and therefore received) at regular intervals. This is beneficial for time-sensitive applications, such as packetized voice, video, or multimedia.

The standards for frame relay have been defined by the International Telecommunications Union Telecommunications Standardization Sector (ITU-T) and the American National Standards Institute (ANSI). Cell relay standards have been defined by the ITU-T as part of its work in Broadband Integrated Services Digital Network (B-ISDN) and Asynchronous Transfer Mode (ATM) technologies. In addition, the Institute of Electrical and Electronics Engineers (IEEE) has defined a Metropolitan Area Network (MAN) standard for cell relay, IEEE 802.6. A subset of the IEEE 802.6 work forms the basis for Switched Multimegabit Data Service (SMDS), a network service developed by Bell Communications Research Inc. (also called Bellcore).

The attributes of frame relay and cell relay technology are listed in the lower portion of Figure 1–4. The following sections describe these characteristics in more detail.

1.3 Switching Technologies

Traditional internetworks consisted of a collection of workstations, hosts, and LANs connected by WAN links such as leased lines. Two types of technologies make the connection: switching technologies and services that connect the end-user equipment to the network.

Broadband technologies use three types of switching technologies: circuit switching, packet switching, and cell switching (see Figure 1–5 and Reference [1–3]).

The earliest technology, circuit-switched networks, guarantees the end user a predetermined amount of bandwidth. A telephone circuit is an example of a circuit-switched connection. When you place a telephone call, the various Local Exchange Carrier (LEC) and Inter-Exchange Carrier (IXC) switching systems establish a connection between the calling and called parties. Once all the switches have set up the connection, the remote telephone begins ringing. The end-to-end connection is completed when the called party answers.

A circuit connection may consist of a physical and a virtual path. The physical connection is the electrical or optical transmission path through the various switching elements. This path may change with network conditions such as link failures, congested routes, and so on. The virtual connection describes the path between end points, but not necessarily with reference to the physical path. So, a physical path between Denver and New York may have an intermediate switch in Chicago, but the virtual connection remains Denver to New York. The end user does not need to know about the intermediate stop as long as it does not affect the communication parameters, such as delay and throughput.

There are two types of virtual connections: permanent and switched. A permanent virtual connection (PVC) is analogous to a leased line that the carrier establishes and always keeps connected. To change a PVC, you need to call the carrier, who then changes the network configuration. A switched virtual connection (SVC) is similar to a telephone call; it is initiated by call-setup messages sent by the calling party.

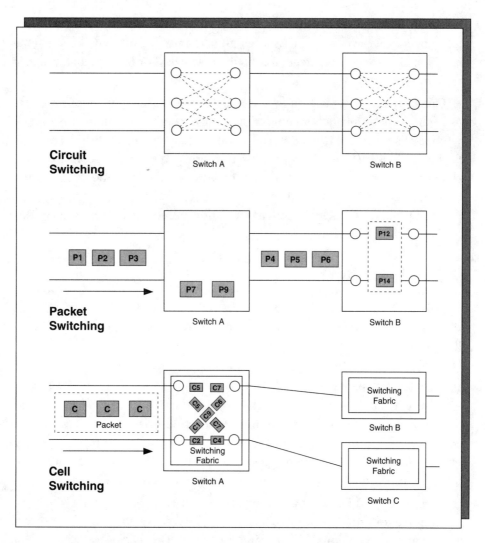

Figure 1–5. Primary switching technologies *(Courtesy of Cisco Systems Inc.)*

Packet-switched networks improved circuit switching by allowing dynamic sharing of the available LAN or WAN bandwidth. Workstations transmit packets of information, which are switched into and out of hubs, servers, bridges, and so on, until they reach their destination. The packet length may vary, depending on the transmission speed, network protocols, and other factors inherent in the network.

Today, administrators primarily compare packet switching to cell-switching technologies. Cell switching fixes the length of the packets at a small value. This technology offers the advantage of a predictable delay, or latency, and a higher throughput.

One of two services is used to connect the end user's equipment to the network: connection-oriented or connectionless. Connection-oriented service, used by frame relay and ATM, requires call-setup procedures to establish the path. A telephone call is an example of a connection-oriented service. In contrast, connectionless service, used by SMDS, relies on addressing information within each packet that each switching node examines to determine the appropriate path. Mailing a letter, which includes both a destination and source address, is an example of connectionless service.

1.4 Broadband Networks

Frame relay, SMDS, and ATM are the three currently available broadband technologies. Each has different technical characteristics, and may not be available in all regions.

1.4.1 Frame relay networks

Frame relay is a streamlined Data Link Layer protocol, which is often compared to X.25. Frame relay provides a simple, connection-oriented frame-transport service, and is commonly used for private-line replacements in mesh topology networks (see Figure 1–6). Higher layer protocols in end-user devices must provide other protocol requirements, such as flow control or error recovery.

Most LECs and IXCs provide frame relay service as either a tariffed or special assembly offering. Both intra- and inter-LATA service is available. Access rates range from Fractional T1 (*n x* 56/64 Kbps) to DS1 (1.544 Mbps), to even higher rates such as DS3 (44.736 Mbps). Pricing is typically based on the access-line rate, the number of PVCs assigned to the access line, and the Committed Information Rate (CIR) associated with the access line.

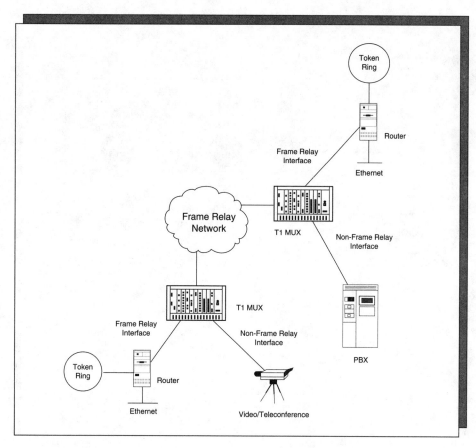

Figure 1–6. A hybrid frame relay network *(Courtesy of Cisco Systems Inc.)*

1.4.2 Switched Multimegabit Data Service

SMDS was developed by Bellcore, the research and development organization that serves many of the Bell Operating Companies. SMDS is a connectionless subset of the Distributed Queue Dual Bus (DQDB), a MAN technology defined by the IEEE 802.6 standard (see Figure 1–7). SMDS features include any-to-any connectivity, group addressing and multicasting, and addressing similar to telephone numbers, which is defined by ITU-T Recommendation E.164. Its similarities to analog telephone service have prompted some analysts to call SMDS "dialtone for data." Enhanced features include call blocking, call validation, and call screening, which provide virtual private network services.

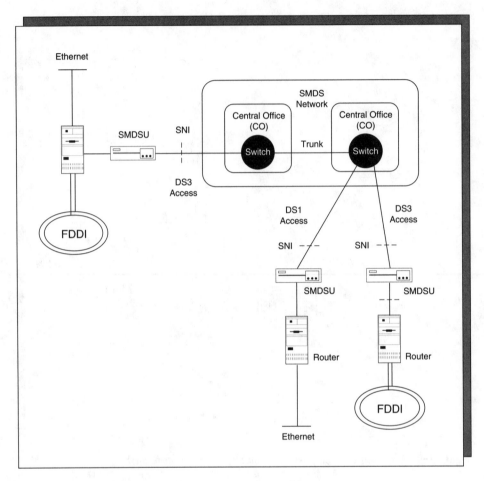

Figure 1–7. An SMDS internetworking scenario *(Courtesy of Cisco Systems Inc.)*

Applications for SMDS include LAN interconnection; high-speed, remote database access; packet audio and video; resource sharing by educational institutions; image transfer; and teleradiology.

Most LECs and the IXC MCI provide SMDS. Access lines are typically available at the DS1 and DS3 rates, with subrate speeds (*n x 56/64* Kbps) emerging in some areas. The cost of SMDS is typically a flat rate, insensitive to usage, and defined by an access class. The access class is determined by the Sustained Information Rate (SIR), which is the service limit on an access line and can range from 1.17 Mbps. to 34 Mbps.

1.4.3 Asynchronous Transfer Mode

A connection-oriented service for both LAN and WAN applications (see Figure 1–8), ATM is unique among the three broadband technologies. All ATM applications share a foundation in cell switching, based on 53 octet cells. A number of interfaces operating at 25 Mbps to 622 Mbps have been defined. The 100 Mbps interface is used for LANs. Currently, the 45 Mbps and 155 Mbps for WANs are the most popular. Nearly all major internetworking vendors, LECs, and IXCs currently develop ATM products and services. Presently, ATM is undergoing field trials and testing. Most carriers have not widely publicized their service characteristics and pricing yet.

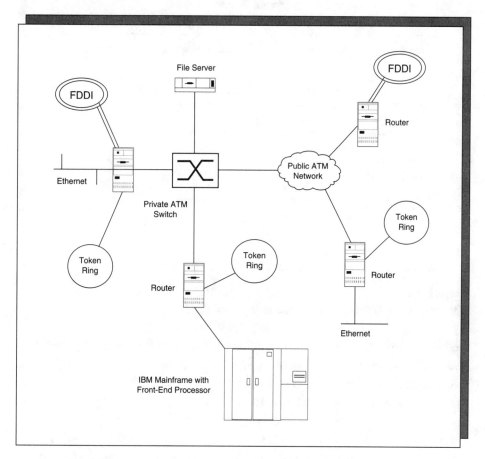

Figure 1–8. A practical ATM architecture *(Courtesy of Cisco Systems Inc.)*

1.5 Selecting the Broadband Technology

Each broadband technology has its strengths and weaknesses. So, each is best suited to a particular application. For example, Infonetics Research's studies indicate that frame relay service is most readily available in Europe and South America (see Figure 1–9a). SMDS is often chosen for its cost-effectiveness (see Figure 1–9b). ATM's great strength is its ability to consolidate multiple signals, such as voice, data, and video (see Figure 1–9c).

Frame Relay	
Why Chosen	Why Not Chosen
Speed, performance, bandwidth	Don't know enough to evaluate it
Cost-effectiveness	Too much bandwidth for our needs
Reliability, high availability	Unproven technology, too new
Consolidate lines for data, voice image	Will wait for SMDS or ATM
Availablilty in Europe and S. America	Lack of availability
Virtual network with upgrade path for technology and bandwidth	No need
Low-entry price point	Too little bandwidth
More efficient bandwidth allocation	Satellite was less expensive
Multiprotocol services	We have small bursts, not large bursts
T1 muxes waste bandwidth, frame relay does not	Lack of ubiquitous service
Replacing X.25 network with frame relay	We will pick speed in smaller increments on T1

Figure 1–9a. Why users choose frame relay for large sites (© 1993 Infonetics Research Inc. "The Branch Office Explosion: LAN Interconnection in the '90s")

Deploying broadband technologies takes considerable investment by the LECs and IXCs. User demand and willingness to pay are key factors in the LECs' and IXCs' decision to invest in these new services. For network managers, the projected revenues from these broadband services give us some clues as to the likelihood that one service will be financially stronger than another (see Figure 1–10). Frame relay service should have a steady, linear growth until 1997. SMDS experienced growth in the early 1990s, and will taper off later in the decade. ATM has had a slow start, but should begin growing rapidly in 1995.

SMDS	
Why Chosen	Why Not Chosen
Bandwidth performance Cost-effective Can handle data, image, voice	Unaware or never evaluated Too much bandwidth for our needs Not cost-effective Only available in limited locations

Figure 1–9b. Why users choose SMDS for large sites (© 1993 Infonetics Research Inc. "The Branch Office Explosion: LAN Interconnection in the '90s")

ATM	
Why Chosen	Why Not Chosen

More speed, more bandwidth
Consolidation (voice, video, data)
Handles video
Cost/megabit is attractive
Easier than point-to-point network
Most stable of emerging technologies
It is or will be a standard
Handles high burst speeds
Can go desktop-to-desktop
Will handle document imaging and
  multimedia
More reliable than other technologies
	Technology is too new, unproven
	Reliability is suspect—new technology
	Costs too much
	Too much bandwidth for our needs
	We haven't evaluated ATM yet
	Not as cost-effective as frame relay
	Downsizing is our priority—we don't
	  have money for new technology
	Don't want to change existing
	  technology
	Not available yet

Figure 1–9c. Why users choose ATM for large sites (© 1993 Infonetics Research Inc. "The Branch Office Explosion: LAN Interconnection in the '90s")

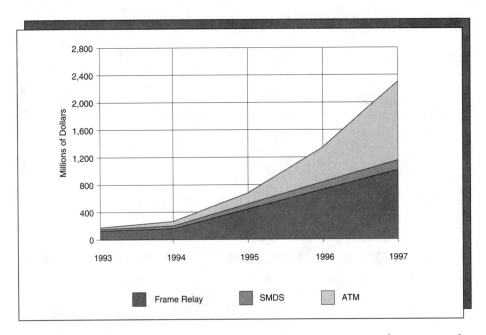

Figure 1–10. Worldwide aggregate service revenues, 1993 to 1997 (© 1993 Infonetics Research Inc. "The Branch Office Explosion: LAN Interconnection in the '90s")

1.6 Broadband Networks

The broadband networking industry is unique in the widespread support of frame relay, SMDS, and ATM from users and vendors.

The Frame Relay Forum (FRF) was founded in May 1991 as a consortium of users, vendors, and carriers [1–4]. All members (currently more than 100 people) share an interest in promoting frame relay technology for both private networking and as a public carrier service. The FRF focuses on promoting acceptance and interoperability of frame relay technology. To achieve such goals, the FRF promotes the ANSI and ITU-T standards for frame relay and develops Implementation Agreements (IAs) that further define how those standards will be adopted. Adherence to both international standards and the IAs provide a greater likelihood of multivendor interoperability. FRF efforts are divided among a number of committees, including the Technical Committee, the Inter-Carrier Committee, the Testing and Interoperability Committee, and the Marketing and Education Committee.

The SMDS Interest Group (SIG) was founded in late 1990 to advance SMDS as an interoperable, worldwide data-connectivity technology [1–5]. Currently, the SIG has more than 60 members, including users, consultants, equipment vendors, and carriers. These organizations collaborate in three working groups. The Technical Working Group promotes interoperability between SMDS and other major networking protocols such as AppleTalk, DECnet, NetWare, and TCP/IP. The Intercarrier and Network Management Working Group promotes cooperation between LECs and IXCs, including network maintenance and management concerns. The Public Relations and User-Awareness Working Group promotes SMDS at conferences, trade shows, and in the networking press.

The ATM Forum was founded in October 1991 to speed the development of ATM technology, while assuring interoperability between various vendor products [1–6]. The more than 425 members include computer manufacturers, internetworking vendors, LECs and IXCs, semiconductor manufacturers, research organizations, and users. The ATM Forum working groups include: the Technical Committee, Market Awareness and Education, the European Activity Committee, and the Enterprise Network Roundtable, which is a users' group.

The ATM Forum does not duplicate the work of the international standards bodies, such as the ITU-T, but instead develops specifications based on standards created by those groups. Examples include the ATM User-Network Interface, the Broadband Intercarrier Interface, and the Data Exchange Interface.

1.7 Frame Relay Applications

R.W. Beck, an engineering firm headquartered in the Pacific Northwest with 10 offices nationwide, selected frame relay service as its backbone transport. The firm's broadband requirements included bursty data transfers, including reports, proposals, CAD drawings, and office-automation functions such as spreadsheets.

In the 1970s, the company implemented a WAN to handle remote host access and electronic mail (e-mail). Remote users at five locations were connected to host computers at the headquarters location via multiplexers and 9.6 Kbps leased lines (see Figure 1–11). These users also used dial-up lines to connect to a mini-computer-based e-mail system. So, field offices could communicate with headquarters and one another via headquarters, but not directly with each other.

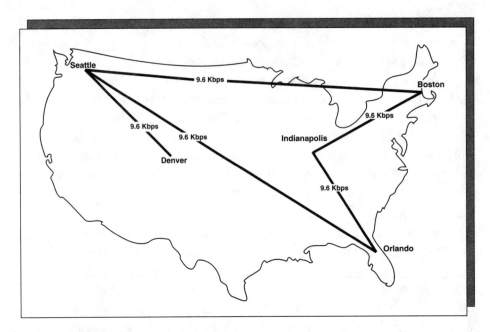

Figure 1–11. R.W. Beck point-to-point network

In the early 1990s, the company chartered a task force to re-evaluate its internetworking requirements. This group recommended that the company install Ethernet LANs using Microsoft Corp.'s LAN Manager network operating system in each office, ensuring companywide compatibility. It selected TCP/IP as the common internetworking protocol, and applied for Class C IP addresses for each location.

The firm selected frame relay as the technology basis for the broadband internetwork and WilTel of Tulsa, Okla., as the frame relay IXC provider. LECs in each city provided the connection between the R.W. Beck offices and the WilTel network (see Figure 1–12).

The company began its conversion to frame relay service in January 1993, and completed it in six months. Each field location was connected with 56/64 Kbps PVCs, while the headquarters was connected at 256 Kbps. Each location has PVCs to at least two other locations from a single serial port on the routers, which were supplied by Advanced Computer Communications (ACC). If a location requires communication to other locations, routers at intermediate locations complete the connection to the selected destination. The combination of routers and multiple PVCs provided any-to-any connectivity between all locations.

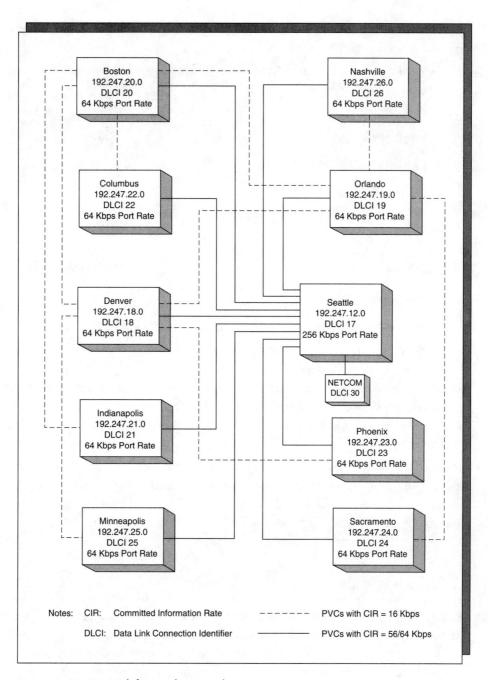

Figure 1–12. R.W. Beck frame relay network

Currently, e-mail (Microsoft Mail), file transfer, and remote-host access are the primary applications.

The total cost for the frame relay network included the following:

10 ACC Nile routers	$42,350
4 Digital Link DSUs (DS1)	$ 6,000
6 Adtran DSUs (DS0)	$ 3,300
Cables and Miscellaneous	$ 1,250
Total	$52,900

Annual router maintenance contract:	$ 1,500 per year
LEC and IXC installation charges:	$ 5,000
LEC and IXC recurring charges:	$ 8,000 per month

The most immediate improvement has been an increase in throughput, any-to-any connectivity between locations, and a reduction in monthly telecommunication expenses from $10,000 to $8,000. When an Internet connection was required, the company was able to add the link as another PVC without additional hardware.

R.W. Beck officials view the network as a strategic tool that enhances and enriches its relationships with clients and lets it provide superior services. By achieving the network implementation—taking advantage of dispersed resource capabilities—the firm has facilitated the exchange of ideas and collaborative thinking throughout the firm. (References [1–7] through [1–13] are journal articles about frame relay pricing and applications issues.)

1.8 SMDS Application

When the University of Delaware ran out of capacity on its leased-line network, it chose SMDS from Bell Atlantic to meet its bandwidth requirements. The university's network, called UDelnet, connects its main campus with seven other facilities. Each location has an Ethernet LAN, which is connected to the other campuses using Wellfleet routers. Applications on UDelnet are centered on TCP/IP access from remote campuses, including TELNET, FTP, e-mail, and Internet access.

The original network consisted of 56 Kbps leased lines connecting each location with the main campus (see Figure 1–13). A combination of multiplexers and routers linked the main campus Ethernet to similar networks in the other locations. The university used TCP/IP to access databases at the remote campuses, such as an Ocean Database at the Marine Studies facility in Lewes, Del.

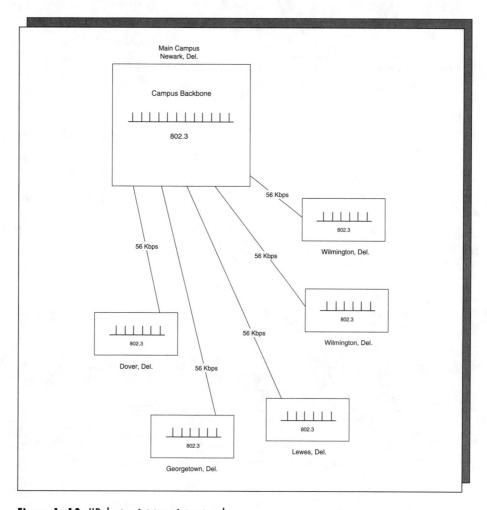

Figure 1–13. UDelnet point-to-point network

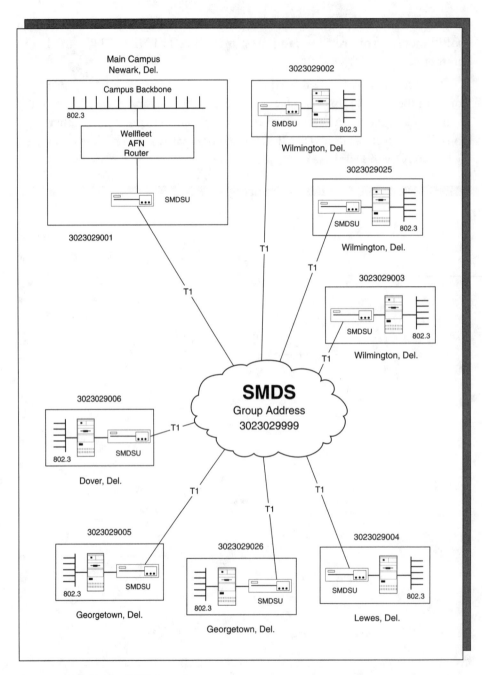

Figure 1–14. UDelnet SMDS network

SMDS was installed in November 1993, and implementation took approximately six months (see Figure 1–14). The total costs for the SMDS service were as follows:

Hardware

Digital Link SMDSU (8 at $4,400 each):	$35,200
Wellfleet AFN Routers (8 at $3,600 each):	$28,800
Total hardware costs:	$64,000

Circuits

Per location (8 at $475 per month):	$ 3,800
Annualized:	$45,600
Total first-year cost of the SMDS network:	$82,200

The major advantages of the SMDS network were a savings of $2,000 per month over the previous leased-line solution, and an increase in transport speed from 56 Kbps to 1.17 Mbps. This savings was attributed to the distance-insensitive pricing on which the Bell Atlantic SMDS offering was tariffed. The increase in transport speed greatly improved the response times for many applications, but it was a particular improvement for the Ocean Database, which is accessed worldwide. (References [1–14] through [1–16] are journal articles about SMDS availability and design issues.)

1.9 ATM Application

Image transfer, one of the most frequently touted ATM applications, is one of the key features of the FISHnet, a fiber-optic system designed by Cablevision Systems Corp. of Woodbury, N.Y., that links physicians and researchers at Brookhaven National Laboratory, SUNY-Stony Brook, and Grumman Data Systems (see Figure 1–15). FISHnet, which stands for Fiber Optic, Island-Wide,

Super High-speed Network, currently links medical and environmental researchers at the three institutions.

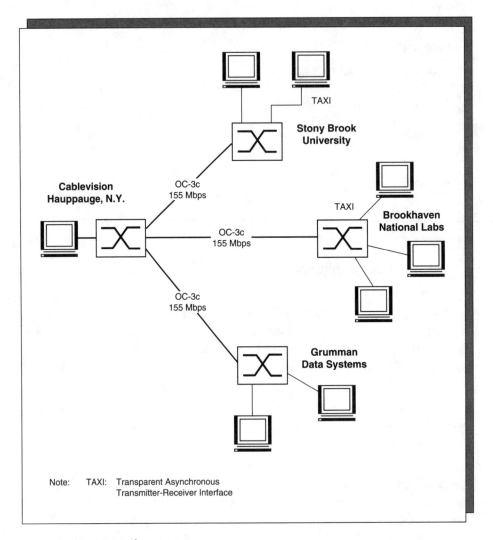

Figure 1–15. FISHnet Phase 1

An optical backbone, operating at the OC-3c rate of 155 Mbps, connects ATM switches from Fore Systems Inc. of Warrendale, Pa., at each location. Sun workstations connect to the ATM switches using a 100Mbps TAXI interface.

Currently, the FISHnet system lets doctors at Stonybrook Hospital read patient X-rays taken at Brookhaven almost as soon as they have been taken. If the doctor needs additional diagnostics, such as a different X-ray position, the X-ray can be retaken immediately.

A second application visually models the horizontal spread of groundwater contamination, showing the effects of contaminated leakage over a 20-year period. The visualization tool lets researchers view the information many different ways. Researchers can see it in different colors, and they can slice through the image at different points. An animation mode displays the data at successive time intervals to illustrate the dynamics of the contaminants' movement. The system stores data, which includes more than 200,000 irregularly spaced grid points, in a Paragon computer at Stony Brook. Yet, researchers at Brookhaven can access and examine that data using visualization software on their local Sun workstation. Currently, FISHnet is an experimental network that interconnects major research organizations on Long Island, N.Y. But when fully deployed, it will offer high-speed connectivity for multimedia data to all of Long Island's businesses, medical centers, and educational institutions.

The next wave of expansion is expected to be university hospitals and publishing companies (see Figure 1–16). Many of these organizations have large investments in legacy LAN architectures. To protect this investment, the system will first implement LAN connectivity into ATM on the WAN, and only gradually migrate to ATM at the desktop. So, ATM-capable hubs and routers will play an interim role in this connectivity plan. ATM switches will be deployed at each premise only when the application requirements can justify the hardware expense. (References [1–17] through [1–21] are journal articles about ATM technology and field trials.)

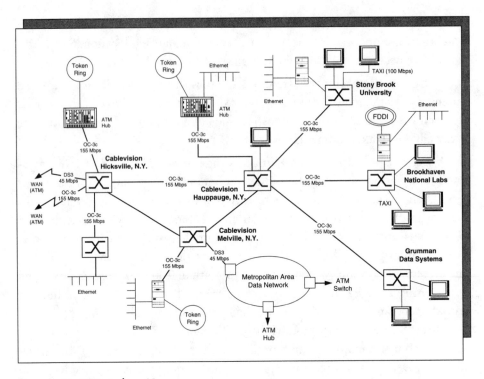

Figure 1–16. FISHnet phase 11

1.10 Comparing Broadband Technologies

This chapter has examined the technologies and applications of broadband networks. Figure 1–17 summarizes the various attributes that we have discussed, such as transmission rates, information unit size, connection orientation, and so on. In many cases, the type of application data to be transmitted gives an advantage to one technology over another. In other situations, the selection of one broadband technology over another boils down to a question of availability—not all of these services are offered by every LEC or IXC.

The rest of this book examines broadband networking technology from three perspectives. The first chapter of each section discusses architectural issues for frame relay, SMDS, and ATM (Chapters 2, 5, and 8). The second chapter of each section provides technical details on the protocols (Chapters 3, 6, and 9). The third chapter in each section includes several case studies illustrating the operation of the protocols (Chapters 4, 7, and 10). Chapter 11 looks at the management of broadband networks.

Feature	X.25	Frame Relay	SMDS	ATM
Standardized By	ITU-T, ISO, and others	ITU-T, ANSI, IEEE 802.2	Bellcore, ETSI	ITU-T
Current Typical Speeds	9.6–64 Kbps	56 Kbps–2 Mbps	1–34 Mbps	45–155 Mbps
Information Unit Size	Variable (up to 4,096 octets)	Variable (up to 4,096 octets)	Variable (up to 9,188 octets)	Fixed (53 octets)
Multicasting	No	Yes (not widely implemented)	Yes	Proposed
Addressing	X.121 Variable length (up to 14 decimal digit, IDNs commonly extended to 15 digits)	Fixed length (10-bit DLCIs)	Variable length (10 to 15 digits, based on telephone numbers)	Fixed length (24-bit VPI/VCI)
Connectionless	No	No	Yes	No
PVCs	Yes	Yes	N/A	Yes
SVCs	Yes	Proposed	N/A	Yes
Explicit, per-virtual-circuit flow control	Yes	No	N/A	No
Data Link Level Error Correction	Yes	No	No	No

Figure 1–17. Comparison of packet-service technologies *(Courtesy of Cisco Systems Inc.)*

1.11 References

[1–1]   Infonetics Research Inc. "Critical Network Management Tools: What Network Managers Really Need," 1992.

[1–2]   Infonetics Research Inc. "The Branch Office Explosion: LAN Interconnection in the '90s," 1993.

[1–3]   Cisco Systems Inc. "Integrating LANs with Public and Private Packet Networks." Cisco document 031201, 1994.

[1–4]   A Guide to Frame Relay. *Business Communications Review Supplement* (October 1991): 1–39.

[1–5]   SMDS Today Networks in Action. *Business Communications Review Supplement* (September 1993): 1–31.

[1–6]   ATM, Views of the New Frontier. *Business Communications Review Supplement* (February 1993): 1–15.

[1–7]   Minoli, Dan. "The New Wide Area Networking Technologies: Frame Relay." *Network Computing* (May 1991): 102–106.

[1–8]   Dougherty, Elizabeth. "The Forerunners." *LAN Magazine* (May 1992): 77–83.

[1–9]   Merritt, John. "Frame Relay Technology." Network Computing (November 1, 1992): 75–76.

[1–10] Malone, Richard J. "Are You a Candidate for Frame Relay?" *Business Communications Review* (January 1993): 27–31.

[1–11] Gasparro, Daniel M. and William A. DeMartini. "Booz, Allen Buys a Frame Relay Network." *Data Communications* (July 1993): 70–84.

[1–12] Malone, Richard. "Frame Relay Service Pricing: Contrasting the Competitors." *Business Communications Review* (August 1993): 32–36.

[1–13] Finn, Chris and Chris Heckart. "Frame Relay Grows Up." *Network World* (February 7, 1994): 33–40.

[1–14] Minoli, Dan. "The New Wide Area Technologies: SMDS and BISDN." *Network Computing* (August 1991): 88–92.

[1–15]   Harrison, Bradford T. "The Quick Link." *DEC Professional* (October 1992): 22–32.

[1–16]   Briere, Daniel. "SMDS: The Silent Contender." *Network World* (November 29, 1993): 39–49.

[1–17]   Minoli, Dan. "ATM Protocols: Let's Get Technical." *Network Computing* (November 15, 1992): 156–163.

[1–18]   Wallace, Bob. "The Impact of ATM." *Network World* (November 1, 1993): 44–56.

[1–19]   Sammartino, Fred. "The Future of ATM: Moving Beyond the Hype." *Telecommunications* (January 1994): 27–28.

[1–20]   Booker, Ellis. "ATM Faces High Expectations." *Computerworld* (January 24,1994): 49–51.

[1–21]   Naegle, John H. et. al. "Developing an ATM Network at Sandia National Laboratories." *Telecommunications* (February 1994): 21–24.

 **Frame Relay Architecture**

Frame relay has become a very popular broadband WAN service. Inter-Exchange Carriers (IXCs) offering frame relay include AT&T, Cable and Wireless Communications, CompuServe, MCI, Sprint, and WilTel. Local Exchange Carriers (LECs) offering frame relay service include Ameritech, Bell Atlantic, BellSouth, NYNEX, Pacific Bell, Southwestern Bell, and US West. Appendix F lists addresses and telephone numbers for these and other broadband carriers. This chapter examines frame relay architecture; Chapter 3 details frame relay protocol; and Chapter 4 explores case studies of frame relay networks under real-life conditions.

2.1 Frame Relay Network Service

The ITU-T standards for Integrated Services Digital Network (ISDN) define a number of services. The ITU-T services relevant to this discussion are the ITU-T bearer services, which let end-user devices transfer information via the network. Bearer services transfer data using either circuit mode, which provides a circuit-switched connection or packet mode, which provides a packet-switched connection. *Frame relay*, defined by ANSI T1.606 [2–1], is an ISDN packet-mode bearer service that transfers frames of information from the network side of one user-network interface (UNI) to the network side of another UNI. The UNI is the demarcation point, between the terminal equipment (controlled by the end user) and the transport facility (controlled by the network provider), as shown in Figure 2–1. The frame relay access device (FRAD), which is also called the frame relay assembler/deassembler, or some other device performing this function, indicates the terminal equipment. The frame relay network device (FRND), or other device performing its function, designates the network's access equipment. Depending upon the design of the FRAD, other interfaces, such as the V.35, may provide a connection to a Data Service Unit/Channel Service Unit (DSU/CSU), which then connects to the network.

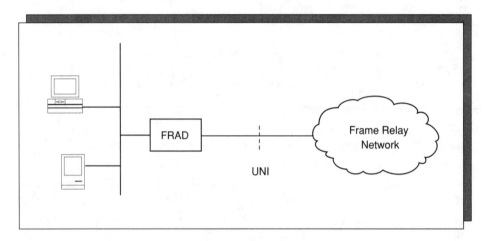

Figure 2–1. The UNI *(© 1990, Digital Equipment Corp., Northern Telecom, Inc., and Stratacom, Inc.)*

The frame relay standards clearly define the bearer service provided by the network, so the design requirements for each side of the UNI are unambiguous. The bearer-service definition includes:

▼ bidirectional frame transfer

▼ preservation of the frame order

▼ detection of transmission, format, and operational errors

▼ transparent transport of the user data, with modification to the Address and Error-Control fields only

▼ no frame acknowledgment.

So, a frame relay network provides only a simple, connection-oriented frame transport service. Higher layer protocols in the FRADs handle other network-protocol requirements, such as flow control or error recovery. T1.606, Section 1.2 describes applications that might benefit from frame relay's streamlined transport service. These include:

▼ block-interactive data applications, such as high-resolution graphics or CAD/CAM

▼ file transfers for large amounts of data

▼ multiplexing low bit-rate applications onto one high-speed channel

▼ character-interactive traffic, such as text editing, which requires short frames, low delays, and low throughput.

References [2–2] through [2–6] discuss applications for frame relay technology. References [2–7] through [2–9] compare frame relay costs with those of other WAN technologies, such as T1. References [2–10] through [2–15] discuss vendor products and carrier services that support the technology.

2.2 Frame Relay Standards

Before discussing the frame relay protocols and architecture in greater detail, you should first examine the governing standards. Three different organizations have written the documents that govern current frame relay implementations: ANSI, ITU-T, and the Frame Relay Forum (FRF). Both ANSI and the ITU-T frame relay standards are based on the ISDN architecture. The FRF documents address implementation issues, assuring the interoperability of multivendor networks.

Standards documents from these organizations describe four areas: architecture and services, access signaling, data transfer, and circuit management. The architecture- and service-description documents define frame relay functions. The data-transfer documents describe the formats used to transfer user information; that is, they describe the core of the frame relay interface's Data Link layer service. The management documents deal with management of the interface between the end-user equipment and the network, as well as control of network congestion. Finally, the access-signaling documents define the messages used to establish and disconnect a frame relay connection. The following are the documents that the ITU-T and ANSI have produced:

Subject	ITU-T Standard	ANSI Standard
Architecture and Service Description	I.233	T1.606
Data Link Layer Core Aspects	Q.922 Annex A	T1.618
Permanent Virtual Circuit (PVC) Management	Q.933 Annex A	T1.617 Annex D
Congestion Management	I.370	T1.606a
Switched Virtual Connection (SVC) Signaling	Q.933	T1.617

Other ITU-T/ANSI standards, primarily those defining ISDN architecture and protocols are also relevant. These include:

Standard	Description
Q.920 (T1.602)	Concepts, terminology, and description of the Link-Access Procedure on the D channel (LAPD).
Q.921 (T1.602)	LAPD frame structure, elements of procedure, field formats, and operational procedures.

To order any of the ANSI or ITU-T standards, see Appendix A. Because national and international standards, such as ANSI and ITU-T, do not always specify individual protocol parameters, such as the maximum transmitted frame size, a number of carriers and vendors formed the FRF in 1991 to address such implementation issues. The FRF works to develop frame relay technologies, improve existing standards, and facilitate multivendor interoperability. The organization's formal documents are called Implementation Agreements (IAs). The FRF IAs heavily reference ITU-T standards. Currently available IAs are as follows:

Standard	Description
FRF.1	The User-Network Interface (UNI)
FRF.2	The Network-to-Network Interface (NNI)
FRF.3	Multiprotocol encapsulation
FRF.4	Switched Virtual Circuit (SVC)
FRF:5	Frame Relay/ATM Network Interworking
FRF:6	Frame Relay Service Customer Network Management

To obtain IAs, contact the FRF at the address given in Appendix A. When reading through the standards documents listed above, you'll notice that many of the standards from the ITU-T, ANSI, and FRF are closely related. In fact, some of the FRF IAs are derived from those of the ITU-T and ANSI. ITU-T Q.931 (ANSI T1.607), for example, is an ISDN Layer 3 standard for basic call control. A subset of that standard, ITU-T Q.933 (ANSI T1.617) specifies frame mode basic call control. The forum's implementation agreement, FRF.4, which details SVC service offerings at the user-to-network interface, is derived from both of these standards. So, to fully understand FRF.4, you'll need copies of Q.933 and Q.931. Although this may seem circular, referring to previous standards prevents unnecessary repetition of information. Tom Nolle's excellent paper, "Frame Relay— Standards Advance" [2–16], puts these key standards issues into perspective.

2.3 Comparing Frame Relay and X.25

When frame relay networks were first introduced, the only similar WAN service was X.25. Therefore, these two services are often compared.

Figure 2–2 compares both the frame relay and X.25 architectures to the Open Systems Interconnection (OSI) Reference Model. As you can see, X.25 encompasses the lower three layers of the model, using various Physical layer standards such as EIA-232 or X.21, the Link Access Procedure—Balanced (LAPB) at the Data Link layer, and the Packet Layer Protocol (PLP) at the Network layer.

Protocols above the Network layer do not interact with the X.25 protocols; rather, higher layer information passes transparently between end-user equipment via the network.

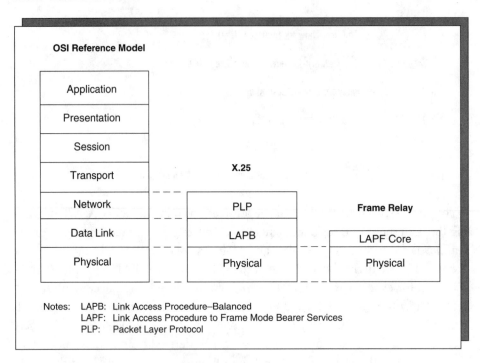

Figure 2–2. Comparing OSI, X.25, and frame relay architectural models.

The frame relay protocols use industry-standard interfaces, such as EIA-232, V.35, and DS1 at the Physical layer. The Data Link layer uses elements, called the core procedures, defined by Q.922, ISDN Data Link Layer Specification for Frame Mode Bearer Services. This specification is based on an extension to the LAPD, defined in Q.921. Because the procedures apply to frame relay services, the Q.922 protocol is called Link Access Procedures to Frame Mode Bearer Services (LAPF). In the next section, we'll discuss these core procedures, which provide the functions necessary for basic frame transport. The frame relay protocols offer no network or higher layer functions.

Figure 2–3, which shows how X.25 and frame relay process frames and packets, illustrates further functional differences between X.25 and frame relay. (In this text, I use the term *frame* to represent a Data Link layer unit of information, and the term *packet* to represent a Network layer unit of information. Note that in Figure 2–3, the frame relay operates only on frames because the protocol includes no Network layer functionality.)

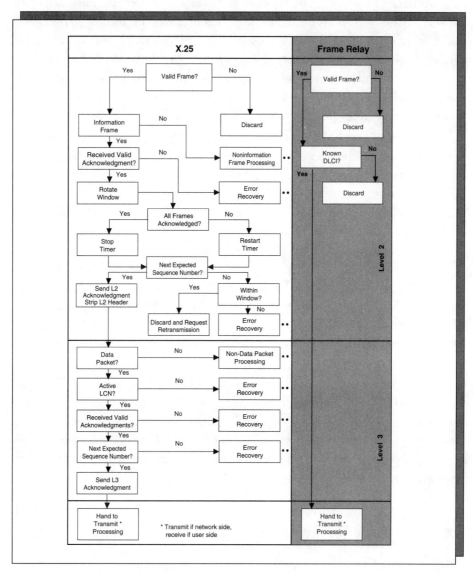

Figure 2–3. Comparing X.25 and frame relay processing. *(Courtesy of Netrix Corporation)*

As you can see, X.25 processing is far more complex than that of frame relay. It begins at Level 2 by testing for a valid frame and checking whether the frame contains user data or control information. The two X.25 end-user devices also invoke functions, such as flow control, sequence control, acknowledgments, and error recovery. Similar functions occur at Level 3, but the terminal equipment performs these operations on the PLP packets in the LAPB frames. Data is also multiplexed onto one of the many possible Logical Channel Numbers (LCNs) at this layer. Note that many network-layer functions, such as sequence control, error recovery, and acknowledgments, are parallel with functions performed at the Data Link layer. When the frame and packet processing is complete, the packet is handed to the upper layer protocol (ULP) process for further decoding.

Frame relay uses a different, simpler approach. As Figure 2–2 shows, the frame relay architecture consists of a limited Data Link layer and no Network layer. The frame-processing sequence illustrates frame relay's simplicity. The LAPF core functions first determine whether the frame is valid (that is, whether it is the correct format, length, and so on). They then test the Frame Check Sequence (FCS). If the frame is valid, processing continues; if not, the frame is discarded. Next, these functions examine the Data Link Connection Identifier (DLCI) or channel number within the frame for validity. The DLCI performs logical multiplexing, allowing multiple logical channels to exist on a single physical channel. Unlike X.25, which handles this function at the Network layer, frame relay does it at the Data Link layer. If the DLCI is known, the contents of the frame are handed to the ULP for further processing; otherwise, the frame is discarded.

Frame relay technology is able to use such a streamlined approach to frame and packet processing because it assumes that Physical layer channels, based on ISDN, are relatively error free. If few errors occur, elaborate and/or duplicated error-control mechanisms are unnecessary. Eliminating redundant functions saves development costs and data communication overhead. References [2–17] through [2–20] consider the relative advantages and disadvantages of X.25 and frame relay architectures.

2.4 Frame Relay Service Architecture

The frame relay service architecture is defined as two planes: the C-Plane performs control functions, and the U-Plane interacts with the user functions (see

Figure 2–4). The C-Plane and the U-Plane share Physical layer connections, defined by standards such as ANSI T1.601 [2–21].

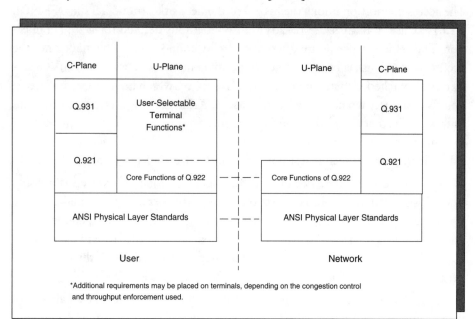

Figure 2–4. ANSI UNI protocol architecture *(Source: ANSI T1.606, reproduced with permission of Alliance for Telecommunications Industry Solutions)*

The C-Plane uses the ISDN D channel, a 16- or 64-Kbps channel carrying control and signaling information. The C-Plane protocols perform call-control, parameter-negotiation, administration, and maintenance functions. Protocols used on the C-Plane include ITU-T Q.931 [2–22], Q.921 [2–23], and Q.922 [2–24]. The U-Plane may use ISDN B (64 Kbps), D (16 or 64 Kbps) or H (384, 1,472, or 1,536 Kbps) channels. The core functions of Q.922 form the basis of the U-Plane capabilities. The Q.922 standard defines functions such as frame delimiting, alignment, and transparency; virtual-circuit multiplexing/demultiplexing using the address field; frame inspection for an integral number of octets; frame inspection for the correct length; and detection of transmission, format, and operational errors. One core function, found in Q.922 but not in Q.921, is congestion control. User terminals may also implement functions such as error recovery; these functions are not included in the core Q.922 functions.

2.5 Accessing Frame Relay Service

The access connection hooks the FRAD to the network's frame handler (FRND). T1.617, Case A and Case B [2–25] are two methods defined for access connection. The standard also defines two frame relay connections to be made once the access connection has been completed: permanent virtual connection (PVC) service and switched virtual connection (SVC) service, which are used with Case A; and SVC service, which is used with Case B. Although this section describes all of these defined-access and frame relay connections for the sake of completeness, the only frame relay carrier offering currently in use is the PVC service over non-ISDN access lines, which is not illustrated in Figures 2–5a or 2–5b.

Case A access is a two-step process (see Figure 2–5a). The first step establishes a circuit-switched (or dial-up) connection between the user equipment and a remote frame handler (RFH) using ISDN B or H channels. Once the access connection is established, in-band signaling procedures, also defined in T1.617 and using DLCI 0, establish the frame relay connection. This step is not necessary if there is a semi-permanent connection between the user equipment and the RFH.

Case B access is a one-step process that occurs when the local exchange provides frame handler (FH) capability, as shown in Figure 2–5b. This frame relay connection is established using a SETUP message on the D channel, which is also defined in T1.617. Data transfer then occurs on either a B or H channel. Once data transfer is complete, the frame relay connection terminates using D-channel signaling.

For PVC service, the end user and the network determine the bandwidth, number, and location of the logical channels necessary to carry the data to the various endpoints. The network then assigns a fixed number of DLCIs in the prescribed user locations. Once the local FRAD knows which DLCI will reach a remote FRAD, communication may proceed. ANSI T1.618 [2–26] defines data transfer over PVC service and ANSI T1.617 Annex D defines the management (addition, deletion, and so on) of those circuits.

In contrast, SVC service assigns DLCIs dynamically, based on end-user requirements. Digital signaling messages between the FRAD and the network, which are similar to the ringing and busy signals of an analog telephone, establish the SVC. The signaling messages are transmitted on DLCI 0, which is reserved for that purpose, or on the ISDN D channel. Once the call is established, data transfer follows the procedures of T1.618. These messages are defined in standards Q.933 (T1.607),

Q.931 (T1.617), and FRF.4. Chapter 3 details the procedures defined by the FRF to establish SVC service connections.

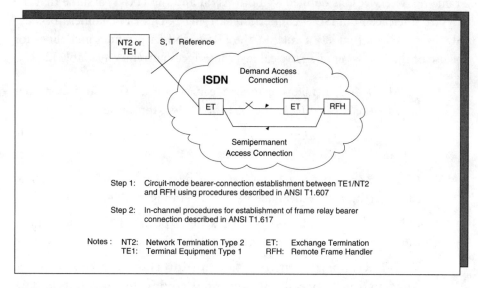

Figure 2–5a. Case A: Two-step frame mode call establishment *(Source: ANSI T1.617, reproduced with permission of Alliance for Telecommunications Industry Solutions)*

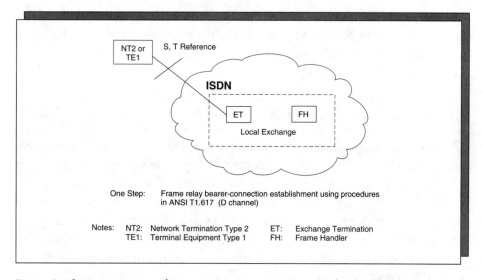

Figure 2–5b. Case B: Integrated access *(Source: ANSI T1.617, reproduced with permission of Alliance for Telecommunications Industry Solutions)*

2.6 Physical Layer Options

Frame relay services, as defined by both ANSI and the ITU-T, assume that the physical interface is an ISDN connection carrying B, D, or H channels. Because ISDN service is not widely available, the FRF's UNI IA provides guidelines for the use of the following five Physical layer interfaces currently available [2–27]:

▼ *ANSI T1.403,* a metallic interface between carriers and customer installations, operating at the DS1, or 1.544 Mbps, rate

▼ *ITU-T Recommendation V.35,* a full duplex interface that typically operates at 56 Kbps over leased lines

▼ *ITU-T Recommendation G.703,* a description of the electrical characteristics for a metallic interface operating at 2.048 Mbps

▼ *ITU-T Recommendation G.704,* a description of the synchronous frame structure for transmission at 2.048 Mbps

▼ *ITU-T Recommendation X.21,* an interface for synchronous transmission between data-terminal equipment and public data networks.

In addition to these guidelines, the UNI IA acknowledges that other interfaces, such as ISDN, may be used as appropriate. For example, MCI currently offers frame relay as a switched digital service at 56/64 Kpbs, and also as a fractional T1 service, Nx56 or Nx64 Kpbs.

2.7 The T1.618 Frame Format

As its name implies, the frame relay protocol relays frames of information across the LAN, MAN, or WAN, as well as the internetworking devices that connect those elements. The word that best describes the objective of the frame relay protocol is *simplicity.* The protocol is designed to transfer frames of information with the least possible overhead. To do so, it uses a subset of the High Level Data Link Control (HDLC) frame format, which has been incorporated into many other data communication systems, including mainframe environments, X.25 WANs, and ISDN. This frame format, defined in T1.618, is shown in Figure 2–6a. The frame consists of five fields: beginning and ending Flags, an Address field, an

Information field, and a FCS. It does not include the Control field, commonly found in HDLC, that normally comes after the Address and before the Information fields. Frame relay includes some control functions in the Address field and omits others, such as sequence control.

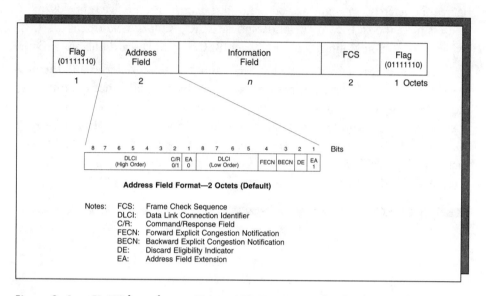

Figure 2–6a. T1.618 frame format *(Source: ANSI T1.618, reproduced with permission of Alliance for Telecommunications Industry Solutions)*

The Flag field is a 1-octet, fixed sequence consisting of 01111110 (binary) or 7EH. The Flag marks the beginning and end of each frame. If a transmitter were to send a 7EH in the Information field, the receiver would become confused, thinking it had received the end of the frame. To prevent this, the transmitter performs a function known as zero-bit insertion. In this process, the transmitter scans the sender's data, looking for the sequence 011111. If it finds this sequence, it inserts a zero immediately after the fifth one. As shown below, a complementary process in the receiver removes the extra zero before delivering the data to the receiver process:

Data from Sender	01111110
Transmitted Sequence	011111010
Received Sequence	011111010
Data to Receiver	01111110

43

Note that this process works regardless of the value of the subsequent bit (one or zero) that follows the 011111 sequence. Address is a field that includes address and control functions for the frame. The default length is 2 octets (as shown in Figure 2–6a), although longer fields have been defined, as in Figure 2–6b. Subsequent figures and references assume a 2–octet Address field. There are five subfields in the Address field: the DLCI, Command/Response (C/R), Address field extension (EA), Explicit Congestion Notification (FECN and BECN), and Discard Eligibility (DE).

The DLCI represents a single logical channel between the user and the network through which data can pass. DLCIs have local significance only; that is, they apply only to the physical interface between the user (FRAD) and the network, not to the end-to-end relationship between two end users. In Figure 2–7, the frame relay connection between User A and User B uses different DLCIs at each end (DLCI 575 at User A and DLCI 441 at User B). The end-to-end connection is called a virtual circuit between A and B.

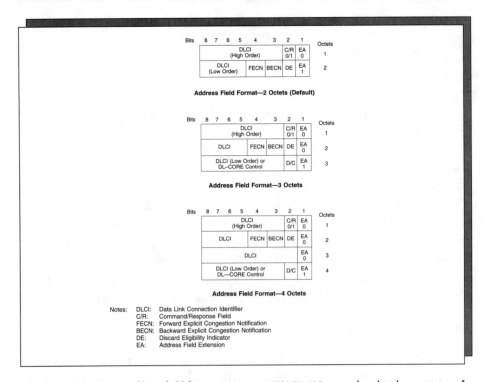

Figure 2–6b. T1.618 Address field formats *(Source: ANSI T1.618, reproduced with permission of Alliance for Telecommunications Industry Solutions)*

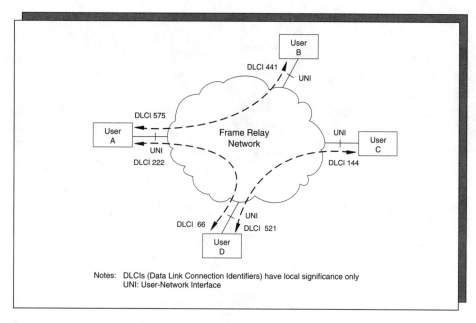

Figure 2–7. Frame relay DLCIs

With 10 bits of address space available, up to 1,024 DLCIs, numbered from 0 to 1,023, may be assigned. As discussed below, some of these DLCIs are reserved for special purposes (see Figure 2–8).

The C/R field is provided for use by the higher layer protocols; the frame relay protocol does not examine it. End-user devices (FRADs) may use this single-bit field for signaling and/or control. The EA bits extend the addressing structure beyond the 2–octet default to either 3 or 4 octets (see Figure 2–6b). The values are EA = 0; more address octets follow, EA = 1; last address octet. Note that in the 2–octet example (see Figure 2–6a), each octet ends with an EA bit. The EA in the first octet has the value of zero; the value in the second octet is one. The first EA indicates that another octet follows; the second EA marks the last octet of the address field. For example, if 4-octet addressing were used, the first three octets would have EA = 0, while the fourth octet would have EA = 1 (see Figure 2–6b).

DLCI Values	Function
0	Reserved for Call-Control Signaling (In-Channel)
1–15	Reserved
16–1,007	Assignable to Frame Relay PVCs
1,008–1,022	Reserved
1,023	Local Management Interface (LMI)

DLCI Assignment (Consortium)

DLCI Values	Function
0	In-Channel Signaling
1–15	Reserved
16–991	Assigned Using Frame Relay Connection Procedures
992–1,007	Layer 2 Management of Frame Relay Bearer Service
1,008–1,022	Reserved
1,023	In-Channel Layer Management

DLCI Values for B-Channel and H-Channel Applications (ANSI T1.618)

DLCI Values	Function
512–991	Assigned Using Frame Relay Connection Procedure

DLCI Values for D Channel (ANSI T1.618)

Figure 2–8. DLCI assignments *(Source: ANSI T1.618, reproduced with permission of Alliance for Telecommunications Industry Solutions)*

The network sets the ECN bits to indicate the direction of the network's congestion. The Forward Explicit Congestion Notification (FECN) bit indicates congestion in the direction of traffic flow. The Backward Explicit Congestion Notification (BECN) indicates congestion in the direction opposite the flow of traffic. The DE bit indicates the relative importance of the frame, and whether it can be discarded in the event of network congestion. Either the user or the network may set this bit. The Information field carries higher layer protocol information, such as client/server data from a LAN or inter-router communication on an internetwork. This field is passed transparently from source to destination; no intermediate frame relay devices examine it. ANSI T1.618 recommends a maximum-negotiated Information field length of at least 1,600 octets to minimize segmentation and reassembly functions with LAN traffic. The FRF implementation agreement (FRF.1) requires that both the network and the user support the field length of 1,600 octets. The FCS implements a 2–octet Cyclic Redundancy Check (CRC) sequence, using the CRC-16 polynomial. This polynomial provides error detection for frames up to 4,096 octets in length.

2.8 Operation Support: The Local Management Interface

The Consortium of companies comprised of Cisco Systems Inc., Digital Equipment Corp., Northern Telecom, and StratCom Inc. developed and published the Local Management Interface (LMI) protocol in 1990 to provide support and management for the UNI [2–28]. Derivatives of the Consortium LMI were formally adopted as T1.617 Annex D and Q.933 Annex A. However, differences in these three standards, such as the DLCI and the message formats, render them mutually incompatible. The LMI defines a polling protocol between the FRAD and the network for exchanging information about the status of the interface and its defined PVCs. The T1.617 standard defines the following four purposes of this protocol:

- ▼ notification of the addition of a PVC
- ▼ detection of the deletion of a PVC
- ▼ notification of the availability or unavailability of a configured PVC
- ▼ verification of the integrity of the link (UNI).

The LMI procedures define an asymmetric protocol; the FRAD periodically issues a STATUS ENQUIRY message; and the network responds with a STATUS message (see Figure 2–9). The polling period is a negotiable parameter, with a default of 10 seconds. The first poll requests a link integrity verification response to determine the status of the in-channel signaling link. (The original LMI specification defines DLCI 1023 for the LMI; the Annex D standard assigns DLCI 0 for this function. This revision aligns the LMI functions with previously defined ISDN specifications that assign DLCI 0 for signaling functions. The Annex D assignment is most widely accepted.)

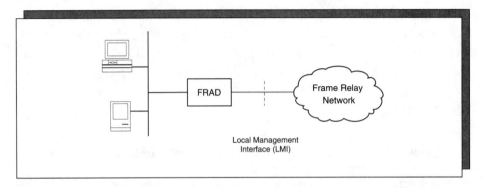

Figure 2–9. The LMI *(© 1990, Digital Equipment Corp., Northern Telecom, Inc., and Stratacom, Inc.)*

After several (typically six) link integrity verification polls have been issued, the user requests the status of all PVCs on the interface. The resulting full status message response contains information on every PVC configured on that bearer channel. The information includes the recent history of that PVC (already present or new), and its availability (inactive or active). Periodic polling, as described in T1.617 Annex D, also detects error conditions, such as reliability errors of the in-channel signaling link (DLCI 0), signaling-link protocol errors, or internal network problems.

2.9 Frame Relay Network Design Issues

As with any other data communication transport facility, end users and network managers of frame relay networks want good response time. The key to optimizing performance is to minimize the network congestion that occurs when more data enters the network than it can handle. This section looks at some of the design issues that affect network performance.

2.9.1 Design parameters

An addendum to T1.606 addresses principles of congestion management that affect the design of frame relay networks [2–29]. Some parameters and functions you should consider when designing these networks include:

▼ *Access Rate (AR)*, the data rate in bits per seconds of the user-access channel (D, B, or H channel)

▼ *Measurement Interval (T),* the time interval over which rates and burst sizes are measured

▼ *Committed Burst Size (Bc),* the maximum amount of data in bits that a network agrees to transfer under normal conditions, over a measurement interval T

▼ *Excess Burst Size (Be),* the maximum amount of uncommitted data in bits that the network will attempt to deliver over measurement interval T (the network may mark excess burst data as DE)

▼ *Discard Eligibility Indicator (DE),* a 1-bit field in the T1.618 Address field, which indicates a frame that may be discarded to relieve congestion

▼ *Committed Information Rate (CIR),* the rate in bits per second at which the network transfers information under normal conditions

▼ *Offered Load,* the bits that an end user offers the network for delivery to the selected destination

▼ *Explicit Congestion Notification,* the process by which the network signals end users, notifying them of network congestion

▼ *Implicit Congestion Notification,* an inference by user equipment that the network is congested. It is based on a determination by protocol entities operating above the data link core sublayer that one or more frames has been lost.

The parameters described in this section affect the principal operational characteristic of frame relay networks, congestion control. References [2–30] through [2–33] further consider the impact of these parameters on operating networks.

2.9.2 Congestion control

Congestion-control strategies operate in the U-Plane for frame relay bearer services, and their objective is to provide high performance consistently for end-user applications. Figures 2–10a and 2–10b illustrate performance for both network throughput and delay. As traffic enters the network, the network throughput increases linearly, and the delay increases slightly (see Region I in Figure 2–10). Until Point A, the network meets its negotiated quality of service parameters, such as throughput, delay, or frame loss. But at Point A, an increasing offered load causes unacceptable transit delays (Region II). If the load continues to increase, the network will experience severe congestion (see Point B). Such severe congestion decreases throughput dramatically and increases delays significantly (see Region III).

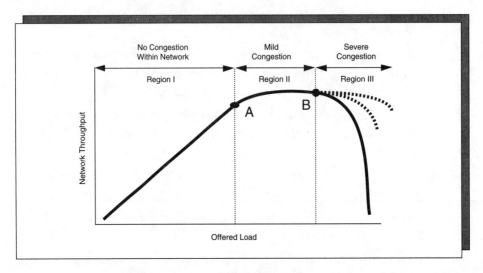

Figure 2–10a. Relationship of network throughput to offered load *(Source: ANSI T1.616, reproduced with permission of Alliance for Telecommunications Industry Solutions)*

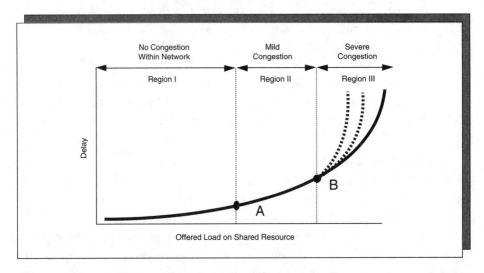

Figure 2–10b. Relationship of network delay to offered load *(Source: ANSI T1.606, reproduced with permission of Alliance for Telecommunications Industry Solutions)*

Frame relay networks have two ways of notifying the network of and/or controlling congestion: explicit congestion notification and implicit congestion notification. ECN uses the FECN and BECN bits included in the T1.618 Address field (review Figure 2–6) to notify the network of congestion. The location of the transmitter control determines the use of these bits. If the data transmitter is controlled at the data's destination, the FECN bit is sent in same direction as the data flow (see Figure 2–11). If the data transmitter is controlled at the data's source, the BECN bit is sent in the direction opposite the flow of the data.

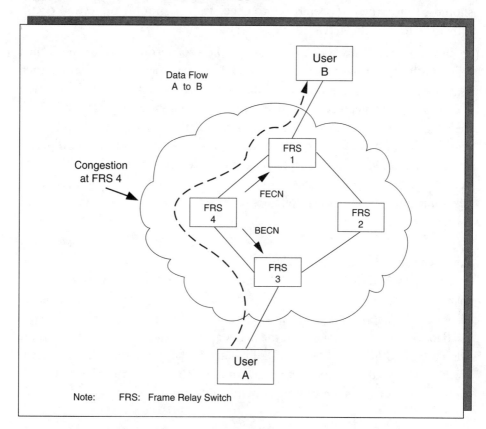

Figure 2–11. Frame relay congestion notification *(Courtesy of Netrix Corporation)*

If no data is flowing in the backward direction, the BECN is rendered unusable and the congested node generates a Consolidated Link Layer Management (CLLM) message and sends it to the data transmitter. The CLLM message is sent on DLCI 1023, which is reserved for that purpose. The contents of the message describe a cause for the congestion, such a structure is defined in T1.618. The CLLM may be used alone or in conjunction with the BECN bit. Although CLLM messages are not widely used, Section 3.5 describes their structure. Once a frame relay network's control mechanisms have been notified of congestion via explicit congestion notification, they return the network to Region I from Region III (or keep it in Region I) by using frame discarding. Frame discarding employs the frame's DE indicator, which indicates whether a particular frame should be discarded in preference to other frames should congestion occur. Either the user or the network may set the DE bit.

A frame relay network can also use implicit congestion notification, which relies on the upper layer protocols in the FRADs or other terminal device, such as a host, to control the amount of data entering the network. This function is generally implemented by a transport layer flow-control mechanism in both the transmitter and receiver. The transmitting device is allowed to send a limited amount of data, but is constrained from further transmission until it has received acknowledgments from the remote device. Processes within these devices monitor the network conditions, such as frame loss. The Implicit Congestion Notification process controls the traffic, which, in turn, controls the congestion.

2.9.3 Committed Information Rate

As defined in Section 2.9.1, the CIR is a static user-specified network parameter that defines the normal information transfer rate in bits per second. The user estimates the CIR, and the network guarantees it (see Figure 2–12). If the transmitted data rate is less than the CIR, the network does not change the status of the DE bit. If the CIR is exceeded, the DE bit is set on the excess frames, and the network may discard those frames. If a maximum rate is exceeded, the entry node discards excess frames, preventing network congestion.

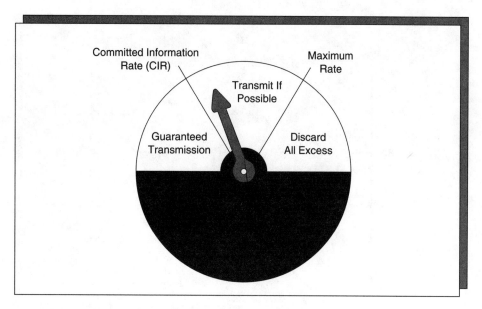

Figure 2–12. Frame relay CIR *(Courtesy of Netrix Corporation)*

2.9.4 Network-capacity management

When a frame relay PVC or SVC is established, the user and the network negotiate the CIR, *Bc*, and *Be*. A measurement interval, *T*, is defined as the period
over which the rates and burst sizes are measured. The excess burst-rate parameter (*Be*) lets users exceed the CIR for brief periods, as required by such "bursty"
applications as LANs. The access rate, measured at the physical interface to the
network, provides an upper limit to the rate at which users may offer data to the
network. Figure 2–13 shows the relationships between various capacity parameters, measured over interval *T*, with four frames of user activity (Frames 1, 2,
3, and 4). Because the total data in the first two frames (measured in bits) is less
than *Bc*, no frame discarding occurs. Adding Frame 3 exceeds *Bc*, but is less than
Bc + *Be*, so it is marked as discard eligible (DE = 1). This frame is transmitted,
and the network delivers it if possible. When Frame 4 is added, the total data
now exceeds *Bc* + *Be*. Frame 4 will be discarded at the network's ingress node.
The area above the *Bc* + *Be* line is called the region of rate enforcement.

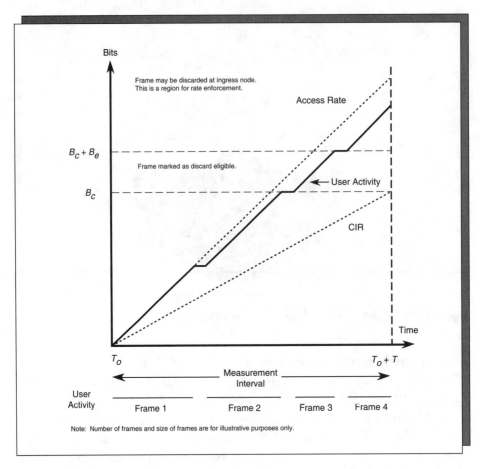

Figure 2–13. Relationships between frame relay parameters *(Source: ANSI T1.606, reproduced with permission of Alliance for Telecommunications Industry Solutions)*

2.10 The Network-to-Network Interface

Until now, the discussion has focused on the relationship between a single user and a single network, or UNI. To extend the user's communication beyond a single frame relay network, the FRF has developed a NNI specification [2–34]. This specification is built upon multinetwork PVC service, which is a concatenation of two or more PVC segments (see Figure 2–14). Note that the NNIs are defined between adjacent networks; UNIs are defined between access and egress networks.

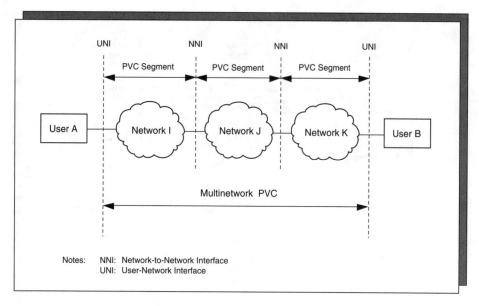

Figure 2–14. Multinetwork PVC *(Courtesy of Frame Relay Forum)*

The LMI defined an out-of-band PVC status-signaling procedure at the UNI, using DLCI 0. Recall that the user periodically issues a STATUS ENQUIRY message, and the network responds with a STATUS message, thus communicating the current status of and/or recent configuration changes to the link in question. With a multinetwork PVC, network-to-network signaling must be added to this status signaling. Each side of the network must issue both the STATUS ENQUIRY message (acting as the user and initiating polling), and the STATUS message (acting as the network and responding to the poll). These additional provisions are called bidirectional procedures. Figure 2–15 shows two users and two networks. Notice that this multinetwork PVC requires three DLCIs (x, y, and z) and two PVC segments (A and B). For DLCIs x and z, the UNI procedures apply, with Users A and B initiating the polling, and Networks J and K responding. For DLCI y, bidirectional procedures apply. Networks J and K implement both the user-side and the network-side procedures, providing status signaling in both directions. For further information, see the FRF NNI specification FRF.2 [2–34], which includes examples of polling sequences for various network conditions.

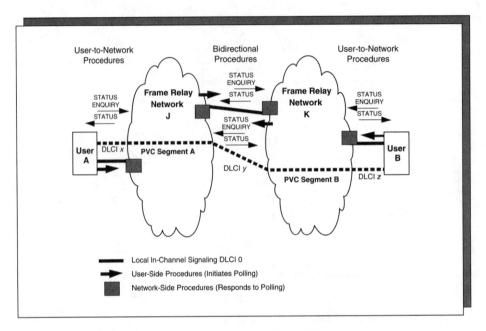

Figure 2–15. NNI bidirectional procedures *(Courtesy of Frame Relay Forum)*

2.11 Frame Relay Customer Network

Networks that include high-speed data-transport systems, such as frame relay, place heavy demands on network management systems. They, therefore, require a comprehensive network management strategy that can accommodate their high-speed transport facilities. However, because different parties—the customer and the carrier—own different parts of the system, a collaborative effort is required.

To facilitate network management, the FRF has defined a Customer Network Management (CNM) IA in FRF.6 [2–35]. The CNM IA lets customers query the configuration, monitor the performance, and detect faults in their frame relay service. Bell Communications Research Inc. (Bellcore) has also defined a CNM service offering, described in TA-NWT-001371 [2–36] and Reference [2–37].

Many LANs are managed via a manager/agent paradigm, which uses the Simple Network Management Protocol (SNMP) for communication. Because of the popularity of this protocol for LAN management, and the need for an industry-standard interface in existing network management systems, the FRF has based its CNM IA, in part, on SNMP. The frame relay service provider makes an SNMP proxy agent available to the customer's network management console. Associated with that proxy agent is a Management Information Base (MIB) of managed objects that directly applies to frame relay service. The console uses SNMP to communicate with the proxy agent to obtain information about network configuration, performance, and so on (see Figure 2–16).

Chapter 11 discusses the management of all broadband networks, including Switched Multimegabit Data Service (SMDS) and Asynchronous Transfer Mode (ATM), and the MIBs relevant to each technology.

This chapter has laid the foundation for our study of the frame relay protocols which, as References [2–38] through [2–40] attest, has achieved widespread use and acceptance.

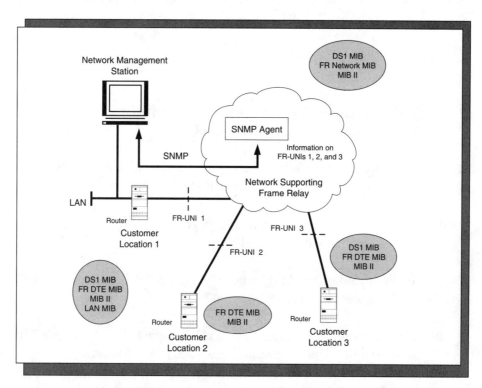

Figure 2–16. Frame relay CNM agent role (SNMP example) *(Source: Brown and Kostick, "And CNM for all: Customer Network Management Services for Broadband Data Services". Proceedings of the 18th Annual Conference on Local Computer Networks, © 1993, IEEE)*

2.12 References

[2–1]   American National Standards Institute. Telecommunications—Integrated Services Digital Network (ISDN)—Architectural Framework and Service Description for Frame-Relaying Bearer Service. ANSI T1.606, 1990.

[2–2]   Taylor, Steven. "Plain Talk About Frame Relay." *Networking Management* (January 1992): 56–70.

[2–3]   Ali, M. Irfan. "Frame Relay in Public Networks." *IEEE Communications Magazine* (March 1992): 72–78.

[2–4]   Finn, Chris and Chris Heckart. "Frame Relay Grows Up." *Network World* (February 7, 1994): 33–40.

[2–5]   Krivda, Cheryl. "A Work in Progress." *LAN Magazine* (February 1993): 93–98.

[2–6]   Garciamendez-Budar, Edsel. "The Emergence of Frame Relay in Public Data Networks." *Telecommunications* (May 1992): 24–32.

[2–7]   Lippis, Nick. "Frame Relay Redraws the Map for Wide Area Networks." *Data Communications* (July 1990): 80–94.

[2–8]   Layland, Robin. "Public Frame Relay: The Price Is Right." *Data Communications* (January 1992): 50–58.

[2–9]   Fitzgerald, Susan and Larry Kraft. "A New Model for Frame Relay." *LAN Magazine* (August 1993): 61–67.

[2–10] Johnson, Johna Till. "Coping with Public Frame Relay: A Delicate Balance." *Data Communications* (January 21, 1992): 31–38.

[2–11] Finn, Chris. "DataCom Buyer's Guide—Frame Relay." *Network World* (February 3, 1992): 31–37.

[2–12] Heywood, Peter and Elke Gronert. "Public Frame Relay Goes Global." *Data Communications* (March 1992): 77–80.

[2–13] Johnson, Johna Till. "Special Report—Frame Relay Products." *Data Communications* (May 1992): 69–86.

[2–14] Heywood, Peter. "Global Public Frame Relay: Risky Business." *Data Communications* (November 1992): 85–90.

[2–15] Fitzgerald, Susan. "Outfit Your WAN." *LAN Magazine* (August 1993): 52–59.

[2–16] Nolle, Thomas. "Frame Relay: Standards Advance." *Business Communications Review Supplement* (October 1991): 22–26.

[2–17] Jones, Tom, Ellen Jennings, and Ken Rehbehn. *The Buyer's Guide to Frame Relay Networking*. Netrix Corp. Herndon, Virginia, 1991.

[2–18] Korpi, Nancy. "Evaluating Frame Relay—Part 1." *Telecommunications* (October 1991): 54–57.

[2–19] Ritzenthaler, Sylvie. "Life After X.25: The Evolution to Frame Relay and Cell Relay." *Internetworking Technology Trends* (June 1992): 62–67.

[2–20] Hume, Sharon and Alison Seaman. "X.25 and Frame Relay: Packet Switched Technologies for Wide Area Connectivity." *3TECH, the 3Com Technical Journal* (Winter 1992): 33–45.

[2–21] American National Standards Institute. ISDN Basic Access Interface for Use on Metallic Loops for Application on the Network Side of the NT. ANSI T1.601, 1992.

[2–22] International Telecommunication Union—Telecommunication Standardization Sector. Digital Subscriber Signaling System No. 1 (DSS 1). Signaling Specification for Frame Mode Call Control. Recommendation Q.931, 1991.

[2–23] International Telecommunication Union—Telecommunication Standardization Sector. Committee. ISDN User-Network Interface Data Link Layer Specifications. Recommendation Q.921, 1991.

[2–24] International Telecommunication Union—Telecommunication Standardization Sector. Committee. ISDN Data Link Layer Specification for Frame Mode Bearer Services. Recommendation Q.922, 1991.

[2–25] American National Standards Institute. Telecommunications—Integrated Services Digital Network (ISDN)—Signaling Specification for Frame Relay Bearer Service for Digital Subscriber Signaling System Number 1 (DSS1). ANSI T1.617, 1991.

[2–26] American National Standards Institute. Telecommunications—Integrated Services Digital Network (ISDN)—Core Aspects of Frame Protocol for Frame Relay Bearer Service. ANSI T1.618, 1991.

[2–27] Frame Relay Forum. Use-to-Network Interface (UNI) Implementation Agreement. FRF.1, 1991.

[2–28] Digital Equipment Corp., Northern Telecom Inc., and StrataCom Inc. Frame Relay Specification with Extensions Based on Proposed T1S1 Standards, Document 001–208966, September 18, 1990.

[2–29] American National Standards Institute. Integrated Services Digital Network (ISDN)—Architectural Framework and Service Description for Frame Relaying Bearer Service (Congestion Management and Frame Size). T1.606a, 1992.

[2–30] Opderbeck, Holger. "Frame Relay Networks: Not as Simple as They Seem." *Data Communications* (December 1990): 109–114.

[2–31] Cavanagh, James P. "Applying the Frame Relay Interface to Private Networks." *IEEE Communications Magazine* (March 1992): 48–64.

[2–32] Brown, Jim and Stan Fry. "Designs Make or Break Frame Relay Switches." *Network World* (September 14, 1992): 39–60.

[2–33] Baker, H.Charles. "In Frame Relay Applications, Frame Length Is the Key to Network Delays." *Telecommunications* (June 1993): 37.

[2–34] Frame Relay Forum. Frame Relay Network-to-Network Phase I Implementation Agreement. FRF.2, August 26, 1992.

[2–35] Frame Relay Forum. Frame Relay Service Customer Network Management Implementation Agreement. FRF.6, 1994.

[2–36] Bell Communications Research Inc. Generic Requirements for Phase 1 Frame Relay PVC Customer Network Management Service. TA-NWT-001371, September 1993.

[2–37] Brown, Tracy A. and Deirdre C. Kostick. "And CNM for All: Customer Network Management Services for Broadband Data Services." Proceedings of the IEEE 18th Annual Conference on Local Computer Networks, October 1993.

[2–38] Merritt, John. "The Future of Frame Relay." *TE&M* (January 1, 1992): 33–45.

[2–39] Malone, Richard J. "Are You a Candidate for Frame Relay?" *Business Communications Review* (January 1993): 27–31.

[2–40] Gasparro, Daniel M. and William A. DeMartini. "Case Study: Booz, Allen Buys a Frame Relay Network." *Data Communications* (July 1993): 71–84.

 # Frame Relay Protocols

Although frame relay networks use streamlined protocols built on the Data Link layer of the OSI Reference Model and are transparent to the higher layer protocols, these protocols are not simplistic. Frame relay protocols provide mechanisms to manage permanent virtual circuits, establish switched virtual circuits, and encapsulate higher layer protocols. This chapter reviews the frame format, and discusses the signaling messages and user data that a frame may transport.

3.1 The T1.618 Frame Format

The T1.618 frame format is the fundamental frame-transmission unit used by frame relay. As noted in Section 2.4, the T1.618 frame format is derived from the HDLC framing structure, although it lacks some typical Data Link layer characteristics, such as sequence numbers and retransmissions. Figure 3–1 shows that the T1.618 frame format consists of Address, Information, and FCS fields, delimited by flag characters. The Address field carries the DLCI, plus several flag bits that provide a C/R indication, signal the presence of congestion, and optionally extend the Address field. The Information field carries one of two types of communication: signaling and congestion control messages. The FCS fields provide error control.

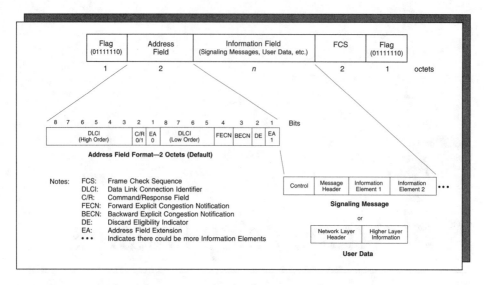

Figure 3–1. T1.618 frame format *(Reproduced with permission of ATIS)*

3.2 Frame Relay Signaling and Congestion Control Messages

A frame relay terminal device communicates with the network to transfer user data and to establish and manage the data link. The nondata communication, sometimes called *signaling*, sets up the connection, determines its status, and controls network congestion. Frame relay networks use four categories of signaling messages: LMI messages (discussed in the next section); T1.617 Annex D Messages (explained in Section 3.4); CLLM messages (discussed in Section 3.5); and SVC messages (covered in Section 3.6). The LMI is a management-message specification published by the Consortium of companies comprised of Cisco Systems Inc., Digital Equipment Corp., Northern Telecom, and StrataCom Inc. The LMI uses DLCI 1023. LMI messages are similar to the T1.617 Annex D messages, and are included for completeness. The T1.607 Annex D messages, published some time after the LMI was published by the Consortium, also manage the link between the data terminal equipment (DTE) and the network, but use DLCI 0. T1.618 defines a congestion notification message structure known as CLLM, which was introduced in the previous chapter. The CLLM messages signal congestion or other abnormal conditions on the network. Because CLLM messages use DLCI

1023, they are incompatible with LMI, but may be used with Annex D messages. Finally, the FRF has defined signaling procedures to establish SVC connections. Each of the four categories of signaling messages use a common header format, but carry different information and parameters.

3.2.1 The Q.931 header

The four categories of signaling messages use a format that is defined for ISDN and found in ITU-T Q.931 [3–1]. The message consists of a header and discrete information elements that convey the signaling commands and parameters (see Figure 3–2). The Q.931 header contains 4 octets with three fields. The Protocol Discriminator field (1 octet) identifies the format of the messages that follow. The value 08H indicates messages defined by the ANSI T1.607 standard, while value 09H identifies a Consortium message, such as an LMI message. The next two fields define the length (4 bits) and the contents (1 octet) of the Call Reference Value, which is a temporary identifier for this service request.

Messages that do not relate to the establishment, disconnection, or status of a call use a Dummy Call Reference, with the field filled with all zeros (00H). The final octet of the Q.931 header contains a Message Type identifier, which specifies the function being performed. T1.607 defines 16 messages divided into three categories: Call Establishment, Call Clearing, and Miscellaneous. Not all of these messages are currently in use. Eleven messages are defined in T1.617 for frame relay connection control; of these, the FRF implementation agreement defines eight for SVC service. Figure 3–2 also shows specific message types and their encodings.

3.2.2 Information Elements

Following the Q.931 header in the signaling messages, Information Elements (IEs) convey message details and parameters, which vary depending on the implementation. Figure 3–3 shows three IE formats and their coding structure. There are two types of single-octet IEs, which may appear anywhere in the message. Type 1 IEs use bits 7, 6, and 5 for the IE identification, and bits 4 through 1 for the IE contents; Type 2 IEs use bits 7 through 1 for the IE identification and have no IE contents. Variable length IEs contain at least three octets: the first octet is the IE identifier and the second octet indicates the length of the IE's contents, beginning with the third octet. The length is expressed as a binary number.

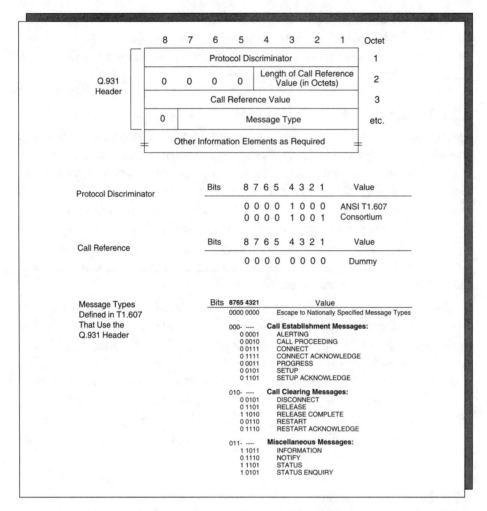

Figure 3–2. Q.931 message format *(Source: ANSI T1.607, reproduced with permission of ATIS)*

All of the standards (ANSI, ITU-T, and FRF) provide an octet label on the right-hand side of the IE octet. You will notice that these labels are not necessarily numbered sequentially. (For your convenience, I show the sequential numbering of the IE octets on the left-hand side of each IE figure.) Some octets, such as those containing addresses, are grouped and denoted by an octet label such as 3a, 3b, 3c, and so on. The octet group is formed using an extension mechanism, usually in bit eight of each octet. The extension bit equals zero if the group continues to the next octet; and the extension equals one if this octet is the last in the group. If an octet label contains an asterisk, the octet is optional. For more information on optional conditions, consult the applicable standard for that IE. So in summary, messages are comprised of a header plus applicable information elements. Some IEs are mandatory, others optional; this is noted by the designations M (mandatory) and O (optional) that appear next to each IE.

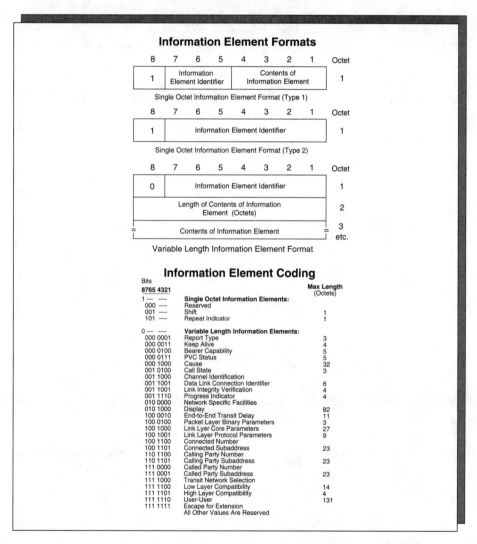

Figure 3–3. IEs used with frame relay *(Source: ANSI T1.607, reproduced with permission of ATIS)*

3.3 Local Management Interface (LMI) Messages

In September 1990, the original four members of the Consortium (Cisco Systems, Digital Equipment, Northern Telecom, and StrataCom) published extensions to the frame relay specification that defined an enhanced interface between the end-user equipment (FRAD) and the network, see Figure 3–4 and Reference [3–2]. These extensions, the LMI (review Section 2.8), specified a protocol and a set of Q.931-based signaling messages for configuring and maintaining the UNI. Although ANSI T1.617 Annex D, discussed in the next section, has superseded the original LMI specifications, some FRADs still implement the LMI protocol.

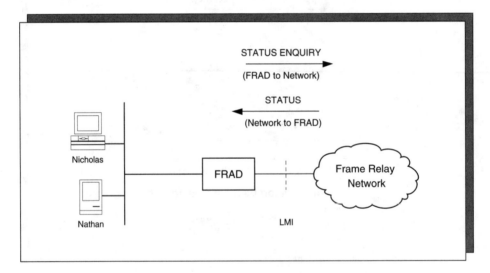

Figure 3–4. Status reporting via the LMI

The Consortium designed the LMI protocol to perform the following three functions:

▼ to let the network notify the FRAD about the active and present DLCIs

▼ to let the network notify the FRAD if a DLCI is removed or fails

▼ to monitor the status of the FRAD-to-network link in real time via keep alive messages.

The LMI defines two messages: STATUS ENQUIRY, which the FRAD sends, and STATUS, which is the network's response (see Figure 3–5). Both messages are sent in HDLC Unnumbered Information (UI) frames, with a Control field value of 03H. The LMI message header, based on Q.931, is three octets in length. Other fields include the Protocol Discriminator = 09H; the Call Reference Value = 00H, which is the Dummy Call Reference; and the Message Type, indicating which of the two messages is being sent. The STATUS ENQUIRY is encoded as Message Type = 75H, and the STATUS message is encoded as Message Type = 7DH. Following the LMI message header are the IEs each message requires.

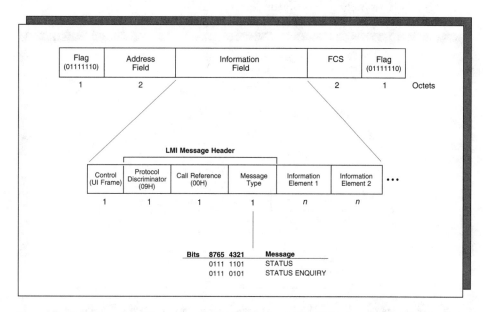

Figure 3–5. Frame relay LMI message format (Consortium) *(© 1990, Digital Equipment Corp., Northern Telecom, Inc., and Stratacom, Inc.)*

3.3.1 The LMI STATUS ENQUIRY message
The LMI protocol operates a heartbeat process, in which the FRAD periodically polls the network using the STATUS ENQUIRY messages. The LMI document defines the polling period as the variable $nT1$, which may range from 5 to 30 seconds, with a default of 10 seconds. The STATUS ENQUIRY message contains two IEs: Report Type and Keep Alive Sequence (see Figure 3–6). When used with

the STATUS ENQUIRY message, the Report Type IE indicates the type of enquiry the DTE has requested (see Figure 3–7). When used by the STATUS message, the Report Type IE defines the contents of the network's STATUS message. The Report Type IE is identified by a 01H in the first octet, and is 3 octets long. The second octet specifies the length of the contents (1 octet), and the third octet specifies the Report Type. A Report Type = 00H indicates a full status message; while a value of 01H indicates a sequence number exchange, which verifies the integrity of the link. (Note from Figure 3–7 that the format of this IE is also used for the Annex D Report Type IE. The difference is that Annex D defines an additional report, the Single PVC Asynchronous Status report [02H].)

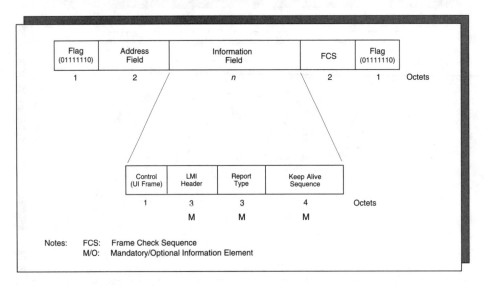

Figure 3–6. Frame relay STATUS ENQUIRY message (Consortium) *(© 1990, Digital Equipment Corp., Northern Telecom, Inc., and Stratacom, Inc.)*

The Keep Alive Sequence IE is identified by a 03H in the first octet, and is 4 octets long (see Figure 3–8). The second octet specifies the length of the contents (2 octets). Both the DTE and the network maintain sequence numbers for link integrity verification. Each time the DTE or network sends a STATUS ENQUIRY message, it increments its internal sequence number, and places the value in the Current Sequence field (octet three). The last sequence number received from the other end of the link is placed in the Last Received Sequence field (octet four). These counters operate modulo 256, but skip sequence number zero.

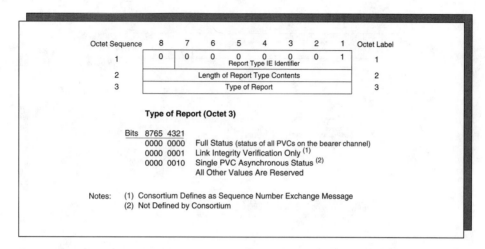

Figure 3–7. Report Type IE (Consortium and T1.617 Annex D) (© 1990, Digital Equipment Corp., Northern Telecom, Inc., and Stratacom, Inc.)

Octet Sequence	8	7	6	5	4	3	2	1
1	0	0	0	0	0	0	1	1
			Keep Alive Sequence IE Identifier					
2	0	0	0	0	0	0	1	0
			Length of Keep Alive Contents					
3			Current Sequence Number					
4			Last Received Sequence Number					

Figure 3–8. Keep Alive Sequence IE (Consortium) (© 1990, Digital Equipment Corp., Northern Telecom, Inc., and Stratacom, Inc.)

Less frequently, the DTE requests a full STATUS message, which adds one PVC Status IE for each PVC configured on the interface. This polling period is defined by the variable $nN1$, which ranges from 1 to 255 intervals of $nT1$, with a default of six intervals.

3.3.2 The LMI STATUS message

The network sends the STATUS message to the DTE in response to the STATUS ENQUIRY message (see Figure 3–9). The Report Type and Keep Alive Sequence IEs are always transmitted with the STATUS message. PVC Status IEs are added, one per configured PVC, to the STATUS message when a full STATUS message is requested.

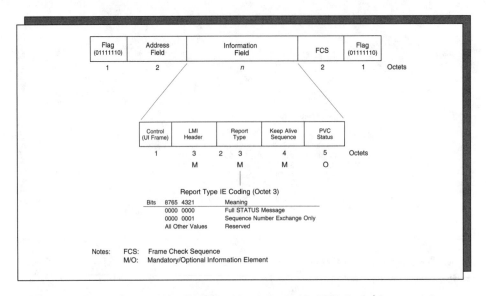

Figure 3–9. Frame relay LMI STATUS message (Consortium) *(© 1990, Digital Equipment Corp., Northern Telecom, Inc., and Stratacom, Inc.)*

The PVC Status IE is identified by a 07H in the first octet, and is either 5 or 8 octets long (see Figure 3–10). The second octet specifies the length of the contents (3 or 6 octets). The third and fourth octets carry the DLCI for this PVC. The fifth octet contains status-bit codings that tell whether that PVC is new (N = 1) and/or active (A = 1). The Consortium has defined octets 6 through 8 to optionally carry a 24-bit number representing the minimum bandwidth in bits per second that the network has allocated to this PVC.

3.4 T1.617 Annex D Messages

In Annex D of T1.617 [3–3], ANSI presents a management signaling scheme derived from the Consortium's LMI. (To avoid confusion, I will refer to the former as LMI and the latter as Annex D). These messages also implement a heartbeat function, use the Q.931 message structure, and are transmitted in HDLC UI frames. While LMI uses DLCI 1023, Annex D messages use DLCI 0, with the FECN, BECN, and DE bits set to zero. Within the Q.931 header of the Annex D messages, the Protocol Discriminator field = 08H, while the LMI sets this field at 09H (see Figure 3–11). LMI and Annex D use identical Dummy Call Reference and Message Type fields. Unlike LMI, Annex D adds the Locking Shift IE (see Figure 3–12), which specifies the use of codeset 5, to the message header.

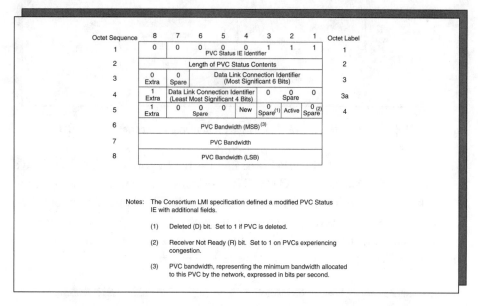

Figure 3–10. PVC status IE (Consortium and T1.617 Annex D) *(Reproduced with permission of ATIS)*

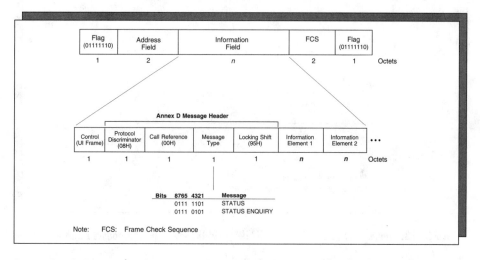

Figure 3–11. Frame relay T1.617 Annex D message format *(Reproduced with permission of ATIS)*

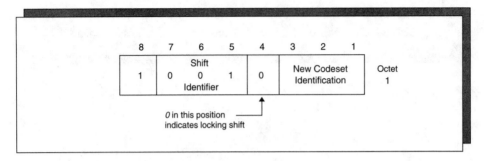

Figure 3–12. Locking Shift IE *(Source: ANSI T1.607, reproduced with permission of ATIS)*

While the LMI STATUS ENQUIRY messages use the Report Type and Keep Alive Sequence IEs, the Annex D STATUS ENQUIRY message contains Report Type and Link Integrity Verification IEs (see Figure 3–13). The Annex D Report Type IE adds a Single PVC Asynchronous Status report (type = 02H) to the Report Type IE used with the LMI. The Link Integrity Verification IE for Annex D is virtually identical to the LMI Keep Alive IE (see Figure 3–14).

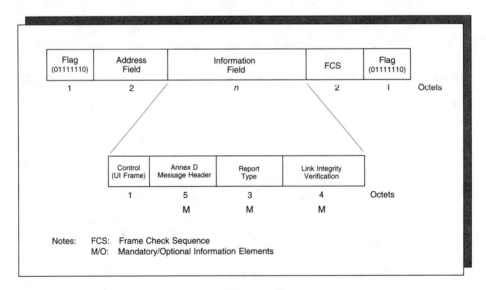

Figure 3–13. Frame relay T1.617 Annex D STATUS ENQUIRY message *(Reproduced with permission of ATIS)*

Octet Sequence	8	7	6	5	4	3	2	1	Octet Label
1	0	0	0	0	0	0	1	1	1
				Link Integrity Verification IE Identifier					
2			Length of Link Integrity Verification Contents						2
3			Send Sequence Number						3
4			Receive Sequence Number						4

Figure 3–14. Link Integrity Verification IE (T1.617 Annex D) *(Reproduced with permission of ATIS)*

The Annex D STATUS message uses the same format as its LMI counterpart, except for differences in the DLCI, header, and Link Integrity Verification IE noted above (see Figure 3–15). One additional difference is noted in the PVC Status IE, where the Consortium adds three fields (review Figure 3–10).

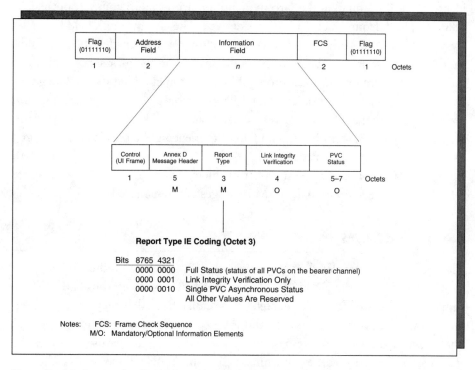

Figure 3–15. Frame relay T1.617 Annex D STATUS message *(Reproduced with permission of ATIS)*

3.5 CLLM Messages

Under most conditions, the FECN and BECN bits within the T1.618 frame (review Figure 3–1) signal congestion within the frame relay network. However, when a frame relay device has no data to send in one direction (for instance, eastbound) no frames are generated in that direction. So, there is no way to notify the eastern devices of problems. The CLLM message format, included in ANSI T1.618, addresses this problem (see Section 8 of Reference [3–4]). CLLM messages are sent on DLCI 1023, of the physical channel that supports the frame relay service. By designating a unique DLCI, all frame relay devices can distinguish these messages from routine traffic. Currently, LMI is more widely implemented than CLLM. Figure 3–16 illustrates the CLLM message format, beginning with the frame relay Address field. Within the Address field, the standard specifies DLCI = 1023 and C/R = R. CLLM messages are sent within HDLC XID (exchange identification) frames, therefore, a single octet Control field (Control = AFH) follows the Address field. A Format identifier (130 decimal) and a Group identifier (15 decimal) come from the ISO 8885 standard, from which CLLM was derived. The Group length field (2 octets) specifies the length of the parameters that follow. Parameter identifier = 0, indicating that the source of the parameters is conveyed in the message. In this case, the parameters are for the I.122 protocol [3–5]. Parameter identifier = 2 identifies the cause of the network problem. Examples of causes include short- or long-term congestion, equipment failure, or maintenance actions. The final parameter, Parameter = identifier 3, identifies the DLCI(s) experiencing the problem. Each DLCI uses 2 octets, and the parameter length field has a maximum value of 255 (1 octet). So, a single CLLM message can report problems for up to 127 DLCIs. If more DLCIs are affected, additional CLLM messages are transmitted.

3.6 SVC Messages

The FRF recently completed an implementation agreement to address the requirements of an SVC at the UNI [3–6]. The procedures used to establish an SVC are similar to those used for making a telephone call, except that they use digital signaling messages between the user and the network, rather than more familiar analog messages, such as ringing and busy signals. The calling user initiates the message sequence for call establishment, sending a SETUP message to the network (see Figure 3–17a). The network forwards this SETUP message to the user called, and returns a CALL PROCEEDING message to the calling user. The called user sends a CONNECT message to the network to indicate call acceptance, which is passed to the calling user. At that point, the SVC is established.

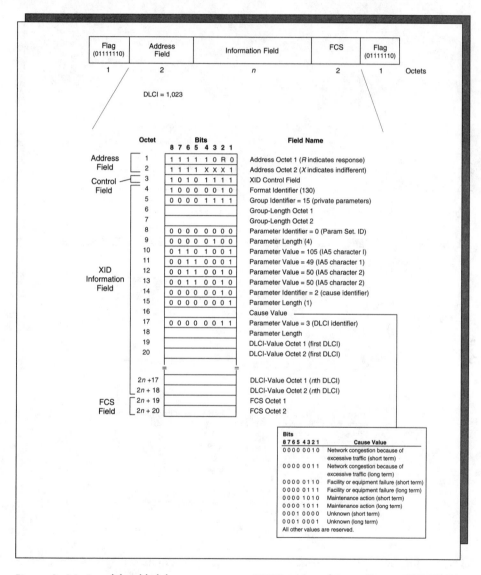

Figure 3–16. Consolidated link layer management (CLLM) message format *(Source: ANSI T1.618, reproduced with permission of ATIS)*

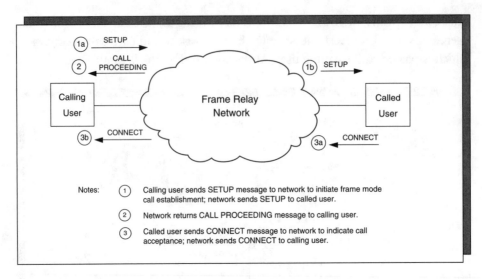

Figure 3–17a. Frame relay SVC call establishment sequence

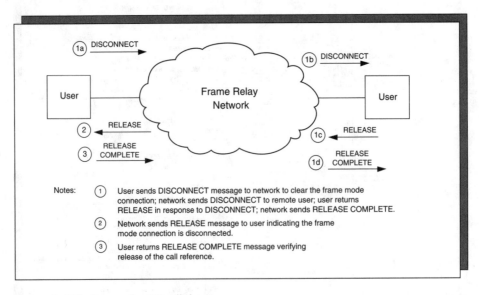

Figure 3–17b. Frame relay SVC call clearing sequence

The message sequence for call clearing is similar. It is initiated when one user sends a DISCONNECT message to the network (see Figure 3–17b). The network passes this DISCONNECT to the distant user, who in turn sends a RELEASE message to the network, acknowledging that the frame mode connection has been disconnected. Both the network and the originating user then send a RELEASE COMPLETE message, verifying the release of the call reference. The FRF SVC implementation agreement is defined for user equipment attached to a non-ISDN network, or to an ISDN network using Case A (review Figure 2-5a). It uses a subset of the frame mode connection-control messages defined in ITU-T Q.933 [3–7] (review Figure 3–2). These messages are SETUP, CONNECT, and CALL PROCEEDING for call establishment; DISCONNECT, RELEASE, and RELEASE COMPLETE for call clearing; plus the STATUS ENQUIRY and STATUS messages for call state information. The format for the SVC signaling messages is similar to that defined for the LMI and Annex D (see Figure 3–18). The SVC signaling messages are sent in information frames, as defined by Q.922, followed by the Q.931 header. The header contains the Protocol Discriminator field (1 octet, 08H), the Call Reference Value field (3 octets) and the Message Type field (1 octet).

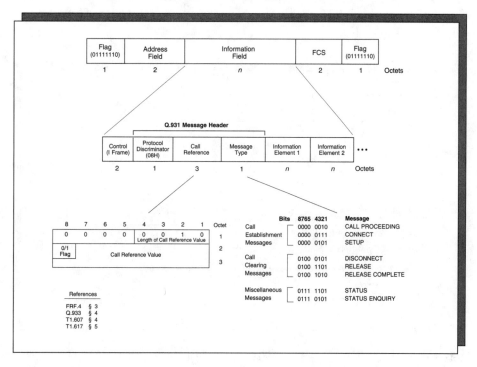

Figure 3–18. Frame relay SVC control message format *(Source: ANSI T1.607, reproduced with permission of ATIS)*

Note that the Call Reference field has a meaningful value, not a dummy value. Call Reference identifies the call, facility registration, or cancellation request at the local UNI that pertains to the message being sent. Like DLCIs, CRVs have local, not end-to-end, significance. Figure 3–18 shows values for the eight defined Message Types. A variable number of IEs, whose contents depend on the purpose of the message, follow the Q.931 header. The following sections discuss these messages and their associated IEs individually. You can find additional information on these messages and IEs in Section 3 of Q.933 and Section 3.4 of the FRF SVC implementation agreement.

3.6.1 SVC SETUP message

The SETUP message, which the calling user sends to the network and the network sends to the called user, signals the initiation of a frame mode call. So, it is one of the more complex SVC messages. The SETUP consists of the I Control field (2 octets), the Q.931 header (5 octets), and up to 10 IEs (see Figure 3–19), which are detailed below.

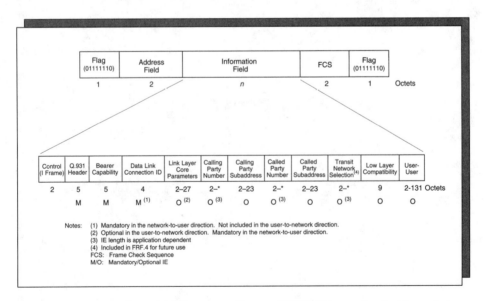

Figure 3–19. Frame relay SVC SETUP message *(Source: ANSI T1.607, reproduced with permission of ATIS)*

The Bearer Capability IE, which is 5 octets long, is mandatory. It asks the network to provide a frame mode bearer service (see Figure 3–20). Its fields define the coding standard (ITU-T); information-transfer capability (unrestricted digital information); transfer mode (frame mode); and User Information Layer 2 protocol.

Octet Sequence	8	7	6	5	4	3	2	1	Octet Label
1	0	0	0	0 Bearer Capability IE identifier	0	1	0	0	1
2	Length of Bearer Capability Contents								2
3	1 Ext	Coding Standard	Information-Transfer Capability						3
4	1 Ext	Transfer Mode	0	0	0 Reserved	0	0		4
5	1 Ext	1 0 Layer 2 Ident	User Information Layer 2 Protocol						6

Figure 3–20. Bearer Capability IE *(ANSI T1.607, reproduced with permission of ATIS)*

The Data Link Connection Identifier IE (see Figure 3–21) is mandatory in the network-to-user direction and is not included in the user-to-network direction. It is 4 octets long when used with 10-bit, 2-octet format DLCIs. The Data Link Connection Identifier IE identifies the DLCI section option (preferred or exclusive) and the DLCI requested or assigned. In the FRF SVC implementation agreement, the value of the Pre/Exc field is always one (exclusive), meaning that this IE indicates the assigned DLCI.

Octet Sequence	8	7	6	5	4	3	2	1	Octet Label
1	0	0	0	1 DLCI IE Identifier	1	0	0	1	1
2	Length of Data Link Connection Identifier Contents								2
3	0 Ext	1 Pre/Exc	Data Link Connection Identifier (Most Significant 6 Bits)						3
4	1 Ext	Data Link Connection Identifier (Second Most Significant 4 Bits)		0	0 Reserved	0			3a

Figure 3–21. Data Link Connection Identifier IE (2-octet format) *(Source: ANSI T1.617, reproduced with permission of ATIS)*

The Link Layer Core Parameters IE is optional in the user-to-network direction, mandatory in the network-to-user direction, and 27 octets long (see Figure 3–22). This IE indicates which core service and quality parameter values should be used for the frame relay call. There are four possible parameters: the maximum Frame Mode Information Field (FMIF) size in octets, the Throughput for the call, the Committed Burst Size (or amount of data per unit of time) that the network agrees to transfer under normal conditions, and the Excess Burst Size that the network will attempt to deliver.

The Calling Party Number IE is optional and of variable length (see Figure 3–23). This IE identifies the origin of the call. Its parameters include the type of number, the numbering-plan identification (ISDN, E.164 or data numbering, X.121), presentation of the calling party number to the called party and screening of the call, and the number digits.

The Calling Party Subaddress IE is optional and of variable length (see Figure 3–24). This IE identifies a subaddress associated with the origin of the call and is of variable length. When included in the user-to-network direction, it indicates the calling party subaddress; in the network-to-user direction, it indicates that the calling party included this IE in its SETUP message.

The Called Party Number IE is optional and of variable length (see Figure 3–25). The user includes it to convey calling party information to the network, and the network uses it to convey called party information to the user. The parameters are similar to those used in the Calling Party Number IE, except that it does not use the Presentation and Screening indicators.

The Called Party Subaddress IE is optional and of variable length (see Figure 3–26). In the user-to-network direction, it indicates the called party subaddress and in the network-to-user direction, it indicates whether the calling user included this IE in its SETUP message.

	Octet Sequence	8	7	6	5	4	3	2	1	Octet Label
	1	0	1	0	0	1	0	0	0	1
			Link Layer Core Parameters IE Identifier							
	2	Length of Link Layer Core Parameters Contents								2
FRIF Size	3	0	0	0	0	1	0	0	1	3
			Maximum Frame Relay Information Field (FRIF) Size							
	4	0 Ext	Outgoing Maximum FRIF Size							3a
	5	0/1 Ext	Outgoing Maximum FRIF Size (Continued)							3b
	6	0 Ext	Incoming Maximum FRIF Size							3c
	7	0/1 Ext	Incoming Maximum FRIF Size (Continued)							3d
Throughput	8	0	0	0	0	1	0	1	0	4
			Throughput							
	9	0 Ext	Outgoing Magnitude			Outgoing Multiplier				4a
	10	0/1 Ext	Outgoing Multiplier (Continued)							4b
	11	0 Ext	Incoming Magnitude			Incoming Multiplier				4c
	12	1 Ext	Incoming Multiplier (Continued)							4d
	13	0	0	0	0	1	0	1	1	5
			Minimum Acceptable Throughput							
	14	0 Ext	Outgoing Magnitude			Outgoing Multiplier				5a
	15	0/1 Ext	Outgoing Multiplier (Continued)							5b
	16	0 Ext	Incoming Magnitude			Incoming Multiplier				5c
	17	1 Ext	Incoming Multiplier (Continued)							5d
Committed Burst Size	18	0	0	0	0	1	1	0	1	6
			Committed Burst Size							
	19	0 Ext	Outgoing Committed Burst Size Value							6a
	20	0/1 Ext	Outgoing Committed Burst Size Value (Continued)							6b
	21	0 Ext	Incoming Committed Burst Size Value							6c
	22	1	Incoming Committed Burst Size Value (Continued)							6d
Excess Burst Size	23	0	0	0	0	1	1	1	0	7
			Excess Burst Size							
	24	0 Ext	Outgoing Excess Burst Size Value							7a
	25	0/1 Ext	Outgoing Excess Burst Size Value (Continued)							7b
	26	0 Ext	Incoming Excess Burst Size Value							7c
	27	1 Ext	Incoming Excess Burst Size Value (Continued)							7d

Figure 3–22. Link Layer Core Parameters IE *(Source: ANSI T1.617, reproduced with permission of ATIS)*

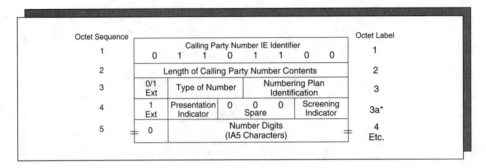

Figure 3–23. Calling Party Number IE *(Source: ANSI T1.607, reproduced with permission of ATIS)*

Octet Sequence	8	7	6	5	4	3	2	1	Octet Label
1	0	1	1	0	1	1	0	1	1
				Calling Party Subaddress IE Identifier					
2	Length of Calling Party Subaddress Contents								2
3	1 Ext	Type of Subaddress		Odd/Even Indicator	0	0 Spare	0		3
4	Subaddress Information								4 etc.

Figure 3–24. Calling Party Subaddress IE *(Source: ANSI T1.607, reproduced with permission of ATIS)*

Octet Sequence									Octet Label
1	0	1	1	1	0	0	0	0	1
				Called Party Number IE Identifier					
2	Length of Called Party Number Contents								2
3	1	Type of Number		Numbering Plan Identification					3
4	0	Number Digits (IA5 Characters)							4 etc.

Figure 3–25. Called Party Number IE *(Source: ANSI T1.607, reproduced with permission of ATIS)*

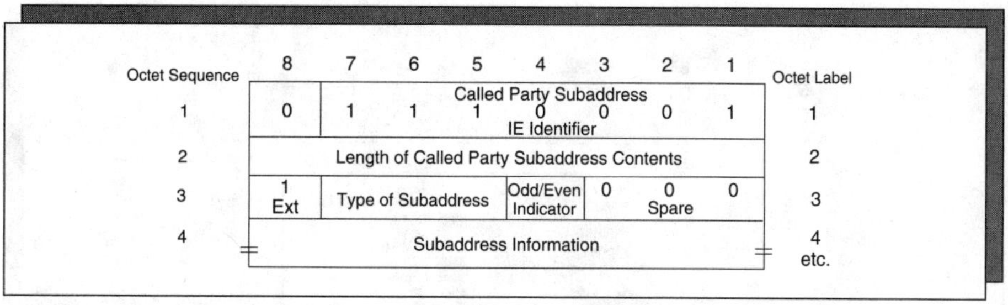

Figure 3–26. Called Party Subaddress IE *(Source: ANSI T1.607, reproduced with permission of ATIS)*

The Transit Network Selection IE is optional and included in the FRF SVC implementation agreement for future use (see Figure 3–27). This IE is of variable length. Its parameters identify one requested transit network.

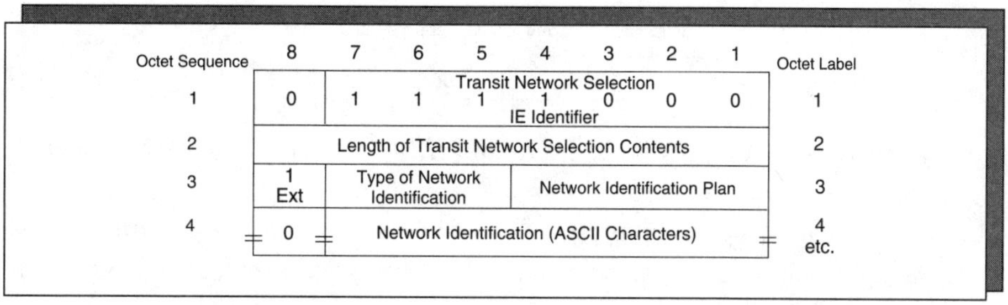

Figure 3–27. Transit Network Selection IE *(Source: ANSI T1.607, reproduced with permission of ATIS)*

The Low Layer Compatibility IE is optional, and 8 octets long (see Figure 3–28). In the user-to-network direction, it indicates that the calling user wants to pass Low Layer Compatibility information to the called user. In the network-to-user direction, it indicates that the calling user included this IE in the SETUP message. The network passes this information transparently between the end users. These compatibility parameters include the Coding Standard/Information Transfer Capability (ITU-T coding with unrestricted digital information); Transfer mode (frame mode); Address included or encapsulated; and User information Layer 3 protocol (such as X.25, ISO CONS, and so on.)

Octet Sequence	8	7	6	5	4	3	2	1	Octet Label
1	0	1	1	Low Layer Compatibility 1 1 1 0 0 IE Identifier					1
2	Length of Low Layer Compatibility Contents								2
3	0/1 Ext	0 0 Coding Std	0 0 0 0 0 Information Transfer Capability						3
4	1 Ext	Transfer Mode	0 0 0 0 0 Reserved						4
5	0/1 Ext	1 0 Layer 2 Ident	User Information Layer 2 Protocol						6*(1)
6	1 Ext	0 0 0 0 0					Address Inclusion		6a(1)
	1 Ext	User Specified							6a(2)
7	0/1 Ext	1 1 Layer 3 Ident	User Information Layer 3 Protocol						7
8	1 Ext	Optional Layer 3 Protocol Information							7a

Notes: (1) This octet is included when a Layer 2 address is included
             in the frame relay information field.
        (2) This octet may be present only if Octet 6 indicates a user-
             specified Layer 2 protocol.

Figure 3–28. Low Layer Compatibility IE *(Source: ANSI T1.607, reproduced with permission of ATIS)*

The User-User IE is optional and of variable length, up to a maximum of 131 octets (Figure 3–29). It carries information between end users, and is not interpreted by the network. The Protocol Discriminator field (octet 3) defines the protocol contained within the IE, such as OSI, X.25, ASCII characters, and so on.

Octet Sequence	8	7	6	5	4	3	2	1	Octet Label
1	0	1	1	User-User 1 1 1 1 0 IE Identifier					1
2	Length of User-User Contents								2
3	Protocol Discriminator								3
4	User Information								4 etc.

Figure 3–29. User-User IE *(Source: ANSI T1.607, reproduced with permission of ATIS)*

3.6.2 SVC CALL PROCEEDING message

The called user can send the CALL PROCEEDING message to the network, or the network can send it to the calling user (see Figure 3–30). This message indicates that the call requested via the SETUP message has been initiated, and that no more call establishment information will be accepted. The message consists of the I-Frame Control field, the Q.931 header, and a Data Link Connection Identifier IE (review Figure 3–21).

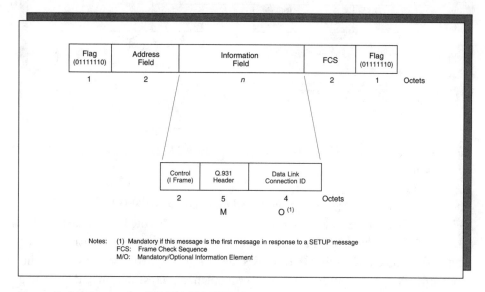

Figure 3–30. Frame relay SVC CALL PROCEEDING message *(Source: ANSI T1.617, reproduced with permission of ATIS)*

3.6.3 SVC CONNECT message

The CONNECT message completes the SVC call establishment sequence (see Figure 3–31). The called user sends the CONNECT message to the network, or the network sends it to the calling user. The CONNECT message consists of the I-Control field, the Q.931 header, and up to five IEs. The Data Link Connection Identifier and Link Layer Core Parameters specify the DLCI and protocol parameters for the call, respectively. The Connected Number, Connected Subaddress, and User-User IEs are optional.

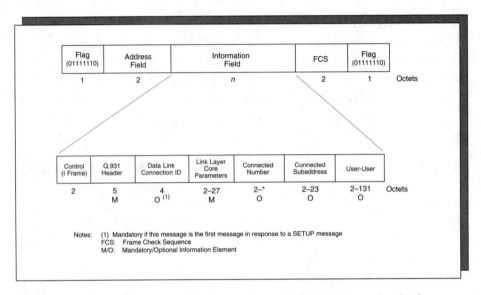

Figure 3–31. Frame relay SVC CONNECT message *(Source: ANSI T1.617, reproduced with permission of ATIS)*

The Connected Number IE is optional, and may have a variable length (see Figure 3–32). This IE identifies the party responding to the call. (Note for comparison that the Called Party Number IE, as shown in Figure 3–25, identified the called party, while the Connected Number IE identifies the responding party.) Parameters in this IE identify the type of number and numbering plan, the Presentation and Screening indicators, and the number itself, again similar to the Connected Number IE.

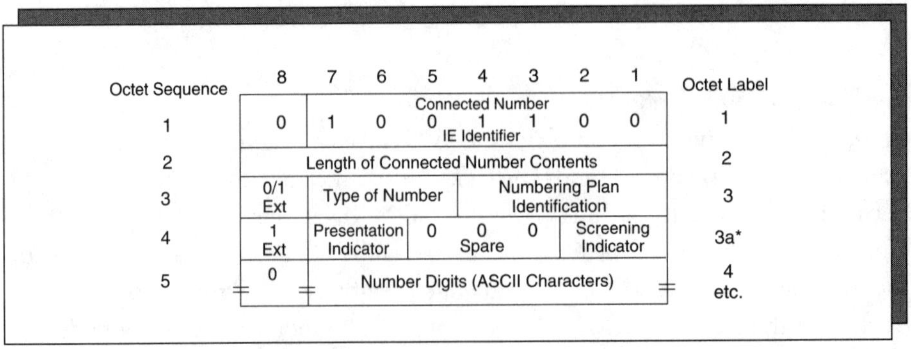

Figure 3–32. Connected Number IE *(Source: ANSI T1.607, reproduced with permission of ATIS)*

The Connected Subaddress IE is optional, and may have a variable length (see Figure 3–33). This IE identifies the subaddress of the party responding to a call. Note for comparison that this IE and its parameters are very similar to the Calling Party Subaddress IE discussed above (review Figure 3–24).

Octet Sequence	8	7	6	5	4	3	2	1	Octet Label
1	0	1	0	0	1	1	0	1	1
				Connected Subaddress IE Identifier					
2	Length of Connected Subaddress Contents								2
3	1 Ext	Type of Subaddress		Odd/Even Indicator	0	0 Spare	0		3
4	Subaddress Information								4 etc.

Figure 3–33. Connected Subaddress IE *(Source: ANSI T1.607, reproduced with permission of ATIS)*

3.6.4 SVC DISCONNECT message

When the users have completed a SVC call, either end of the connection may initiate the call clearing sequence (review Figure 3–17b). That sequence begins with a DISCONNECT message, as shown in Figure 3–34. The DISCONNECT message consists of the I-Frame Control field, the Q.931 header, and a Cause IE.

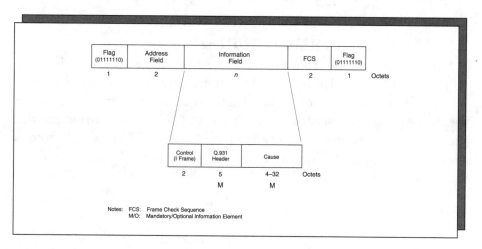

Figure 3–34. Frame relay SVC DISCONNECT message *(Source: ANSI T1.617, reproduced with permission of ATIS)*

The Cause IE is mandatory, and may be up to 32 octets in length (see Figure 3–35). The Cause IE describes the reason that certain messages, such as the DISCONNECT, were generated, and provides diagnostic information to locate the sources of the errors. Parameters within this IE include the coding standard (ITU-T), the location of the originator of this message (such as a private or public network serving a local or remote user), and a Cause value (normal call clearing, network out of order, service or option not implemented, protocol error, and so on). An optional Diagnostics field provides further information.

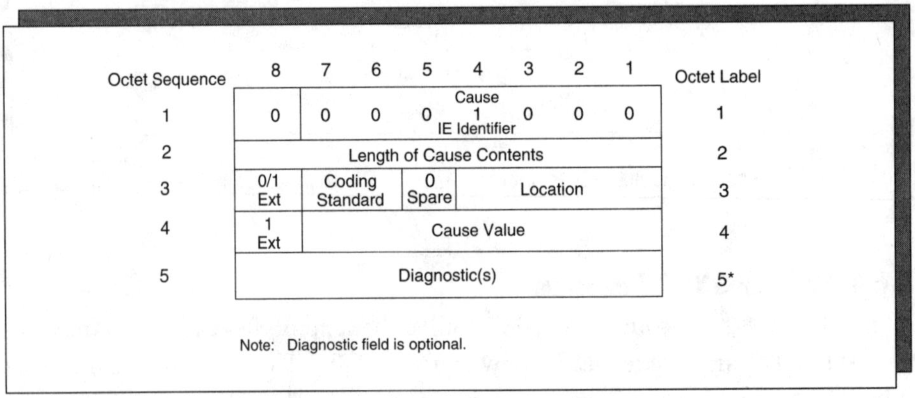

Figure 3–35. Cause IE *(Source: ANSI T1.607, reproduced with permission of ATIS)*

3.6.5 SVC RELEASE and RELEASE COMPLETE messages

When the user receives a DISCONNECT message, he or she responds with a RELEASE message (see Figure 3–36). Either the user or the network can send this message, and it indicates that the sender has released the call reference. In response, the user or the network sends a RELEASE COMPLETE message to indicate that the sender has released the call reference (see Figure 3–37). Note that both of these messages have an identical format, consisting of the I-Control field, the Q.931 header, and a Cause IE.

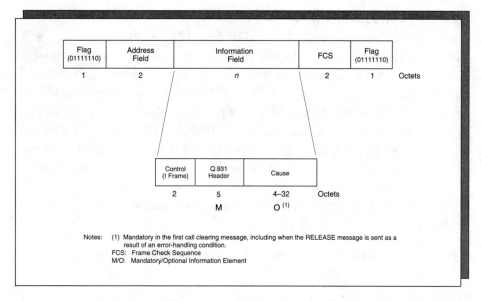

Figure 3–36. Frame relay SVC RELEASE message *(Source: ANSI T1.607, reproduced with permission of ATIS)*

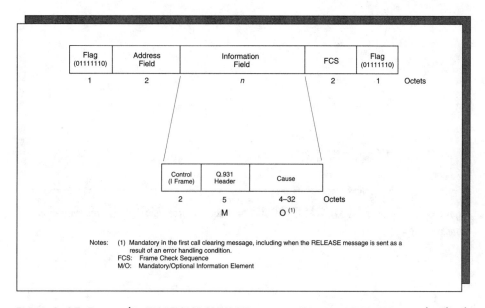

Figure 3–37. Frame relay SVC RELEASE COMPLETE message *(Source: ANSI T1.607, reproduced with permission of ATIS)*

3.6.6 SVC STATUS ENQUIRY and STATUS messages

The user or the network sends the STATUS ENQUIRY message to solicit a STA-TUS message from its peer. The STATUS message may be sent at any time to report error conditions, such as an invalid Protocol Discriminator, Call Reference Value, or out-of-sequence IEs. The STATUS ENQUIRY message includes the I-Frame Control field and the Q.931 header (see Figure 3–38). The STATUS message includes mandatory Cause and Call State IEs (see Figure 3–39). The Call State IE is 3 octets in length, and describes the current status of the call, as shown Figure 3–40. Two parameters are transferred with this IE: the coding standard (ITU-T) and a Call State value. The various states are defined for both the user and network side of the interface and include Call Initiated, Call Present, Disconnect Request, Release Request, and so on.

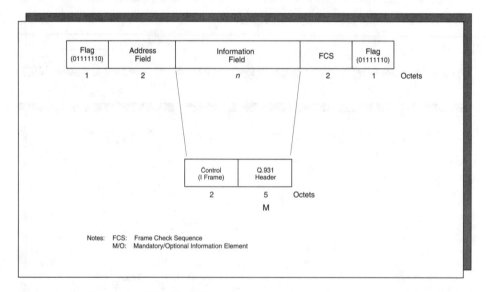

Figure 3–38. Frame relay SVC STATUS ENQUIRY message *(Source: ANSI T1.617, reproduced with permission of ATIS)*

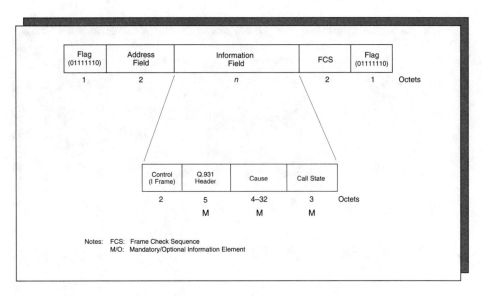

Figure 3–39. Frame relay SVC STATUS message *(Source: ANSI T1.617, reproduced with permission of ATIS)*

Octet Sequence	8	7	6	5	4	3	2	1	Octet Label
1	0	0	0	1	Call State 0 IE Identifier	1	0	0	1
2	Length of Call State Contents								2
3	0 0 Coding Standard		Call State Value/Global Interface State Value (state value is coded in binary)						3

Figure 3–40. Call State IE *(Source: ANSI T1.607, reproduced with permission of ATIS)*

Figure 3–41 is a summary of all LMI, Annex D, and SVC messages discussed in this chapter, plus the included IEs.

	Protocol Discriminator	Call Reference Value	Message Type	Shift	Repeat Indicator	Bearer Capability	Cause	Call State	Channel Identification	Data Link Connection Identifier	Progress Indicator	Network Specific Facilities	Display	End-to-End Transit Delay	Packet Layer Binary Parameters	Link Layer Core Parameters	Link Layer Protocol Parameters	Connected Number	Connected Subaddress	Calling Party Number	Calling Party Subaddress	Called Party Number	Called Party Subaddress	Transit Network Selection	Low Layer Compatibility	High Layer Compatibility	User-User	Escape for Extension	Locking Shift	Report Type	Link Integrity Verification	PVC Status	Keep Alive
ANSI Reference Section	T1.617 6.2	T1.617 6.3	T1.617 6.4	T1.607 4.5.3	T1.617 6.5.25	T1.617 6.5.5	T1.617 6.5.11	T1.607 5.6	T1.607 4.5.12	T1.617 6.5.15	T1.607 4.5.21	T1.607 4.5.19	T1.607 4.5.16	T1.617 6.5.17	T1.617 6.5.23	T1.617 6.5.19	T1.617 6.5.20	T1.607 4.5.13	T1.607 4.5.14	T1.607 4.5.9	T1.607 4.5.10	T1.607 4.5.7	T1.607 4.5.8	T1.607 4.5.25	T1.617 6.5.21	T1.617 6.5.16	T1.607 4.5.26	T1.607 4.5.2	T1.617 4.5.3	T1.617 D.3.1	T1.617 D.3.2	T1.617 D.3.3	Consortium LMI
ITU-T Reference Section	Q.931 4.2	Q.931 4.3	Q.933 4.4	Q.933 4.5.3	Q.933 4.5.25	Q.933 4.5.5	Q.931 4.5.12	Q.931 4.5.7	Q.931 4.5.13	Q.933 4.5.15	Q.931 4.5.23	Q.931 4.5.21	Q.931 4.5.16	Q.933 4.5.17	Q.933 4.5.23	Q.933 4.5.19	Q.933 4.5.20	Q.951 5.4.1	Q.951 5.4.2	Q.931 4.5.10	Q.931 4.5.11	Q.931 4.5.8	Q.931 4.5.9	Q.931 4.5.29	Q.933 4.5.21	Q.931 4.5.17	Q.931 4.5.30	Q.931 4.5.2	Q.931 4.5.3	Q.933 A.3.1	Q.933 A.3.2	Q.933 A.3.3	N/A
LMI Messages (Consortium)																																	
STATUS	M	M	M																											M		O	M
STATUS ENQUIRY	M	M	M																											M			M
ANNEX D Messages (ANSI T1.617)																																	
STATUS	M	M	M																											M	M	O	O
STATUS ENQUIRY	M	M	M																											M	M	M	
SVC Control Messages (FRF.4)																																	
CALL PROCEEDING	M	M	M							M																							
CONNECT	M	M	M							M								O	O								O						
SETUP	M	M	M			M				M						O				O	O	O	O	O	O		O						
DISCONNECT	M	M	M				M																										
RELEASE	M	M	M				M																										
RELEASE COMPLETE	M	M	M				M																										
STATUS	M	M	M				M	M																									
STATUS ENQUIRY	M	M	M																														

M = Mandatory   O = Optional

Figure 3–41. Frame relay control messages and IEs

3.7 Frame Relay Support for Upper Layer Protocols

Two issues involving support for higher layer protocols remain in this discussion of the frame relay protocol: multiprotocol support and fragmentation. Multiprotocol support refers to the techniques used to encapsulate higher layer protocols, such as LAN traffic, inside the T1.618 frame. Fragmentation, which is one aspect of multiprotocol encapsulation, divides a long Network layer packet into multiple T1.618 frames, then reassembles the packet at the receiving end of the connection. The Request for Comments (RFC) document, RFC 1490, published by the Internet Engineering Task Force (IETF) [3–8] addresses both of these topics. Elements of that RFC have been incorporated into Q.933 Annex E, and the T1.617 Annex F frame relay documents [3–9]. Annex G of T1.617 discusses encapsulation of X.25/X.75 traffic inside a T1.618 frame. The next three sections discuss these multiprotocol topics in greater detail.

3.7.1 Multiprotocol encapsulation

Frame relay networks carry two types of LAN interconnect data: routed packets and bridged packets. End-user systems, such as host computers, may receive data on numerous DLCIs and on other communication links such as LANs. It is, therefore, necessary to identify the packet type, routed or bridged, inside the T1.618 frame to the host. The identification scheme, known as multiprotocol encapsulation and documented in RFC 1490, defines additional fields within the frame relay Information field for identification. Up to four fields may be added to the T1.618 frame (see Figure 3–42). The Q.922 Control field specifies an UI frame, with a value of 03H. (Frame relay stations may also use XID frames to negotiate various parameters at circuit-initialization time, as discussed in RFC 1490.) The Pad field aligns the rest of the frame on a 2-octet boundary and contains up to 1 octet with a value of 00H. The ISO and ITU-T administers the Network Layer Protocol ID (NLPID), which identifies the encapsulation or protocol that follows. ISO/IEC TR 9577 [3–10], provides specific values for this field. Common NLPID values include Q.933 (08H), the Subnetwork Access Protocol, or SNAP, (80H); ISO Connectionless Network Protocol, or CLNP, (81H); and the Internet Protocol, or IP, (CCH, an NLPID value of CC in hexadecimal). In some cases, Layer 2 and Layer 3 Protocol IDs, or a SNAP header follow the NLPID.

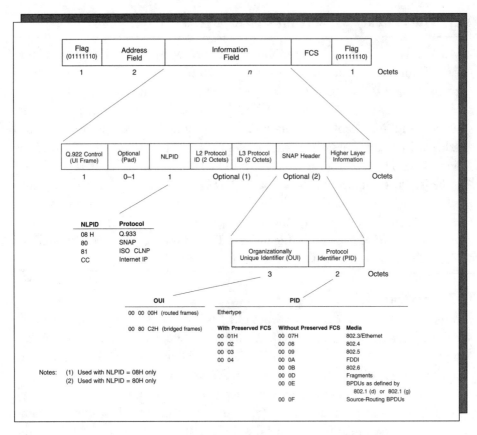

Figure 3–42. Frame relay multiprotocol encapsulation format using NLPID and SNAP
(Source: ANSI T1.617a Draft, subject to change. Reproduced with permission of ATIS)

When ISO/IEC TR 9577 defines the Network layer protocol in use, the frame relay network may use direct NLPID encapsulation. For example, when encapsulating ISO CLNP, the Information field contains the Q.922 Control field (03H), an NLPID identifying CLNP (81H), and the CLNP Protocol Data Unit (PDU). An optional pad may be added to align the rest of the frame on a 2-octet boundary. No further control information, such as protocol IDs or a SNAP header, is required.

If the Network layer protocol in use is not defined in ISO/IEC TR 9577, the network has two encapsulation alternatives. The first alternative uses NLPID = 08H (Q.933), followed by 2-octet protocol IDs for both the Layer 2 and Layer 3 protocols. The values of these protocol IDs are the same as those defined for the Low Layer Compatibility IE (review Figure 3–28). The second encapsulation technique is used when the Network layer protocol in use is not defined in ISO/IEC TR 9577, but a SNAP address is defined [3–11]. This technique is used for either routed or bridged packets that contain LAN interconnect (LAN-to-LAN) traffic. NLPID = 80H identifies the SNAP method and is followed by a 5-octet SNAP header (note in Figure 3–42 that the L2 and L3 Protocol ID field would not be included in this case). The SNAP header contains two fields: a Organizationally Unique Identifier, or OUI, (3 octets) and a Protocol Identifier, or PID, (2 octets). The OUI identifies the organization that defines the PID, so these two fields define a specific protocol. Routed packets use OUI 00 00 00H, followed by an Ethertype to identify the protocol. (The Ethertype is a 2-octet protocol identifier that was part of the original Ethernet frame format. The current IETF Assigned Numbers document, presently RFC 1340, lists the assigned Ethertype values.) Bridged packets use OUI 00 80 C2H to identify IEEE 802.1. Each media type, such as Ethernet or FDDI, have specific PIDs assigned (see Figure 3–42). There are two additional values for most media types, one that preserves the frame's original FCS, and one that does not. For example, suppose you want to transmit routed Novell Inc. NetWare packets across a frame relay network. NetWare does not have an assigned NLPID, but it does have an assigned Ethertype (8137H). As you review Figure 3–42, notice that the NLPID would be 80H (SNAP). The SNAP header would consist of the OUI 00 00 00H plus the Ethertype (8137H). If that traffic were bridged across an IEEE 802.3 network, not routed, the SNAP header would change to OUI 00 80 C2H (802.1 bridging) with PID 00 01H (FCS preserved). The next section of the Information field would contain the bridged frame, beginning with the Destination Address.

3.7.2 Fragmentation
In many cases, the upper layer protocol Information field contains more than a single T1.618 frame can transmit. For example, while the network may support a maximum frame size of 262 octets, an IP datagram could be 500 octets in length. To remedy this situation, a fragmentation protocol, also defined in RFC 1490, is added to the encapsulation technique. When a packet must be fragmented, the fragmentation protocol adds an encapsulation header to it, and divides the packet into as many fragments as the network requires. Each of these fragments receives a fragmentation header, and the resulting data elements are trans-

mitted on the network. The Fragmentation header consists of four fields: a Sequence field (2 octets) that is incremented with each new message; Reserved field (4 bits, all set to zero); Final bit (set to zero for the initial fragments, and one for the last fragment); and the Offset field (an 11-bit value that represents the logical offset of this fragment divided by 32). The first fragment has Offset = 0).

RFC 1490 gives an example of the fragmentation of a large IP datagram over a frame relay network (see Figure 3–43). The Encapsulation header (2 octets) is added to the beginning of the IP datagram, which is then divided into two fragments. Each fragment contains an NLPID, a SNAP header, a Fragmentation header, and the Fragmentation data. (Note the change of the Final bit between Fragment 1 and 2, and that the same sequence number [n] identifies both fragments.)

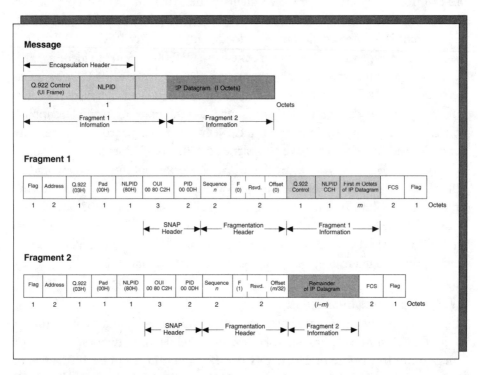

Figure 3–43. Fragmented IP datagram within frame relay frames *(Source: ANSI T1.617a Draft, subject to change. Reproduced with permission of ATIS)*

3.7.3 X.25/X.75 Encapsulation

T1.617 Annex G [3–12] addresses the encapsulation of X.25/X.75 traffic within a T1.618 frame. This standard defines an interworking function (IWF) that encapsulates and decapsulates the X.25/X.75 LAPB frames within the T1.618 frames. The IWF also provides for congestion avoidance. This IWF is best illustrated with an example (see Figure 3–44).

An X.25 DTE contains its native protocols, LAPB and PLP. It connects to a network provider that supports both the X.25 and frame relay protocols or, in other words, an imbedded IWF. The frame relay network may be accessed from that access point. The remote X.25 DTE must also contain the IWF to extract the LAPB frame from the T1.618 frame and pass it to the distant X.25 DTE.

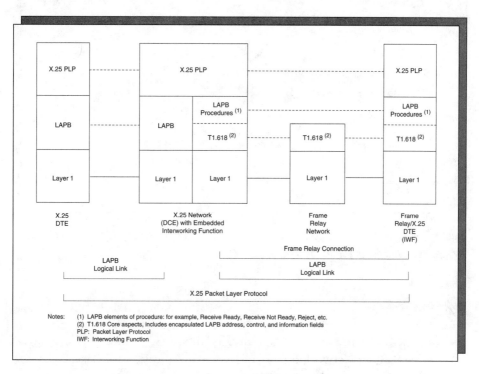

Figure 3–44. Frame relay/X.25 protocol diagram with embedded IWF *(Source: ANSI T1.617a Draft, subject to change. Reproduced with permission of ATIS)*

The encapsulation process places the LAPB Address, Control and Information fields inside a T1.618 frame (see Figure 3–45). A new FCS is then calculated on the entire T1.618 frame, including the DLCI. A reverse process (decapsulation) is performed before delivery of the X.25 packet to the remote X.25 DTE.

This chapter has looked at the frame relay protocols in detail, examining issues of interface management, the establishment of switched virtual circuits, and multiprotocol support. The following chapter looks at case studies taken from live networks that illustrate the frame relay protocols in action.

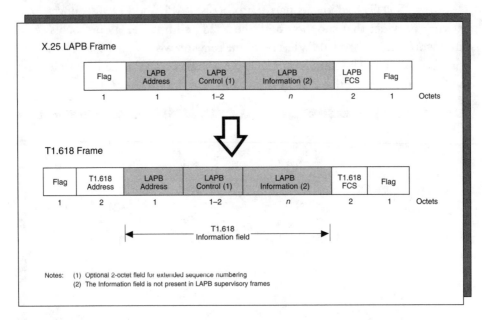

Figure 3–45. Frame relay encapsulation of X.25 frames *(Source: ANSI T1.617a Draft, subject to change. Reproduced with permission of ATIS)*

3.8 References

[3–1]   The International Telegraph and Telephone Consultative Committee. ISDN User-Network Interface Layer 3 Specification for Basic Call Control, Recommendation Q.931, 1991.

[3–2]   Digital Equipment Corp., Northern Telecom Inc., and StrataCom Inc. Frame Relay Specification with Extensions Based on Proposed T1S1 Standards, Document 001-208966, September 18, 1990.

[3–3]   American National Standards Institute. Integrated Services Digital Network (ISDN)—Signaling Specification for Frame Relay Bearer Service for Digital Subscriber Signaling System Number 1 (DSS1), ANSI T1.617 Annex D, 1991.

[3–4]   American National Standards Institute. Telecommunications. Integrated Services Digital Network (ISDN)—Core Aspects of Frame Protocol for Frame Relay Bearer Service, ANSI T1.618, 1991.

[3–5]   The International Telegraph and Telephone Consultative Committee. Framework for Providing Additional Packet-Mode Bearer Services, Recommendation I.122, 1988.

[3–6]   Frame Relay Forum. Frame Relay User-to-Network SVC Implementation Agreement, FRF.4, June 1993.

[3–7]   International Telecommunication Union—Telecommunication Standardization Sector. ISDN Signaling Specification for Frame Mode Bearer Services, Recommendation Q.933, 1991.

[3–8]   Bradley, T., et.al. Multiprotocol Interconnect over Frame Relay, RFC 1490, July 1993.

[3–9]   Frame Relay Forum. Multiprotocol-Encapsulation Implementation Agreements, FRF.3, 1993.

[3–10]   International Organization for Standardization. Information Technology. Telecommunications and Information Exchange Between Systems—Protocol Identification in the Network Layer, ISO/IEC TR 9577, 1990.

[3–11]   Institute of Electrical and Electronics Engineers. IEEE Standards for Local and Metropolitan Area Networks: Overview and Architecture, IEEE 802, 1990.

[3–12]   American National Standards Institute. Encapsulation of ITU-T X.25/X.75 over Frame Relay. ANSI T1.617a Annex G, 1993.

# Frame Relay Analysis

This chapter presents case studies that show the frame relay architecture and protocols discussed in Chapters 2 and 3 in action. To gather the data for this section, I used the Expert Sniffer Internetwork Analyzer from Network General Corp. of Menlo Park, Calif. (see Figure 4–1). This internetwork analyzer provides diagnostic capabilities that help managers maintain, troubleshoot, fine-tune, and expand bridge/router-based leased-line, frame relay, and X.25 internetworks. This analyzer captures data transmitted at up to 2.048 Mbps and analyzes the LAN protocols encapsulated within WAN dataframes.

Using an analyzer such as the Expert Sniffer Internetwork Analyzer, you can observe your network, learn its unique characteristics, and automatically uncover a variety of problems. By identifying critical problem areas within multilayered LANs and WANs more quickly, expert analysis reduces network downtime.

If you are unfamiliar with the Sniffer Analyzer's display, the following information will be helpful. The Sniffer Analyzer works by capturing and decoding frames of information transmitted on the LAN or WAN. These frames come from either the DTE (the user equipment or FRAD) or the DCE (Data Communications Equipment, or the network). The analyzer numbers frames sequentially, and then stores them in sequential order. When displaying frames, you can choose the desired amount of detail in the decode, showing all the layers of protocol or just one. The minimum level of detail is a single summary line that briefly describes the contents of a single frame. A more detailed display describes each field within the frame. The maximum level of detail is a hexadecimal representation of each field or bit that the analyzer receives over the wire.

Figure 4–1. The Expert Sniffer Internetwork Analyzer *(Courtesy of Network General Corp.)*

4.1 Using the LMI

To introduce you to the techniques of frame relay analysis, the first case study shows how the LMI operates under typical network conditions. Recall from Section 3.3 and Figure 3-4 that the LMI communicates status information between the FRAD and the frame relay network. There are small differences between the Consortium's original LMI definition, the ANSI version found in T1.617 Annex D, and the ITU-T version found in Q.933 Annex A. One of these differences is the reserved DLCI used: DLCI 0 (defined by T1.617 Annex D and Q.933 Annex A) or DLCI 1023 (defined by the Consortium).

In Trace 4.1a, the analyzer has captured data transmitted between the DTE (FRAD) and the DCE (network). The trace contains several columns of information. The first column is a sequential numbering of the frames as they were captured. Notice that not all numbers appear on the trace; some of the captured frames did not contain frame relay information and were excluded, or filtered

out. The Delta T column measures the time (in seconds) between the frames'
arrival at the analyzer. The Destination and Source fields indicate the Destination
and Source addresses of the frame and the DLCI in use, respectively. The Summary column presents the analyzer's interpretation of the frame's function.

In this example, DLCI 0 is used for LMI communication, which means that the
Annex D (or Q.933 Annex A) implementation is being followed (see Figure 4–2 and
Trace 4.1a). The DTE sends a STATUS ENQUIRY message approximately every 10
seconds (see the Delta T field), requesting a link integrity verification. From this,
you can see that the link integrity verification polling timer (variable *T391*) is set
for 10 seconds (the default). After five of these polls, the DTE issues a STATUS
ENQUIRY requesting the full status of all PVCs on the channel. From this you can
determine that the full-status polling timer (variable *N391*) is set for five polling
cycles (the default is six polling cycles). Let's look at these two messages in detail.

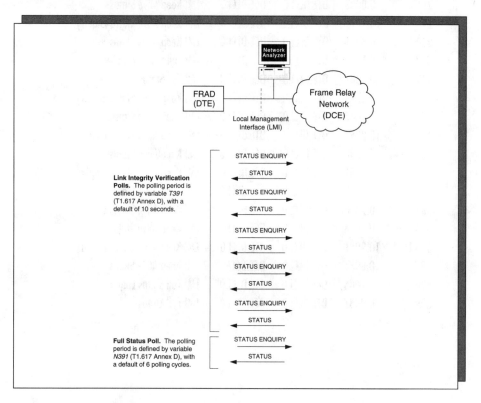

Figure 4–2. LMI message polling

Trace 4.1a. LMI messages (summary)

Sniffer Internetwork Analyzer data, 22-Aug-93 at 19:10:00, OAT1.SYC Pg 1

SUMMARY	Delta T	Destination	Source	Summary
44		DCE.DLCI.0	DTE.DLCI.0	LMI Keep Alive Status Enquiry
45	0.0086	DTE.DLCI.0	DCE.DLCI.0	LMI Keep Alive Status
120	10.1765	DCE.DLCI.0	DTE.DLCI.0	LMI Keep Alive Status Enquiry
121	0.0080	DTE.DLCI.0	DCE.DLCI.0	LMI Keep Alive Status
171	10.2058	DCE.DLCI.0	DTE.DLCI.0	LMI Keep Alive Status Enquiry
172	0.0081	DTE.DLCI.0	DCE.DLCI.0	LMI Keep Alive Status
220	10.1982	DCE.DLCI.0	DTE.DLCI.0	LMI Keep Alive Status Enquiry
221	0.0083	DTE.DLCI.0	DCE.DLCI.0	LMI Keep Alive Status
297	10.1799	DCE.DLCI.0	DTE.DLCI.0	LMI Keep Alive Status Enquiry
298	0.0081	DTE.DLCI.0	DCE.DLCI.0	LMI Keep Alive Status
348	10.1434	DCE.DLCI.0	DTE.DLCI.0	LMI Full Status Enquiry
349	0.0087	DTE.DLCI.0	DCE.DLCI.0	LMI Full Status
395	10.1794	DCE.DLCI.0	DTE.DLCI.0	LMI Keep Alive Status Enquiry
396	0.0082	DTE.DLCI.0	DCE.DLCI.0	LMI Keep Alive Status
465	10.2357	DCE.DLCI.0	DTE.DLCI.0	LMI Keep Alive Status Enquiry
466	0.0080	DTE.DLCI.0	DCE.DLCI.0	LMI Keep Alive Status
516	10.1651	DCE.DLCI.0	DTE.DLCI.0	LMI Keep Alive Status Enquiry
517	0.0079	DTE.DLCI.0	DCE.DLCI.0	LMI Keep Alive Status
565	10.2028	DCE.DLCI.0	DTE.DLCI.0	LMI Keep Alive Status Enquiry
566	0.0086	DTE.DLCI.0	DCE.DLCI.0	LMI Keep Alive Status
636	10.2081	DCE.DLCI.0	DTE.DLCI.0	LMI Keep Alive Status Enquiry
637	0.0081	DTE.DLCI.0	DCE.DLCI.0	LMI Keep Alive Status
698	10.1685	DCE.DLCI.0	DTE.DLCI.0	LMI Full Status Enquiry
699	0.0087	DTE.DLCI.0	DCE.DLCI.0	LMI Full Status

.
.
.

T1.618 frames carry LMI messages over the serial link between the FRAD and the network DTE and DCE (review Figure 3-11). The Data Link Control addresses (DLC prefix in Trace 4.1b) are indicated in the beginning of the frame. The frame relay Address field (FRELAY prefix in the trace) of Frame 44 has a value of 0001H. It identifies the DLCI in use (0), that there is no forward or backward congestion (FECN = 0 and BECN = 0), and that the frame cannot be discarded (DE = 0). The T1.618 frame Information field (shown with the LMI prefix in the trace) contains a Control field that specifies a UI frame with a value of 03H.

The Annex D header, which has four fields, is transmitted next. These fields include a Protocol Discriminator (transmitted as 08H to specify LMI, although the hexadecimal encoding is not shown in the trace); a Call Reference (the Dummy Call Reference, with a transmitted value of 0); a Message Type (STATUS ENQUIRY, transmitted as 75H); and a Locking Shift (ANSI Codeset 5, transmitted as 95H). The Locking Shift IE indicates that this is a T1.617 Annex D message, not a Q.933 Annex A message. Annex A does not include the Locking Shift IE in either its STATUS ENQUIRY or STATUS messages.

Two IEs are transmitted next. The Report Type IE specifies a link integrity verification, which is a sequential number exchange (review Figure 3-7). The Link Integrity Verification IE (review Figure 3-14) contains the numbers for the DTE, the current sequence number (68), and the last received sequence number (154). The network's response (Frame 45) contains almost identical fields and information. The only difference is in the DCE sequence numbers: the current sequence number is 155, and the last received sequence number is 68. By comparing these numbers with ones sent by the DTE (Frame 45), we can confirm that the DCE received the DTE's current number (68) and incremented its own (155).

Trace 4.1b. LMI STATUS ENQUIRY/STATUS messages (keep alive)

Sniffer Internetwork Analyzer data, 22-Aug-93 at 19:10:00, OAT1.SYC, Pg 1

- - - - - - - - - - - - - - - - Frame 44 - - - - - - - - - - - - - - - - -

DLC: ----- DLC Header -----
DLC:

DLC: Frame 44 arrived at 17:54:46.1838; frame size is 14 bytes.
DLC: This frame is dated 2 day(s) after capture started.
DLC: Destination = DCE
DLC: Source   = DTE
DLC:
FRELAY: ----- Frame Relay -----
FRELAY:
FRELAY: Address word = 0001
FRELAY: 0000 00.. 0000 ....   = DLCI 0 (Signaling)
FRELAY: .... ..0. ....   = Response
FRELAY: .... 0...   = No forward congestion
FRELAY: .... .0..   = No backward congestion
FRELAY: ....0.   = Not eligible for discard
FRELAY:
LMI: ----- Local Management Interface -----
LMI:
LMI: Unnumbered Information
LMI: Local In-channel Signaling Protocol
LMI: Call reference
LMI: Message type = 75 (Status Enquiry)
LMI: Locking shift to ANSI Codeset 5
LMI:
LMI: Information element 01 (Report type)
LMI: Report type 01 (Sequence number exchange only)
LMI:
LMI: Information element 03 (Keep alive)
LMI: Current sequence number   = 68
LMI: Last received sequence number = 154

- - - - - - - - - - - - - - - - Frame 45 - - - - - - - - - - - - - - - - -

DLC: ----- DLC Header -----
DLC:
DLC: Frame 45 arrived at 17:54:46.1924; frame size is 14 bytes.
DLC: This frame is dated 2 day(s) after capture started.
DLC: Destination = DTE

```
DLC:  Source    = DCE
DLC:
FRELAY: ----- Frame Relay -----
FRELAY:
FRELAY: Address word = 0001
FRELAY: 0000 00.. 0000 ....  = DLCI 0 (Signaling)
FRELAY: .... ..0. .... ....  = Response
FRELAY: .... .... .... 0...  = No forward congestion
FRELAY: .... .... .... .0..  = No backward congestion
FRELAY: .... .... .... ..0.  = Not eligible for discard
FRELAY:
LMI:   ----- Local Management Interface -----
LMI:
LMI:   Unnumbered Information
LMI:   Local In-channel Signaling Protocol
LMI:   Call reference
LMI:   Message type = 7D (Status)
LMI:   Locking shift to ANSI Codeset 5
LMI:
LMI:   Information element 01 (Report type)
LMI:     Report type 01 (Sequence number exchange only)
LMI:
LMI:   Information element 03 (Keep alive)
LMI:     Current sequence number    = 155
LMI:     Last received sequence number = 68
```

After five Link Integrity Verification message polls, the DTE requests a Full Status Enquiry (review Trace 4.1a and see Trace 4.1c). The full STATUS ENQUIRY message (Frame 348) includes the DLC, FRELAY, and LMI fields as before, but with two differences. First, the Report Type IE requests a FULL STATUS message (type 00H). Second, the sequence numbers have been incremented as follows: current sequence number (DTE) = 73, and the last received sequence number (from DCE) = 159.

The network's response (Frame 349) contains six IEs: Report Type, Link Integrity Verification, and four PVC STATUS messages. The Report Type specifies a FULL STATUS message. The Link Integrity Verification contains the sequence numbers, current sequence number (DCE) = 160, and last received sequence number (from DTE) = 73. Next, four PVC status IEs convey the information on the current PVCs (review Figure 3-10, noting that this PVC Status IE is 5 octets long per Annex D, and does not include the optional PVC bandwidth fields).

The first two octets of each PVC Status IE contain the identifier (07H) and the length of the contents (03H octets, not shown in the trace). The next two octets contain the DLCI of the PVC in question (DLCI 30, DLCI 31, and so on). Note that DLCIs 30–33 were the only ones active when this data was captured. The final octet contains two flag bits: the New flag (bit 4) and the Active flag (bit 2). The New flag indicates whether the PVC is present (New = 0) or whether the PVC is new (New = 1). The Active flag indicates whether the PVC is inactive (Active = 0) or active (Active = 1). Note that for each DLCI reported, the channel is present and active.

This case study demonstrates the use of the LMI and LMI messages transmitted between the FRAD and the network.

Trace 4.1c. LMI STATUS ENQUIRY/STATUS messages (full status)

Sniffer Internetwork Analyzer data, 22-Aug-93 at 19:10:00, OAT1.SYC, Pg 1

---------------- Frame 348 -----------------

DLC: ----- DLC Header -----
DLC:
DLC: Frame 348 arrived at 17:55:37.1285; frame size is 14 bytes.
DLC: This frame is dated 2 day(s) after capture started.
DLC: Destination = DCE
DLC: Source   = DTE
DLC:
FRELAY: ----- Frame Relay -----
FRELAY:
FRELAY: Address word = 0001
FRELAY: 0000 00.. 0000 .... = DLCI 0 (Signaling)

```
FRELAY:  .... ..0. .... ....    = Response
FRELAY:  .... .... ... 0...     = No forward congestion
FRELAY:  .... .... .... .0..    = No backward congestion
FRELAY:  .... .... .... ..0.    = Not eligible for discard
FRELAY:
LMI:    ----- Local Management Interface -----
LMI:
LMI:    Unnumbered Information
LMI:    Local In-channel Signaling Protocol
LMI:    Call reference
LMI:    Message type = 75 (Status Enquiry)
LMI:    Locking shift to ANSI Codeset 5
LMI:
LMI:    Information element 01 (Report type)
LMI:       Report type 00 (Full status message)
LMI:
LMI:    Information element 03 (Keep alive)
LMI:       Current sequence number    = 73
LMI:       Last received sequence number = 159
```

- - - - - - - - - - - - - - - Frame 349 - - - - - - - - - - - - - - - -

```
DLC:  ----- DLC Header -----
DLC:
DLC:  Frame 349 arrived at  17:55:37.1372; frame size is 34 bytes.
DLC:  This frame is dated 2 day(s) after capture started.
DLC:  Destination = DTE
DLC:  Source     = DCE
DLC:
FRELAY: ----- Frame Relay -----
FRELAY:
FRELAY: Address word = 0001
FRELAY:  0000 00.. 0000 ....    = DLCI 0 (Signaling)
FRELAY:  .... ..0. .... ....    = Response
FRELAY:  .... .... .... 0...    = No forward congestion
FRELAY:  .... .... .... .0..    = No backward congestion
```

FRELAY: ....0 .   = Not eligible for discard
FRELAY:
LMI: ----- Local Management Interface -----
LMI:
LMI: Unnumbered Information
LMI: Local In-channel Signaling Protocol
LMI: Call reference
LMI: Message type = 7D (Status)
LMI: Locking shift to ANSI Codeset 5
LMI:
LMI: Information element 01 (Report type)
LMI: Report type 00 (Full status message)
LMI:
LMI: Information element 03 (Keep alive)
LMI: Current sequence number   = 160
LMI: Last received sequence number = 73
LMI:
LMI: Information element 07 (PVC status)
LMI: PVC DLCI   = 30
LMI: PVC status = X2
LMI: .... 0... = Channel is present
LMI: .... ..1 . = Channel is active
LMI:
LMI: Information element 07 (PVC status)
LMI: PVC DLCI   = 31
LMI: PVC status = X2
LMI: .... 0... = Channel is present
LMI: .... ..1 . = Channel is active
LMI:
LMI: Information element 07 (PVC status)
LMI: PVC DLCI   = 32
LMI: PVC status = X2
LMI: .... 0... = Channel is present
LMI: .... ..1 . = Channel is active
LMI:
LMI: Information element 07 (PVC status)

```
LMI:    PVC DLCI   = 33
LMI:    PVC status = X2
LMI:    .... 0...  = Channel is present
LMI:    .... ..1.  = Channel is active
```

4.2 Encapsulating LAN Data Within T1.618 Frames

Section 3.7.1 explained how to encapsulate ULP information within T1.618 frames. As noted, a Q.922 UI frame (review Figure 3-42) carries the encapsulated information. A NLPID identifies the data carried within the frame and the encapsulation format. This case study investigates several of these alternative formats.

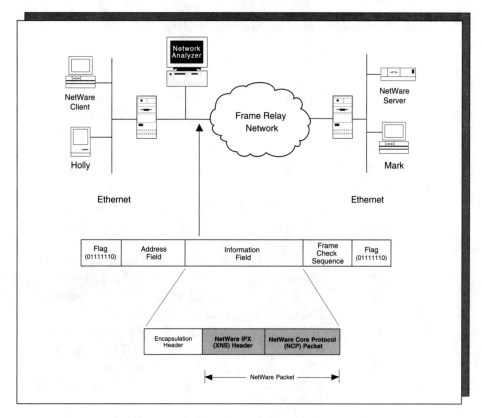

Figure 4–3. Higher layer protocols encapsulated in T1.618 frame

Trace 4.2a shows a number of higher layer protocols being transmitted across the frame relay interface (see Figure 4–3). These include the Xerox Network Systems (XNS) Routing Information Protocol (RIP), the NetWare Core Protocol (NCP), and the NetWare diagnostic protocol (NDIAG) that are used with Novell's NetWare operating system. TCP/IP-based internetworks use the RIP to convey information between routers. The SNAP transmits other information, such as LAN data. This trace also includes the LMI STATUS ENQUIRY and STATUS messages (Frames 44–45) discussed in the previous example. (Source and Destination IP addresses have been disguised with an X and Y in the first 2 octets to maintain the anonymity of the source.)

Trace 4.2a. Multiprotocol traffic over frame relay

Sniffer Internetwork Analyzer data, 22-Aug-93 at 19:10:00, OAT1.SYC Pg 1

SUMMARY	Delta T	Destination	Source	Summary
1		44135044.FFFF	44135044.Wllf	XNS RIP response: 10 networks, 20850301 at 2 hops, 20850302 at 2 hops, ...
2	0.1982	BOOMER1	9943AC.3Com	NCP C Create Connection
3	0.0624	9943AC.3Com	BOOMER11	NCP R OK
4	0.3588	000000219001	000000219002	SNAP Ethernet Type=80FF
5	0.0732	BRUTUS1	9943AC.3Com	NCP C Create Connection
6	0.0917	9943AC.3Com	BRUTUS1	NCP R OK
7	1.0991	000000218001	000000218002	SNAP Ethernet Type=80FF
8	0.1960	000000208501	000000208502	SNAP Ethernet Type=80FF
9	0.1039	BUSTER1	9943AC.3Com	NCP C Create Connection
10	0.0788	9943AC.3Com	BUSTER1	NCP R OK
11	0.1228	000000225001	000000225002	SNAP Ethernet Type=80FF
12	0.3411	BOOMER1	9943AC.3Com	NCP C Create Connection
13	0.0639	9943AC.3Com	BOOMER1	NCP R OK
14	0.1651	000000208502	000000208501	SNAP Ethernet Type=80FF
15	0.1342	000000208501	000000208502	SNAP Ethernet Type=80FF
16	0.1297	BRUTUS1	9943AC.3Com	NCP C Create Connection
17	0.0867	9943AC.3Com	BRUTUS1	NCP R OK

18	0.3134	000000219001	000000219002	SNAP Ethernet Type=80FF
19	0.2690	000000225002	000000225001	SNAP Ethernet Type=80FF
20	0.1020	000000225001	000000225002	SNAP Ethernet Type=80FF
21	0.7196	BUSTER1	9943AC.3Com	NCP C Create Connection
22	0.0780	9943AC.3Com	BUSTER1	NCP R OK
23	0.0950	000000218001	000000218002	SNAP Ethernet Type=80FF
24	0.2452	[X.Y.1.255]	[X.Y.1.2]	RIP R Routing entries=10
25	0.1244	BOOMER1	9943AC.3Com	NCP C Create Connection
26	0.0654	9943AC.3Com	BOOMER1	NCP R OK
27	0.3716	[X.Y.1.255]	[X.Y.1.2]	RIP R Routing entries=10
28	0.0559	BRUTUS1	9943AC.3Com	NCP C Create Connection
29	0.0919	9943AC.3Com	BRUTUS1	NCP R OK
30	0.2400	000000208501	000000208502	SNAP Ethernet Type=80FF
31	0.3212	000000225001	000000225002	SNAP Ethernet Type=80FF
32	0.2201	000000219001	000000219002	SNAP Ethernet Type=80FF
33	0.6175	BUSTER1	9943AC.3Com	NCP C Create Connection
34	0.0791	9943AC.3Com	BUSTER1	NCP R OK
35	0.4636	BOOMER1	9943AC.3Com	NCP C Create Connection
36	0.0623	9943AC.3Com	BOOMER1	NCP R OK
37	0.0395	000000218001	000000218002	SNAP Ethernet Type=80FF
38	0.2718	44135044.FFFF	44135044.Wllf	XNS RIP response:
				12 networks,
				00210101 at 2 hops,
				00210102 at 2 hops, ...
39	0.1194	BRUTUS1	9943AC.3Com	NCP C Create Connection
40	0.0870	9943AC.3Com	BRUTUS1	NCP R OK
41	0.2379	NFIDC08	4.1	XNS NetWare Security
42	0.1271	701B.00608CB8	7107F2.1	NDIAG IPX Config request
43	0.3489	000000208501	000000208502	SNAP Ethernet Type=80FF
44	0.2054	DCE.DLCI.0	DTE.DLCI.0	LMI Keep Alive Status Enquiry
45	0.0086	DTE.DLCI.0	DCE.DLCI.0	LMI Keep Alive Status
46	0.1015	000000225001	000000225002	SNAP Ethernet Type=80FF
47	0.2326	000000219001	000000219002	SNAP Ethernet Type=80FF
48	0.1418	BUSTER1	9943AC.3Com	NCP C Create Connection
49	0.0782	9943AC.3Com	BUSTER1	NCP R OK
50	0.4645	BOOMER1	9943AC.3Com	NCP C Create Connection

Let's examine these protocols separately. First, consider the NetWare packets transmitted in Frames 2 and 3 (see Trace 4.2b). In Frame 2, a NetWare client requests a connection with a NetWare server (BOOMER1). Frame 3 returns the server's response. The frame relay address field specifies the DLCI in use (32) and indicates that there are no congestion problems. The first 2 octets of the Information field contain the Q.922 Control field (set to 03H to indicate a UI frame), and one octet of padding (00H) to align the message. The NLPID field indicates SNAP (80H), followed by the 5 octets of the SNAP header. The Sniffer does not display the OUI, 00 00 00H (routed frames), although it does display the Novell Ethertype (8137H). The rest of Frame 2 contains the NetWare "Create Service Connection" packet, which contains a NetWare Internetwork Packet Exchange (IPX) header (another name for the XNS header shown in the trace), and an NCP packet. Frame 3 contains the corresponding NetWare "Create Service Connection" Reply packet.

Trace 4.2b. Novell NetWare over frame relay

Sniffer Internetwork Analyzer data, 22-Aug-93 at 19:10:00, OAT1.SYC Pg 1

- - - - - - - - - - - - - - - - Frame 2 - - - - - - - - - - - - - - - - -

```
DLC: ----- DLC Header -----
DLC:
DLC:  Frame 2 arrived at 17:54:37.1041; frame size is 48 (0030 hex) bytes.
DLC:  This frame is dated 2 day(s) after capture started.
DLC:  Destination = DCE
DLC:  Source     = DTE
DLC:
FRELAY: ----- Frame Relay -----
FRELAY:
FRELAY: Address word = 0801
FRELAY: 0000 10.. 0000 ....     = DLCI 32
FRELAY: .... ..0. .... ....     = Response
FRELAY: .... .... .... 0...     = No forward congestion
FRELAY: .... .... .... .0..     = No backward congestion
FRELAY: .... .... .... ..0.     = Not eligible for discard
```

FRELAY:
FRELAY: ----- Multiprotocol over Frame Relay -----
FRELAY:
FRELAY: Control, pad(s) = 0300
FRELAY: NLPID = 0x80 (SNAP)
FRELAY:
SNAP: ----- SNAP Header -----
SNAP:
SNAP: Type = 8137 (Novell)
SNAP:
XNS: ----- XNS Header -----
XNS:
XNS: Checksum = FFFF
XNS: Length = 37
XNS: Transport control   = 02
XNS: 0000 .... = Reserved
XNS: .... 0010 = Hop count
XNS: Packet type = 17 (Novell NetWare)
XNS:
XNS: Dest   network.node = 219003F5.1 (BOOMER1), socket = 1105 (NetWare)
XNS: Source network.node = 9943AC.3Com 4BB9C9, socket = 16387 (4003)
XNS:
XNS: ----- Novell Advanced NetWare -----
XNS:
XNS: Request type = 1111 (Create Connection)
XNS: Seq no=0   Connection no=255 Task no=4
XNS:
NCP: ----- Create Service Connection -----
NCP:
NCP: [Normal end of NetWare "Create Service Connection" packet.]
NCP:

- - - - - - - - - - - - - - - Frame 3 - - - - - - - - - - - - - - - - -

DLC: ----- DLC Header -----
DLC:
DLC: Frame 3 arrived at 17:54:37.1665; frame size is 48 bytes.
DLC: This frame is dated 2 day(s) after capture started.
DLC: Destination = DTE
DLC: Source   = DCE
DLC:
FRELAY: ----- Frame Relay -----
FRELAY:
FRELAY: Address word = 0801
FRELAY: 0000 10.. 0000 .... = DLCI 32
FRELAY: .... ..0. .... = Response
FRELAY: .... 0... = No forward congestion
FRELAY: .... .0.. = No backward congestion
FRELAY: ....0. = Not eligible for discard
FRELAY:
FRELAY: ----- Multiprotocol over Frame Relay -----
FRELAY:
FRELAY: Control, pad(s) = 0300
FRELAY: NLPID = 0x80 (SNAP)
FRELAY:
SNAP: ----- SNAP Header -----
SNAP:
SNAP: Type = 8137 (Novell)
SNAP:
XNS: ----- XNS Header -----
XNS:
XNS: Checksum = FFFF
XNS: Length = 38
XNS: Transport control = 01
XNS: 0000 .... = Reserved
XNS: .... 0001 = Hop count
XNS: Packet type = 17 (Novell NetWare)
XNS:

```
XNS:  Dest   network.node = 9943AC.3Com  4BB9C9, socket = 16387 (4003)
XNS:  Source network.node = 219003F5.1 (BOOMER1), socket = 1105 (NetWare)
XNS:
XNS:  ----- Novell Advanced NetWare -----
XNS:
XNS:  Request type = 3333 (Reply)
XNS:  Seq no=0   Connection no=1   Task no=1
XNS:
NCP:  ----- Create Service Connection Reply -----
NCP:
NCP:  Completion code = 00 (OK)
NCP:  Connection status flags = 00 (OK)
NCP:  [Normal end of NetWare "Create Service Connection Reply" packet.]
NCP:
```

The second example of multiprotocol encapsulation illustrates the format for bridged frames (Trace 4.2c). In Frames 7 and 8, the frame relay Address field has the same format as the previous example, except for a different DLCI (33). The NLPID indicates SNAP encapsulation, with an OUI indicating 802.1 bridged frames (transmitted as 00 80 C2H, but not delineated in the trace). The PID, or Type, as shown in the trace, has a value of 00 07H, which specifies 802.3/Ethernet media with a preserved FCS (review the table on Figure 3-42).

The higher layer information includes one short IEEE 802.3 frame inside the T1.618 frame. The 802.3 frame consists of Source and Destination addresses (6 octets each); a Length field (2 octets); a Logical Link Control (LLC) header (3 octets), which contains Destination and Source Service Access Point Addresses (DSAP and SSAP, 1 octet each) and a Control field; a SNAP header (5 octets), plus 2 octets of data. The total length of this encapsulated frame (beginning with the LLC header) is 10 octets: 3 + 5 + 2. Also note the dual use of SNAP, once in conjunction with the NLPID to define the encapsulation and a second time to define the information within the encapsulated frame.

Trace 4.2c. Bridged Ethernet frames over frame relay

Sniffer Internetwork Analyzer data, 22-Aug-93 at 19:10:00, OAT1.SYC Pg 1

- - - - - - - - - - - - - - - Frame 7 - - - - - - - - - - - - - - - -

DLC: ----- DLC Header -----
DLC:
DLC: Frame 7 arrived at 17:54:38.7894; frame size is 34 bytes.
DLC: This frame is dated 2 day(s) after capture started.
DLC: Destination = DTE
DLC: Source   = DCE
DLC:
FRELAY: ----- Frame Relay -----
FRELAY:
FRELAY: Address word = 0811
FRELAY: 0000 10.. 0001 .... = DLCI 33
FRELAY: .... ..0. .... = Response
FRELAY: .... 0... = No forward congestion
FRELAY: .... .0.. = No backward congestion
FRELAY: ....0. = Not eligible for discard
FRELAY:
FRELAY: ----- Multiprotocol over Frame Relay -----
FRELAY:
FRELAY: Control, pad(s) = 0300
FRELAY: NLPID = 0x80 (SNAP)
FRELAY:
SNAP: ----- SNAP Header -----
SNAP:
SNAP: Vendor ID = IEEE 802.1
SNAP: Type = 0007 (802.3/Ethernet)
SNAP:
ETHER: ----- Ethernet Header -----
ETHER:
ETHER: Destination = Station 000000218001
ETHER: Source   = Station 000000218002

ETHER: 802.3 length = 10
ETHER:
LLC: ----- LLC Header -----
LLC:
LLC: DSAP = AA, SSAP = AA, Command, Unnumbered frame: UI
LLC:
SNAP: ----- SNAP Header -----
SNAP:
SNAP: Type = 80FF (Unknown)
SNAP: [2 byte(s) of data]

- - - - - - - - - - - - - - - Frame 8 - - - - - - - - - - - - - - - -

DLC: ----- DLC Header -----
DLC:
DLC: Frame 8 arrived at 17:54:38.9854; frame size is 34 bytes.
DLC: This frame is dated 2 day(s) after capture started.
DLC: Destination = DTE
DLC: Source   = DCE
DLC:
FRELAY: ----- Frame Relay -----
FRELAY:
FRELAY: Address word = 04E1
FRELAY: 0000 01.. 1110 .... = DLCI 30
FRELAY: .... ..0. .... = Response
FRELAY: .... 0...   = No forward congestion
FRELAY: .... .0.. = No backward congestion
FRELAY: ....0. = Not eligible for discard
FRELAY:
FRELAY: ----- Multiprotocol over Frame Relay -----
FRELAY:
FRELAY: Control, pad(s) = 0300
FRELAY: NLPID = 0x80 (SNAP)
FRELAY:
SNAP: ----- SNAP Header -----
SNAP:

```
SNAP: Vendor ID =  IEEE 802.1
SNAP: Type = 0007 (802.3/Ethernet)
SNAP:
ETHER: ----- Ethernet Header -----
ETHER:
ETHER: Destination = Station 000000208501
ETHER: Source    = Station 000000208502
ETHER: 802.3 length = 10
ETHER:
LLC:  ----- LLC Header -----
LLC:
LLC:  DSAP = AA, SSAP = AA, Command, Unnumbered frame: UI
LLC:
SNAP: ----- SNAP Header -----
SNAP:
SNAP: Type = 80FF (Unknown)
SNAP: [2 byte(s) of data]
```

The final encapsulation example illustrates the use of the NLPID to transport IP-based information (refer to Trace 4.2d). The NIPID format was designed to be as general as possible, assigning specific values for commonly used protocols, and providing other mechanisms, such as SNAP, for less frequently used cases. One of the protocols with a direct NLPID assignment is the IP, with NLPID = CCH, as shown in Frame 24.

The frame relay Address field uses DLCI 30. The Information field contains a Q.922 Control field set for a UI frame as before, but it does not require a pad for octet alignment of the message. The NLPID is transmitted next (shown as 0xCC, meaning CC hexadecimal), without either of the optional L2/L3 or SNAP headers (review Figure 3–42).

The Higher Layer Information field begins with the IP header (20 octets), followed by a RIP packet. The RIP packet contains information about 10 IP-based networks. Note that two of these networks are one hop away (routing Frames 3 and 4) and the others are unreachable via this router.

Trace 4.2d. Internet Protocol (IP) packets over frame relay

Sniffer Internetwork Analyzer data, 22-Aug-93 at 19:10:00, OAT1.SYC Pg 1

- - - - - - - - - - - - - - - - Frame 24 - - - - - - - - - - - - - - - - -

```
DLC: ----- DLC Header ----- DLC:
DLC: Frame 24 arrived at  17:54:42.0339; frame size is 236 bytes. DLC:  This frame is dated 2 day(s)
after capture started.
DLC:  Destination = DTE
DLC:  Source      = DCE
DLC:
FRELAY: ----- Frame Relay -----
FRELAY:
FRELAY: Address word = 04E1
FRELAY:  0000 01..  1110 ....   = DLCI 30
FRELAY:  ....  ..0. .... ....   = Response
FRELAY:  ....   ....   ....  0...   = No forward congestion
FRELAY:  ....   ....   ....  .0..   = No backward congestion
FRELAY:  ....   ....   ....  ..0.   = Not eligible for discard
FRELAY:
FRELAY: ----- Multiprotocol over Frame Relay -----
FRELAY:
FRELAY: Control, pad(s) = 03
FRELAY: NLPID = 0xCC (Internet IP)
FRELAY:
IP:  ----- IP Header -----
IP:
IP:  Version = 4, header length = 20 bytes
IP:  Type of service = 00
IP:     000.    ....     = routine
IP:     ...0    ....     = normal delay
IP:     ....   0...    = normal throughput
IP:     ....   .0..    = normal reliability
IP:  Total length = 232 bytes
IP:  Identification = 48478
IP:  Flags = 0X
```

```
IP:    .0.. .... = may fragment
IP:    ..0. .... = last fragment
IP:    Fragment offset = 0 bytes
IP:    Time to live = 30 seconds/hops
IP:    Protocol = 17 (UDP)
IP:    Header checksum = D6FC (correct)
IP:    Source address = [X.Y.1.2]
IP:    Destination address = [X.Y.1.255]
IP:    No options
IP:
UDP:   ----- UDP Header -----
UDP:
UDP:   Source port = 520 (Route)
UDP:   Destination port = 520
UDP:   Length = 212
UDP:   Checksum = BB70 (correct)
UDP:
RIP:   ----- RIP Header -----
RIP:
RIP:   Command = 2 (Response)
RIP:   Version = 1
RIP:   Unused  = 0
RIP:
RIP:   Routing data Frame 1
RIP:      Address family identifier = 2 (IP)
RIP:      IP Address = [X.Y.1.0]
RIP:      Metric    = 16 (Unreachable)
RIP:
RIP:   Routing data Frame 2
RIP:      Address family identifier = 2 (IP)
RIP:      IP Address = [X.Y.10.0]
RIP:      Metric    = 16 (Unreachable)
RIP:
RIP:   Routing data Frame 3
RIP:      Address family identifier = 2 (IP)
RIP:      IP Address = [X.Y.1.0]
RIP:      Metric    = 1
```

```
RIP:
RIP:  Routing data Frame 4
RIP:    Address family identifier = 2 (IP)
RIP:    IP Address = [X.Y.3.0]
RIP:    Metric    = 1
RIP:
RIP:  Routing data Frame 5
RIP:    Address family identifier = 2 (IP)
RIP:    IP Address = [X.Y.1.0]
RIP:    Metric    = 16 (Unreachable)
RIP:
RIP:  Routing data Frame 6
RIP:    Address family identifier = 2 (IP)
RIP:    IP Address = [X.Y.3.0]
RIP:    Metric    = 16 (Unreachable)
RIP:
RIP:  Routing data Frame 7
RIP:    Address family identifier = 2 (IP)
RIP:    IP Address = [X.Y.1.0]
RIP:    Metric    = 16 (Unreachable)
RIP:
RIP:  Routing data Frame 8
RIP:    Address family identifier = 2 (IP)
RIP:    IP Address = [X.Y.3.0]
RIP:    Metric    = 16 (Unreachable)
RIP:
RIP:  Routing data Frame 9
RIP:    Address family identifier = 2 (IP)
RIP:    IP Address = [X.Y.1.0]
RIP:    Metric    = 16 (Unreachable)
RIP:
RIP:  Routing data Frame 10
RIP:    Address family identifier = 2 (IP)
RIP:    IP Address = [X.Y.3.0]
RIP:    Metric    = 16 (Unreachable)
RIP:
```

4.3 Measuring Differing Bandwidth Requirements

End-user applications determine the bandwidth requirements for DLCIs. In this example, a local network needs to communicate with two remote locations (see Figure 4–4). The protocols on each remote network are different. Remote Network A runs AppleTalk, DECnet, and TCP/IP. Remote Network B uses only AppleTalk and TCP/IP. These differing traffic patterns produce the differing bandwidth requirements.

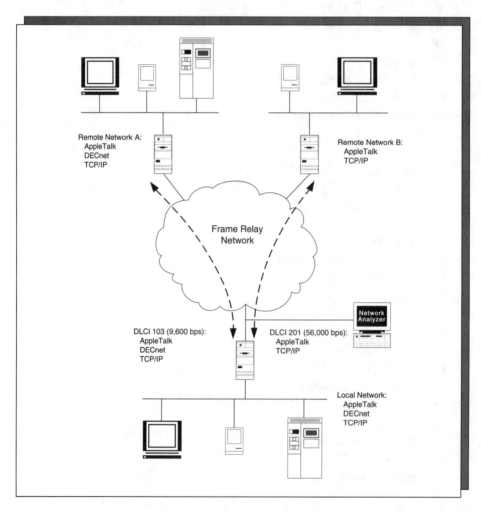

Figure 4–4. Multi-location bandwidth requirements

A summary trace of the traffic transmitted to and from the local network reveals the sources of the protocol traffic, and the DLCIs in use (refer to Trace 4.3a). AppleTalk traffic (LAP) is found in Frames 3, 4, 9, 17, 25, and 26. DECnet traffic, a DECnet Routing Protocol (DRP) packet, is seen in Frame 30. TCP/IP transports SNMP messages in Frames 2, 6, 7, and others, and Open Shortest Path First (OSPF) messages in Frames 8, 12, 18, and 19. Bridge protocol data units (BPDUs) are sent in Frames 1, 5, 10, 11, 14, and others. Finally, frame relay LMI messages are found in Frames 20 and 21.

By reconfiguring the output of the Sniffer Analyzer, you can see that the same traffic shows the DLCIs used for each protocol (refer to Trace 4.3b). In this trace, you see that DLCI 103 carries AppleTalk (LAP), DECnet (DRP), and IP (SNMP) traffic, while DLCI 201 carries only AppleTalk and TCP/IP. DLCI 1023 carries LMI messages, indicating Consortium-defined signaling (not shown in Figure 4–4).

Trace 4.3a. Multiprotocol traffic (summary)

Sniffer Internetwork Analyzer data 17-Mar-93 at 15:07:58 DDPRELAY.SYC Pg 1

SUMMARY	Delta T	Destination	Source	Summary
1		DTE.DLCI.201	DCE.DLCI.201	BPDU S:Pri=FFFF Port=8003 Root:Pri=0001 Addr=DECnet000904 Cost=100
2	0.0007	[X.Y.231.20]	[X.Y.241.9]	SNMP Got ifOperStatus = down
3	1.9219	DCE.DLCI.103	DTE.DLCI.103	LAP D=0 S=32 Type=0 NULLP
4	0.0015	DCE.DLCI.201	DTE.DLCI.201	LAP D=0 S=32 Type=0 NULLP
5	0.1044	DTE.DLCI.201	DCE.DLCI.201	BPDU S:Pri=FFFF Port=8003 Root:Pri=0001 Addr=DECnet000904 Cost=100

6	1.3053	[X.Y.231.20]	[X.Y.241.9]	SNMP Got ifInErrors .. ifOutOctets (11 items)
7	0.0006	[X.Y.231.20]	[X.Y.241.9]	SNMP Got ifOperStatus = up
8	0.5331	[X.Y.0.5]	[X.Y.240.232]	OSPF Hello ID=[X.Y.0.232]
9	0.1082	DTE.DLCI.201	DCE.DLCI.201	LAP D=0 S=44 Type=0 NULLP
10	0.0865	DTE.DLCI.201	DCE.DLCI.201	BPDU S:Pri=FFFF Port=8003 Root:Pri=0001 Addr=DECnet000904 Cost=100
11	2.0276	DTE.DLCI.201	DCE.DLCI.201	BPDU S:Pri=FFFF Port=8003 Root:Pri=0001 Addr=DECnet000904 Cost=100
12	0.4153	[X.Y.0.5]	[X.Y.240.242]	OSPF Hello ID=[X.Y.0.242]
13	0.0963	[X.Y.231.20]	[X.Y.241.9]	SNMP Got ifInErrors .. ifOutOctets (11 items)
14	1.5155	DTE.DLCI.201	DCE.DLCI.201	BPDU S:Pri=FFFF Port=8003 Root:Pri=0001 Addr=DECnet000904 Cost=100
15	0.0076	[X.Y.231.20]	[X.Y.241.9]	SNMP Got ifInOctets .. ifOutErrors (4 items)
16	0.0755	[X.Y.231.20]	[X.Y.241.9]	SNMP Got sysUpTime = 16765812 ticks
17	0.6122	DTE.DLCI.103	DCE.DLCI.103	LAP D=0 S=32 Type=0 NULLP
18	0.1099	[X.Y.0.5]	[X.Y.240.241]	OSPF Hello ID=[X.Y.0.241]
19	0.0015	[X.Y.0.5]	[X.Y.240.241]	OSPF Hello

				ID=[X.Y.0.241]
20	0.2211	DCE.DLCI.1023	DTE.DLCI.1023	LMI Full Status Enquiry
21	0.0010	DTE.DLCI.1023	DCE.DLCI.1023	LMI Full Status
22	1.0007	DTE.DLCI.201	DCE.DLCI.201	BPDU S:Pri=FFFF
				Port=8003
				Root:Pri=0001
				Addr=DECnet000904
				Cost=100
23	1.8227	[X.Y.231.20]	[X.Y.241.1]	SNMP Got ipForwDatagrams
				ipInDelivers (3 items)
24	0.0805	[X.Y.231.20]	[X.Y.241.1]	SNMP Got ifNumber ..
				ipInDiscards (4 items)
25	0.0180	DCE.DLCI.103	DTE.DLCI.103	LAP D=0 S=32 Type=0 NULLP
26	0.0015	DCE.DLCI.201	DTE.DLCI.201	LAP D=0 S=32 Type=0 NULLP
27	0.0411	[X.Y.231.20]	[X.Y.241.1]	SNMP Got ifAdminStatus,
				ifOperStatus
28	0.0543	[X.Y.231.20]	[X.Y.241.1]	SNMP Got ifAdminStatus,
				ifOperStatus
29	0.0090	DTE.DLCI.201	DCE.DLCI.201	BPDU S:Pri=FFFF
				Port=8003
				Root:Pri=0001
				Addr=DECnet000904
				Cost=100
30	1.2827	DTE.DLCI.103	12.1010	DRP ROUTER Hello
				S=12.1010 BLKSZ=1498

Trace 4.3b. Multiprotocol traffic by DLCI

Sniffer Internetwork Analyzer data 17-Mar-93 at 15:07:58 DDPRELAY.SYC Pg 1

SUMMARY	Delta T	Destination	Source	Summary
1		DTE.DLCI.201	DCE.DLCI.201	BPDU S:Pri=FFFF
2	0.0007	DCE.DLCI.201	DTE.DLCI.201	SNMP Got ifOperStatus =
3	1.9219	DCE.DLCI.103	DTE.DLCI.103	LAP D=0 S=32 Type=0

4	0.0015	DCE.DLCI.201	DTE.DLCI.201	LAP D=0 S=32 Type=0
5	0.1044	DTE.DLCI.201	DCE.DLCI.201	BPDU S:Pri=FFFF
6	1.3053	DCE.DLCI.201	DTE.DLCI.201	SNMP Got ifInErrors ..
7	0.0006	DCE.DLCI.201	DTE.DLCI.201	SNMP Got ifOperStatus =
8	0.5331	DTE.DLCI.201	DCE.DLCI.201	OSPF Hello
9	0.1082	DTE.DLCI.201	DCE.DLCI.201	LAP D=0 S=44 Type=0
10	0.0865	DTE.DLCI.201	DCE.DLCI.201	BPDU S:Pri=FFFF
11	2.0276	DTE.DLCI.201	DCE.DLCI.201	BPDU S:Pri=FFFF
12	0.4153	DTE.DLCI.103	DCE.DLCI.103	OSPF Hello
13	0.0963	DCE.DLCI.201	DTE.DLCI.201	SNMP Got ifInErrors ..
14	1.5155	DTE.DLCI.201	DCE.DLCI.201	BPDU S:Pri=FFFF
15	0.0076	DCE.DLCI.201	DTE.DLCI.201	SNMP Got ifInOctets ..
16	0.0755	DCE.DLCI.201	DTE.DLCI.201	SNMP Got sysUpTime =
17	0.6122	DTE.DLCI.103	DCE.DLCI.103	LAP D=0 S=32 Type=0
18	0.1099	DCE.DLCI.103	DTE.DLCI.103	OSPF Hello
19	0.0015	DCE.DLCI.201	DTE.DLCI.201	OSPF Hello
20	0.2211	DCE.DLCI.1023	DTE.DLCI.1023	LMI Full Status Enquiry
21	0.0010	DTE.DLCI.1023	DCE.DLCI.1023	LMI Full Status
22	1.0007	DTE.DLCI.201	DCE.DLCI.201	BPDU S:Pri=FFFF
23	1.8227	DCE.DLCI.201	DTE.DLCI.201	SNMP Got ipForwDatagrams
24	0.0805	DCE.DLCI.201	DTE.DLCI.201	SNMP Got ifNumber ..
25	0.0180	DCE.DLCI.103	DTE.DLCI.103	LAP D=0 S=32 Type=0 NULLP
26	0.0015	DCE.DLCI.201	DTE.DLCI.201	LAP D=0 S=32 Type=0 NULLP
27	0.0411	DCE.DLCI.201	DTE.DLCI.201	SNMP Got ifAdminStatus,
28	0.0543	DCE.DLCI.201	DTE.DLCI.201	SNMP Got ifAdminStatus,
29	0.0090	DTE.DLCI.201	DCE.DLCI.201	BPDU S:Pri=FFFF
30	1.2827	DTE.DLCI.103	DCE.DLCI.103	DRP ROUTER Hello

A more detailed look at the LMI messages reveals the traffic patterns between these two locations. The analyst first captures all the LMI messages and notes that they were transmitted on DLCI 1023, which indicates conformance with the Consortium (not T1.617 Annex D) standard (see Trace 4.3c). Also notice that the Keep Alive polls occur every 10 seconds, and that a Full Status Enquiry is issued after every five polls; these are both consistent with the Consortium specifications.

The details of the Full Status message show the bandwidth of each DLCI (refer to Trace 4.3d). Note that the modified PVC Status IE, defined by the Consortium, is in use (review Figure 3-10). The first PVC Status IE reports on DLCI 103. Recall from Figure 3-10 that the fifth octet of the PVC Status IE indicates a number of channel conditions. The analyzer displays this information as a "X2", meaning that the first octet is irrelevant, and the second octet is a hexadecimal 2, or 0010 in binary. You can, therefore, see that the channel is present, not new (New bit = 0); the channel is active (Active bit = 1); and the channel is below the buffer threshold (Receiver Not Ready bit = 0). The bandwidth for this PVC is given as 9,600 bps. The status of DLCI 201 reports similar information, but with a bandwidth of 56,000 bps.

Returning to Figure 4–4, note that DLCI 103 is the local end of the logical connection to Remote Network A. A bandwidth of 9,600 bps is adequate for this traffic. But more traffic is expected on the logical connection to Remote Network B, which requires a bandwidth of 56,000 bps.

Trace 4.3c. LMI messages (summary)

Sniffer Internetwork Analyzer data, 17-Mar-93 at 15:07:58 DDPRELAY.SYC Pg 1

SUMMARY	Delta T	Destination	Source	Summary
20		DCE.DLCI.1023	DTE.DLCI.1023	LMI Full Status Enquiry
21	0.0010	DTE.DLCI.1023	DCE.DLCI.1023	LMI Full Status
41	10.1398	DCE.DLCI.1023	DTE.DLCI.1023	LMI Keep Alive Status Enquiry
42	0.0011	DTE.DLCI.1023	DCE.DLCI.1023	LMI Keep Alive Status
61	10.1397	DCE.DLCI.1023	DTE.DLCI.1023	LMI Keep Alive Status Enquiry
62	0.0007	DTE.DLCI.1023	DCE.DLCI.1023	LMI Keep Alive Status
78	10.1451	DCE.DLCI.1023	DTE.DLCI.1023	LMI Keep Alive Status Enquiry
79	0.0007	DTE.DLCI.1023	DCE.DLCI.1023	LMI Keep Alive Status
101	10.1461	DCE.DLCI.1023	DTE.DLCI.1023	LMI Keep Alive Status Enquiry
102	0.0008	DTE.DLCI.1023	DCE.DLCI.1023	LMI Keep Alive Status
126	10.1601	DCE.DLCI.1023	DTE.DLCI.1023	LMI Keep Alive Status Enquiry

128	0.0009	DTE.DLCI.1023	DCE.DLCI.1023	LMI Keep Alive Status
149	10.1213	DCE.DLCI.1023	DTE.DLCI.1023	LMI Full Status Enquiry
150	0.0009	DTE.DLCI.1023	DCE.DLCI.1023	LMI Full Status
171	10.1419	DCE.DLCI.1023	DTE.DLCI.1023	LMI Keep Alive Status Enquiry
172	0.0010	DTE.DLCI.1023	DCE.DLCI.1023	LMI Keep Alive Status
192	10.1393	DCE.DLCI.1023	DTE.DLCI.1023	LMI Keep Alive Status Enquiry

Trace 4.3d. LMI messages (details)

Sniffer Internetwork Analyzer data, 17-Mar-93 at 15:07:58 DDPRELAY.SYC Pg 1

- - - - - - - - - - - - - - - Frame 149 - - - - - - - - - - - - - - - - -

LMI: ----- Local Management Interface -----
LMI:
LMI: Unnumbered Information
LMI: Local Management Interface (LMI)
LMI: Call reference
LMI: Message type = 75 (Status Enquiry)
LMI:
LMI: Information element 01 (Report type)
LMI: Report type 00 (Full status message)
LMI:
LMI: Information element 03 (Keep alive)
LMI: Current sequence number   = 199
LMI: Last received sequence number = 184

- - - - - - - - - - - - - - - Frame 150 - - - - - - - - - - - - - - - - -

LMI: ----- Local Management Interface -----
LMI:
LMI: Unnumbered Information
LMI: Local Management Interface (LMI)
LMI: Call reference
LMI: Message type = 7D (Status)
LMI:

```
LMI:   Information element 01 (Report type)
LMI:     Report type 00 (Full status message)
LMI:
LMI:   Information element 03 (Keep alive)
LMI:     Current sequence number     = 185
LMI:     Last received sequence number = 199
LMI:
LMI:   Information element 07 (PVC status)
LMI:     PVC DLCI    = 103
LMI:     PVC status = X2
LMI:     .... 00..  = Channel is present
LMI:     .... ..1.  = Channel is active
LMI:     .... ...0  = Below buffer threshold
LMI:     Bandwidth   = 9600 bits/second
LMI:
LMI:   Information element 07 (PVC status)
LMI:     PVC DLCI    = 201
LMI:     PVC status = X2
LMI:     .... 00..  = Channel is present
LMI:     .... ..1.  = Channel is active
LMI:     .... ...0  = Below buffer threshold
LMI:     Bandwidth   = 56000 bits/second
```

4.4 Congestion Notification

Section 2.9.2 describes how implicit and explicit processes communicate network congestion. Explicit or implicit protocol procedures communicate congestion in three ways. One, Explicit Congestion Notification uses 2 bits within the T1.618 frame, FECN and BECN. The FECN (forward) bit notifies the network of congestion in the same direction as the data flow; the BECN (backward) bit notifies it of congestion in the direction opposite to the data flow (review Figure 2-11). Two, the CLLM protocol, defined in T1.618, can explicitly send a congestion-notification message on DLCI 1023. Currently, CLLM is not widely implemented. Third, implicit congestion notification relies on the upper layer protocol, such as the Transmission Control Protocol (TCP), to recognize and correct the problem.

This case study examines explicit congestion control using the the FECN and BECN bits. The next case study explores the implicit method. In this example, several DLCIs have been configured between end-user processes and the network, connecting a local Ethernet with a remote Ethernet (see Figure 4–5). One of the host-application processes is experiencing response-time problems, prompting the network manager to suspect network congestion.

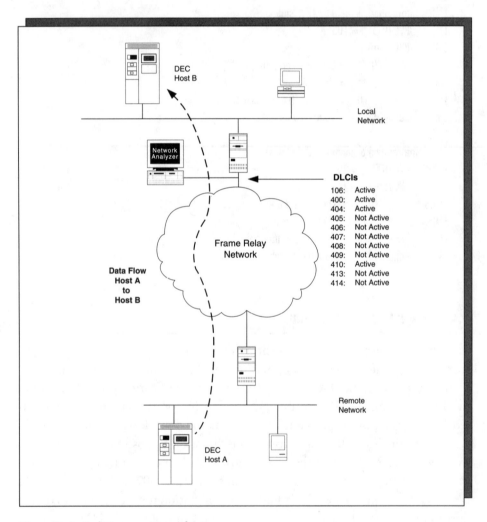

Figure 4–5. Explicit congestion notification

To begin analyzing this problem, the network analyst looks at the overall traffic between the local Ethernet and the network. As you can see in Trace 4.4a, the analyst finds two protocols, Ethernet and RIP.

Trace 4.4a. Multiple DLCIs in use

Sniffer Internetwork Analyzer data 7-May-92 at 10:20:40, KP1.SYC Pg 1

SUMMARY	Delta T	Destination	Source	Summary
1		DTE.DLCI.410	DCE.DLCI.410	Ethertype=0400
2	0.0033	DTE.DLCI.410	DCE.DLCI.410	Ethertype=0400
3	0.0033	DTE.DLCI.410	DCE.DLCI.410	Ethertype=0400
4	0.0033	DTE.DLCI.410	DCE.DLCI.410	Ethertype=0400
5	0.0033	DTE.DLCI.410	DCE.DLCI.410	Ethertype=0400
6	0.0033	DTE.DLCI.410	DCE.DLCI.410	Ethertype=0400
7	0.0033	DTE.DLCI.410	DCE.DLCI.410	Ethertype=0400
8	0.0033	DTE.DLCI.410	DCE.DLCI.410	Ethertype=0400
9	0.0033	DTE.DLCI.410	DCE.DLCI.410	Ethertype=0400
10	0.0033	DTE.DLCI.410	DCE.DLCI.410	Ethertype=0400
11	0.0033	DTE.DLCI.410	DCE.DLCI.410	Ethertype=0400
12	0.0033	DTE.DLCI.410	DCE.DLCI.410	Ethertype=0400
13	0.0020	DTE.DLCI.410	DCE.DLCI.410	Ethertype=0400
14	0.1834	DCE.DLCI.410	DTE.DLCI.410	Ethertype=0400
15	0.0075	DCE.DLCI.410	DTE.DLCI.410	Ethertype=0400
16	1.2105	[255.255.255.255]	DCE.DLCI.31.129]	RIP R Routing entries=25
17	0.0037	[255.255.255.255]	DCE.DLCI.31.129]	RIP R Routing entries=25
18	0.0036	[255.255.255.255]	DCE.DLCI.31.129]	RIP R Routing entries=25
19	0.0011	[255.255.255.255]	DCE.DLCI.31.129]	RIP R Routing entries=6
20	2.3283	DTE.DLCI.0	DCE.DLCI.0	LMI Keep Alive Status Enquiry

21	0.0009	DCE.DLCI.0	DTE.DLCI.0	LMI Keep Alive Status
.				
.				
.				
36	0.0017	[255.255.255.255]	DCE.DLCI.31.244]	RIP R Routing entries=11
37	0.0017	[255.255.255.255]	DCE.DLCI.31.244]	RIP R Routing entries=11
38	0.4242	DTE.DLCI.0	DCE.DLCI.0	LMI Full Status Enquiry
39	0.0013	DCE.DLCI.0	DTE.DLCI.0	LMI Full Status
40	0.1465	DCE.DLCI.410	DTE.DLCI.410	Ethertype=0400
41	0.0113	DCE.DLCI.410	DTE.DLCI.410	Ethertype=0400
42	0.0110	DCE.DLCI.410	DTE.DLCI.410	Ethertype=0400
43	0.0377	DCE.DLCI.410	DTE.DLCI.410	Ethertype=0400
44	0.0055	DTE.DLCI.106	DCE.DLCI.106	Ethertype=0400
45	0.0005	DTE.DLCI.400	DCE.DLCI.400	Ethertype=0400
46	0.0004	DTE.DLCI.404	DCE.DLCI.404	Ethertype=0400
47	0.0005	DTE.DLCI.410	DCE.DLCI.410	Ethertype=0400
48	0.0735	DCE.DLCI.400	DTE.DLCI.400	Ethertype=0400
49	0.0031	DCE.DLCI.400	DTE.DLCI.400	Ethertype=0400
50	0.0717	DCE.DLCI.410	DTE.DLCI.410	Ethertype=0400
51	0.0697	DCE.DLCI.400	DTE.DLCI.400	Ethertype=0400
52	0.0009	DCE.DLCI.410	DTE.DLCI.410	Ethertype=0400
53	0.0980	DCE.DLCI.410	DTE.DLCI.410	Ethertype=0400
54	0.0913	DCE.DLCI.400	DTE.DLCI.400	Ethertype=0400
55	0.0944	DCE.DLCI.400	DTE.DLCI.400	Ethertype=0400
56	0.0921	DCE.DLCI.400	DTE.DLCI.400	Ethertype=0400
57	0.1072	DCE.DLCI.400	DTE.DLCI.400	Ethertype=0400
58	0.0029	DCE.DLCI.400	DTE.DLCI.400	Ethertype=0400
59	0.0568	DTE.DLCI.106	DCE.DLCI.106	Ethertype=0400
60	0.0004	DTE.DLCI.400	DCE.DLCI.400	Ethertype=0400

Next, the analyst looks at the LMI messages and determines the current status of all the DLCIs (Trace 4.4b). The LMI Full Status message in Frame 39 reveals the following DLCIs:

DLCI	Channel Status
106	Active
400	Active
404	Active
405	Not active
406	Not active
407	Not active
408	Not active
409	Not active
410	Active
413	Not active
414	Not active

Trace 4.4b. LMI Full Status message

Sniffer Internetwork Analyzer data 7-May-92 at 10:20:40, KP1.SYC Pg 1

- - - - - - - - - - - - - - - Frame 38 - - - - - - - - - - - - - - - - -

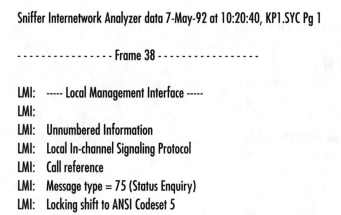

```
LMI:    ----- Local Management Interface -----
LMI:
LMI:    Unnumbered Information
LMI:    Local In-channel Signaling Protocol
LMI:    Call reference
LMI:    Message type = 75 (Status Enquiry)
LMI:    Locking shift to ANSI Codeset 5
```

```
LMI:
LMI:    Information element 01 (Report type)
LMI:        Report type 00 (Full status message)
LMI:
LMI:    Information element 03 (Keep alive)
LMI:        Current sequence number    = 134
LMI:        Last received sequence number = 169


- - - - - - - - - - - - - - - - Frame 39 - - - - - - - - - - - - - - - -


LMI:    ----- Local Management Interface -----
LMI:
LMI:    Unnumbered Information
LMI:    Local In-channel Signaling Protocol
LMI:    Call reference
LMI:    Message type = 7D (Status)
LMI:    Locking shift to ANSI Codeset 5
LMI:
LMI:    Information element 01 (Report type)
LMI:        Report type 00 (Full status message)
LMI:
LMI:    Information element 03 (Keep alive)
LMI:        Current sequence number    = 170
LMI:        Last received sequence number = 134
LMI:
LMI:    Information element 07 (PVC status)
LMI:        PVC DLCI    = 106
LMI:        PVC status = X2
LMI:        .... 0...  = Channel is present
LMI:        .... ..1.  = Channel is active
LMI:
LMI:    Information element 07 (PVC status)
LMI:        PVC DLCI    = 400
LMI:        PVC status = X2
LMI:        .... 0...  = Channel is present
LMI:        .... ..1.  = Channel is active
```

```
LMI:
LMI:    Information element 07 (PVC status)
LMI:    PVC DLCI   = 404
LMI:    PVC status = X2
LMI:    .... 0...   = Channel is present
LMI:    .... ..1.   = Channel is active
LMI:
LMI:    Information element 07 (PVC status)
LMI:    PVC DLCI   = 405
LMI:    PVC status = X0
LMI:    .... 0...   = Channel is present
LMI:    .... ..0.   = Channel is not active
LMI:
LMI:    Information element 07 (PVC status)
LMI:    PVC DLCI   = 406
LMI:    PVC status = X0
LMI:    .... 0...   = Channel is present
LMI:    .... ..0.   = Channel is not active
LMI:
LMI:    Information element 07 (PVC status)
LMI:    PVC DLCI   = 407
LMI:    PVC status = X0
LMI:    .... 0...   = Channel is present
LMI:    .... ..0.   = Channel is not active
LMI:
LMI:    Information element 07 (PVC status)
LMI:    PVC DLCI   = 408
LMI:    PVC status = X0
LMI:    .... 0...   = Channel is present
LMI:    .... ..0.   = Channel is not active
LMI:
LMI:    Information element 07 (PVC status)
LMI:    PVC DLCI   = 409
LMI:    PVC status = X0
LMI:    .... 0... = Channel is present
LMI:    .... ..0. = Channel is not active
```

139

```
LMI:
LMI:    Information element 07 (PVC status)
LMI:        PVC DLCI   = 410
LMI:        PVC status = X2
LMI:        .... 0...   = Channel is present
LMI:        .... ..1.   = Channel is active
LMI:
LMI:    Information element 07 (PVC status)
LMI:        PVC DLCI   = 413
LMI:        PVC status = X0
LMI:        .... 0...   = Channel is present
LMI:        .... ..0.   = Channel is not active
LMI:
LMI:    Information element 07 (PVC status)
LMI:        PVC DLCI   = 414
LMI:        PVC status = X0
LMI:        .... 0...   = Channel is present
LMI:        .... ..0.   = Channel is not active
```

By comparing the active DLCIs with the applications currently running, the analyst isolates the end user's response time complaint to DLCI 410. Next, the analyst captures the data on DLCI 410 and displays a summary of all protocol layers (Trace 4.4c). Traffic on this DLCI consists of encapsulated Ethernet frames of moderate size (all less than 500 octets in length). In the first eight frames, the network sends an FECN to the end user, warning of network congestion. The FECN goes away in Frame 9. By examining the relative time between Frame 1 and Frame 9, you can see that the network took 0.0263 seconds to recover from the congestion. While end users may not notice this short amount of time as a response-time delay, multiple occurrences could degrade performance. Trace 4.4d provides a more detailed look.

Trace 4.4c. Congestion notification (summary)

Sniffer Internetwork Analyzer data 7-May-92 at 10:20:40, KP1.SYC Pg 1

SUMMARY	Rel Time	Destination	Source	Summary
1	0.0000	DTE.DLCI.410	DCE.DLCI.410	DLC Length=494 FRELAY DLCI=410 FECN ETHER Type=0400, size=490
2	0.0033	DTE.DLCI.410	DCE.DLCI.410	DLC Length=494 FRELAY DLCI=410 FECN ETHER Type=0400, size=490
3	0.0065	DTE.DLCI.410	DCE.DLCI.410	DLC Length=494 FRELAY DLCI=410 FECN ETHER Type=0400, size=490
4	0.0098	DTE.DLCI.410	DCE.DLCI.410	DLC Length=494 FRELAY DLCI=410 FECN ETHER Type=0400, size=490
5	0.0131	DTE.DLCI.410	DCE.DLCI.410	DLC Length=494 FRELAY DLCI=410 FECN ETHER Type=0400, size=490
6	0.0164	DTE.DLCI.410	DCE.DLCI.410	DLC Length=494 FRELAY DLCI=410 FECN ETHER Type=0400, size=490
7	0.0197	DTE.DLCI.410	DCE.DLCI.410	DLC Length=494 FRELAY DLCI=410 FECN ETHER Type=0400, size=490
8	0.0230	DTE.DLCI.410	DCE.DLCI.410	DLC Length=494 FRELAY DLCI=410 FECN ETHER Type=0400, size=490
9	0.0263	DTE.DLCI.410	DCE.DLCI.410	DLC Length=494 FRELAY DLCI=410 ETHER Type=0400, size=490
10	0.0295	DTE.DLCI.410	DCE.DLCI.410	DLC Length=494 FRELAY DLCI=410 ETHER Type=0400, size=490

11	0.0328	DTE.DLCI.410	DCE.DLCI.410	DLC Length=494
				FRELAY DLCI=410
				ETHER Type=0400, size=490
12	0.0361	DTE.DLCI.410	DCE.DLCI.410	DLC Length=494
				FRELAY DLCI=410
				ETHER Type=0400, size=490
13	0.0381	DTE.DLCI.410	DCE.DLCI.410	DLC Length=302
				FRELAY DLCI=410
				ETHER Type=0400, size=298
14	0.2215	DCE.DLCI.410	DTE.DLCI.410	DLC Length=494
				FRELAY DLCI=410
				ETHER Type=0400, size=490
15	0.2290	DCE.DLCI.410	DTE.DLCI.410	DLC Length=366
				FRELAY DLCI=410
				ETHER Type=0400, size=362

The details of Frames 1 and 9 show the contents of the T1.618 Address field, and the changed FECN bit. Note that the network (DCE) is the source of the data in both cases. Also of interest is the DE bit (not set in Frame 1), which indicates that the end user considers this a priority frame and that the traffic to the network has not exceeded the committed burst size measured in bits (variable Bc, as shown in Figure 2-13). From this, the analyst can conclude that the congestion was temporary and that the network has recovered. Further investigation, possibly at different times and/or on different days, would be necessary to determine the cause of the congestion.

Trace 4.4d. FECN and DE bit details

Sniffer Internetwork Analyzer data 7-May-92 at 10:20:40, KP1.SYC, Pg 1

- - - - - - - - - - - - - - - Frame 1 - - - - - - - - - - - - - - - - -

DLC: ----- DLC Header ----- DLC:
DLC: Frame 1 arrived at 10:24:44.4797; frame size is 494 (01EE hex) bytes.
DLC: Destination = DTE
DLC: Source = DCE

DLC:
FRELAY: ----- Frame Relay -----
FRELAY:
FRELAY: Address word = 64A9
FRELAY: 0110 01.. 1010 ....   = DLCI 410
FRELAY: .... ..0. ....   = Response
FRELAY: .... 1...   = Forward congestion
FRELAY: .... .0..   = No backward congestion
FRELAY: ....0.   = Not eligible for discard
FRELAY:
FRELAY: ----- Multiprotocol over Frame Relay -----
FRELAY:
FRELAY: Control, pad(s) = 03
FRELAY: NLPID = 0xCE (EtherType)
FRELAY:
ETYPE: Ethertype = 0400 (Unknown)
ETYPE:
???: ----- Unknown Ethertype data -----
???:
???: No protocol interpreter is installed for this Ethertype.
???: [488 bytes of data]

    .
    .
    .

- - - - - - - - - - - - - - - - Frame 9 - - - - - - - - - - - - - - - -

DLC: ----- DLC Header -----
DLC:
DLC: Frame 9 arrived at 10:24:44.5060; frame size is 494 (01EE hex) bytes.
DLC: Destination = DTE
DLC: Source   = DCE
DLC:
FRELAY: ----- Frame Relay -----
FRELAY:
FRELAY: Address word = 64A1

```
FRELAY: 0110 01.. 1010 ....  = DLCI 410
FRELAY: .... ..0. .... ....  = Response
FRELAY: .... .... ....  0...  = No forward congestion
FRELAY: .... .... .... .0..   = No backward congestion
FRELAY: .... .... .... ..0.   = Not eligible for discard
FRELAY:
FRELAY: ----- Multiprotocol over Frame Relay -----
FRELAY:
FRELAY: Control, pad(s) = 03
FRELAY: NLPID = 0xCE (EtherType)
FRELAY:
ETYPE: Ethertype  = 0400 (Unknown)
ETYPE:
???: ----- Unknown Ethertype data -----
???:
???:  No protocol interpreter is installed for this Ethertype.
???:  [488 bytes of data]
```

4.5 Error Recovery Using Upper Layer Protocol Procedures

The final example looks at error-recovery procedures occurring in end-user systems that use protocols in layers higher than frame relay. In this case, a local workstation has a remote-terminal (or TELNET) connection with a remote host. The end user has complained of response-time problems, so the network analyst captures data going from the local router to the frame relay network and back (see Figure 4–6). The challenge is to determine whether the source of the response-time delays is a congested network or a slow host.

The first step in a complex analysis such as this is to clearly define the problem. To do so, the analyst looks at all of the traffic on the link from the DTE to the DCE into the frame relay network. The analyst discovers that the user complaints come from the traffic carried on DLCI 31 (see Trace 4.5a). Notice that the trace has been filtered to display only the traffic on DLCI 31, so the FRELAY DLCI = 31 notation in the summary section of every frame. Also note that an IP header, 20 octets in length, and a TCP header, also 20 octets in length, precede every TELNET message. Of greater importance are the special flags, inserted by the Expert Sniffer, that indicate the detection of a problem. In this case, Frames 45, 61, 68, and 79 show the flag "Transport retransmissions," which indicate that an upper layer protocol (TCP, in this case), had to retransmit data. Now, we must determine the cause of these retransmissions.

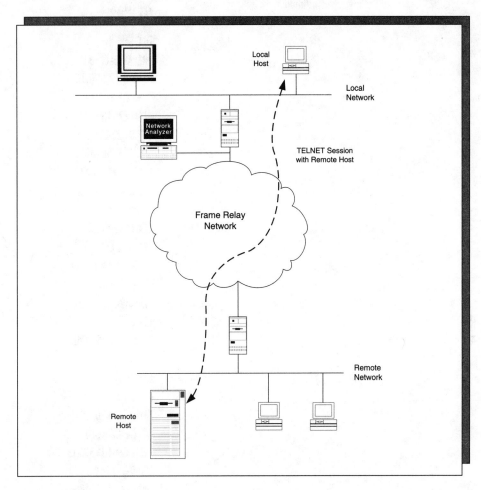

Figure 4–6. Host retransmission

Trace 4.5a. TELNET retransmissions (summary)

Sniffer Internetwork Analyzer data 10-Nov-92 at 14:28:24, FR1.SYC, Pg 1

SUMMARY	Delta T	Destination	Source	Summary
12		DTE	DCE	DLC Length=50
				FRELAY DLCI=31
				IP D=[X.Y.200.10]
				S=[X.Y.204.12]
				LEN=21 ID=2121
				TCP D=23 S=11069
				ACK=575826873
				SEQ=147196479
				LEN=1 WIN=422
				Telnet C PORT=11069 0
15	0.0155	DCE	DTE	DLC Length=50
				FRELAY DLCI=31
				IP D=[X.Y.204.12]
				S=[X.Y.200.10]
				LEN=20 ID=52644
				TCP D=11069 S=23
				ACK=147196480
				WIN=3265
16	0.0006	DCE	DTE	DLC Length=50
				FRELAY DLCI=31
				IP D=[X.Y.204.12]
				S=[X.Y.200.10]
				LEN=21 ID=52645
				TCP D=11069 S=23
				ACK=147196480
				SEQ=575826873
				LEN=1 WIN=3265
				Telnet R PORT=11069 0

25	0.0990	DTE	DCE	DLC Length=50
				FRELAY DLCI=31
				IP D=[X.Y.200.10]
				S=[X.Y.204.12]
				LEN=21 ID=2122
				TCP D=23 S=11069
				ACK=575826874
				SEQ=147196480
				LEN=1 WIN=421
				Telnet C PORT=11069 1
30	0.0119	DCE	DTE	DLC Length=50
				FRELAY DLCI=31
				IP D=[X.Y.204.12]
				S=[X.Y.200.10]
				LEN=20 ID=52647
				TCP D=11069 S=23
				ACK=147196481 WIN=3264
32	0.0019	DCE	DTE	DLC Length=50
				FRELAY DLCI=31
				IP D=[X.Y.204.12]
				S=[X.Y.200.10]
				LEN=20 ID=52648
				TCP D=11069 S=23
				ACK=147196481 WIN=3264
33	0.0006	DCE	DTE	DLC Length=50
				FRELAY DLCI=31
				IP D=[X.Y.204.12]
				S=[X.Y.200.10]
				LEN=21 ID=52649
				TCP D=11069 S=23
				ACK=147196481
				SEQ=575826874
				LEN=1 WIN=3264
				Telnet R PORT=11069 1

39	0.1542	DTE	DCE	DLC Length=50
				FRELAY DLCI=31
				IP D=[X.Y.200.10]
				S=[X.Y.204.12]
				LEN=20 ID=2123
				TCP D=23 S=11069
				ACK=575826875 WIN=420
41	0.0096	DCE	DTE	DLC Length=50
				FRELAY DLCI=31
				IP D=[X.Y.204.12]
				S=[X.Y.200.10]
				LEN=20 ID=52650
				TCP D=11069 S=23
				ACK=147196481 WIN=3264
42	0.0024	DTE	DCE	DLC Length=50
				FRELAY DLCI=31
				IP D=[X.Y.200.10]
				S=[X.Y.204.12]
				LEN=21 ID=2124
				TCP D=23 S=11069
				ACK=575826875
				SEQ=147196481
				LEN=1 WIN=420
				Telnet C PORT=11069 0
43	0.0096	DCE	DTE	DLC Length=50
				FRELAY DLCI=31
				IP D=[X.Y.204.12]
				S=[X.Y.200.10]
				LEN=20 ID=52651
				TCP D=11069 S=23
				ACK=147196482 WIN=3263
44	0.0015	DCE	DTE	DLC Length=50
				FRELAY DLCI=31
				IP D=[X.Y.204.12]
				S=[X.Y.200.10]
				LEN=21 ID=52652

				TCP D=11069 S=23
				ACK=147196482
				SEQ=575826875
				LEN=1 WIN=3263
				Telnet R PORT=11069 0
45	0.0325	DTE	DCE	Transport retransmissions
				DLC Length=50
				FRELAY DLCI=31
				IP D=[X.Y.200.10]
				S=[X.Y.204.12]
				LEN=21 ID=2125
				TCP D=23 S=11069
				ACK=575826875
				SEQ=147196481
				LEN=1 WIN=420
				Telnet C PORT=11069 0
47	0.0142	DCE	DTE	DLC Length=50
				FRELAY DLCI=31
				IP D=[X.Y.204.12]
				S=[X.Y.200.10]
				LEN=20 ID=52653
				TCP D=11069 S=23
				ACK=147196482
				WIN=3263
61	0.1305	DTE	DCE	Transport retransmissions
				DLC Length=50
				FRELAY DLCI=31
				IP D=[X.Y.200.10]
				S=[X.Y.204.12]
				LEN=21 ID=2126
				TCP D=23 S=11069
				ACK=575826875
				SEQ=147196481
				LEN=1 WIN=420
				Telnet C PORT=11069 0

62	0.0222	DCE	DTE	DLC Length=50
				FRELAY DLCI=31
				IP D=[X.Y.204.12]
				S=[X.Y.200.10]
				LEN=20 ID=52654
				TCP D=11069 S=23
				ACK=147196482
				WIN=3263
67	0.0417	DTE	DCE	DLC Length=50
				FRELAY DLCI=31
				IP D=[X.Y.200.10]
				S=[X.Y.204.12]
				LEN=21 ID=2127
				TCP D=23 S=11069
				ACK=575826876
				SEQ=147196482
				LEN=1 WIN=419
				Telnet C PORT=11069 2
68	0.0036	DTE	DCE	Transport retransmissions
				DLC Length=50
				FRELAY DLCI=31
				IP D=[X.Y.200.10]
				S=[X.Y.204.12]
				LEN=21 ID=2128
				TCP D=23 S=11069
				ACK=575826876
				SEQ=147196482
				LEN=1 WIN=419
				Telnet C PORT=11069 2
69	0.0059	DCE	DTE	DLC Length=50
				FRELAY DLCI=31
				IP D=[X.Y.204.12]
				S=[X.Y.200.10]
				LEN=20 ID=52656
				TCP D=11069 S=23
				ACK=147196483 WIN=3262

70	0.0015	DCE	DTE	DLC Length=50
				FRELAY DLCI=31
				IP D=[X.Y.204.12]
				S=[X.Y.200.10]
				LEN=20 ID=52657
				TCP D=11069 S=23
				ACK=147196483 WIN=3262
71	0.0006	DCE	DTE	DLC Length=50
				FRELAY DLCI=31
				IP D=[X.Y.204.12]
				S=[X.Y.200.10]
				LEN=21 ID=52658
				TCP D=11069 S=23
				ACK=147196483
				SEQ=575826876
				LEN=1 WIN=3262
				Telnet R PORT=11069 2
72	0.0044	DCE	DTE	DLC Length=50
				FRELAY DLCI=31
				IP D=[X.Y.204.12]
				S=[X.Y.200.10]
				LEN=20 ID=52659
				TCP D=11069 S=23
				ACK=147196483 WIN=3262
79	0.1304	DTE	DCE	Transport retransmissions
				DLC Length=50
				FRELAY DLCI=31
				IP D=[X.Y.200.10]
				S=[X.Y.204.12]
				LEN=21 ID=2129
				TCP D=23 S=11069
				ACK=575826876
				SEQ=147196482
				LEN=1 WIN=419
				Telnet C PORT=11069 2

80	0.0123	DCE	DTE	DLC Length=50
				FRELAY DLCI=31
				IP D=[X.Y.204.12]
				S=[X.Y.200.10]
				LEN=20 ID=52660
				TCP D=11069 S=23
				ACK=147196483 WIN=3262
88	0.1286	DTE	DCE	DLC Length=50
				FRELAY DLCI=31
				IP D=[X.Y.200.10]
				S=[X.Y.204.12]
				LEN=20 ID=2130
				TCP D=23 S=11069
				ACK=575826877 WIN=418
89	0.0111	DCE	DTE	DLC Length=50
				FRELAY DLCI=31
				IP D=[X.Y.204.12]
				S=[X.Y.200.10]
				LEN=20 ID=52661
				TCP D=11069 S=23
				ACK=147196483 WIN=3262
100	0.1613	DTE	DCE	DLC Length=50
				FRELAY DLCI=31
				IP D=[X.Y.200.10]
				S=[X.Y.204.12]
				LEN=21 ID=2131
				TCP D=23 S=11069
				ACK=575826877
				SEQ=147196483
				LEN=1 WIN=418
				Telnet C PORT=11069 -
103	0.0345	DCE	DTE	DLC Length=50
				FRELAY DLCI=31
				IP D=[X.Y.204.12]
				S=[X.Y.200.10]
				LEN=20 ID=52662

104	0.0006	DCE	DTE	TCP D=11069 S=23
				ACK=147196484 WIN=3261
				DLC Length=50
				FRELAY DLCI=31
				IP D=[X.Y.204.12]
				S=[X.Y.200.10]
				LEN=21 ID=52663
				TCP D=11069 S=23
				ACK=147196484
				SEQ=575826877
				LEN=1 WIN=3261
119	0.1752	DTE	DCE	Telnet R PORT=11069 -
				DLC Length=50
				FRELAY DLCI=31
				IP D=[X.Y.200.10]
				S=[X.Y.204.12]
				LEN=20 ID=2132
				TCP D=23 S=11069
				ACK=575826878 WIN=417
120	0.0096	DCE	DTE	DLC Length=50
				FRELAY DLCI=31
				IP D=[X.Y.204.12]
				S=[X.Y.200.10]
				LEN=20 ID=52666
				TCP D=11069 S=23
				ACK=147196484 WIN=3261

The first step is to look at the LMI frames transmitted during the analysis period. (These messages do not appear in Trace 4.5a for two reasons. First, the LMI messages were transmitted on DLCI 1023, and Trace 4.5a was filtered to show only DLCI 31. Second, the LMI messages were not transmitted until Frame 175, which occurred after Trace 4.5a.) During the analysis period, only a Keep Alive Status message, not the more informative Full Status message has been sent. Therefore the LMI information derived is limited. Nevertheless, the sequence numbers increment properly, indicating no problems with the FRAD interface into the network (Trace 4.5b).

Trace 4.5b. LMI messages (detail)

Sniffer Internetwork Analyzer data 10-Nov-92 at 14:28:24 FR1.SYC Pg 1

---------------- Frame 175 -----------------

```
LMI:   ----- Local Management Interface ----- LMI:
LMI:   Unnumbered Information
LMI:   Local Management Interface (LMI)
LMI:   Call reference
LMI:   Message type = 75 (Status Enquiry)
LMI:
LMI:   Information element 01 (Report type)
LMI:      Report type 01 (Sequence number exchange only)
LMI:
LMI:   Information element 03 (Keep alive)
LMI:      Current sequence number    = 14
LMI:      Last received sequence number = 13
```

---------------- Frame 176 -----------------

```
LMI:   ----- Local Management Interface -----
LMI:
LMI:   Unnumbered Information
LMI:   Local Management Interface (LMI)
LMI:   Call reference
LMI:   Message type = 7D (Status)
LMI:
LMI:   Information element 01 (Report type)
LMI:      Report type 01 (Sequence number exchange only)
LMI:
LMI:   Information element 03 (Keep alive)
LMI:      Current sequence number    = 14
LMI:      Last received sequence number = 14
```

The third step is to look at some of the retransmitted frames for a clue. Next, the analyst examines the frame relay Address fields to see whether any network congestion is present. The analyst examines a few frames before the first retransmission, but finds no congestion (Trace 4.5c).

Trace 4.5c. Frame relay header (details)

Sniffer Internetwork Analyzer data 10-Nov-92 at 14:28:24 FR1.SYC Pg 1

- - - - - - - - - - - - Frame 41 (Source = DTE) - - - - - - - - - - - -

FRELAY: ----- Frame Relay -----
FRELAY:
FRELAY: Address word = 04F1
FRELAY: 0000 01.. 1111 .... = DLCI 31
FRELAY: .... ..0. .... = Response
FRELAY: .... 0... = No forward congestion
FRELAY: .... .0.. = No backward congestion
FRELAY: ....0. = Not eligible for discard
FRELAY:
FRELAY: ----- Multiprotocol over Frame Relay -----
FRELAY:
FRELAY: Control, pad(s) = 03
FRELAY: NLPID = 0xCC (Internet IP)
FRELAY:

- - - - - - - - - - - - Frame 42 (Source = DCE) - - - - - - - - - - - -

FRELAY: ----- Frame Relay -----
FRELAY:
FRELAY: Address word = 04F1
FRELAY: 0000 01.. 1111 .... = DLCI 31
FRELAY: .... ..0. .... = Response
FRELAY: .... 0... = No forward congestion
FRELAY: .... .0.. = No backward congestion
FRELAY: ....0. = Not eligible for discard

```
FRELAY:
FRELAY: ----- Multiprotocol over Frame Relay -----
FRELAY:
FRELAY: Control, pad(s) = 03
FRELAY: NLPID = 0xCC (Internet IP)
FRELAY:


- - - - - - - - - - - Frame 43 (Source = DTE) - - - - - - - - - - - -


FRELAY: ----- Frame Relay -----
FRELAY:
FRELAY: Address word = 04F1
FRELAY:  0000 01.. 1111 ....   = DLCI 31
FRELAY:  .... ..0. .... ....   = Response
FRELAY:  .... .... .... 0...   = No forward congestion
FRELAY:  .... .... .... .0..   = No backward congestion
FRELAY:  .... .... .... ..0.   = Not eligible for discard
FRELAY:
FRELAY: ----- Multiprotocol over Frame Relay -----
FRELAY:
FRELAY: Control, pad(s) = 03
FRELAY: NLPID = 0xCC (Internet IP)
FRELAY:


- - - - - - - - - - - Frame 44 (Source = DTE) - - - - - - - - - - - -


FRELAY: ----- Frame Relay -----
FRELAY:
FRELAY: Address word = 04F1
FRELAY:  0000 01.. 1111 ....   = DLCI 31
FRELAY:  .... ..0. .... ....   = Response
FRELAY:  .... .... .... 0...   = No forward congestion
FRELAY:  .... .... .... .0..   = No backward congestion
FRELAY:  .... .... .... ..0.   = Not eligible for discard
FRELAY:
FRELAY: ----- Multiprotocol over Frame Relay -----
```

```
FRELAY:
FRELAY: Control, pad(s) = 03
FRELAY: NLPID = 0xCC (Internet IP)
FRELAY:


- - - - - - - - - - - - Frame 45 (Source = DCE) - - - - - - - - - - - -


FRELAY: ----- Frame Relay -----
FRELAY:
FRELAY: Address word = 04F1
FRELAY:  0000 01.. 1111 ....  = DLCI 31
FRELAY:  .... ..0. .... ....  = Response
FRELAY:  .... .... ... 0...   = No forward congestion
FRELAY:  .... .... .... .0..  = No backward congestion
FRELAY:  .... .... .... ..0.  = Not eligible for discard
FRELAY:
FRELAY: ----- Multiprotocol over Frame Relay -----
FRELAY:
FRELAY: Control, pad(s) = 03
FRELAY: NLPID = 0xCC (Internet IP)
FRELAY:
```

Moving up the protocol stack, the analyst looks at the IP and TCP headers and discovers no abnormal conditions in the IP process. In Trace 4.5d, the TCP sequence and acknowledgment numbers reveal what has occurred. The following condensation will help you follow what has occurred in Trace 4.5d. Note that the Acknowledgment number is the next octet expected from the other end of the link, and the Sequence number is the current number of the octet being transmitted:

Frame	Source	Action	Notes
41	DTE	ACK = 147196481	DTE ready to receive
42	DCE	SEQ = 147196481	DCE initial transmission
43	DTE	ACK = 147196482	DTE receives Frame 42

44	DTE	ACK = 147196482	DTE ready for more data,
		SEQ = 575826875	one octet transmitted
45	DCE	SEQ = 147196481	DCE retransmits Frame 42
47	DTE	ACK = 147196482	DTE ready for more data
61	DCE	SEQ = 147196481	DCE retransmits Frame 42
62	DTE	ACK = 147196482	DTE ready for more data
67	DCE	SEQ = 147196482	DCE transmits more data,
			plus ACK for Frame 61
68	DCE	SEQ = 147196482	DCE retransmits more data
69	DTE	ACK = 147196483	DTE receives Frame 68

You can make several observations from the previous table. First, all of the retransmissions come from the network (DCE) side of the frame relay interface. Second, because the network transparently sends information, you know that the remote host is the source of these retransmissions.

You also know that the local host is willing to receive the information because it resends periodic acknowledgments in Fames 44, 47, and 62. The size of the transmitted message (only 1 octet of TELNET data) is considerably less than the receiver's window size. This indicates that both the DTE and DCE have enough buffer space for these messages. Also note that you never see Window = 0, which would indicate that the opposite end of the connection is requesting a halt in data transmission.

You can also see that the local host is transmitting TELNET data. The DTE transmits one octet of TELNET data in Frame 44 (SEQ = 575826875), which is not acknowledged until Frame 67 (ACK = 575826876). Also in Frame 67, the remote host transmits another octet of TELNET data (SEQ = 147196482), indicating that it received the local host's acknowledgment (ACK = 147196482) sent in Frames 44, 47, and 62.

Therefore, it is possible to conclude that neither the local host nor internal network problems are causing the data retransmissions. The culprit must be the TCP or TELNET processes within the remote host. Further testing would require another analyzer at the remote end and coordination between the local and remote analysts. While these tests have not been conclusive, they have eliminated the local end of the connection as the point of failure.

Trace 4.5d. TCP retransmissions (details)

```
Sniffer Internetwork Analyzer data 10-Nov-92 at 14:28:24 FR1.SYC Pg 1

- - - - - - - - - - - - Frame 41 (Source = DTE) - - - - - - - - - - - - -

TCP: ----- TCP header -----
TCP:
TCP: Source port = 23 (Telnet)
TCP: Destination port = 11069
TCP: Sequence number = 575826875
TCP: Acknowledgment number = 147196481
TCP: Data offset = 20 bytes
TCP: Flags = 10
TCP: ..0. .... = (No urgent pointer)
TCP: ...1 .... = Acknowledgment
TCP: .... 0... = (No push)
TCP: .... .0.. = (No reset)
TCP: .... ..0. = (No SYN)
TCP: .... ...0 = (No FIN)
TCP: Window = 3264
TCP: Checksum = C281 (correct)
TCP: No TCP options
TCP:

- - - - - - - - - - - - Frame 42 (Source = DCE) - - - - - - - - - - - - -

TCP: ----- TCP header -----
TCP:
TCP: Source port = 11069
TCP: Destination port = 23 (Telnet)
TCP: Sequence number = 147196481
```

```
TCP:  Acknowledgment number = 575826875
TCP:  Data offset = 20 bytes
TCP:  Flags = 18
TCP:  ..0. ....  = (No urgent pointer)
TCP:  ...1 ....  = Acknowledgment
TCP:  .... 1...  = Push
TCP:  .... .0..  = (No reset)
TCP:  .... ..0.  = (No SYN)
TCP:  .... ...0  = (No FIN)
TCP:  Window = 420
TCP:  Checksum = 9D94 (correct)
TCP:  No TCP options
TCP:  [1 byte(s) of data]
TCP:
Telnet:----- Telnet data -----
Telnet:
Telnet:0
Telnet:


- - - - - - - - - - - Frame 43 (Source = DTE) - - - - - - - - - - - -


TCP:  ----- TCP header -----
TCP:
TCP:  Source port = 23 (Telnet)
TCP:  Destination port = 11069
TCP:  Sequence number = 575826875
TCP:  Acknowledgment number = 147196482
TCP:  Data offset = 20 bytes
TCP:  Flags = 10
TCP:  ..0. ....  = (No urgent pointer)
TCP:  ...1 ....  = Acknowledgment
TCP:  .... 0...  = (No push)
TCP:  .... .0..  = (No reset)
TCP:  .... ..0.  = (No SYN)
TCP:  .... ...0  = (No FIN)
TCP:  Window = 3263
```

TCP: Checksum = C281 (correct)
TCP: No TCP options
TCP:

- - - - - - - - - - - Frame 44 (Source = DTE) - - - - - - - - - - - -

TCP: ----- TCP header -----
TCP:
TCP: Source port = 23 (Telnet)
TCP: Destination port = 11069
TCP: Sequence number = 575826875
TCP: Acknowledgment number = 147196482
TCP: Data offset = 20 bytes
TCP: Flags = 18
TCP: ..0. .... = (No urgent pointer)
TCP: ...1 .... = Acknowledgment
TCP: .... 1... = Push
TCP: .... .0.. = (No reset)
TCP: .... ..0. = (No SYN)
TCP: ....0 = (No FIN)
TCP: Window = 3263
TCP: Checksum = 9278 (correct)
TCP: No TCP options
TCP: [1 byte(s) of data]
TCP:
Telnet:----- Telnet data -----
Telnet:
Telnet:0
Telnet:

- - - - - - - - - - - Frame 45 (Source = DCE) - - - - - - - - - - - -

TCP: ----- TCP header -----
TCP:
TCP: Source port = 11069
TCP: Destination port = 23 (Telnet)

TCP: Sequence number = 147196481
TCP: Acknowledgment number = 575826875
TCP: Data offset = 20 bytes
TCP: Flags = 18
TCP: ..0. .... = (No urgent pointer)
TCP: ...1 .... = Acknowledgment
TCP: .... 1... = Push
TCP: .... .0.. = (No reset)
TCP: .... ..0. = (No SYN)
TCP: ....0 = (No FIN)
TCP: Window = 420
TCP: Checksum = 9D94 (correct)
TCP: No TCP options
TCP: [1 byte(s) of data]
TCP:
Telnet:----- Telnet data -----
Telnet:
Telnet:0
Telnet:
- - - - - - - - - - - - Frame 47 (Source = DTE) - - - - - - - - - - - - -

TCP: ----- TCP header -----
TCP:
TCP: Source port = 23 (Telnet)
TCP: Destination port = 11069
TCP: Sequence number = 575826876
TCP: Acknowledgment number = 147196482
TCP: Data offset = 20 bytes
TCP: Flags = 10
TCP: ..0. .... = (No urgent pointer)
TCP: ...1 .... = Acknowledgment
TCP: .... 0... = (No push)
TCP: .... .0.. = (No reset)
TCP: .... ..0. = (No SYN)
TCP: ....0 = (No FIN)
TCP: Window = 3263

```
TCP:  Checksum = C280 (correct)
TCP:  No TCP options
TCP:


- - - - - - - - - - - Frame 61 (Source = DCE) - - - - - - - - - - - -


TCP:  ----- TCP header -----
TCP:
TCP:  Source port = 11069
TCP:  Destination port = 23 (Telnet)
TCP:  Sequence number = 147196481
TCP:  Acknowledgment number = 575826875
TCP:  Data offset = 20 bytes
TCP:  Flags = 18
TCP:  ..0.  .... = (No urgent pointer)
TCP:  ...1  .... = Acknowledgment
TCP:  ....  1... = Push
TCP:  ....  .0.. = (No reset)
TCP:  ....  ..0. = (No SYN)
TCP:  ....  ...0 = (No FIN)
TCP:  Window = 420
TCP:  Checksum = 9D94 (correct)
TCP:  No TCP options
TCP:  [1 byte(s) of data]
TCP:
Telnet:----- Telnet data -----
Telnet:
Telnet:0
Telnet:


- - - - - - - - - - - Frame 62 (Source = DTE) - - - - - - - - - - - -


TCP:  ----- TCP header -----
TCP:
TCP:  Source port = 23 (Telnet)
TCP:  Destination port = 11069
```

```
TCP:  Sequence number = 575826876
TCP:  Acknowledgment number = 147196482
TCP:  Data offset = 20 bytes
TCP:  Flags = 10
TCP:  ..0. .... = (No urgent pointer)
TCP:  ...1 .... = Acknowledgment
TCP:  .... 0... = (No push)
TCP:  .... .0.. = (No reset)
TCP:  .... ..0. = (No SYN)
TCP:  .... ...0 = (No FIN)
TCP:  Window = 3263
TCP:  Checksum = C280 (correct)
TCP:  No TCP options
TCP:
```

----------- Frame 67 (Source = DCE) ------------

```
TCP:  ----- TCP header -----
TCP:
TCP:  Source port = 11069
TCP:  Destination port = 23 (Telnet)
TCP:  Sequence number = 147196482
TCP:  Acknowledgment number = 575826876
TCP:  Data offset = 20 bytes
TCP:  Flags = 18
TCP:  ..0. .... = (No urgent pointer)
TCP:  ...1 .... = Acknowledgment
TCP:  .... 1... = Push
TCP:  .... .0.. = (No reset)
TCP:  .... ..0. = (No SYN)
TCP:  .... ...0 = (No FIN)
TCP:  Window = 419
TCP:  Checksum = 9B93 (correct)
TCP:  No TCP options
TCP:  [1 byte(s) of data]
TCP:
```

Telnet:----- Telnet data -----
Telnet:
Telnet:2
Telnet:

- - - - - - - - - - - - Frame 68 (Source = DCE) - - - - - - - - - - - -

TCP: ----- TCP header -----
TCP:
TCP: Source port = 11069
TCP: Destination port = 23 (Telnet)
TCP: Sequence number = 147196482
TCP: Acknowledgment number = 575826876
TCP: Data offset = 20 bytes
TCP: Flags = 18
TCP: ..0. .... = (No urgent pointer)
TCP: ...1   .... = Acknowledgment
TCP: .... 1... = Push
TCP: .... .0.. = (No reset)
TCP: .... ..0. = (No SYN)
TCP: ....0 = (No FIN)
TCP: Window = 419
TCP: Checksum = 9B93 (correct)
TCP: No TCP options
TCP: [1 byte(s) of data]
TCP:
Telnet:----- Telnet data -----
Telnet:
Telnet:2
Telnet:

- - - - - - - - - - - - Frame 69 (Source = DTE) - - - - - - - - - - - -

TCP: ----- TCP header -----
TCP:
TCP: Source port = 23 (Telnet)

TCP: Destination port = 11069

TCP: Sequence number = 575826876

TCP: Acknowledgment number = 147196483

TCP: Data offset = 20 bytes

TCP: Flags = 10

TCP: ..0. ....   = (No urgent pointer)

TCP: ...1   ....   = Acknowledgment

TCP: .... 0...   = (No push)

TCP: .... .0..   = (No reset)

TCP: .... ..0.   = (No SYN)

TCP: 0   = (No FIN)

TCP: Window = 3262

TCP: Checksum = C280 (correct)

TCP: No TCP options

TCP:

4.6 Possible Frame Relay Error Conditions

The frame relay protocol, based on ISDN, provides new challenges to those more familiar with testing analog, than digital, WAN circuits (see Reference [4–1]. Table 4–1, from Reference [4–2], summarizes typical frame relay errors.

Table 4–1. Errors encountered by subscriber and network

Error Condition	Source	Description
Octet 1 EA bit not 1	Frame relay header	A frame has been received with the value 0 for the EA bit in the second octet, indicating an extended address.
Octet 0 EA bit not 0	Frame relay header	A frame has been received with the value 1 for the EA bit in the first octet, indicating end-of-address prematurely.
Data received from an unmapped DLCI	Frame relay header	A frame has been received with a DLCI value that had a last defined status of Inactive.

Data received from DLCI *xxx* while set to Inactive	Frame relay header	A frame has been received with a DLCI value that had a last defined status of Inactive.
FECN/BECN/DE set on LMI DLCI	Frame relay header	Message received on LMI DLCI in which one or more of FECN, BECN, or DE has been set to 1.
Invalid Protocol Discriminator field	LMI message header	Message received on LMI DLCI in which value of Protocol Discriminator field is not 8 or 9.
Invalid Call Reference field	LMI message header	Message received on LMI DLCI in which value of Call Reference field is not 0.
Length of Keep Alive not equal to 2	Keep Alive IE	Message received with value of Length field for Keep Alive IE not equal to 2.
Last Received Sequence Number unequal to last Sequence Number sent	Keep Alive IE	Message received with value of Last Received Sequence number not equal to last value of Current Sequence number sent.
Sequence number = *xx* Expected = *yy*	Keep Alive IE	Message received with Current Sequence number not equal to Last Received Sequence number plus 1 (mod 256, skipping the value 0).
Remote Restart Last Received Sequence number = 0	Keep Alive IE	Message received with value of 0 for Last Received Sequence number implies LMI restart by the remote end.
Remote Restart	Keep Alive IE	Message received with value of 0 for Current Sequence number; indicates LMI restart by the remote end.
Length of Report Type is not equal to 1.	Report Type IE	Message received with value of Length field for Report Type IE not equal to 1.
Unknown or invalid Message code *xx*	Message Type IE	Message received in which value of Message Type IE is neither STATUS ENQUIRY nor STATUS.

Table 4–2. Errors encountered by the subscriber

Error Condition	Source	Description
No response to STATUS ENQUIRY	LMI procedures	Timer *nT1* has expired without receipt of a STATUS message.
Unknown or Invalid Message code *xx*	Report Type IE	Message received in which value of Report Type IE is not STATUS.
Length of PVC Status IE not equal to 3 (for Annex D) or 6 (for Consortium)	PVC Status IE	STATUS message received with value of Length field for PVC Status IE not equal to 3 (for Annex D) or 6 (for Consortium).
DLCI *xx* is new, but *N* bit is 0	PVC Status IE	STATUS message received containing PVC Status IE for previously undefined PVC with *N* bit set to 0 (denotes previously defined PVC).
DLCI *xx* is not new, but *N* bit is 1	PVC Status IE	STATUS Message received containing PVC Status IE for previously defined PVC with *N* bit set to 1 (denotes new PVC).

Table 4–3. Errors encountered by the network

Error Condition	Source	Description
No STATUS ENQUIRY received in *nT2* seconds	LMI procedures	Timer *nT2* has expired without receipt of a STATUS ENQUIRY from the subscriber.
PVC Status IE received from subscriber	PVC Status IE	Network has received a PVC Status IE from the subscriber; Illegal IE, unless using the T1.617 Annex D (D.6) Bidirectional procedures.
Unknown or invalid message code *xx*	Report Type IE	Message received with value of Report Type IE not equal to STATUS ENQUIRY, unless using the T1.617 Annex D bidirectional procedures.

4.7 References

[4–1]   Kocen, Ross. "Is the Test Sector Ready for Frame Relay?" *Telephone Engineer and Management* (January 1, 1992): 43–45.

[4–2]   Telenex Corp. *An Introduction to Useful Frame Relay Testing.* August 1991.

 **SMDS Architecture**

The SMDS is a broadband networking technology developed by Bellcore, which is the research and development organization for many of the Bell Operating Companies. SMDS is a subset of the IEEE 802.6 Distributed Queue Dual Bus (DQDB) metropolitan area networking (MAN) technology. In this chapter, we'll examine both the SMDS and DQDB architectures, then explore the details of the SMDS interfaces used by internetworking hardware.

5.1 SMDS Applications and Support

SMDS is a high-speed service that currently offers access at rates up to Digital Signal Level 3, or DS3 (44.736 Mbps), and plans to increase these rates to the Optical Carrier Level 3, or OC3 (155.520 Mbps). SMDS has many applications, including LAN interconnection; high-speed, remote-database access; packet audio and video; resource sharing by educational institutions, image transfer; and teleradiology [5–1]. References [5–2] through [5–4] detail other innovative applications.

Currently, you can access SMDS through most of the regional Bell Operating Companies, including Ameritech, Bell Atlantic, BellSouth, Pacific Telesis Group, and US West. Southwestern Bell plans to offer SMDS in the future. NYNEX, however, has announced that it will bypass an SMDS offering, and move directly to ATM.

Among the independent (non-Bell) LECs, GTE Telephone Operations offers SMDS [5–5]. Inter-exchange carrier MCI has also announced an SMDS service [5–6] as well as an agreement with Bell Atlantic to provide local-to-long distance SMDS connections [5–7]. In addition, many European carriers have either field tested or announced their own SMDS service [5–8].

In 1991, telecommunications service providers, equipment vendors, and users united to further this technology by chartering the SMDS Interest Group (SIG). References [5–9] through [5–11] are examples of the many publications and documents that the SIG has published.

Bellcore has defined the technical deployment of SMDS in three phases, along with target time frames [5–12]. Phase 1, 1991 through 1993, defined the service, access protocols, operational characteristics, and administrative issues, such as billing. In 1994, Phase 2 will extend SMDS to both local and inter-exchange service, and define plans for CNM. Phase 3, scheduled to begin in 1995, will include ISDN and Synchronous Optical Network (SONET) interfaces and CNM enhancements.

In brief, SMDS operates by accepting high-speed customer data in increments of up to 9,188 octets and divides it into 53-octet cells for transmission through the service provider's network. The receiving end reassembles these cells into customer data. To help you better understand these processes, I will now detail the SMDS architecture. In addition, Russell Sharer's "The SMDS Express" [5–13] is an excellent introduction to SMDS technology.

5.2 SMDS Architecture

Bellcore designed SMDS to be a "high-speed, connectionless, public, packet-switching service to extend LAN-like performance beyond the subscriber's premises, across a MAN or WAN" [5–14].

Several key user requirements have spurred SMDS development. LAN popularity has resulted in a need for inter-LAN communication. Yet, traditional interconnectivity solutions, such as dedicated point-to-point T1 facilities operating at 1.544 Mbps, can be costly. As the number of locations and wide-area bandwidth requirements increase, companies need alternative solutions to point-to-point architectures. In addition, when computing power is distributed among multiple LANs, timely access to remote data is also a requirement. After all, having access to remote data is of little value if it takes too long to communicate that data.

An SMDS network, therefore, must provide a cost-effective solution that removes the traditional geographical constraints of LANs and provides acceptable response times. It must also communicate with other broadband technologies, such as frame relay, and provide a migration path to ATM.

To allow for network access (see Figure 5–1a), SMDS has defined a Subscriber Network Interface (SNI) and an SMDS Interface Protocol (SIP) based on DQDB. The network incorporates a number of internal systems and functions, including Switching Systems (SS), Inter-Switching System Interfaces (ISSI), Operations Systems (OS), and Data Communications Network (DCN). An Inter-exchange Carrier Interface (ICI), as shown in Figure 5–1b, offers a connection between two SMDS-based networks. When both intra- and inter-Local Area Transport Area (LATA) carriers help provide SMDS service, the term *Exchange Access SMDS* (XA-SMDS) is used. Because I am focusing on SMDS service, rather than internal SMDS design, the next sections concentrate on the users' interface to the service—the SNI and SIP.

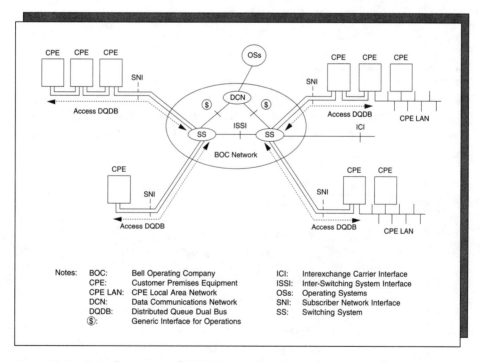

Figure 5–1a. Network in support of SMDS (*Source: TR-TSV-000772, ©1991, Bell Communications Research, Inc., reprinted with permission*)

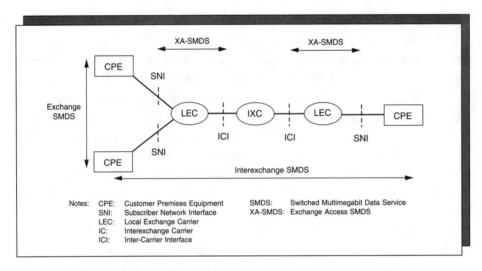

Figure 5–1b. Relationship of SMDS services *(Source: TR-TSV-001240, ©1993, Bell Communications Research, Inc., reprinted with permission)*

5.3 SMDS Standards

Bellcore documents have two designations: Technical Advisories (TA) are preliminary documents that are subject to change and revision, and Technical References (TR), which are the final versions of TAs. Key SMDS documents include the following:

Document	Subject
TR-TSV-000772	Generic system requirements for SMDS
TR-TSV-000773	Local access system requirements, objectives, and interfaces for SMDS
TR-TSV-000774	SMDS operations-technology network element generic requirements
TR-TSV-000775	Usage measurement requirements in support of billing for SMDS
TA-TSV-001059	SMDS networking requirements

TR-TSV-001060	SMDS requirements for exchange access and intercompany serving arrangements
TA-TSV-001061	Operations-technology network-element requirements for interswitch and exchange access
TR-TSV-001062	Phase 1 SMDS Customer Network Management service requirements
TR-TSV-001063	Operations-technology generic criteria in support of exchange-access SMDS and intercompany serving arrangements
TR-TSV-001064	SMDS generic criteria on operations interfaces (information model and usage)
TR-TSV-001239	Generic requirements for low-speed SMDS access
TA-TSV-001240	Generic requirements for frame relay access to SMDS

Information for obtaining these documents is in Appendix A.

The SIG has also defined a number technical specifications that address implementation issues, such as AppleTalk over SMDS and DECnet over SMDS. The European SIG has also tailored SMDS requirements for the European marketplace. The principal SIG documents include:

Document	Subject
SIG-TS-001 (1991)	Data Exchange Interface (DXI) Specification
SIG-TS-002 (1992)	Local Management Interface (LMI) Specification
SIG-TS-003 (1992)	DECnet over SMDS Specification

Many of the SIG documents are available via anonymous File Transfer Protocol (FTP) on host *ftp.acc.com*, in directory *pub/smds*.

5.4 IEEE 802.6 Architecture

The 802.6 standard was designed under the auspices of the IEEE project 802 architecture to interconnect DQDB subnetworks within MANs. These DQDB subnetworks may provide data concentration, routing, or switching functions, or they may interconnect workstations, hosts, and LANs over a MAN.

The IEEE 802.6 standard, *DQDB Subnetwork of a MAN* [5–15], is a member of a family of LAN and MAN standards (see Figure 5–2a). These standards deal only with OSI Data Link and Physical layer functions, or as the 802.6 standard states, they act as a "high-speed shared medium access protocol for use of a dual, counter-flowing, unidirectional bus subnetwork." The systems that use the 802.6 standards, such as a router or a host, define the network through Application layer functions and processes.

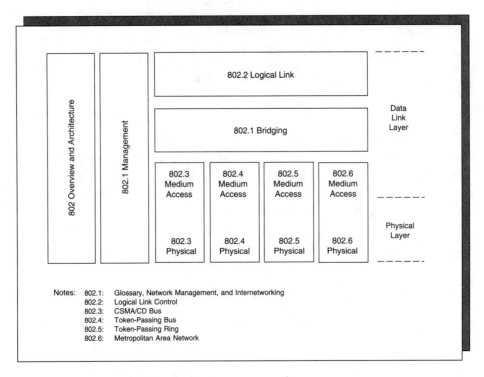

Figure 5–2a. IEEE LAN/MAN standards (© 1993 IEEE, Std 802.6–1990)

To perform its functions, 802.6 defines two layers (DQDB and Physical), which in turn provide three functions (a Medium Access Control, or MAC, service to support LLC; a connection-oriented service; and an isochronous service, see Figure 5–2b). The MAC sublayer service to LLC is a connectionless service that provides compatibility with other networks that use the LLC (802.2) protocol, including Ethernet, FDDI, and token-ring networks. The connection-oriented data service is asynchronous, and can transport bursty data such as signaling. Isochronous support is a connection-oriented service that transports data with a time-dependent arrival, such as digitized voice transmission.

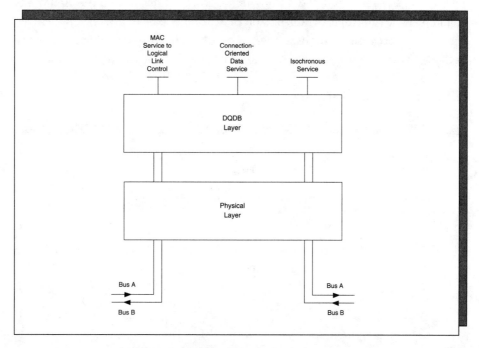

Figure 5–2b. Scope of IEEE 802.6 (© 1993 IEEE, Std 802.6–1990)

SMDS is a high-speed, connectionless data service, while 802.6 is an IEEE standard for MANs. Customer networks access SMDS via the SIP, which uses a subset of the 802.6 protocol. 802.6 defines the DQDB as its network transport technology. Current SMDS implementations are point-to-point connections, not DQDB, though this may change in the future. The following section provides more details of DQDB operation.

5.5 Distributed Queue Dual-Bus Architecture

The DQDB network is a dual-bus architecture, with each unidirectional bus operating independent of the other. Nodes using the bus for data transport connect to both buses. The data itself is transmitted in fixed-length slots, each 53 octets long, a length compatible with ATM services. In the next sections, we'll examine each element of the DQDB architecture, beginning with the bus.

5.5.1 Dual-Bus Architecture

The two buses of the DQDB dual-bus architecture are designated Bus A and Bus B, and provide full-duplex transmission between any pair of attached nodes (see Figure 5–3). Because both buses operate simultaneously, the aggregate capacity of the network is twice the transmission rate of one bus. The nodes at the ends of the bus, which are called the Head of Bus A (HOB A) and Head of Bus B (HOB B), initiate the transmission slots.

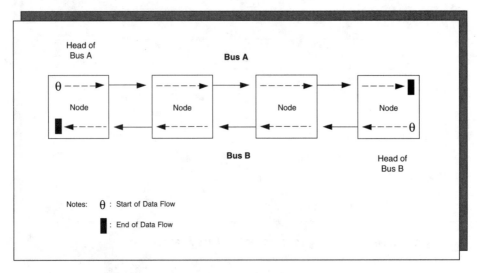

Figure 5–3. Dual-bus architecture (© 1993 IEEE, Std 802.6–1990)

When the two endpoints of the bus are located at the same node, a looped-bus topology results (see Figure 5–4). The resulting topology is called a looped bus. Note that while this topology looks like a ring, it isn't a true ring because the data does not flow through to the head of the same bus.

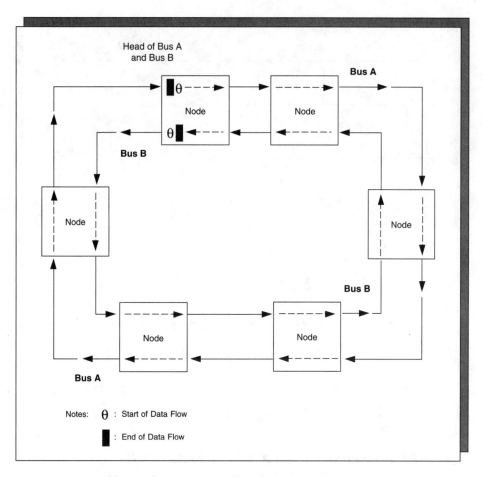

Figure 5–4. Looped-bus topology (© 1993 IEEE, Std 802.6–1990)

If a bus failure occurs, a healing mechanism in the bus repositions the normal bus break to the location of the physical break (see Figure 5–5). In other words, HOB functions move to the nodes adjacent to the break (the two lower nodes in Figure 5–5). If the nodes adjacent to the break do not support the HOB function, the next-adjacent node assumes the HOB role, and the node lacking the HOB functions is disconnected from the rest of the network.

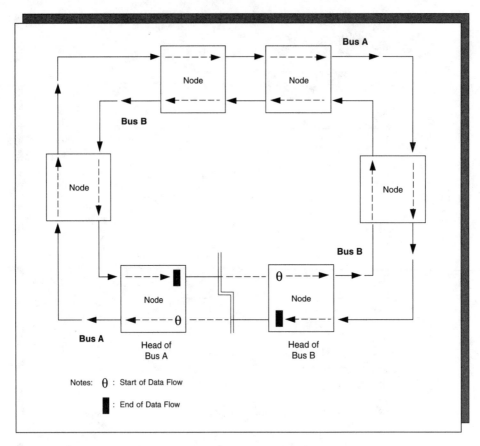

Figure 5–5. Subnetwork reconfiguration (© 1993 IEEE, Std 802.6–1990)

5.5.2 Node architecture

Each node consists of an access unit, which implements the DQDB layer functions, and a physical attachment to the A and B buses, which implements the Physical layer functions (see Figure 5– 6). Each access unit may attach to the bus via active or passive connections. Note that the Read and Write functions for each bus are independent. The Read function is placed ahead of the Write function to allow the access unit to copy all incoming data from the bus before writing anything to the bus. To generate the outgoing data (thereby writing to the bus), the access unit performs a logical OR function on the incoming data with the data to be transmitted.

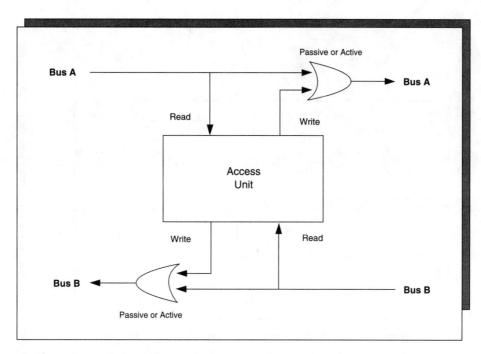

Figure 5–6. Example access-unit attachment (© 1993 IEEE, Std 802.6–1990)

Bus Input	Write Value	Bus Output
0	0	0
0	1	1
1	0	1
1	1	1

So, a zero on the bus input may change to a one at the bus output, but the converse is not true. This function is used in conjunction with the Busy and Request bits, discussed below.

The node architecture includes DQDB and Physical layer functions (see Figure 5–7). Two Service Access Points (SAPs) provide Physical layer service to the DQDB layer entity at a node. Each SAP is associated with one duplex transmission link connecting the node to an adjacent node.

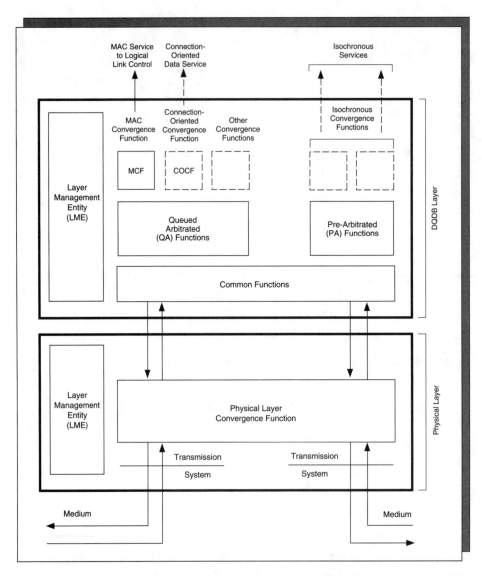

Figure 5–7. DQDB node functional architecture *(© 1993 IEEE, Std 802.6–1990)*

The Physical layer contains three functions: transmission, Physical layer convergence, and layer management. The transmission system provides the interface from the nodes to the communication link. 802.6 transmission systems offer DS1 (1.544 Mbps) and DS3 (44.736 Mbps) rates, plus the synchronous digital hierarchy (SDH) rates. The Physical Layer Convergence Function (PLCF) provides the interface between the DQDB layer and the Physical layer, giving the two layers some independence. Each type of transmission system requires the definition of a unique Physical Layer Convergence Procedure (PLCP). The Layer Management Entity (LME) provides remote management of the physical subsystem. The IEEE 802.1B standard addresses management of IEEE 802 LANs/MANs more fully.

The DQDB Layer performs four functions: common functions, access-control functions, convergence functions, and layer-management functions. Common functions relay the DQDB information to the Physical layer entity, perform the Head of Bus function, and perform a configuration-control function that ensures all nodes are configured into a correct dual-bus topology. The Access Control functions provide access to transmission slots. Two Access Control functions are defined based on the type of data transfer required. The Queued Arbitrated (QA) functions, which transfer 48-octet data segments, are used for asynchronous (nontime-sensitive) data transfer. SMDS, which is a connectionless service, uses the QA functions. For isochronous (time-sensitive) data transfer, the Pre-Arbitrated (PA) functions provide access control for the connection-oriented transfer of an octet stream. The Convergence functions provide one of the three services discussed previously: MAC to LLC, connection-oriented data service, or isochronous service. Finally, the LME provides local and remote management of the DQDB layer resources.

5.5.3 DQDB segmentation units

The MAC Convergence Function (MCF) implements a segmentation and reassembly protocol within the DQDB layer. This protocol takes a long message from the upper layer protocols, and segments it into smaller units for transmission via the DQDB bus. The reassembly process does the opposite, taking smaller units from the bus and delivering a complete message to the upper layer receiver.

Figure 5–8 illustrates the segmentation process, beginning with the receipt of a MAC Service Data Unit (MSDU) from LLC. The first step is to form an Initial MAC Protocol Data Unit (IMPDU), which adds a header and trailer to the MSDU. The IMPDU header includes a Common PDU header, a MAC Convergence Protocol (MCP) header, and an optional header extension. The trailer contains an optional PAD field to assure 32-bit alignment, a CRC-32, and a Common PDU trailer. The

IMPDU is then fragmented into fixed-length segmentation units, called Derived MAC Protocol Data Units (DMPDUs), and includes a header and trailer. Segmentation units are further identified by their position within the message, as a beginning of message (BOM), continuation of message (COM) or end of message (EOM). The segmentation units are transferred in QA segment payloads within slots.

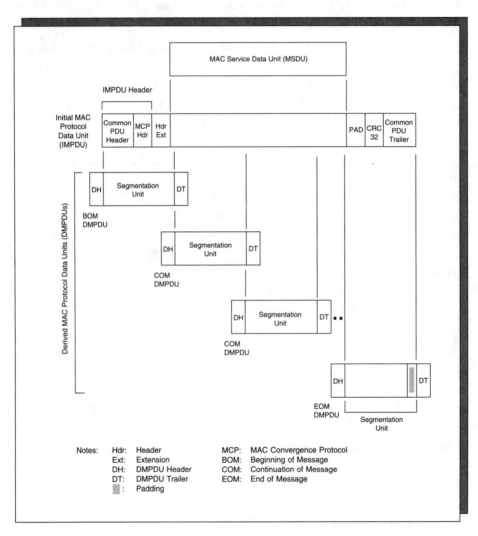

Figure 5–8. Segmentation of an IMPDU into DMPDUs (© *1993 IEEE, Std 802.6–1990*)

The slot, which is 53 octets in length (see Figure 5–9), is the basic unit of data transfer. The slot contains a PDU being transferred from one node to another via the bus. There are two types of slots: a QA slot and PA slot. The QA slot transfers a QA segment, and the PA slot transfers isochronous service octets.

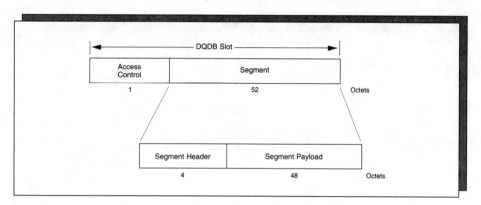

Figure 5–9. DQDB slot format (© 1993 IEEE, Std 802.6–1990)

The 53-octet slot consists of two fields. The Access Control field contains subfields that control access to the bus. The Segment field contains the data. Two segment types are defined: a QA segment, which is the PDU transferred in a QA slot, and a PA segment, which is the isochronous-service octets transferred in the PA segment. Both QA and PA segments contain two fields, a 4-octet segment header and a 48-octet segment payload.

5.5.4 The Distributed Queuing Algorithm

Because many nodes may be attached to the bus, the network needs a mechanism to control access to assure that one node will not overwrite another's data. This process, governed by the Distributed Queuing Algorithm, is called access control.

The DQDB layer provides two access-control modes: PA for isochronous data and QA for nonisochronous data. With PA, the node at the head of the bus controls access to the slots. Because SMDS uses QA, this section focuses on this control mode. For further information on PA access, refer to 802.6, Section 2.1.2.2.

For QA, the Distributed Queue Access Protocol controls access to the transmission media. It uses two subfields within the Access Control field of the slot. These two subfields are the Busy (B) bit and the Request (REQ) bit.

Figure 5–10 illustrates the way the Distributed Queuing Algorithm enables access to a single bus (Bus A, in this case). We assume that Bus A is the forwad bus with data flowing from left to right, and that Bus B is the reverse bus. (An identical and independent process exists for Bus B, which for simplicity, is not illustrated in the figure.)

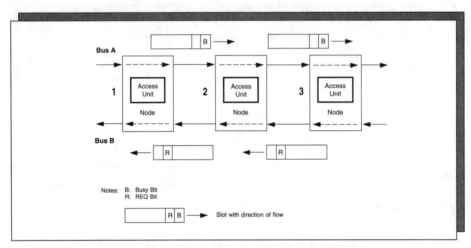

Figure 5–10. Queue formation on Bus A (© 1993 IEEE, Std 802.6–1990)

The state of the Busy and REQ bits indicate control of an individual slot. Busy bits indicate that a slot is currently in use, while REQ bits signal when a QA segment is queued on the reverse bus. (Note that there are three REQ bits, allowing for multiple access priorities. For the sake of simplicity, assume that only one priority is implemented.)

When it needs to access the forward bus (Bus A, in this case) and send a QA segment, an Access Unit (AU) sends a single REQ on the reverse bus (Bus B). The REQ is written into the next free REQ bit on the reverse bus (Bus B), using the logic OR function shown in Figure 5–6. Sending the REQ on the reverse bus informs the requesting AU's upstream nodes that a QA segment is queued for transmission. Only one QA segment (per priority level) may be queued for each bus.

Returning to Figure 5–10, assume that AU 2 wants to transmit a segment. It would send a REQ on Bus B to signal its upstream AUs (only AU 1, in this case) that a segment is queued for access.

Once the AU has informed the upstream AUs that the segment is ready for transmission, additional mechanisms queue the segments using the Request Counter (RQ) and the Countdown Counter (CD) (shown in Figure 5–11). The RQ counts the number of REQ bits that pass on the reverse bus (see Figure 5– 11a), which measures the number of segments queued downstream from that AU. So, for each REQ that passes an AU on the reverse bus, the RQ is incremented by one.

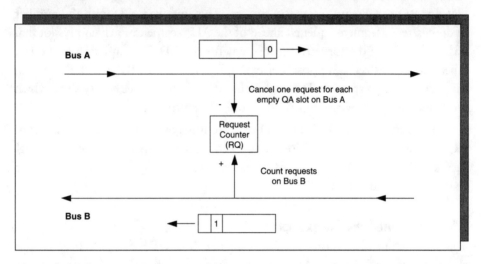

Figure 5–11a. Node not queued to send (Bus A) *(© 1993 IEEE, Std 802.6–1990)*

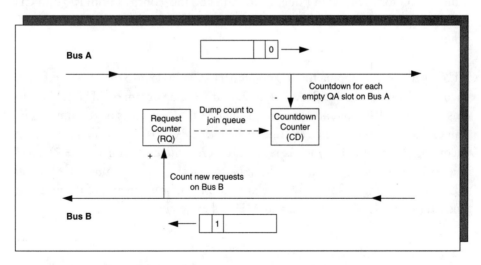

Figure 5–11b. Node queued to send (Bus A) *(© 1993 IEEE, Std 802.6–1990)*

Even when the AU's transmitter is not queued to send, it affects the next algo-rithm function. In this case, the RQ counter is decremented by one for each empty slot that passes on the forward bus. In other words, the RQ increments for each slot requested and decrements when one of these requests is fulfilled.

If the AU is queued to send, the algorithm also uses the CD (see Figure 5–11b). When the AU issues a REQ on the reverse bus, it transfers the contents of the value of RQ to CD and resets RQ to zero. This initializes CD with the number of downstream segments queued ahead of the AU's segment. Each empty slot that passes the AU on the forward bus decrements the CD. Transmission is allowed when CD equals zero. Suppose, for example, the value of RQ was three. When this value is transferred to CD, it forces the AU to bypass three empty slots, which were reserved by downstream AUs, before transmitting.

Also, note that the RQ and CD operate independently. After the value of RQ is transferred to CD, RQ continues to count newly queued downstream seg-ments. CD governs the sending of the current segment, also independent of the then-current value of RQ.

5.5.5 Distributed queuing example
To conclude our discussion of 802.6, consider the DQDB bus with five AUs, as shown in Figure 5–12. The AUs are numbered one to five. The figure shows the value of RQ for each AU not queued to send and the values of both RQ and CD for AUs queued to send. I have assumed that the initial values of all RQ and CD counters are zero.

AU5 queues first, dumping the RQ count (0) to CD. AU5 also overwrites the next incoming REQ bit on Bus B. AUs 4, 3, 2, and 1 are upstream of AU5 (relative to Bus A), see the REQ bit, and increment their RQ. AU2 queues next, dumping its value of RQ (1) to CD, and resetting the value of RQ = 0. AU2 also sets the next incoming REQ bit = 1, which is read and incremented at AU1 (RQ = 2). AU3 queues last, following the same pattern. Note that the counter values of AU4 and AU5 did not change, as these were relative to Bus B, or upstream, of the unit that queued (AU3). The RQ of AU2 and AU1 did increment, however.

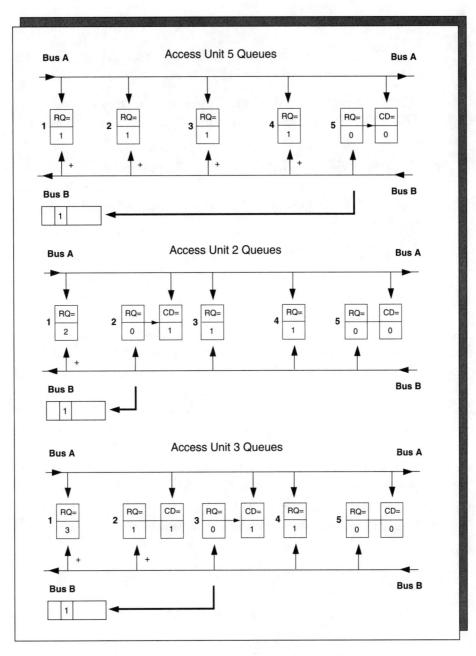

Figure 5–12. Queuing for access (Bus A) *(© 1993 IEEE, Std 802.6–1990)*

We can make the following observations from the final state of the counters:

▼ *AU1.* Three downstream AUs have QA segments queued for access (relative to Bus A), as represented by RQ = 3

▼ *AU2.* One downstream AU has a QA segment queued for access before AU2 (CD = 1), and one downstream AU is queued for access after AU2 (RQ = 1)

▼ *AU3.* One downstream AU has a QA segment queued for access before AU3 (CD = 1). From AU3's perspective, no AUs are queued for access after AU3 because RQ = 0 (AU2's REQ was only registered at AU1)

▼ *AU4.* There is one downstream AU, with a QA segment queued for access (RQ=1)

▼ *AU5.* AU5 is the end of the bus, with no downstream AUs (RQ = 0, CD = 0).

Figure 5–13 illustrates the access sequence for the queued nodes. An empty slot (Busy = 0) on Bus A causes the RQ of the nonqueued AUs and the CD for queued AUs to be decremented. The empty slot then reaches AU5. That node gains access because CD = 0, overwrites the Busy bit (B = 1), and sends a seg-ment. Now, AU2 and AU3 both have CD = 0. AU2 gains access first, because it is the most upstream node. AU3 gains access last, depleting the sending queue (not shown in Figure 5–13). Comparing the sequences for Figures 5–12 and 5–13, note that the order of queuing (AU5, AU2, and AU3) is the same as the order of access.

Now that you understand the DQDB architecture, slot format, and queuing algorithm, the next section shows how SMDS implements these elements.

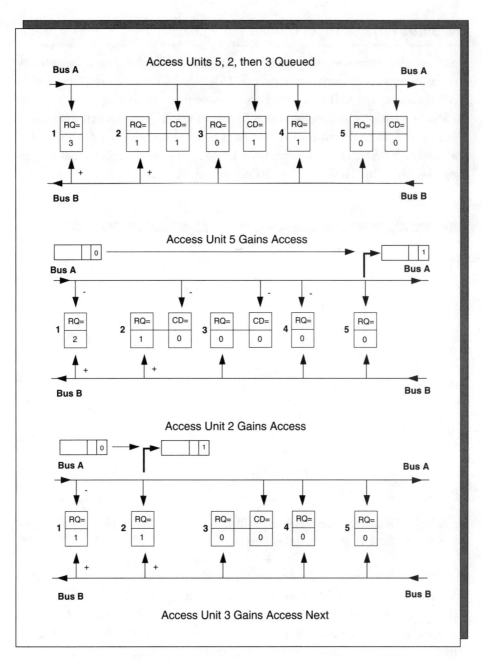

Figure 5–13. Gaining access (Bus A) (© 1993 IEEE, Std 802.6–1990)

5.6 SMDS Physical Layer Options

SMDS requires point-to-point, digital transmission facilities between the network and customer's equipment (see Figure 5–14). A Subscriber Access Termination (SAT) represents the SMDS protocol processes at the customer equipment side of the SNI. A Switching System Exchange Termination (SET) resides in the network's central office. Digital transmission facilities connect the SAT with the SET. The link may be a DS1 channel operating at 1.544 Mbps; or a DS3 channel operating at 44.736 Mbps. Bellcore also defines low-speed access to SMDS, operating at 56/64 Kbps.

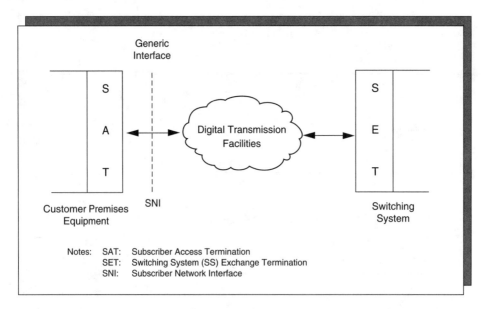

Figure 5–14. Local access system supporting SMDS *(Source: TR-TSV-000773, ©1991, Bell Communications Research, Inc., reprinted with permission)*

The DS1 channel may be a repeatered T1 circuit (see Figure 5–15). To access that circuit, the SNI would be connected to a Digital Signal Cross-Connect Level 1 (DSX-1) frame, which may also terminate other T1 circuits used for voice, video, or other services. Similarly, a DS3 channel would terminate on a DSX-3 frame for connection into a Fiber-Optic Transmission System (FOTS), as shown in Figure 5–16.

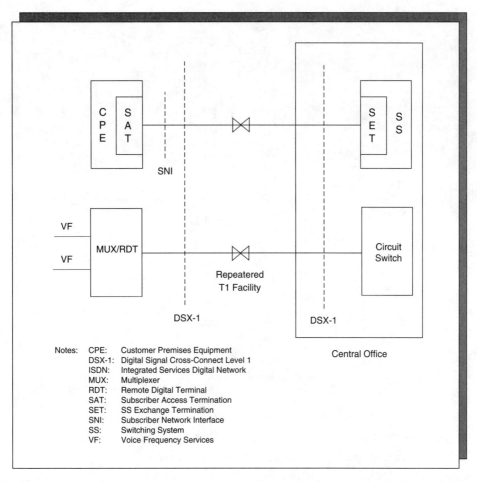

Figure 5–15. SMDS local access system and DS1 Transport *(Source: TR-TSV-000773, ©1991, Bell Communications Research, Inc., reprinted with permission)*

Chapter 6 discusses the use and formats of the DS1 and DS3 channels in greater detail. For further information on T1 and T3 circuits and their applications, see Reference [5–16].

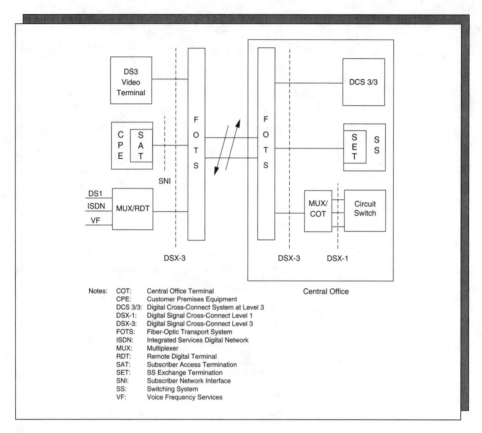

Figure 5–16. SMDS local access system and integrated DS3 Transport *(Source: TR-TSV-000773, ©1991, Bell Communications Research, Inc., reprinted with permission)*

5.7 SMDS Interfaces

While the SMDS network provider needs to understand the internal network operations, end users are more concerned with the interface to the network. There are two ways to connect customer premises equipment (CPE) to an SMDS network, either through the SIP or the Data Exchange Interface (DXI). The following sections provide an overview of these interfaces, while Chapter 6 examines these protocols in depth. Bertil Lindberg's "Switched Broadband Network Interfaces" [5–17] provides a good overview of interfaces between terminal equipment and MANs.

5.7.1 The SMDS Interface Protocol (SIP)

The SNI is the demarcation point that Bellcore has defined between the CPE and the network. At the SNI, the CPE connects to the network via a dedicated transmission link. A "dedicated" link transports data from single customer, and is not shared with other customers. The physical connections currently defined for SMDS include DS0 (56/64 Kbps), DS1 (1.544 Mbps), and DS3 (44.736 Mbps) transmission rates.

There are two possible access configurations, single CPE access and multi-CPE access (see Figure 5–17). The network side terminates in a SS. Note that the SMDS access bus operates as a DQDB open bus, not looped-bus, topology. The SS operates as the Head of Bus A, while the CPE operates as the Head of Bus B. Current SMDS implementations operate as a single CPE, not a multi-CPE, arrangement.

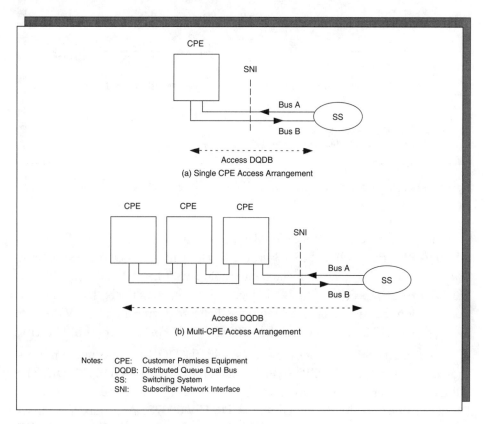

Figure 5–17. SMDS access configurations (Source: TR-TSV-000772, ©1991, Bell Communications Research, Inc., reprinted with permission)

SIP is the protocol operating on the SNI, and it is based on the 802.6 DQDB protocol. The operation of SIP across the SNI is defined as "access DQDB" to distinguish it from other uses of the DQDB protocol. SIP is a three-level protocol implemented in both the CPE and the SS (see Figure 5–18) using the MAC service to LLC (connectionless service) defined in 802.6. The three levels of SIP are grouped for design convenience and do not correspond to the lower three layers of the OSI Reference Model. SIP Level 3 handles addressing and error detection; SIP Level 2 handles framing and error detection; and SIP Level 1 handles the physical transport. So, the functions of these three levels perform OSI Physical and Data Link layer operations.

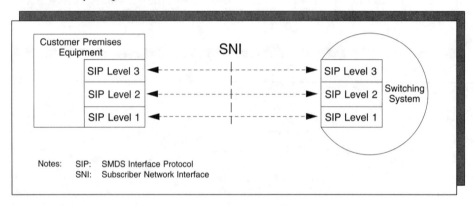

Figure 5–18. SIP protocol stack (Source: TR-TSV-000772, ©1991, Bell Communications Research, Inc., reprinted with permission)

ULP information, such as application data, comprises an SMDS Service Data Unit (SDU) (see Figure 5–19). A Level 3 Protocol Data Unit (L3_PDU) transports the SDU. The L3_PDU is then segmented into multiple SIP Level 2 PDUs (L2_PDUs). The SIP Level 1 process (not shown in Figure 5–19) handles the bit-level transmission functions across the physical interface. Bellcore document TR-TSV-000772 [5–14] defines SIP Levels 3 and 2, while TR-TSV-00773 [5–18] defines SIP Level 1.

Compare the SIP segmentation process with the DQDB segmentation process shown in Figure 5–8. The SIP L3_PDU compares with the DQDB IMPDU. The SIP L2_PDU compares with the DQDB DMPDU, segments, and slots. The SIP L1_PDU compares with the DQDB PLCP. TR-TSV-000772 Appendix A discusses these comparisons in greater detail. Chapter 6 discusses specific details of the SIP protocol.

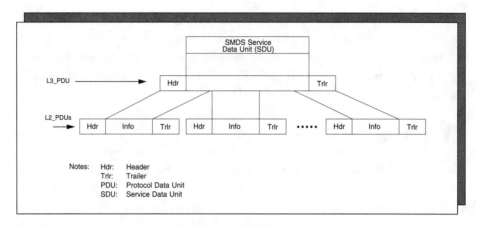

Figure 5–19. Encapsulation of user information by the layers of SIP *(Source: TR-TSV-000772, ©1991, Bell Communications Research, Inc., reprinted with permission)*

5.7.2 Data Exchange Interface (DXI)

The SIP functionality is divided between a DSU that connects to the network and a bridge or router that connects to the customer's network (see Figure 5–20). SIG developed this interface, called the DXI, which provides an open interface between CPE and DSU, allowing the three levels of SIP to be split between these two devices in a vendor-independent manner [5–19].

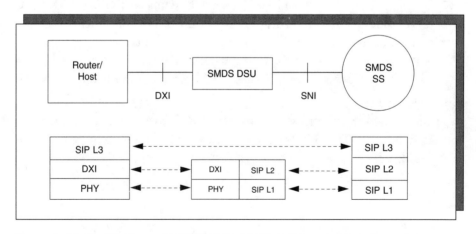

Figure 5–20. The DXI *(Source: TR-TSV-001239, ©1991, Bell Communications Research, Inc., reprinted with permission)*

DXI defines another protocol, based on the ISO HDLC protocol, to replace SIP Level 1 and SIP Level 2 on the link between the router, host or other CPE, and the DSU. SIP Level 3 operates only in the CPE and network. When you implement DXI, support for SMDS by the CPE can be handled by a software upgrade, which maximizes the acceptance of SMDS.

5.8 SMDS Internetworking

Customers of broadband services typically have substantial investment in their current internetworking hardware and software. Carriers should be aware of these investments, and cause as little disruption as possible to the customer's architecture with their new service offerings (see [5–20] and [5–21]). SMDS-based network designs provide for internetworking with the IEEE 802 bridges, the Defense Advanced Research Projects Agency (DARPA) protocols, and frame relay devices. The following sections explore these alternatives.

5.8.1 SMDS and IEEE 802 LANs

Some LAN protocols, such as Digital Equipment Corp.'s Local Access Terminal (LAT) protocol or the Network Basic Input/Output System (NetBIOS) protocol do not contain Network layer functions, and must therefore be bridged, not routed. In this case, the Data Link layer handles the internetworking functions (see Figure 5–21 and Reference [5–22]). A bridge connects to the LAN's MAC layer on one side and the SMDS network on the other. The end-system protocols, such as TCP, IP, and LLC, which are above SIP, pass transparently through the SMDS network. Figure 5–21 also illustrates the similar functions provided by the MAC and SIP protocols (note that these two protocols are the only ones that operate in the bridge).

    IEEE 802.1d [5–23] gives standards for MAC-layer bridges. Supplements to that standard, 802.1i [5–24] and 802.1k [5–25] address requirements for 802.6 bridges.

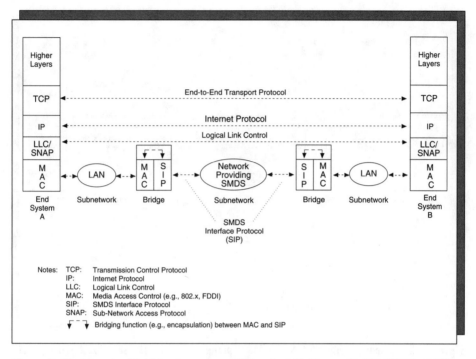

Figure 5–21. Scenario of bridging between an SMDS and a LAN *(Source: TR-TSV-000772, ©1991, Bell Communications Research, Inc., reprinted with permission)*

5.8.2 SMDS and TCP/IP

The TCP/IP suite developed by DARPA is one of the most popular internetworking solutions. Details on SMDS support for TCP/IP are detailed in RFC 1209 "The Transmission of IP Datagrams over the SMDS Service" [5–26], and in Bellcore's TR-TSV-000772.

In the scenario shown in Figure 5–22, the logical connection between the LAN and the SMDS network is made at the Network layer. End System A includes the higher layers, TCP, IP, LLC, and the MAC layer specific to the attached LAN. End System B includes the higher layers, TCP, IP, and LLC, but the lower layer connects to the SMDS network using SIP. A router ties together the LAN and SMDS network, connecting to the LAN MAC layer on one side and to the SMDS SIP layers on the other. Note that the higher protocols starting at LLC pass transparently through the SMDS network.

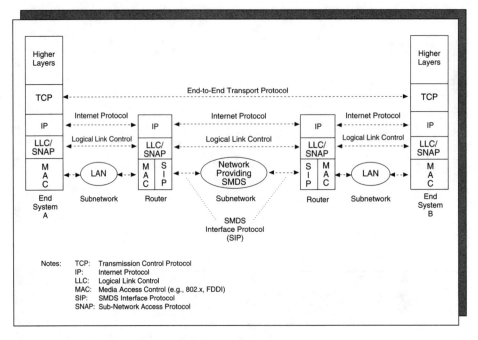

Figure 5-22. Scenario of using SMDS with DARPA protocols *(Source: TR-TSV-000772, ©1991, Bell Communications Research, Inc., reprinted with permission)*

5.8.3 Frame relay access to SMDS

Because of economics, not all broadband networking technologies can serve all locations. Suppose Location A has subscribed to frame relay service, but must communicate with Location B, which only uses SMDS. There are two alternatives: provide frame relay and SMDS for Location A or provide a way for frame relay to access the SMDS network. Because the first alternative may not be economically feasible, the SIG has defined an interface called the SIP Relay Interface (SRI), described in SIG-TS-006, and Bellcore's TA-TSV-001240 [5–27] to provide a solution.

SIP Relay provides frame relay PVC access to SMDS networks. This allows communication with the local SMDS network, or other SMDS locations using XA-SMDS. The SIP Relay Interface (SRI) demarcates between the SMDS network and the frame relay terminal equipment. The SIP Relay protocols allow a frame relay T1.618 frame to carry a SMDS L3_PDU. So, a user with a frame relay interface can purchase additional software supporting SIP, subscribe to the SIP Relay service, and communicate with a SIP-based SMDS user.

Figure 5–23 illustrates the resulting communication flexibility. Location A communicates with Location B via the frame relay network using frame relay PVCs. To communicate with Location C, which is supported by SMDS, not frame relay, a SRI PVC is established. Note that Location B cannot communicate with Location C because the terminal equipment at Location B does not support the SRI.

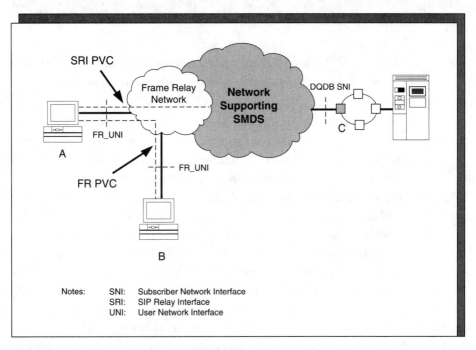

Figure 5–23. Frame Relay and SMDS communications *(Source: TR-TSV-001240, ©1991, Bell Communications Research, Inc., reprinted with permission)*

5.9 SMDS Customer Network Management (CNM)

As networks have evolved in complexity and speed in the last few years, they have placed additional requirements on network management systems. When the network topology includes high-speed data-transport systems, such as SMDS, a comprehensive network management strategy must include these transport facilities as well. The only complication is that different parties—the customer and the carrier—own these systems, thus requiring collaborative efforts.

Bellcore has solved this challenge for SMDS-based internetworks by defining a CNM service described in TR-TSV-001062 [5–28] and References [5–29] and [5–30]. Because of the popularity of the SNMP protocol for LAN management, and the need to provide an industry standard interface into existing network management systems, Bellcore based its CNM standard, in part, on SNMP. A manager/agent paradigm, using the SNMP protocol as the communication mechanism, manages many LANs.

The LEC offers CNM service that provides network management several ways, including as a CPE-based network management application, proprietary monitoring protocols, or remote-user access to network-specific information such as usage details.

In one of the CNM support alternatives, the LEC provides a CNM agent, shown in Figure 5–24, that the customer's network management system can access. To assure interoperability, both the manager and the agent are SNMP-based. The CNM agent gathers information regarding all SNIs at all customer locations. This information is comprehensive and divided according to the three levels of the SIP, plus DS1 and DS3 transport systems. The information specific to a particular layer or function is called a Management Information Base (MIB). Examples of information contained in these MIBs would be the SNI location, access classes, subscriber addresses, and group addresses. DS1 and DS3 performance statistics are also included. By using the manager/agent model upon which SNMP is based, the customer can utilize existing network management consoles, plus integrate the management of the SMDS network elements alongside other elements such as LANs, routers, and hosts. Chapter 11 explores the issue of network-service management, plus the SMDS-related MIBs in greater detail.

This chapter has begun our study of SMDS and the IEEE 802.6 protocols upon which that service is based. We will take a detailed look at these protocols in Chapter 6, and then study their use in Chapter 7.

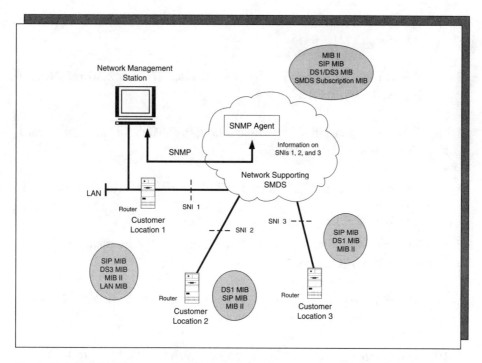

Figure 5–24. SMDS CNM agent role (SNMP example) *(Source: Brown and Kostick, "And CNM for all: Customer Netowork Management Services for Broadband Data Services". Proceedings of the 18th Annual Conference on Local Computer Networks, ©1993, IEEE)*

5.10 References

[5–1]   McCabe, James D. "SMDS: A User's Perspective." *Business Communications Review Supplement* (September 1993): 18–19.

[5–2]   Cox, Tracy, Frances Dix, Christine Hemrick and Josephine McRoberts. "SMDS: The Beginning of WAN Superhighways." *Data Communications* (April 1991): 105–110.

[5–3]   Sharp, Betsy and John Cromett. "Closing the Electronic Loop with SMDS." *Telecommunications* (July 1991): 27–30.

[5–4]   Spiegleman, Alan J. "SMDS Has Arrived." *Networking Management* (October 1992): 40–45.

[5–5]   Briere, Daniel. "SMDS: The Silent Contender." *Network World* (November 29, 1993): 39–49.

[5–6]   Johnson, Johna Till. "The Missing Link for SMDS." *Data Communications* (January 1993): 55–56.

[5–7]   Wexler, Joanie. "SMDS in cross fire." *Network World* (January 31, 1994): 1,50.

[5–8]   Krishnaswamy, Padma and Mehmet Ulema. "Developments in SMDS." *ConneXions* (October 1991): 24–31.

[5–9]   SMDS Interest Group. "Some Potential User Applications." SIG 2691, 1991.

[5–10] SMDS Interest Group. "Saving Money with SMDS." SIG 4691, 1991.

[5–11] SMDS Interest Group. "A Perspective on SMDS and IEEE 802.6 Market Size." SIG 3691, 1991.

[5–12] Wandel & Goltermann Technologies. "SMDS: How Voice Networks Dial Data." *InterNetworking* (Summer 1992): 9–11.

[5–13] Sharer, Russell. "The SMDS Express." *LAN Magazine* (July 1993): 51–58.

[5–14] Bell Communications Research Inc. Generic System Requirements in Support of Switched Multimegabit Data Service. TR-TSV-000772, May 1991.

[5–15] Institute of Electrical and Electronics Engineers, Inc. Distributed Queue Dual Bus (DQDB) Subnetwork of a Metropolitan Area Network (MAN). IEEE 802.6, 1990.

[5–16]   Taylor, Steven A. "What's New in T1 and T3 Networking." *Networking Management* (July 1992): 32–36.

[5–17]   Lindberg, Bertil C. "Switched Broadband Network Interfaces." *Telecommunications* (October 1991): 47–58.

[5–18]   Bell Communications Research Inc. Local Access System Generic Requirements, Objectives, and Interfaces in Support of Switched Multimegabit Data Service. TR-TSV-000773, June 1991.

[5–19]   Strauss, Paul. "The Implications for CPE." *Business Communications Review Supplement* (June 1992): 18–22.

[5–20]   Mollenauer, James F. "The MAN in the Middle." *Networking Management* (February 1991): 36–42.

[5–21]   Nolle, Tom. "Integrating SMDS Into Existing Networks." *Business Communications Review Supplement* (June 1992) 23–27.

[5–22]   Clapp, George H. "LAN Interconnection Across SMDS." *IEEE Network Magazine* (September 1991): 25–32.

[5–23]   Institute of Electrical and Electronics Engineers, Inc. Media Access Control (MAC) Bridges, 802.1d, 1991.

[5–24]   Institute of Electrical and Electronics Engineers, Inc. Remote LAN Bridging of Metropolitan Area Networks (MANs). IEEE draft 802.1i/D5, 1993.

[5–25]   Institute of Electrical and Electronics Engineers, Inc. Supplement to Media Access Control (MAC) Bridges—IEEE Standard 802.6 Distributed Queue Dual Bus (DQDB) Subnetwork of a MAN. IEEE 802.1k, 1993.

[5–26]   Piscitello, D. and J. Lawrence. "The Transmission of IP Datagrams over the SMDS Service." RFC 1209, March 1991.

[5–27] Bell Communications Research Inc. Generic Requirements for Frame Relay Access to SMDS. TA-TSV-001240, June 1993.

[5–28] Bell Communications Research Inc. Generic Service Requirements for Phase 1 SMDS Customer Network Management Service. TR-TSV-001062 and Revision 1, March 1993 and December 1993.

[5–29] Cox, Tracy, David M. Piscitello and Kaj Tesink. "SNMP Agent Support for SMDS." *IEEE Network Magazine* (September 1991): 33–40.

[5–30] Brown, Tracy A. and Deirdre C. Kostick. "And CNM for All: Customer Network Management Services for Broadband Data Services." Proceedings of the IEEE 18th Annual Conference on Local Computer Networks, October 1993.

 # SMDS Protocols

This chapter further details the features of SMDS service and explores how the SMDS protocols support them. In addition, we will draw comparisons between the SMDS and IEEE 802.6 protocols.

6.1 SMDS Features

SMDS is a public, packed-switched service that lets end users exchange data units of up to 9,188 octets. (Recall that an *octet* is a data unit with a length of eight bits.) Two features affect the delivery of these data units: the SMDS addressing structure and the access classes assigned to the information flow [6–1].

6.1.1 SMDS addresses

Each data unit is transmitted independently, and contains addresses that identify its sender and receiver. The service provider assigns SMDS addresses, which identify the SNI from which the data unit was sent and/or the SNI for which it was intended. There are two types of addresses, individual addresses and group addresses. An individual address is assigned uniquely to a single SNI. Each SNI can have a maximum of 16 addresses assigned. Group addresses, which are analogous to a LAN multicast address, let an SMDS data unit be delivered to multiple SNIs.

The ITU-T E.164 standard, "Numbering Plan for the ISDN Era" defines the address format. In the United States, individual and group SMDS addresses consist of the prefix of the numeral one, followed by a 10-digit number. In other countries, SMDS addresses begin with the appropriate country code. An Address Type field preceding the address identifies whether the address is an individual or a group.

You can use addressing restrictions, called address screens, to create a logical private network. An Individual Address screen scrutinizes destination addresses of data units that the CPE has sent, as well as source addresses of data units to be delivered to the CPE. The screen consists either of a set of allowed addresses or a set of disallowed addresses, but not both. The Group Address screen scrutinizes destination addresses of data units sent by the CPE.

This screen also consists of a set of allowed addresses or disallowed addresses, but not both.

6.1.2 SMDS access classes

The physical path between the customer and the network is a leased line operating at the DS0, DS1, or DS3 rates. Data is transferred on those paths at the maximum effective bandwidth (56/65 Kbps, 1.17 Mbps, or 34 Mbps, respectively) after any overhead is removed.

Because each customer's traffic flow into the network is different, the network requires customers using lines operating at DS3 rates (but not at DS0 or DS1 rates) to predict the amount and duration of traffic flow. This measurement is called the Sustained Information Rate (SIR), measured in megabits per second. One of the following five Access Classes defines SIR traffic enforcement:

Access Class	SIR (Mbps)
1	4
2	10
3	16
4	25
5	34

By defining the Access Class parameter at subscription time, customers ensure that the network can allocate its resources to meet their traffic-flow requirements.

The most commonly used Access Classes support the following networks: Access Classes 1 and 3 support IEEE 802.5 LANs; Access Class 2 supports IEEE 802.3 LANs; and Access Class 5 is the maximum effective bandwidth across a DS3-based SNI. It is not necessary to match the Access Class speed to the LAN media speed, however. For example, Access Classes 1 or 3 may support a 10 Mbps Ethernet LAN. The connecting device, such as a router, manages traffic to and from the SMDS network. Should traffic loads increase, the customer can order a higher Access Class with a correspondingly higher SIR from the network provider.

6.2 The SMDS Interface Protocol

Chapter 5 discussed the SMDS network architecture, including the SNI, SIP, and segmentation of the PDUs. Figure 6–1 summarizes the relationships between these elements.

SIP is a three-level protocol that controls the customer's access to the network. Recall from Chapter 5 that SIP's three levels were derived from the connectionless part of the IEEE 802.6 DQDB standard. SIP Level 3 receives and transports frames of ULP information. SIP Level 2 controls access to the physical medium, and is based on the IEEE 802.6 DQDB standard. SIP Level 1 includes the PLCP, and the transmission system itself. The PLCP converges the cells coming from SIP Level 2 into bits that can be sent on the transmission line, and it performs monitoring and maintenance. Figure 6–2 compares the SIP and DQDB protocol layers. Recall from our discussion in Chapter 5 that SIP Level 1 performs OSI Physical layer functions, while SIP Levels 2 and 3 perform OSI Data Link layer functions.

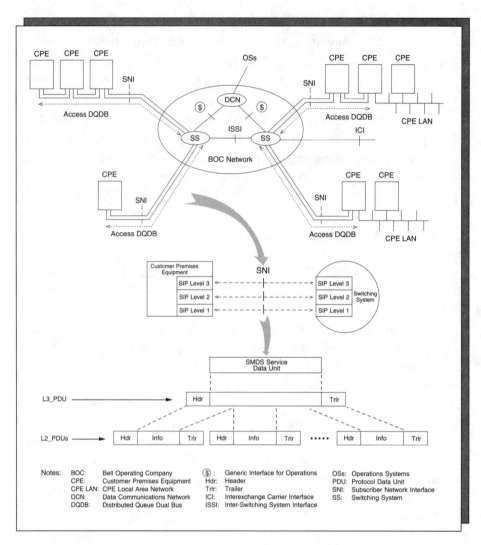

Figure 6–1. SMDS architecture and protocols *(Source: TR-TSV-000772, ©1991, Bell Communications Research, Inc., reprinted with permission)*

The following sections explain the details of SIP from the transmitter's perspective, considering the protocol processing of SIP Level 3 first, then SIP Level 2, and finally SIP Level 1.

SIP	IEEE 802.6
L3_PDU	IMPDU
L2_PDU	DMPDU
	SEGMENT
	SLOT
L1_PDU	PLCP

Figure 6–2. Correlation of protocol layers between SIP and IEEE 802.6 DQDB *(Source: TR-TSV-000772, ©1991, Bell Communications Research, Inc., reprinted with permission)*

6.3 SIP Level 3

Reviewing Figure 6–1, recall that the SMDS SDU, which contains up to 9,188 octets of information, is passed from the ULP process to SIP Level 3 for transmission over the network. SIP Level 3 builds a L3_PDU, which includes a header and trailer (see Figure 6–3). The L3_PDU is then passed to SIP Level 2, where it is segmented into multiple L2_PDUs, each 53 octets long (see Figure 6–4). These L2_PDUs are then passed to the PLCP, and finally to the physical transmission medium.

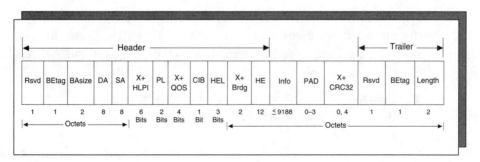

Figure 6–3. SIP Level 3 PDU format *(Source: TR-TSV-000772, ©1991, Bell Communications Research, Inc., reprinted with permission)*

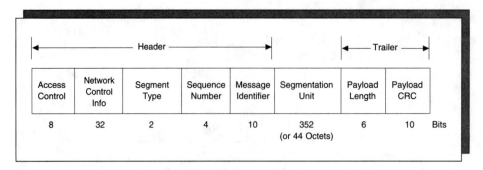

Figure 6–4. SIP Level 2 PDU format *(Source: TR-TSV-000772, ©1991, Bell Communications Research, Inc., reprinted with permission)*

The L3_PDU header is 36 octets long, and contains 12 fields. Fields marked with the symbol *X+* align the SIP and DQDB protocol formats, and are not processed by the network. The L3_PDU header fields are:

▼ *Reserved (Rsvd)*, a 1-octet field that the CPE and the SS fill with zeros.

▼ BEtag, a 1-octet field that contains a beginning/end tag. The BEtag is a binary number with a value between 0–255 that forms an association between the first segment (containing the header) and the last segment (containing the trailer) of an L3_PDU.

▼ *BAsize*, a 2-octet field containing the length in octets of the L3_PDU, from the beginning of the Destination Address field to (and including) the CRC32 field, if present.

▼ *Destination Address (DA)*, an 8-octet field containing the address of the intended recipient of this L3_PDU. This field contains two subfields, Address_Type (the four most significant bits) and Address (the 60 remaining bits).

▼ The *Address_Type* subfield value indicates an Individual address (1100) or a Group address (1110).

▼ The *Address subfield* contains the SMDS address for which the Address subfield L3_PDU is intended. For SMDS implementations in the United States, this subfield contains 0001 (indicating the country code for World Zone 1, North America); has 10 Binary Coded Decimal (BCD) digits (four bits each); and ends with 16 one bits.

▼ *Source Address (SA)*, an 8-octet field that contains the address of the sender of this L3_PDU. This field contains the Address_Type and Address subfields, as in the Destination Address. The value of Address_Type field always indicates an Individual address (1100).

▼ *Higher Layer Protocol Identifier (HLPI)*, a 6–bit field that aligns the SIP and DQDB protocol formats.

▼ *PAD Length (PL)*, a two-bit field that indicates the number of octets in the PAD field, which aligns the L3_PDU on a 32-bit boundary.

▼ *Quality of Service (QOS)*, a 4-bit field that aligns the SIP and DQDB protocol formats.

▼ *CRC32 Indication Bit (CIB)*, a single-bit field that indicates the presence (value = 1) or absence (value = 0) of the CRC32 field.

▼ Header Extension Length (HEL), a 3-bit field that indicates the number of 32-bit words in the Header Extension field. Both CPE and SS populate this field with the value 011, indicating a three-word (or 12-octet) Header Extension field.

▼ *Bridging (Brdg)*, a 2-octet field that aligns the SIP and DQDB Bridging protocol formats.

▼ *Header Extension (HE)*, a 12-octet field that contains version and carrier-selection information presented in a variable number of subfields as follows:

  • *Element Length,* a 1-octet subfield that contains the combined length of the Element Length, Element Type, and Element Value fields in octets

- *Element Type*, a 1-octet subfield that contains a binary value indicating the type of information found in the Element Value field:

Element Type	Meaning
0	Version, the version of SMDS access in use
1	Carrier Selection, which supports the per-L3_PDU carrier-selection feature of exchange access service
2–127	Reserved
128–255	For use by other entities, such as IXCs

- *Element Value*, a variable-length field, with a value that depends on the Element Type and its function.

- *HE PAD*, a variable length field, 0 to 9 octets long, that assures the length of Header Extension field is 12 octets.

▼ *Information field (Info)*, a variable-length field, up to 9,188 octets long, that contains user information, known as a Level 3 SDU.

▼ *PAD*, a variable-length field, 0 to 3 octets long, filled with zeros aligning the entire L3_PDU on a 32-bit boundary, as indicated by the PAD Length field.

▼ *CRC32*, a 2-octet field that performs error detection on the L3_PDU, beginning with the Destination Address field, up to and including the CRC32 field. This field may be absent.

The L3-PDU Trailer is 4 octets long and contains three fields:

▼ *Reserved (Rsvd)*, a 1-octet field that the CPE and SS fills with zeros.

▼ *BEtag*, a 1-octet field that contains a beginning/end tag. The tag is a binary number with a value between 0 to 255 that forms an association between the first segment (containing the header) and the last segment (containing the trailer) of a L3_PDU.

▼ *Length*, a 2-octet field that contains the same value as the BAsize field.

When the L3_PDU processing is complete, it is passed to SIP Level 2 to create one or more L2_PDUs.

6.4 SIP Level 2

SIP Level 2 generates the 53-octet cells transmitted over the PLCP and physical transmission medium. The 53-octet length is compatible with broadband ISDN technologies, such as ATM. The SIP L2_PDU contains a 5-octet header, a 44-octet Segmentation Unit (payload), and a 2-octet trailer (see Figure 6–4).

The L2_PDU header contains five fields:

▼ *Access Control,* an eight-bit field that indicates whether the L2_PDU Access Control contains information (Busy = 1) or is empty (Busy = 0); it may also contain reservation-priority information. This field has two formats, CPE to SS and SS to CPE. For the CPE to SS format, the first bit is the Busy bit, the network does not process the next four bits, and the final three bits represent different DQDB priority levels in the distributed queue. The SS to CPE case uses the Busy bit and sets the remaining seven bits to zero.

▼ *Network Control Information,* a 4-octet field that determines whether Network Control Information of the L2_PDU contains information (value = FFFFF022H) or is empty (value = 0).

▼ *Segment Type.* A 2-bit field that indicates how the receiver should process nonempty L2_PDUs. The possible values are:

Segment Type Value	Meaning
00	Continuation of Message (COM)
01	End of Message (EOM)
10	Beginning of Message (BOM)
11	Single Segment Message (SSM)

▼ *Sequence Number,* a 4-bit number that verifies all the L2_PDUs belonging to a single L3_PDU have been received in the correct order.

215

▼ *Message Identifier,* a 10-bit number that lets the various segments be associated with a single L3_PDU.

▼ *Segmentation Unit,* a 44-octet field that contains a portion of the L3_PDU.

The L2_PDU trailer contains two fields:

▼ *Payload Length*, a 6–bit field that indicates which of the 44 octets in the Segmentation Unit contain actual data. BOM and COM segments always indicate 44 octets. EOM segments indicate between 4 and 44 octets in multiples of 4 octets. SSM segments indicate between 28 and 44 octets in multiples of 4 octets.

▼ *Payload CRC,* a 10-bit CRC that performs error detection on the Segment Type, Sequence Number, Message Identifier, Segmentation Unit, Payload Length, and Payload CRC fields.

Once assembled, SIP L2_PDUs are passed to the PLCP and Physical functions within SIP Level 1 for transmission.

6.5 SIP Level 1

SIP Level 1 transmits the L2_PDUs generated at SIP Level 2. Its transmission functions are divided into two sublayers, an upper PLCP sublayer and a lower Transmission System sublayer (review Figure 5-7). The PLCP sublayer interfaces to the SIP Level 2 functions and supports the transfer of data (L2_PDUs) and control information. The Transmission System sublayer defines characteristics such as the format and speed for transmitted data. The two most common implementations for the Transmission System sublayer, which are both point-to-point connections (review Figure 5-18), are based on existing DS1 (1.544 Mbps) and DS3 (44.736 Mbps) technologies and standards. Bellcore document TR-TSV-000773 [6–2] addresses both of these configurations. The next two sections consider the DS1 and DS3 access options separately. Section 6.7 discusses a third configuration option, called low-speed SMDS access.

6.5.1 DS1 access to SMDS

In the 1970s, Bell Laboratories developed the DS1 signal that operated at a line rate of 1.544 Mbps to support voice communication and eventually data and video transport. The DS1 signal has a capacity to have 24 channels of digitized voice communication over a full-duplex circuit. Many different types of transmission media have been used with the DS1 signal, including copper pairs, fiber optics, as well as infrared and microwave links. When used with copper pairs, the DS1 circuit is called a T1 line.

The DS1 frame format contains 193 bits, with a duration of 125 microseconds. The frame consists of 24 octets (192 bits) of payload and one additional bit (called the F-bit) for framing and overhead. The resulting information payload is 1.536 Mbps.

DS1 signals are carried over high-performance transmission lines. The availability objective is 99.99 percent, which corresponds to a downtime of 53 minutes per year. The Bit Error Ratio (BER) is specified at less than 10^{-9}, which results in a long-term average of 99.86 percent Error Free Seconds (EFS).

To achieve these high-performance objectives, the SMDS specification places certain constraints on the transmission line. One of these is the requirement for the network to maintain the correct *ones density*. The system's key characteristic is its ability to derive a clock signal from the incoming data stream, using it to synchronize the outgoing transmitted data. This clock signal is derived from the data pulses that represent a binary value of one, with a specified number of one pulses present at any given time. This requirement is called the ones density. The network maintains the proper ones density using a coding procedure called Bipolar with 8-ZERO Substitution (B8ZS). In B8ZS coding, data strings that do not contain sufficient ones are substituted for strings with the proper ones density.

When the transmission line and its associated equipment assure a proper ones density, the CPE is relieved of this task. This process is known as Clear Channel Capability (CCC), and lets the entire 192 information bits be devoted to sending user information. TR-TSV-000773 mandates that all DS1 circuits used for SMDS have CCC, and further recommends that the B8ZS coding method be used.

6.5.1.1 DS1 Framing and control overhead

Over the past two decades of DS1 development, the basic signal has been enhanced a number of ways. One of these enhancements was the combining of 24 consecutive DS1 frames into a larger data structure called an Extended Superframe (ESF), with a duration of 3 milliseconds. This larger structure allows for expanded use of the framing and overhead bit (the F-bit). Because each DS1 frame contains one F-bit, an ESF contains 24 F-bits. This series of F-bits performs three functions: framing (6 bits), a CRC-6 for error control (six bits), and a data link (12 bits). The data link forms a 4 Kbps channel between DS1 endpoints, through which end devices may communicate. Two message formats are defined on this data link for SMDS applications, a scheduled performance report and unscheduled messages.

The Performance Report Message (PRM) is communicated between the SAT and SET, using the Q.921/LAPD message format, which was originally defined for ISDN signaling every second (see Figure 6–5). The PRM contains performance statistics and error-notification conditions. A Service Access Point Identifier (SAPI) value of 14 and a Terminal Endpoint Identifier (TEI) value of zero identify these PRMs. The source of the report is identified by the C/R field, either the SET (C/R = 1) or the SAT (C/R = 0). The contents of the message contain a number of individual reports that identify specific conditions and events.

Unscheduled messages may preempt the scheduled messages, and communicate more serious conditions. There are two types of unscheduled messages, priority messages and C/R messages. A priority message is also called a Yellow Alarm, and indicates that the transmitting SET or SAT has lost its incoming signal. The C/R messages place the link hardware, such as the CSU/DSU, in a loopback condition for testing purposes.

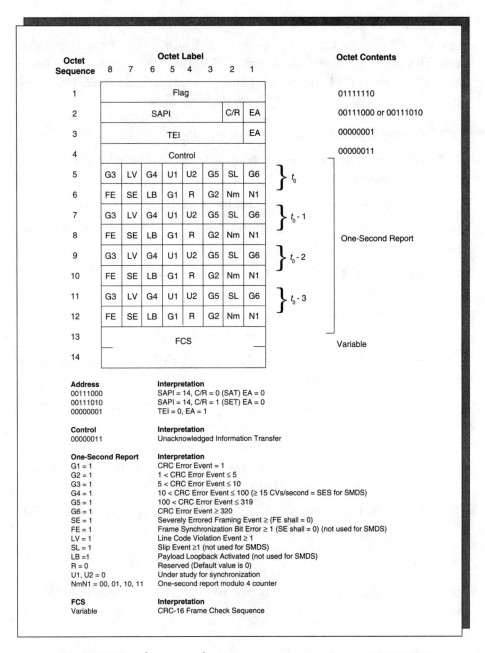

Figure 6–5. SMDS DS1 performance and report-message structure *(Source: TR-TSV-000773, ©1991, Bell Communications Research, Inc., reprinted with permission)*

6.5.1.2 DS1 PLCP payload format

The DS1 PLCP frame is transmitted using the ESF format of 24 frames per super-frame. This results in a superframe length of 576 octets. The contents of the frame include PLCP overhead (40 octets), L2_PDUs (530 octets), and a trailer (six octets) as illustrated in Figure 6–6. The PLCP overhead consists of:

▼ *framing octets* (A1 and A2).

▼ *path overhead identifier octets* identify the row number plus a parity bit (P9 to P0).

▼ *growth octets,* reserved for future use, encoded as all zeros (Z4 to Z1).

▼ *PLCP Path User Channel,* for communication between the SAT and the SET (F1).

▼ *bit-interleaved parity octet (BIP-8),* used for PLCP path-layer error monitoring (B1).

▼ *PLCP Path Status Indicator,* which conveys the near-end PLCP status to the transmitting far end (G1). This octet is encoded as follows:

• *Far-end Block Error, or FEBE,* (Bits 1 to 4) counts the number of blocks with errors.

• *Yellow Signal* (Bit 5) indicates normal (0) or Yellow Alarm (1) condition.

• *Link Status Signal* (Bits 6 to 8) indicates the current status of the received link: Received Link Connected (000), Received Link Down (011), or Received Link Up (110).

▼ *SIP Level 1 Control Information* (M2 to M1) is used by the DQDB nodes to exchange management information.

▼ *Cycle/Stuff Counter,* encoded as all zeros (C1).

The payload of the PLCP frame contains 10 L2_PDUs, followed by a 6–octet trailer.

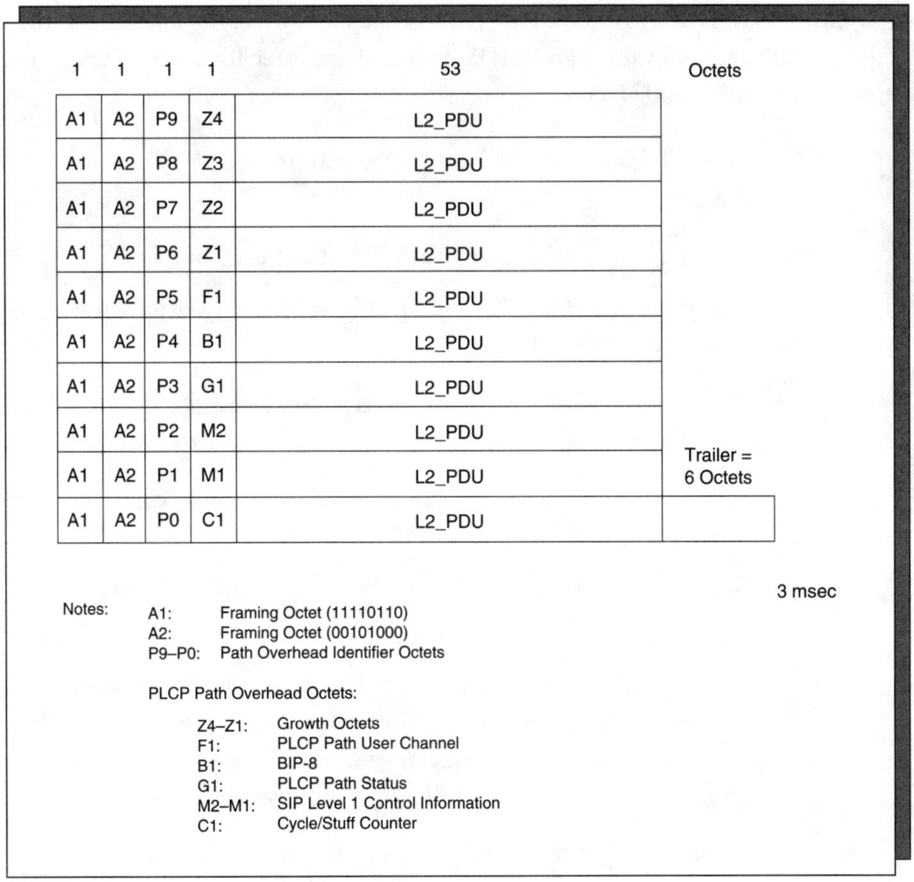

1	1	1	1	53	Octets
A1	A2	P9	Z4	L2_PDU	
A1	A2	P8	Z3	L2_PDU	
A1	A2	P7	Z2	L2_PDU	
A1	A2	P6	Z1	L2_PDU	
A1	A2	P5	F1	L2_PDU	
A1	A2	P4	B1	L2_PDU	
A1	A2	P3	G1	L2_PDU	
A1	A2	P2	M2	L2_PDU	
A1	A2	P1	M1	L2_PDU	Trailer = 6 Octets
A1	A2	P0	C1	L2_PDU	

3 msec

Notes:
A1: Framing Octet (11110110)
A2: Framing Octet (00101000)
P9–P0: Path Overhead Identifier Octets

PLCP Path Overhead Octets:

Z4–Z1: Growth Octets
F1: PLCP Path User Channel
B1: BIP-8
G1: PLCP Path Status
M2–M1: SIP Level 1 Control Information
C1: Cycle/Stuff Counter

Figure 6–6. The DS1 PLCP frame format *(Source: TR-TSV-000773, ©1991, Bell Communications Research, Inc., reprinted with permission)*

6.5.1.3 DS1 performance monitoring

The DS1 and PLCP layers are involved in monitoring the performance of the DS1-based SMDS access line on a periodic basis. The results are stored in registers. This monitoring is mandatory at the SET (the network side) and recommended at the SAT (customer side). The DS1 layer provides information to this monitoring process from the CRC-6 (one of the F-bit functions) and the scheduled performance report messages illustrated in Figure 6–5. The PLCP path layer provides information from this process from the BIP-8 octet (B1) and from the FEBE bits (part of G1). Both DS1 and PLCP parameters measure performance, and may be provided as an output on an SMDS protocol analyzer. The DS1 parameters defined in TR-TSV-000773 are:

▼ *Line Code Violation (LCV)*, a bipolar violation (BPV) or excessive zeros (EXZ).

▼ *Line Errored Seconds (LES)*, any second with at least one LCV.

▼ *Line Severely Errored Seconds (LSES)*, any second with 16 or more LCVs measured at the DS1 rate.

▼ *Code Violation (CV)*, discrepancy between the received CRC-6 and the locally calculated CRC-6.

▼ *Errored Second (ES)*, any second with at least one code violation derived from the received CRC-6 or PRM.

▼ *Severely Errored Second (SES)*, any second with 15 or more code violations measured at the DS1 rate.

▼ *Severely Errored Framing Second (SEFS)*, a count of one-second intervals containing one or more SEF events. SEF events occur when two or more framing-bit errors occur within a 3 millisecond period, or two or more errors occur out of five or less consecutive framing bits.

▼ *Alarm Indication Signal Second (AISS)*, a count of one-second intervals containing one or more incoming AISes.

▼ *Unavailable Second (UAS)*, a count of seconds during which the DS1 layer service is unavailable.

The DS1 PLCP Path Layer performance parameters defined in TR-TSV-000773 are similar to those defined for the DS1 layer parameters, but they may differ in the specific quantities being measured:

▼ *Code Violation*, the occurrence of a received BIP-8 code that is not identical to the corresponding locally calculated code.

▼ *Errored Second*, a second with at least one code violation, derived from received BIP-8 errors or FEBE codes.

▼ *Severely Errored Second (SES)*, any second with 15 or more code violations monitored at the DS1 rate.

▼ *Severely Errored Framing Second (SEFS)*, a count of one-second intervals containing one or more SEF events. SEF events occur when an error in both the A1 and A2 octets or two consecutive invalid and/or nonsequential Path Overhead Identifier octets is detected.

▼ *Unavailable Second (UAS)*, a count of seconds during which the DS1 PLCP Path Layer service is unavailable.

6.5.1.4 DS1 carrier failure alarms

Both ends of the DS1 link—the SET (network) and the SAT (customer)—monitor the health and status of the connection. Both normal and specific error conditions are defined, and called carrier failure alarms (CFAs). SMDS protocol analyzers typically note these CFAs. The DS1 conditions defined in TR-TSV-000773 and the SIP functions (DS1 transmission system or PLCP) to which they apply are:

▼ *Good Signal Definition*, a DS1 signal with a ONEs density of at least 12.5 percent, and no more than 15 consecutive zeros (DS1 level).

▼ *Loss of Signal (LOS)*, when the incoming DS1 signal contains 175±75 consecutive zeros or no pulses (DS1 level).

▼ *Out of Frame (OOF) or Severely Errored Frame (SEF)*, when two or more framing-bit errors within a 3 millisecond period, or two or more errors out of five or less consecutive F-bits, are detected (DS1 level).

▼ *Out of Frame (OOF) or Severely Errored Frame (SEF)*, when an error in both the A1 and A2 octets or two consecutive invalid and/or nonsequential Path Overhead Identifier octets are detected (PLCP level).

▼ *Alarm Indication Signal (AIS)*, an incoming DS1 signal with an all ONEs pattern, but without framing.

▼ *Yellow Alarm*, when the incoming DS1 signal is lost (DS1 level).

▼ *Yellow Alarm*, when the incoming PLCP signal is lost (PLCP level).

TR-TSV-000773 also addresses procedures for the testing and resolution of these alarm conditions.

6.5.2 DS3 access to SMDS

As industry professionals gathered experience with digital transmission facilities and the use of the DS1 signal, higher transmission rates were defined. The DS3 signal operates at the rate of 44.736 Mbps, the functional equivalent of 28 DS1s. This signal transmits 699 octets of data in a 125 microsecond period. Once overhead is subtracted, the nominal information payload is 44.210 Mbps.

6.5.2.1 DS3 framing and overhead

The DS3 frame, which is called the M-frame, consists of 595 octets or 4,760 bits. When formatted, it is divided into seven subframes, each containing 680 bits (see Figure 6–7). These subframes are further divided into eight blocks containing 85 bits. For each block, one bit is allocated to overhead, and 84 bits for the payload. So of the 4,760 bits in the M-frame, 56 bits are used for overhead, and 4,704 bits are available for the PLCP payload. Every 125 microseconds, a payload of 690.78 octets is transmitted (699 octets per DS3 signal format multiplied by the payload efficiency of 84/85).

The DS3 overhead performs several functions, which are designated by the letters *M*, *F*, *P*, *X*, or *C*. The M-bits and F-bits align the M-frame and the M-subframes, respectively. The P-bits are parity bits for monitoring performance. The X-bits indicate a Yellow Alarm, a loss of signal. The C-bits detect an Alarm Indication Signal. Notice that in Figure 6–7 these bits are placed in specific positions between segments of the information payload.

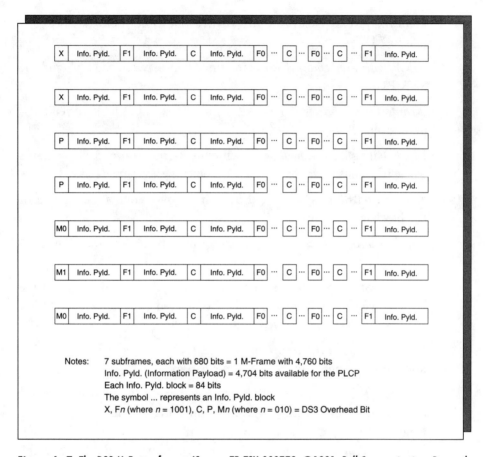

Notes: 7 subframes, each with 680 bits = 1 M-Frame with 4,760 bits
Info. Pyld. (Information Payload) = 4,704 bits available for the PLCP
Each Info. Pyld. block = 84 bits
The symbol ... represents an Info. Pyld. block
X, Fn (where n = 1001), C, P, Mn (where n = 010) = DS3 Overhead Bit

Figure 6–7. The DS3 M-Frame format *(Source: TR-TSV-000773, ©1991, Bell Communications Research, Inc., reprinted with permission)*

6.5.2.2 DS3 PLCP payload format

The DS3 PLCP frame format contains DS3 PLCP overhead (48 octets), payload information (636 octets), and a trailer (6.5 to 7 octets), as illustrated in Figure 6–8. The DS3 PLCP overhead is similar to the overhead defined for the DS1 PLCP. It consists of the following:

▼ *framing octets* (A1 and A2).

▼ *path overhead identifier octets*, which identify the row number and a parity bit (P11 to P0).

225

▼ *growth octets*, reserved for future use, encoded as all zeros (Z6 to Z1).

▼ *PLCP path user channel* for communication between the SAT and the SET (F1).

▼ *bit-interleaved parity octet* (BIP-8), used for PLCP Path Layer error monitoring (B1).

▼ *PLCP path status indicator*, which conveys the near-end PLCP status to the transmitting far end (G1). This octet is encoded as follows:

  • *Far End Block Error, or FEBE* (Bits 1 to 4), counts the number of blocks with errors.

  • *Yellow Signal* (Bit 5) indicates normal (0) or Yellow Alarm (1) condition.

  • *Link Status Signal* (Bits 6 to 8) indicates the current status of the received link: Received Link Connected (000), Received Link Down (011), or Received Link Up (110).

▼ *SIP Level 1 Control Information* (M2 to M1) is used by the DQDB nodes to exchange management information.

▼ *Cycle/Stuff Counter (octet C1)*, which indicates the phase of the 375 microsecond nibble-stuffing opportunity cycle, and therefore the length of the PLCP trailer (13 or 14 nibbles). The first DS3 PLCP frame contains 13 nibbles, the second contains 14 nibbles, and the third contains either 13 or 14 nibbles, depending on the stuffing function.

The payload of the PLCP frame contains 12 L2_PDUs, followed by a 13- or 14-nibble trailer.

1	1	1	1	53	Octets
A1	A2	P11	Z6	L2_PDU	
A1	A2	P10	Z5	L2_PDU	
A1	A2	P9	Z4	L2_PDU	
A1	A2	P8	Z3	L2_PDU	
A1	A2	P7	Z2	L2_PDU	
A1	A2	P6	Z1	L2_PDU	
A1	A2	P5	F1	L2_PDU	
A1	A2	P4	B1	L2_PDU	
A1	A2	P3	G1	L2_PDU	
A1	A2	P2	M2	L2_PDU	
A1	A2	P1	M1	L2_PDU	Trailer = 13–14 Nibbles
A1	A2	P0	C1	L2_PDU	

125 μsec

Notes:
A1:   Framing Octet (11110110)
A2:   Framing Octet (00101000)
P11–P0: Path Overhead Identifier Octets

PLCP Path Overhead Octets:

Z6–Z1:   Growth Octets
F1:   PLCP Path User Channel
B1:   BIP-8
G1:   PLCP Path Status
M2–M1:   SIP Level 1 Control Information
C1:   Cycle/Stuff Counter

Figure 6–8. The DS3 PLCP frame format *(Source: TR-TSV-000773, ©1991, Bell Communications Research, Inc., reprinted with permission)*

6.5.2.3 DS3 performance monitoring

The transmission equipment monitors the performance of the DS3-based SMDS access line on a periodic basis, using a procedure similar to that used for DS1. As before, DS3 and PLCP parameters measure this performance, which may be provided as an output on an SMDS protocol analyzer. The DS3 parameters defined in TR-TSV-000773 are:

▼ Line Code Violation (LCV), a BPV or EXZ.

▼ Line Errored Seconds (LES), any second with at least one LCV.

▼ Line Severely Errored Seconds (LSES), any second with 45 or more LCVs measured at the DS3 rate.

▼ P-Bit Parity Code Violation (CV), the occurrence of a received P-bit code in the DS3 M-frame that differs from the corresponding locally calculated code.

▼ Errored Second (ES), any second with at least one code violation.

▼ Severely Errored Second (SES), any second with 44 or more code violations measured at the DS3 rate.

▼ Severely Errored Framing Second (SEFS), a count of one-second intervals containing one or more SEF events (SEF events occur when three or more errors in 16 or fewer consecutive F-bits occur within a DS3 M-frame).

▼ Alarm Indication Signal Second (AISS), a count of one-second intervals containing one or more incoming alarm indication signals.

▼ Unavailable Second (UAS), a count of seconds during which the DS3 layer service is unavailable.

The DS3 PLCP Path Layer performance parameters defined in TR-TSV-000773 are similar to those defined for the DS3 Layer parameters, but may differ in the specific quantities being measured:

▼ *Code Violation*, the occurrence of a received BIP-8 code that is not identical to the corresponding locally calculated code.

▼ *Errored Second*, a second with at least one code violation, derived from received BIP-8 errors or FEBE codes.

▼ *Severely Errored Second (SES)*, any second with five or more code violations monitored at the DS3 rate.

▼ Severely Errored Framing Second (SEFS), a count of one-second intervals containing one or more SEF events. SEF events occur when an error in both the A1 and A2 octets, or two consecutive invalid and/or nonsequential Path Overhead Identifier octets, is detected.

▼ *Unavailable Second (UAS)*, a count of seconds during which the DS3 PLCP Path Layer service is unavailable.

6.5.2.4 DS3 Carrier failure alarms

As with DS1, DS3 circuit performance is also monitored. TR-TSV-000773 defines the following CFAs for DS3 circuits along with the SIP functions to which they apply (DS3 transmission system or PLCP):

▼ *Good Signal Definition*, a DS3 signal with valid framing and parity and a ones density of at least 33 percent (DS3 level).

▼ *Loss of Signal (LOS)*, when the incoming DS3 signal contains 175±75 consecutive zeros or no pulses (DS3 level).

▼ *Out of Frame (OOF) or Severely Errored Frame (SEF)*, when three or more errors of 16 or fewer consecutive framing F-bits are detected (DS3 level).

▼ *Out of Frame (OOF) or Severely Errored Frame (SEF)*, when an error in both the A1 and A2 octets or two consecutive invalid and/or nonsequential Path Overhead Identifier octets is detected (PLCP level).

▼ *Alarm Indication Signal (AIS)*, an incoming DS3 signal with the information bits set to 1010..., and the C-bits set to zero.

▼ *Yellow Alarm*, when the incoming DS3 signal is lost (DS3 level).

▼ *Yellow Alarm*, when the incoming PLCP signal is lost (PLCP Level).

TR-TSV-000773 also offers procedures for the testing and resolution of these DS3 alarm conditions.

6.6 Data Exchange Interface Protocol

The Data Exchange Interface (DXI) protocol, defined by SIG-TS-001 [6–3], lets LAN internetworking equipment, such as bridges and routers, connect to SMDS network facilities, as shown in Figure 6–9. A DSU provides the physical connection to the network. SIP Level 3 processing occurs at the bridge/router; the SIP Level 2 and 1 processing occurs in the DSU. The bridge/router and DSU communicate using the DXI protocol, improving the likelihood that one vendor's DSU will interoperate with another vendor's bridge/router. Because functionality is split this way, customers can upgrade internetworking equipment via software upgrades and can use existing Physical Layer interfaces, such as DS1 and DS3, with the DSU [6–4].

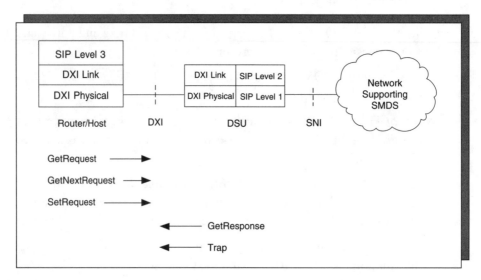

Figure 6–9. DXI protocol

A second protocol, called the DXI Local Management Interface (DXI LMI, not to be confused with the frame relay LMI), operates between the internetworking equipment and the DSU. This protocol, defined in SIG-TS-002 [6–5], is a condensed version of SNMP, and communicates status information between the internetworking equipment and the DSU.

Communication between the internetworking hardware and the DSU requires a special frame format derived from the ISO HDLC protocol. In HDLC parlance, the internetworking hardware functions as the DTE and the DSU functions as the DCE. This DXI frame may contain one of two types of information: data or an LMI PDU. These types are designated as logical links numbering zero and one, respectively. Logical-link zero provides for the transport of an entire L3_PDU between the bridge/router and the DSU. Logical-link one communicates status, control, and diagnostic information concerning the L2_PDU, PLCP, or Physical layer (DS1 or DS3) connection.

The frame format contains four fields enclosed within Flag characters (see Figure 6–10): the Address field, the Control field, the Information field, and a Frame Check Sequence. The Address field identifies the source and destination device for the frame, plus the logical link type within that frame. The Control field identifies the frame type, which may be a UI frame or a test frame. The Information field may carry up to 9,234 octets of data, which may be a L3_PDU (for example, LAN data) or a DXI LMI PDU (management data). The fourth field carries a 2- or 4-octet FCS for error control.

The Address field is further divided into four subfields, designated L, S, CR, and AE. The Logical Link (L) subfield, 5 bits long, defines one of 32 logical links. Current definitions for this field include Data (an L3_PDU) with L = 0 and Link Management (a DMI LMI PDU) with L = 1. All other values (2 to 31 decimal) are reserved for future use. The Station Address (S) subfield defines the transmission direction for that frame, whether the frame is traveling toward the DSU (S = 1) or from the DSU (S = 0). The DCE (or DSU) is designated device zero, while the bridge/router (or DTE) is designated device one. Commands contain the address of the device receiving that command. Responses contain the address of the device responding to the command. For example, a command to the DSU (DCE) uses CR = 0. A response from that DSU would also contain CR = 0. The S-bit is an explicit address that defines the source of the frame as from the DCE (S = 0) or the DTE (S = 1). Finally, the Address Extension (AE) bit is reserved and set to zero.

The Control field identifies either UI frames or test frames. UI frames transfer information, such as a L3_PDU or DXI LMI management request or response. The Control field contains 03H for UI frames. Test frames transfer test information across the link. The Control field includes a Poll/Final bit for test frames. The Poll bit is used when the field is issued as a command; the Final bit is used when it is issued as a response (Poll/Final = 1).

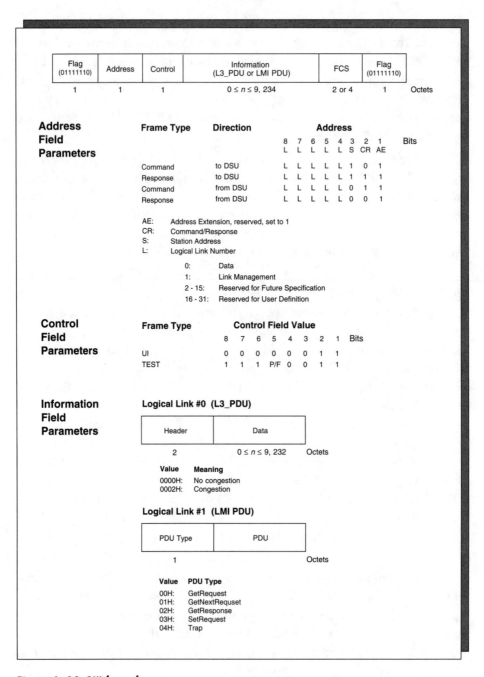

Figure 6–10. DXI frame format

The Information field carries information from one of two logical links. Logical Link 0 uses UI frames to transport entire L3_PDUs. In this case, the Information field contains two subfields: Header (2 octets) and Data (up to 9,232 octets). The Header contains a notification of congested resources, as sent from the DSU to the bridge/router. A value of 0000H indicates no congestion, while a value of 0002H tells the bridge/router that the frames it transmits may encounter congested resources. Use of the Congestion bit from the bridge/router to the DSU is reserved for future specification.

Logical Link 1 uses UI frames to transport DMI LMI PDUs or test frames to transmit test data. In the case of DMI LMI PDUs, the Information field contains two subfields: a 1-octet Header that identifies one of five PDUs and the PDU data.

The DMI LMI PDUs are similar to those defined by SNMP, but have different structures. The GetRequest, GetNextRequest, and SetRequest are sent from the Router/Host to the DSU, while the GetResponse and Trap are sent from the DSU to the Router/Host (see Figure 6–9).

All these PDUs are sent within the DXI LMI frame (see Figure 6–11). The Address and Control fields of the DXI frame indicate that the frame contains LMI information. In the Address field, the L-bits are set equal to 00001 (link management information), while the S-and C/R-bits define the direction and format of the PDU (C/R to/from DSU). The Control field is set for 03H, indicating a UI frame.

The Information field contains one of the five PDUs. Note from Figure 6–11 that the Request and Response PDUs share a common structure, while the Trap PDU is unique. The first field of each PDU defines its type: GetRequest, GetNextRequest, GetResponse, SetRequest, or Trap. The remaining fields contain information specific to the management information being conveyed, and are described in detail in SIG-TS-002.

The DXI LMI protocol extends the capabilities of the SNMP proxy agent that exists on the DTE such as a bridge or router. The SNMP management console is also operational on the network or internetwork that includes the DTE.

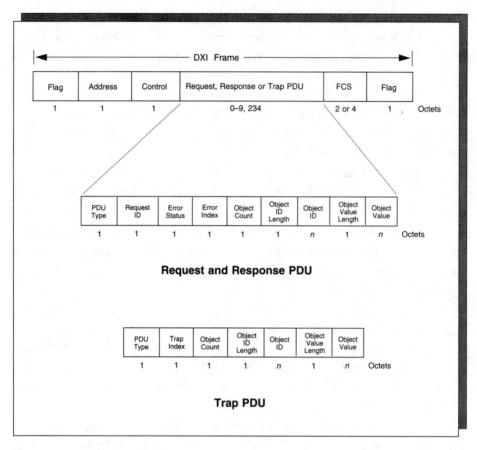

Figure 6–11. DXI LMI PDUs

The DTE's agent is called a proxy agent. The proxy acts on behalf of the DTE's SNMP agent to obtain information from another device (such as the DSU) that would otherwise be unavailable. Suppose the management console needs to retrieve information about the DTE and its connection via the DSU to the SMDS network. The management console would send an SNMP message to the proxy agent within the DTE. The proxy agent would determine whether the requested information resides in the DTE or in the DSU. If the information resides in the DTE, the proxy agent issues an SNMP response to the manager and no further action is required. If the information resides in the DSU, the proxy agent issues the appropriate LMI PDU to the DSU, and the DSU replies with a GetResponse when finished.

The GetRequest and GetNextRequest PDUs originate in the DTE and retrieve the value of a managed object, or element of management information, for the manager. The SetRequest PDU also originates in the DTE, and writes the value of a managed object. The DSU responds with a GetResponse in all three cases. The Trap PDU originates in the DSU, and is sent to the DTE to signal an alarm condition. Standard traps, such as coldStart or linkDown, are indicated by the Trap Index field, and are further defined in the DXI LMI specification.

Logical Link 1 may also transmit test data between the bridge/router and the DSU. This function enables either end of the link to periodically determine the status of the link. The process is called a heartbeat polling procedure, and is further defined in SIG-TS-001 and TR-TSV-001239 [6–6].

6.7 Low-Speed SMDS Access

In addition to the DS1 and DS3 access rates to SMDS, Bellcore has written a low-speed specification, documented in TR-TSV-001239 [6–6], that operates at the DS0 rates of 56 Kbps and 64 Kbps. This specification is based on the SIG specifications for the DXI SIG-TS-001 [6–3] and the DXI/SNI SIG-TS-005 [6–7]. It lets customers integrate locations with a low data traffic volume, such as remote offices, into a corporatewide, SMDS-based internetwork.

The architecture for low-speed access is similar to that defined for DXI (review Figure 5-20), except that for low-speed access, the CSU/DSU implements only the Physical layer protocols, while the bridge, router, or host implements the DXI and SIP Level 3 protocols (see Figure 6–12). The SNI for low-speed access is, therefore, called the DXI/SNI. Because the SIP Level 3 processing occurs at the end-user device, end users see few differences in SMDS functionality. The primary difference is that some of the service features, such as the number of addresses per SNI and number of group addresses associated with an individual address, are reduced from the TR-TSV-000772 specification. In addition, no access classes are defined for this DS0 access as they were for DS3 access. The network implements the Heartbeat Poll procedure, defined in SIG-TS-001 Section 6, but not the the SMDS DXI LMI procedures, defined in SIG-TS-002.

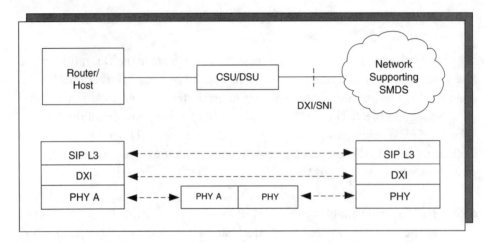

Figure 6–12. Low-speed SMDS access *(Source: TR-TSV-001239, ©1993, Bell Communications Research, Inc., reprinted with permission)*

6.8 SMDS/IEEE 802 Bridging

The IEEE Project 802 has put considerable effort into developing bridging technologies to connect LANs and MANs. This development effort includes architectures for local and remote bridges. Local bridges connect LAN segments directly, while remote bridges connect segments via a transmission facility, such as a leased line. The proposed 802.6i standard on Remote LAN Bridging of Metropolitan Area Networks [6–8] will support SMDS as the remote transmission facility between two IEEE 802 LANs.

Examining the bridge's internal architecture can help you understand its operation and protocols (see Figure 6–13). The bridge contains two interfaces that connect to the two Physical layer interfaces (in this case, an 802 LAN and an 802.6 MAN such as SMDS). A relay function converts the protocols for the dissimilar MAC headers and/or trailers. One significant MAC layer function is address conversion. Recall that IEEE 802 LANs used 48-bit addresses, while the 802.6 standard (and SMDS) specify 60-bit addresses. Higher layer information within those frames is transferred unaltered. The higher layer protocol entities illustrated in Figure 6–13 refer to interbridge communication and management functions, not to the protocols contained within the transferred data frames.

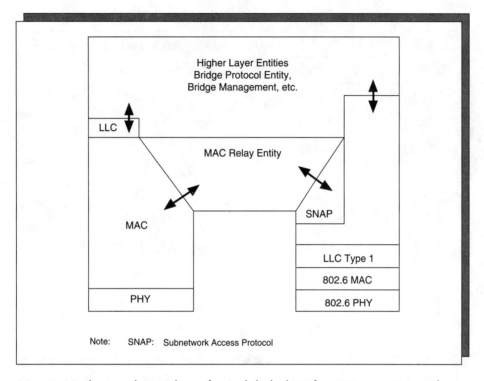

Figure 6–13. The protocol encapsulation of remotely bridged MAC frames *(Source: George H. Clapp, "LAN Interconnection Across SMDS." IEEE Network Magazine (September 1991), ©1991 IEEE.)*

Figure 6–14 illustrates the resulting protocol encapsulation. The incoming MAC frame, such as an 802.5 token-ring frame, may have a maximum length of 9,180 octets. That frame is added in front of the SNAP header and the 802.2 LLC header.

The fields within the SNAP header identify the type of bridged MAC frame the 802.6 frame carries. The OUI field (three octets) contains a value of 0080C2H, which represents the IEEE 802.1 Working Group. The Protocol ID field (two octets) identifies the bridged frame. 802.6i then assigns the following values in hexadecimal:

OUI	PID	Protocol
0080C2	0001	802.3/Ethernet with FCS present
0080C2	0002	802.4 with FCS present
0080C2	0003	802.5 with FCS present
0080C2	0004	FDDI with FCS present
0080C2	0005	802.6 with FCS present
0080C2	0006	802.9 with FCS present
0080C2	0007	802.3/Ethernet with FCS absent
0080C2	0008	802.4 with FCS absent
0080C2	0009	802.5 with FCS absent
0080C2	000A	FDDI with FCS absent
0080C2	000B	802.6 with FCS absent
0080C2	000C	802.9 with FCS absent

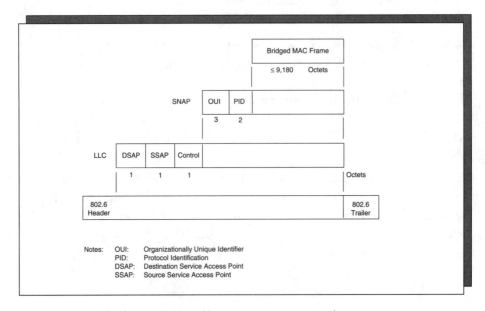

Figure 6–14. Fields of encapsulating sublayers *(Source: George H. Clapp, "LAN Interconnection Across SMDS." IEEE Network Magazine (September 1991), ©1991 IEEE)*

The subfields and values for the LLC header are DSAP (AAH), SSAP (AAH), and Control (03H, indicating UI). The Protocol Identification (PI) field within the 802.6 header indicates that a LLC frame follows (value = 01H). 802.6i provides specific examples of these encodings.

6.9 SMDS/IP Routing

The IETF has developed specific plans to support most LANs and MANs, including ARCNET, FDDI, IEEE 802, and SMDS. RFC 1209 [6–9] details how the IP and the Address Resolution Protocol (ARP) may be implemented within an SMDS environment. IP is a Network layer protocol that performs datagram addressing and delivery functions. ARP is a complementary protocol that translates between the local (Data Link layer) addresses and the IP (or Network layer) addresses. So, ARP is required to map between SMDS and IP addresses.

The IETF work assumes that multiple logical IP subnetworks (LISes) exist, and that the SMDS protocols physically connect these LISes (review Figure 5-22). A single SMDS group address identifies all members of a particular LIS. Furthermore, the internetwork is usually router-based, not bridge-based, and uses IP. The protocol relationships within that router illustrate the interactions between SIP, LLC, and IP/ARP (see Figure 6–15).

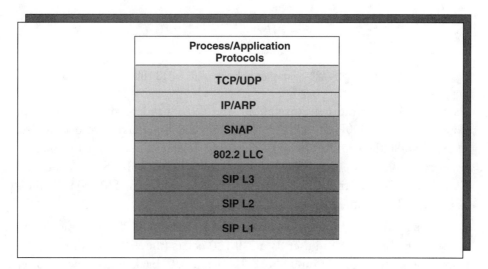

Figure 6–15. Using IP and ARP over SMDS

The SIP encapsulates TCP, higher layer user information, and the associated IP header for transmission via the SMDS-based network (see Figure 6–16). RFC 1209 specifies that the SNAP header (five octets) and the IEEE 802.2 LLC header (three octets) precede this higher layer data, which is then placed within the Information field of the SIP L3_PDU.

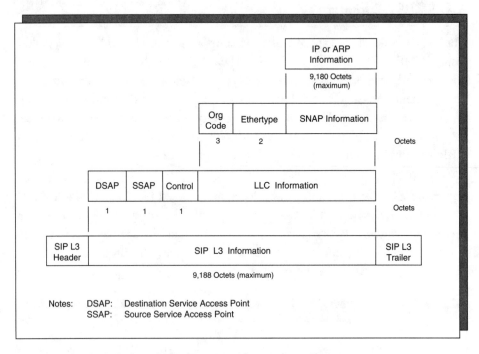

Figure 6–16. Encapsulating IP/ARP information within an SMDS SIP L3-PDU

Starting at the innermost encapsulation—the SNAP header—the Organization Code value is 000000H. The Ethertype defines the upper layer protocol in use, such as IP (0800H) or ARP (0806H). The subfields and values for the LLC header are Destination Service Access Point Address, or DSAP (AAH), SSAP (AAH), and Control (03H, indicating UI). The SIP HLPI field within the SIP L3_PDU indicates that a LLC frame follows (value = 01H).

When an IP datagram is transmitted within the SIP L3_PDU, the maximum length of the IP header and user data is 9,180 octets (the 9,188 maximum SDU length less 8 octets for LLC and SNAP headers). ARP packets are much shorter in length and should never exceed the maximum SDU length. ARP parameters noted in RFC 1209 include: Hardware Type code for SMDS (0EH) and Hardware Address Length for SMDS (8 octets). For additional examples of the address translations and protocol operations refer to RFC 1209. George Clapp's paper, "LAN Interconnection Across SMDS" [6–10] provides an excellent summary of SMDS-based bridged and routed environments.

6.10 Frame Relay Access to SMDS

Bellcore's TA-TSV-001240 [6–11], based upon earlier work by the SIG, permits internetworking between networks supporting frame relay and those supporting SMDS. The defined interface for this configuration is called the SRI, and consists of three levels of protocol: Physical, LAPF, and SIP Level 3 (see Figure 6–17). This architecture provides for the transport of a SIP L3_PDU across a frame relay-based Data Link layer (LAPF).

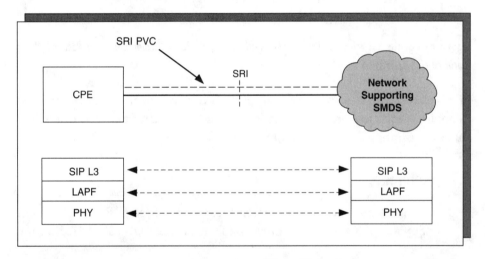

Figure 6–17. SIP relay protocols *(Source: TA-TSV-001240, ©1993, Bell Communications Research, Inc., reprinted with permission.)*

The actual L3_PDU transport is accomplished by encapsulating the L3_PDU within the T1.618 (LAPF) frame (see Figure 6–18). The L3_PDU 23 is contained within the T1.618 Information field, with a maximum length of 9,232 octets. When the remaining fields of the T1.618 frame are added, a maximum length of

9,240 octets results. For more information about Bellcore's implementation of frame relay, refer to TR-TSV-001369 [6–12].

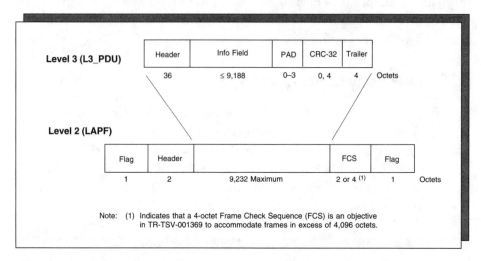

Figure 6–18. The SRI Protocol *(Source: TA-TSV-001240, ©1993, Bell Communications Research, Inc., reprinted with permission.)*

In this chapter, we've discussed details of the SMDS protocol, along with specific examples of internetworking applications for SMDS. The next chapter offers case studies illustrating the operation of these protocols.

6.11 References

[6–1]   Bell Communications Research Inc. Generic System Requirements in Support of Switched Multimegabit Data Service. TR-TSV-000772, May 1991.

[6–2]   Bell Communications Research Inc. Local Access System Generic Requirements, Objectives, and Interfaces in Support of Switched Multimegabit Data Service. TR-TSV-000773, June 1991.

[6–3]   SMDS Interest Group. SMDS Data Exchange Interface Protocol. SIG-TS-001, October 1991.

[6–4] Digital Link Corp. SMDS Strategy Presentation, 1991.

[6–5] SMDS Interest Group. SMDS DXI Local Management Interface. SIG-TS-002, May 1992.

[6–6]   Bell Communications Research Inc. Generic Requirements for Low-Speed SMDS Access. TR-TSV-001239, December 1993.

[6–7] SMDS Interest Group. Frame Based Interface Protocol for SMDS Networks—Data Exchange Interface/Subscriber Network Interface. SIG-TS-005, February 1993.

[6–8] Institute of Electrical and Electronics Engineers, Inc. Remote LAN Bridging of Metropolitan Area Networks. IEEE 802.6i/D5, 1993.

[6–9] Piscitello, D. and J. Lawrence. "The Transmission of IP Datagrams over the SMDS Service." RFC 1209, March 1991.

[6–10] Clapp, George H. "LAN Interconnection Across SMDS." *IEEE Network Magazine* (September 1991): 25–32.

[6–11] Bell Communications Research Inc. Generic Requirements for Frame Relay Access to SMDS. TA-TSV-001240, June 1993.

[6–12] Bell Communications Research Inc. Generic Requirements for Frame Relay PVC Service. TR-TSV-001369, May 1993.

7 SMDS Analysis

Chapter 5 explored DQDB and SMDS architectures; Chapter 6 focused on SIP, DXI, and LMI protocols. This chapter illustrates how these protocols operate and interact with other systems such as LANs.

For this section, I used the Chameleon Open protocol analyzer from Tekelec Corp. of Calabasas, Calif. This analzyer is housed in a UNIX-based portable workstation, and is designed to test LANs, WANs, and internetworks (see Figure 7–1 and Reference [7–1]). The color graphic display provides an X Window Motif user interface. The device supports multiple LAN and WAN interfaces, including Ethernet, token ring, frame relay, ISDN, X.25, SMDS, and ATM. It also provides multiport, simultaneous full-rate simulation and analysis of both LAN and WAN protocols. The SMDS application module captures traffic at up to 34 Mbps and decodes all protocol layers at the SNI and DXI. It can also decode encapsulated LAN traffic, including AppleTalk, Banyan VINES, DECnet, NetWare, TCP/IP, and XNS.

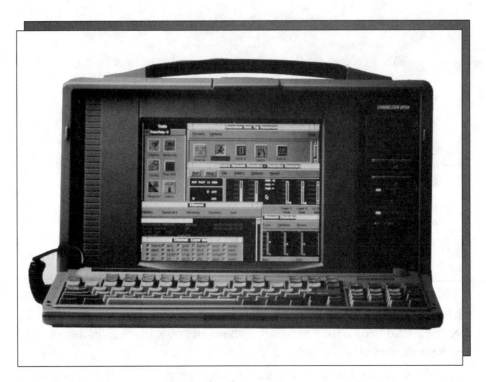

Figure 7–1. The Chameleon Open protocol analyzer

The Chameleon decodes and displays data in either a graphical or text format. The text format, which I used for this chapter, decodes the information one layer at a time. The Chameleon indicates each layer (for example, SIP2 or SIP3) on the left-hand side of the display, and displays the individual fields with their contents one line at a time. Note that the analyzer displays header information for each labeled layer on the lines that precede the label. Now, let's look at SMDS protocol operation.

7.1 Segmenting an SMDS L3_PDU into Multiple L2_PDUs

Chapter 5 noted that an SIP L3_PDU can transmit up to 9,188 octets of ULP information. The ULP information is designated as an SDU and occupies the information field of the L3_PDU (see Figure 7–2). The L3_PDU is then segmented into one or more L2_PDUs. These L2_PDUs consist of a 7–octet header, a 44-octet payload, and a 2-octet trailer, for a total of 53 octets. This case study illustrates how the L3_PDU and L2_PDUs fields are formatted and processed during the segmentation and transmission process.

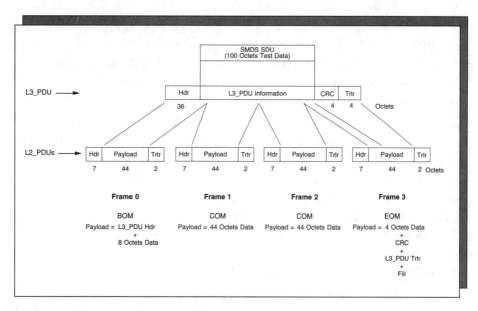

Figure 7–2. Segmenting the SMDS L3_PDU into L2_PDUs

For this example, the Chameleon Open analyzer generates 100 octets of test data to create the SMDS SDU. This data consists of the numbers 0 to 99, expressed in hexadecimal notation: 00, 01, 02, 03, and so on (shown in the lower portion of Trace 7.1a). The L3_PDU header (36 octets) and trailer (4 octets) are added to the SDU prior transmission, completing the L3_PDU.

By examining the details of the L3_PDU, you see the header and trailer fields' values (see Trace 7.1). The Rsvd field is filled with 00H. The beginning and ending BEtags, which associate the various L2_PDU segments of the L3_PDU, contain the same number (01H). Beginning with the Destination Address field, the BAsize field measures the length of the L3_PDU (0088H or 136 decimal), including the data and ending with the CRC field. The Destination and Source Addresses, which indicate individual addresses, are each 8 octets long and begin with a hexadecimal C (1100 binary). The next binary-coded decimal (BCD) digit is the North American prefix (1), followed by 10-digit numbers: (805) 555-1212 and (818) 5555-1212. Each address is filled with 16 ones (FFFFH) to complete the field. The next five fields contain control parameters: Higher Layer Protocol Identifier, or HLPI (00); Pad Length, or PL (0, indicating no padding after the data); Quality of Service, or QOS (0); CRC Indication Bit, or CIB (1, indicating that the CRC field is present); Header Extension Length, or HEL (3H, indicating that the Header Extension field contains three 32-bit words); and Bridging, or BRDG (0000H).

The Header Extension (HE) field contains two elements, a Version and a Carrier Selection. The Version element, 3 octets long, is identified by Element Type = 0. The Element Value = 01, indicating version 1 of SIP. The Carrier Selection element, 4 octets long, is identified by Element Type = 1. For XA-SMDS, you may select a different carrier for each L3_PDU (see TR-TSV-001060). For this L3_PDU, the SMDS Carrier Identification Code (CIC) was the four BCD digits 0222. A Header Pad, with value 00FFFFFFFFH completes the Header Extension field. Note that the pad begins with 1 octet of zeros (00H), and ends with 4 octets of ones (FFFFFFFFH). This completes the SMDS header.

Following the SMDS header fields, the 100 octets of application data, the CRC, and the SMDS trailer fields are transmitted. Within the trailer, the Rsvd field is filled with all zeros (00H), the ending BEtag has the same value as the BEtag in the header (01H), and the Length field has the same value as the BASize field in the header (136 decimal).

The lower portion of Trace 7.1a contains the hexadecimal values of the SIP Level 3 header and the application data.

Trace 7.1a. SMDS L3_PDU

Frame#0 16:41:40 158 494 Len=144

Rsvd=00   Begin BETag=01
BASize=0088
Destination Address C18055551212FFFF
Source Address C18185551212FFFF
HLPI = 00   PL = 0
QOS = 0   CIB = 1
HEL = 3   BRDG = 0000
Header Extension
  Element Length = 3
   Element Type = 0 Version
   Element Value = 01
  Element Length = 4
   Element Type = 1 Carrier
   Element Value = 5678
  Header Pad = 00FFFFFFFF
CRC=354F 4B91
Rsvd=00   End BETag=01
Len=136

SIP3   00010088C18055551212FFFFC1818555
1212FFFF000B00000300010401022200
FFFFFFFF

APPL 000102030405060708090A0B0C0D0E0F
101112131415161718191A1B1C1D1E1F
202122232425262728292A2B2C2D2E2F
303132333435363738393A3B3C3D3E3F
404142434445464748494A4B4C4D4E4F
505152535455565758595A5B5C5D5E5F
60616263

The L3_PDU has an overall length of 144 octets (36 octets in the header, 100 octets of data, 4 octets of CRC, and 4 octets in the trailer). This L3_PDU is passed to the SIP Level 2 process, which segments it into 53 octet L2_PDUs for transmission (review Figure 7–2). Because each L2_PDU can hold 44 octets of payload, four L2_PDU segments are necessary for the entire L3_PDU (see Trace 7.1b).

Frame 0 contains the first L2_PDU. The SIP Layer 2 header (7 octets long) includes the Sequence Number (0), the Message Identifier (33), and the Segment Type field (BOM). Note that the analyzer does not decode the first two fields of the L2_PDU header, which contain Access Control and Network Control Information. The SIP L2_PDU trailer contains a Payload Length value (44 decimal) and a Payload CRC (049H).

The Payload contents are decoded at the lower portion of Frame 0. They include 36 octets of the L3_PDU header, plus 8 octets of application data (values 00 through 07H).

Frames 1, 2, and 3 are constructed in a similar manner. Frame 1 indicates Sequence Number 1 and Message ID 33. The Segment Type is a COM. The 44 octets of payload is all data, with values 08 through 33H. Likewise, Frame 2 is a COM segment with another 44 octets of data (values 34 through 5FH). The final segment, Frame 3, is an EOM segment. This payload contains the final 4 octets of data (values 60 through 63), plus the L3_PDU trailer. The values of the trailer fields are shown in hexadecimal: 354F4B91 (the 4-octet L3_PDU CRC), the Rsvd field (00), the End BEtag (01), and the Length (0088H, or 136 decimal). The remainder of this EOM segment is filled with zeros.

The next case study extends this example by illustrating how upper layer protocol information is encapsulated within the L3_PDU.

Trace 7.1b. Resultant SMDS L2_PDUs

Frame#0 15:05:41 591 653 Len=48
  Sequence Number = 0
  MID = 33   Segment Type = BOM
  Payload Length = 44   Payload CRC = 049

  Rsvd=00   Begin BETag=01
  BASize=0088
  Destination Address C18055551212FFFF
  Source Address C18185551212FFFF
  HLPI = 00   PL = 0
  QOS = 0   CIB = 1
  HEL = 3   BRDG = 0000
  Header Extension
  Element Length = 3
    Element Type = 0 Version
    Element Value = 01
  Element Length = 4
    Element Type = 1 Carrier
    Element Value = 0222
  Header Pad = 00FFFFFFFF
  Application Data   0001020304050607

Frame#1 15:05:41 591 959 Len=48
  Sequence Number = 1
  MID = 33   Segment Type = COM
  Payload Length = 44   Payload CRC = 1CD

  Application Data
  08090A0B0C0D0E0F1011121314151617
  18191A1B1C1D1E1F2021222324252627
  28292A2B2C2D2E2F30313233

Frame#2 15:05:41 592 264 Len=48
   Sequence Number = 2
   MID = 33   Segment Type = COM
   Payload Length = 44   Payload CRC = 18F

   Application Data
   3435363738393A3B3C3D3E3F40414243
   4445464748494A4B4C4D4E4F50515253
   5455565758595A5B5C5D5E5F

Frame#3 15:05:41 592 568 Len=48
   Sequence Number = 3
   MID = 33   Segment Type = EOM
   Payload Length = 12   Payload CRC = 2EF

   Rsvd=00   End BETag=01
   Len=136
   Application Data
   60616263354F4B910001008800000000
   00000000000000000000000000000000
   0000000000000000000000000

7.2 Encapsulating LAN Traffic over SMDS

Because SMDS is derived from the IEEE 802.6 MAN standard, one of its principal applications is LAN interconnection. This case study examines the procedures used to encapsulate LAN traffic inside the SMDS L3_PDU, which is then further segmented into multiple L2_PDUs.

In this example, a user wants to check connectivity to a remote host (see Figure 7–3) via the network providing SMDS. The upper layer protocol used for this test is the Internet Control Message Protocol (ICMP). ICMP is an integral part of the DARPA protocol architecture, and is implemented on every device that implements the IP. Its function is to communicate internal network conditions and test intranetwork connectivity using one of 13 specific messages.

In this example, the station sends an ICMP Echo Request message, or PING. When the remote host receives the message, it responds with an ICMP Echo Reply, or PING REPLY, message.

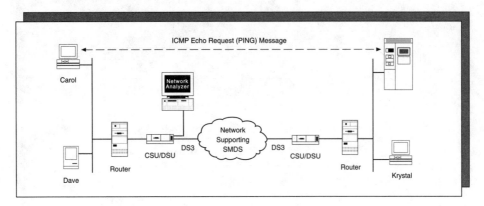

Figure 7-3. Transmitting ICMP messages across SMDS

The ICMP Echo Request message is encapsulated with several other headers prior to placement in the L3_PDU frame (see Figure 7–4). These include the IP header, which includes addressing and datagram delivery information; and the SNAP and LLC headers that identify the upper layer protocol. Finally, the encapsulated ICMP message is placed inside the L3_PDU, which is then segmented into one or more L2_PDUs.

The analysis of the L3_PDU in Trace 7.2a illustrates the protocol layers: SIP3 (the L3_PDU header), LLC, IP, ICMP, and APPL (the application data containing the contents of the ICMP Echo Request message). Note that the overall length of L3_PDU is 148 octets, which includes the L3_PDU header, or 0000000800 (36 octets), the LLC header, or AAAA03 (3 octets), the SNAP header (5 octets), the IP, and the L3_PDU trailer (8 octets). No CRC precedes the L3_PDU trailer, as noted by the value of the CRC indication bit CIB = 0.

The L3_PDU header (again, note that the header precedes the SIP3 label in the trace) contains the fields examined in Section 7.1, including the Destination and Source addresses, HLPI, PL, QOS, and so on. The Header Extension field contains only one element (3 octets), resulting in a Header Pad field 9 octets long.

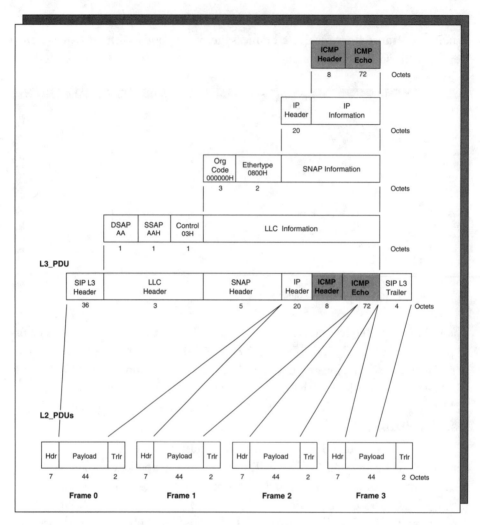

Figure 7–4. Encapsulating ICMP information within a L3_PDU

The LLC and SNAP headers, which total 8 octets long, indicate the next layer of protocol within the L3_PDU. The DSAP and SSAP values indicate that an SNAP header follows, for instance, DSAP = SSAP = AA (or 170 decimal). The LLC Control field contains the value 03H, indicating that this is a UI frame. The SNAP header contains an Organization Code (000000H) and an Ethernet Protocol Type (0800H) that identify the IP as the next highest layer.

The IP header is 20 octets long. Its fields include Version (4); Internet Header Length, or IHL (5, indicating five 32-bit words, for a total of 20 octets); Routine Precedence; Normal Delay (D); Throughput (T) and Reliability (R); a total length of 100 octets (64H); an Identifier of 42194 (A4D2H); Don't Fragment Flag (DF = 0); No More Fragments Flag (MF = 0); Fragment Offset 0 (0000H); Time to Live of 255 seconds or router hops (TTL = 255); Protocol (ICMP = 01H, indicating the next protocol to follow); a Header Checksum (8622H); and finally the Source and Destination IP addresses (4 octets each).

The ICMP header is 8 octets long. Its fields include the Type (ICMP Echo Request message, with value 0080H), a 2-octet Checksum (86BFH), a 4-octet Identifier (4205H), and a 2-octet Sequence number (0012H). (Note that the analyzer uses hexadecimal numbers in some fields and decimals in others. I have noted all the numbers using their hexidecimal value). Following the ICMP header are 72 octets of test data that the remote host will echo to confirm the integrity of the round-trip communication path.

With a calculator, you can check a few numbers. The IP header shows a datagram 100 octets long. This consists of the IP header (20 octets), the ICMP header (8 octets), and the ICMP data (72 octets). To confirm the BASize of 140 octets within the L3_PDU header, add the length of the header (beginning with the Destination Address field, or 32 octets), the length of the LLC and SNAP headers (3 and 5 octets, respectively), and the IP datagram, for a total of 140 octets.

Trace 7.2a. ICMP and IP within an SMDS L3_PDU

Frame#0 16:47:08 002 398 Len=148
    Rsvd=00   Begin BETag=DB
    BASize=008C
    Destination Address C18175551212FFFF
    Source Address C14155551212FFFF
    HLPI = 01   PL = 0
    QOS = 0   CIB = 0
    HEL = 3   BRDG = 0000
    Header Extension
      Element Length = 3

Element Type = 0 Version
Element Value = 01
Header Pad = 000000000000000000
Rsvd=00   End BETag=DB
Len=140

SIP3   00DB008CC18175551212FFFFC1415555
1212FFFF0403000003000100000000000
00000000

DSAP=170   SSAP=170
03 UI   Pro=0   Ether Type= IP

LLC   AAAA030000000800

Ver=4   IHL=5
Precedence Routine
D= Normal T= Normal R= Normal
Len=100   ID=42194
DF=0 MF=0   Offset=0 TTL=255
Protocol= ICMP   Checksum=8622 OK
Source Address   XXX.YYY.10.1
Destination Address XXX.YYY.10.2

IP   45000064A4D20000FF018622XXYY0A01
XXYY0A02

Type: Echo Request
Checksum=86BF OK
Identifier   16901
Sequence Number   18

ICMP   080086BF42050012

```
APPL    1F35EA70ABCDABCDABCDABCDABCDABCD
        ABCDABCDABCDABCDABCDABCDABCDABCD
        ABCDABCDABCDABCDABCDABCDABCDABCD
        ABCDABCDABCDABCDABCDABCDABCDABCD
        ABCDABCDABCD0000
```

As Trace 7.2b illustrates, this L3_PDU (with an overall length of 148 octets, including all the header and trailer fields) is then segmented into four L2_PDUs (one BOM, two COMs, and one EOM), each with a Message ID of 595 (MID = 595). The first L2_PDU contains the complete L3_PDU header (36 octets), the LLC header (3 octets), and the SNAP header (5 octets). The second L2_PDU contains the IP header (20 octets), the ICMP header (8 octets), and the first 16 octets of the data to be echoed. The third L2_PDU contains 44 octets of data. The fourth and final L2_PDU contains the last 12 octets of data and 4 octets of the L3_PDU trailer. The rest of the EOM segment is filled with zeros.

You can make an interesting observation about segment overhead. The overall length of the L3_PDU was 148 octets, including all the upper layer protocol headers (review Figure 7–4). Recall the original ICMP message was 72 octets long. This message was divided between the second, third, and fourth segments, each with 16, 44, and 12 octets, respectively. The total overhead was therefore 76 octets (148–72), resulting in a transmission efficiency of less than 50 percent. This ratio becomes more favorable as the upper layer protocol message length increased.

Trace 7.2b ICMP/IP data within segmented L2_PDUs

Frame#0 16:42:49 749 865 Len=48

      Sequence Number = 13

      MID = 595   Segment Type = BOM

      Payload Length = 44   Payload CRC = 284

SIP2   B653

Rsvd=00   Begin BETag=DB
BASize=008C
Destination Address C18173755001FFFF
Source Address C18173755000FFFF
HLPI = 01   PL = 0
QOS = 0   CIB = 0
HEL = 3   BRDG = 0000
Header Extension
 Element Length = 3
  Element Type = 0 Version
  Element Value = 01
 Header Pad = 000000000000000000

SIP3   00DB008CC18175551212FFFFC1817555
        1212FFFF0403000003000100000000000
        00000000

DSAP=170   SSAP=170
03 UI   Pro=0   Ether Type= IP

LLC   AAAA030000000800

Frame#1 16:42:49 749 875 Len=48

Sequence Number = 14
MID = 595   Segment Type = COM
Payload Length = 44   Payload CRC = 2B7

SIP2   3A53

APPL   45000064A4D20000FF018622XXYY0A01
        XXYY0A02080086BF420500121F35EA70
        ABCDABCDABCDABCDABCDABCD

Frame#2 16:42:49 749 885 Len=48

    Sequence Number = 15
    MID = 595   Segment Type = COM
    Payload Length = 44   Payload CRC = 2D9
SIP2   3E53

APPL   ABCDABCDABCDABCDABCDABCDABCDABCD
       ABCDABCDABCDABCDABCDABCDABCDABCD
       ABCDABCDABCDABCDABCDABCD

Frame#3 16:42:49 749 896 Len=48

    Sequence Number = 0
    MID = 595   Segment Type = EOM
    Payload Length = 16   Payload CRC = 191
SIP2   4253

    Rsvd=00   End BETag=DB
    Len=140

APPL   ABCDABCDABCDABCDABCD000000DB008C
       00000000000000000000000000000000
       000000000000000000000000

7.3 Using the Data Exchange Interface with SIP L3_PDUs

The SMDS DXI protocol provides a way to divide the protocol responsibility between an SMDS DSU and a router or host. Recall from Section 6.6 that the router/host implements SIP Level 3 and places a L3_PDU inside the DXI frame for transmission to the SMDS DSU. The SMDS DSU implements the DXI Link and Physical layers on the router/host side, and SIP Levels 1 and 2 on the network side

259

(review Figure 6-10). The network implements all three SIP layers. Note that only the end systems (router/host and network) implement SIP Level 3.

The DXI frame format is derived from HDLC, and defines two logical links (see Figure 7–5). Logical Link 0 is used to carry data (L3_PDUs), while Logical Link 1 carries link-management information. This example investigates Logical Link 0. Section 7.4 looks at the details of Logical Link 1.

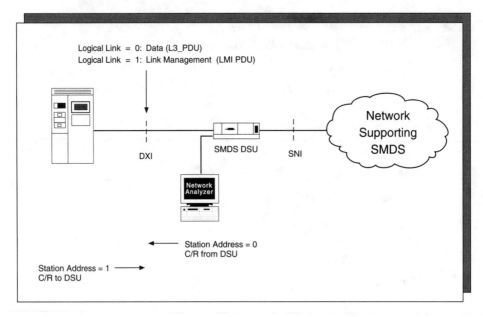

Figure 7–5. Using the DXI

Figure 7–6 shows the DXI frame format with the L3_PDU within the Information field. Trace 7.3 illustrates an L3_PDU transmitted over the DXI. The Tekelec Chameleon Open protocol analyzer indicates the FCS of the frame is EF55H and that the frame is 56 octets long. The DXI Address field contains a binary value of 0000 0001, or 01H. The subfields specify Data (Logical Link = 00000 binary), that the source of the frame was the SMDS DSU (Station Address = 0), and that this frame is a response (Command/Response = 0). The last bit of the Address field is fixed at one (review Figure 6-9.)

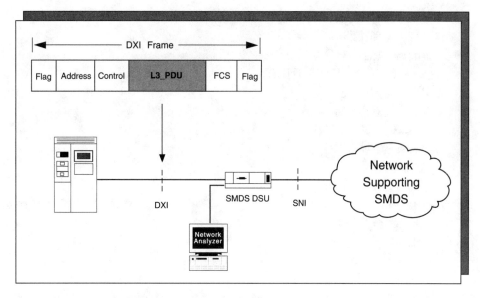

Figure 7-6. Using DXI Logical Link 0: L3_PDU transfer

The Control field has a binary value of 0000 0011, or 03H, indicating a UI frame with the Poll/Final bit = 0.

The Logical Link 0 header contains the value 0002H, indicating to the router/host that any frames it transmits may encounter congested network resources.

The rest of the DXI frame contains a L3_PDU, beginning with the Rsvd field and ending with the Length field, as shown in the previous two examples.

Trace 7.3 L3_PDU within DXI frame

Frame#0   16:03:41 203 000

FCS=EF55 Len=56

C/R = 0   Station Address = 0
Logical Link = 0
Frame Type = UI   Poll/Final = 0
Congestion = 1
DXI   01030002

```
    Rsvd = 00      Begin BETag  =  AA
    BASize  =  002C
  Destination Addr  =  C11111111111FFFF
  Source Address  =  C11111111111FFFF
  HLPI  =  3F   PL  =  3
  QOS  =  7   CIB  =  0
  HEL  =  3   BRDG  =  A1A2
    Header Extension
    Element Length  =  3
    Element Type  =  0  Version
    Element Value  =  01
    Element Length  =  4
    Element Type  =  1  Carrier
    Element Value  =  0222
    Header Pad  =  00FFFFFFFF
  Pad=687D0B
    Rsvd  =  00        End BETag  =  AA
    Len  =  44
```

7.4 Using the DXI Local Management Interface Protocol

The final example in this study of SMDS explores the use of the Data Exchange
Interface Local Management Interface protocol. This protocol is modeled after
the popular Simple Network Management Protocol (SNMP), and defined in SIG-
TS-002 [7–2]. To understand the operation of the DXI LMI, assume that a network management console, running SNMP exists somewhere on the network of
interest. Further, assume that there is an SNMP proxy agent in the router/host
attached to the SMDS DSU. If the manager requests information from the
router/host, some may be resident in the router/host and others in the SMDS DSU.
If the proxy agent is unable to respond completely to the console's request, it
queries the SMDS DSU. The DXI LMI protocol enables communication between
that proxy agent and the SMDS DSU (see Figure 7–7). Note that the GetRequest,
GetNextRequest, and SetRequest PDUs originate at the router/host, while the
GetResponse and Trap PDUs originate at the SMDS DSU.

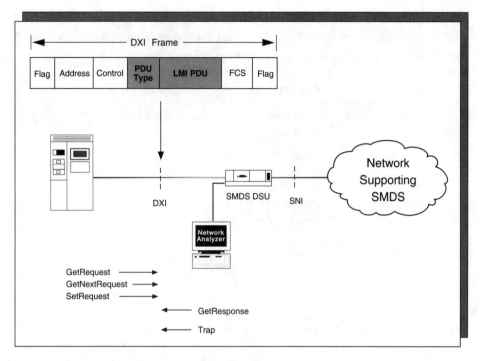

Figure 7–7. Using DXI Logical Link 1: LMI PDU transfer

Trace 7.4 shows four PDU transmissions: GetRequest (Frame 0), GetResponse (Frame 1), SetRequest (Frame 2), and Trap (Frame 3). All these PDUs have a DXI frame header that includes Address and Control fields. In the first PDU, a GetRequest (the Control field) has a value of 0000 1101 binary. This equates to the subfield values Logical Link 1 (00001 binary) and Station Address 1 (a transmission to the DSU), as well as the frame containing a Command (C/R = 0). The Control field has a value of 03H, indicating an UI frame.

The first two hexadecimal characters (00) next to the DXI LMI indicator show that the PDU type is a GetRequest. The Request ID has a value of 0FH, which correlates to the GetResponse returned in Frame 1. The Error Status and Error Index fields indicate that there are no errors. The values of the following three managed objects are requested next: ds1CircuitIdentifier, ds1GgIntervalESs, and ds1GgIntervalUASs. (For additional information on DS1 managed objects, see RFC 1406, Reference [7–3]. Chapter 11 discusses broadband network management in greater detail.)

Note that no values are available in the GetRequest (Frame 0). The GetResponse is returned (Frame 1); these values are complete. These objects, as defined in SIG-TS-002 with their returned values from Trace 7.4, are:

Object	Meaning	Value
CircuitIdentifier	The transmission vendor's circuit identifier	PDX-SEA CCT5
ds1GgIntervalESs	A count of the errored seconds (ESes) in a specified interval	564
ds1GgIntervalUASs	A count of the unavailable seconds (UASes) in a specified interval	35

Frame 2 contains a SetRequest from the router/host to the SMDS DSU to write the value of an object. The object in question is ds1LoopbackConfig, which represents the loopback configuration of the DS1 interface. The object value is five, representing a ds1NetReqLineLoop.

Frame 3 contains a trap, sent from the SMDS DSU to the router/host. A trap is an unsolicited notification, which can notify the router/host that a link is down, as in this case. That link is identified by the index value of the object ds1LineIndex, indicating that the fourth DS1 interface on the SMDS DSU is down. The value of the object (16) indicates the cause of the failure, ds1LossOfSignal. This and other object values are specified in SIG-TS-0002 and RFC 1406.

Trace 7.4 LMI PDUs within SMDS DXI frames

Frame#0   16:05:21 077 200

FCS=00EE Len=54
 C/R = 0   Station Address = 1
 Logical Link = 1
 Frame Type = UI   Poll/Final = 0
DXI   0D03

        PDU Type   GetRequest
        Request ID   0F
        Error Status   noError
        Error Index   00 (noError)
        Obj ID = ds1CircuitIdentifier
         ds1LineIndex = 5
         Obj Value = 0
        Obj ID = ds1GgIntervalESs
         ds1GgIntervalIndex = 5
         ds1GgIntervalNumber = 45
         Obj Value = 0
        Obj ID = ds1GgIntervalUASs
         ds1GgIntervalIndex = 5
         ds1GgIntervalNumber = 45
         Obj Value = 0
DXILMI000F0000030C0103060102010A120101
  0B05000D0103060102010A1206010305
  2D000D0103060102010A12060106052D
  00

APPL   FFFF7E

Frame#1   16:05:21 143 600

FCS=F86A   Len=69
    C/R = 0   Station Address = 0
    Logical Link = 1
    Frame Type = UI   Poll/Final = 0
DXI   0903

    PDU Type   GetResponse
    Request ID   0F
    Error Status   noError
    Error Index   00 (noError)
    Obj ID = ds1CircuitIdentifier
     ds1LineIndex = 5
     Obj Value = PDX-SEA CCT5
    Obj ID = ds1GgIntervalESs
     ds1GgIntervalIndex = 5
     ds1GgIntervalNumber = 45
     Obj Value = 564
    Obj ID = ds1GgIntervalUASs
     ds1GgIntervalIndex = 5
     ds1GgIntervalNumber = 45
     Obj Value = 35

DXILMI020F0000030C0103060102010A120101
    0B050C5044582D53454120434354350D
    0103060102010A12060103052D020234
    0D0103060102010A12060106052D0123

APPL   FFFF7E

Frame#2   16:05:21 170 600

FCS=B097 Len=25
    C/R = 0   Station Address = 1
    Logical Link = 1
    Frame Type = UI   Poll/Final = 0
DXI   0D03

    PDU Type   SetRequest
    Request ID   10
    Error Status   noError
    Error Index   00 (noError)
    Obj ID = ds1LoopbackConfig
     ds1LineIndex = 5
     Obj Value = 5 (ds1NetReqLineLoop)
DXILMI03100000010C0103060102010A120101
    0C050105
APPL   FFFF7E

Frame#3   16:05:21 195 200

    FCS=B4A0 Len=23
    C/R = 1   Station Address = 0
    Logical Link = 1
    Frame Type = UI   Poll/Final = 0
DXI   0B03

    PDU Type   Trap
    Trap Index   linkDown
    Obj ID = ds1LineStatus
     ds1LineIndex = 4
     Obj Value = 16 (ds1LossOfSignal)
DXILMI0402010C0103060102010A1201010D04
    0110

APPL   FFFF7E

7.5 Possible SMDS Error Conditions

The SMDS Interface Protocol is more complex than its IEEE 802 relatives. So when communication or internetworking problems arise, this protocol may require more rigorous analysis. The following sections offer general guidelines for analyzing SIP Level 2 and SIP Level 3 [7–4]. I have listed the Error Conditions according to the SIP_L2 and SIP_L3 PDU formats, highlighting the applicable fields, from left to right across the PDUs. When reading these sections, you may find it helpful to review Figures 6-3 and 6-4.

7.5.1 SIP Level 3 Analysis Guidelines

When analyzing SIP Level 3, check for the following:

▼ the Reserved fields in header and trailer have a value of zero

▼ the Beginning and End tags in the Header and Trailer match

▼ the Buffer Allocation size is correct.

You should examine the address fields for:

▼ a Destination or Source address Type field that is incorrect for the application, such as an Individual address instead of a Group address

▼ a Destination or Source address prefix that does not begin with a binary one

▼ Destination or Source address digits that are not all BCD characters

▼ the last 16 bits of Destination or Source address, and verify the values of FFFFH.

You should also make sure the Pad Length has the correct value.

In the Header Extension field, look for the following:

▼ an incorrect Header Extension Length value

▼ correct values in the Header Extension Version Length, Type, or Value subfields

▼ an error in Header Extension Carrier Selection length

▼ a Header Extension Carrier Selection value that is not a BCD character

▼ the "other" element in the Header Extension, as well as the Length

▼ the type of element that verifies the PAD character is not zero.

The frame length should not deviate from a minimum of 40 octets (a 36-octet header plus a 4-octet trailer) or a maximum of 9,232 octets (a 36-octet header plus 9,188-octets of information, a 4-octet CRC, and a 4-octet trailer. You should also verify that the PAD characters are all zeros. Verify that the CRC-32 value is correct and that the Length field has the correct value.

7.5.2 SIP Level 2 Analysis Guidelines
When analyzing SIP Level 2, check the following.

For Empty cells originating from the SS:

▼ the Network Control Information field must have a value of zero

▼ the Segment Type field must have a value of zero

▼ Single Segment Messages (SSMs), the Message Identifier field must have a value of zero

▼ the Payload must have all octets set with a value of zer

▼ the Payload Length field must have a value of zero

▼ the Payload CRC field must have a value of zero.

For nonempty cells:

▼ the Payload Length must be a multiple of 4 octets

▼ the Payload Length must be 44 octets for BOM and COMs

▼ the Payload Length must be between 4 and 44 octets for EOMs

▼ the Payload Length must be between 28 and 44 octets for SSMs.

You should also verify the following Header fields:

▼ the Access Control Field, as defined by the originator (CPE or SS), for proper syntax

▼ the Network Control Information field should have a value of FFFFF022H for L2_PDUs with information or 00000000H for empty L2_PDUs

▼ the Segment Type field should not have an unexpected BOM, a COM before a BOM, or an EOM before BOM

▼ the Sequence Number field should not indicate a PDU sequence error, such as an invalid sequence number.

When decoding the Message Identifier field, keep the following items in mind:

▼ segments sent from the SS should have a value between 1 and 511

▼ segments sent from the CPE should have a value between 512 and 1023

▼ BOM, COM, and EOM cells cannot have a value of zero

▼ the Payload CRC field should have a correct value.

7.5.3 SIP Level 2 Protocol Errors

You can identify some protocol errors that occur at SIP_L2 by looking at a sequence of PDUs as they are received and processed. Bellcore's TR-TSV-000772 Section 4.2.2.2.2 describes the L2_PDU receive process, and is a useful reference for information about these errors.

An "aborted reassembly error" means that a BOM was received with the same MID as a currently active reassembly process. The previous L2 PDUs are discarded and the reassembly begins again. For example:

```
1. BOM  MID=10    (start reassembly of MID=10)
2. COM  MID=10
3. BOM  MID=10    (restart reassembly of MID=10,
                   abort current reassembly process,
                   and discard PDUs #1 and #2.)
4. COM  MID=10
5. EOM  MID=10    (finish reassembly of MID=10)
```

A "reassembly timeout error" means the time specified in the Message Receive Interval (MRI) has elapsed since the BOM was received (reassembly began), and the EOM, which concludes the reassembly process, was received. This value is 100 milliseconds for a DS3-based access path, and 200 milliseconds for a DS1-based access path.

A "reassembly length error" means the accumulated SIP L2 PDUs exceed the maximum SIP_L3 frame length and occurs when 210 PDUs have been received at the SIP_L2 layer. Because the maximum length of the message would exceed the 9,232-octet limit (210 * 44 = 9,240), it makes no sense to continue reassembly and pass the data on to SIP_L3.

A "too many reassemblies error" means the concurrent reassembly process rules have been violated. Bellcore's TR-TSV-000772 Section 3.2.8 states that there can be one or 16 concurrent reassembly processes. This means SIP_L2 PDUs with up to 16 different MID values can be multiplexed together on the same link. When an EOM is received, its MID is no longer in use. If a 17th BOM is received before any of the other 16 reassembly processes finish, an error occurs.

This chapter concludes our study of SDMS architecture and protocols. The next section looks at an architecture that has been designed as a successor technology to SMDS, Asynchronous Transfer Mode (ATM).

7.5 References

[7–1]   Jander, Mary. "A Jack of All Protocol Analyzer Trades." *Data Communications* (January 1994): 113–114.

[7–2]   SMDS Interest Group. SMDS DXI Local Management Interface. SIG-TS-002, May 1992.

[7–3]   Baker, F. and J. Watt, eds. "Definitions of Managed Objects for the DS1 and E1 Interface Types." RFC 1406, January 1993.

[7–4]   Andrew Scott. Personal communication, March 1994.

# 8 ATM Architecture

ATM is a broadband ISDN technology that has been touted as the next revolution in LAN and WAN communication. Volumes have been written about ATM and its emerging role in corporate networks. References [8-1] through [8-6] provide background on cell-switching and ATM technology. References [8-7] through [8-9] are vendor and analyst reports that discuss trends in the ATM marketplace. References [8–10] through [8–12] provide information on carriers' plans to support ATM. Finally, References [8–13] through [8–19] discuss the integration of LAN and WAN technology. This chapter looks at ATM applications, standards, and interfaces. Chapter 9 discusses the ATM protocols in detail.

8.1 ATM Applications

ATM technology comes from ITU standards that address the worldwide telecommunications infrastructure. Two significant developments preceded ATM: in the early 1980s, the ITU defined ISDN, which is now called Narrowband ISDN (N-ISDN), and in the late 1980s, the ITU enhanced N-ISDN, defining broadband ISDN (B-ISDN). N-ISDN defined two access interfaces: a basic rate operating at 144 Kbps and a primary rate, operating at 1.544 Mbps. These interfaces were designed to carry digital voice, data, and control information. B-ISDN offered transmission rates of up to 622 Mbps. ATM is the technology that implements broadband ISDN.

Figure 8–1 illustrates how ATM transmits data. The ATM cell stream starts with signals from individual users or sources. Signals may include constant bit-rate service, such as a DS1 line; variable bit-rate service, such as compressed video; or bursty data, such as LAN traffic. ATM then segments the signals into 48–octet payloads and prefaces them with a 5-octet header, which contains addressing information. The resulting 53-octet packet is called a cell. At that point, ATM takes cells from various signal sources, mixes them with cells from other sources, and sends them to the ATM switch (see References [8–20 and 8–21]). The switch multiplexes the cells together. The cells then contend for vacant slots in the outgoing ATM cell stream.

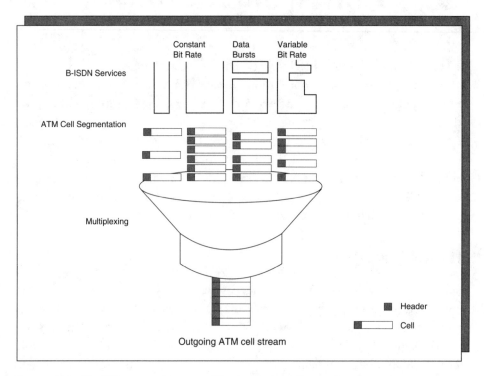

Figure 8–1. The ATM concept *(Courtesy of Hewlett-Packard Company)*

ATM is a connection-oriented service, meaning it requires an established connection before it can transmit data. There are two types of ATM connections: PVCs and SVCs. Two labels identify the endpoint connections: a VPI and a VCI.

The transmission delay for each cell depends on the traffic load from the other input data streams, thus the arrival rate (delay) of each datastream is not periodic. So, the cell transfer is referred to as an asynchronous operation or ATM. In contrast, a synchronous transfer mode has fixed periods for cell transmission and reception.

8.2 ATM Standards

Several sources have defined standards for ATM networks: the ITU-T [8–22], the ATM Forum [8–23], Bellcore [8–24], and ANSI. Both LAN and WAN designs use these cell relay standards (see Figure 8–2 and Reference [8–25]).

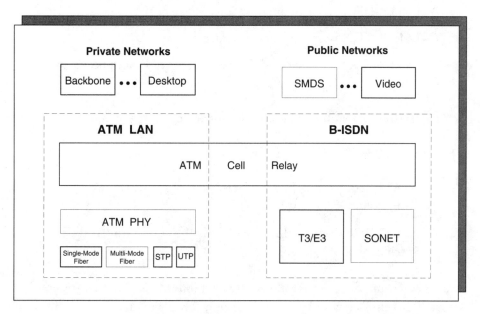

Figure 8–2. ATM standards shared by LANs and WANs *(Courtesy of SynOptics Communications Inc.)*

The key ITU standards are as follows:

▼ I.113 B-ISDN Vocabulary of Terms.

▼ I.121 Broadband Aspects of ISDN.

▼ I.150 B-ISDN ATM Functional Characteristics.

▼ I.211 B-ISDN Service Aspects.

▼ I.311 B-ISDN General Network Aspects.

▼ I.321 B-ISDN Protocol Reference Model.

▼ I.327 B-ISDN Functional Architecture Aspects.

▼ I.361 B-ISDN ATM Layer Specification.

▼ I.362 B-ISDN ATM Adaptation Layer Functional Description.

▼ I.363 B-ISDN ATM Adaptation Layer Specification.

▼ I.413 B-ISDN User-Network Interface.

▼ I.432 B-ISDN User-Network Interface Physical Layer Specification.

▼ I.555 Frame Relay and ATM Interworking.

▼ I.610 B-ISDN Operations and Maintenance Principles and Functions.

ANSI standards for B-ISDN as of this writing include:

▼ T1.624 Broadband ISDN User-Network Interfaces—Rates and Formats Specifications.

▼ T1.627 Broadband ISDN—ATM Layer Functionality and Specification.

The ATM Forum does not develop its own standards, but rather, fosters consensus between users and vendors regarding the use of standards such as the ITU-T recommendations. This process ensures a higher probability of interoperablity between different vendors' products. The key ATM Forum documents are as follows:

▼ ATM UNI Specification, version 3.0 (September 1993),

▼ ATM Broadband Inter-Carrier Interface (B-ICI) Specification, version 1.0 (August 1993), and

▼ ATM DXI Specification, version 1.0 (August 1993).

8.3 Broadband ISDN Architecture

ITU-T Recommendation I.413 provides the reference configuration for the B-ISDN UNI. The reference configuration specifies various functional entities, and the "reference points," interfaces between them (see Figure 8–3a). All interfaces, except for the R interface have a designation beginning with the letter *B*, indicating broadband technology. The R interface may or may not have broadband capabilities (see References [8–26] and [8–27]).

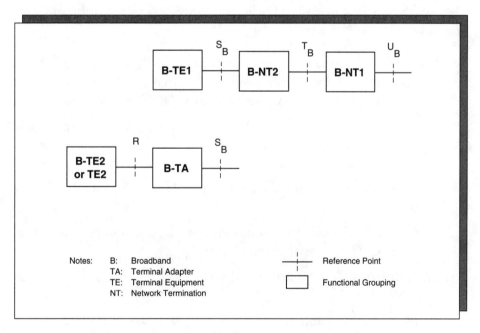

Figure 8–3a. B-ISDN functional reference configuration *(Source: TA-NWT-001112, ©1993, Bell Communications Research, Inc., reprinted with permission)*

8.3.1 B-ISDN reference points

The reference points defined for B-ISDN include:

▼ *R*, the point between non–B-ISDN equipment (TE2 or B-TE2) and a terminal adapter (TA)

▼ *S*, the point between ISDN user equipment (B-TE1 or B-TA) and the customer premises network-termination equipment (B-NT2)

▼ *T*, the point between the customer premises network-termination equipment (B-NT2) and the public network termination (B-NT1)

▼ *U*, the point between the public network termination (B-NT1) and the public network.

8.3.2 B-ISDN functional groups

The B-ISDN functions are grouped to indicate the operations they perform. These groups include:

▼ *B-NT1* (broadband network termination 1), which handles the termination of the transmission line, as well as the Operations and Maintenance (OAM) functions, such as a SONET line termination

▼ *B-NT2* (broadband network termination 2), which may include higher layer functions, such as buffering, multiplexing, and signaling, as well as other examples such as PBX, LAN, or terminal controllers

▼ *B-TE1* (broadband terminal equipment 1), which supports B-ISDN protocols

▼ *B-TE2* (broadband terminal equipment 2), which supports a broadband interface other than B-ISDN

▼ *TE2* (terminal equipment 2), which supports an interface other than ISDN

▼ *TA* (terminal adapter), which lets a B-ISDN user-network interface serve a B-TE2 or TE2.

Figure 8–3b shows an example of a network configuration with the associated reference points.

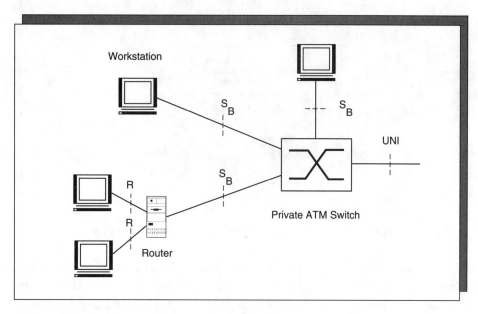

Figure 8–3b. Possible customer premises node configuration *(Source: TA-NWT-001110, ©1993, Bell Communications Research, Inc., reprinted with permission)*

8.3.3 B-ISDN architecture model

The B-ISDN protocol architecture model consists of three planes and four layers (see Figure 8–4). This model differs from the familiar OSI Reference Model in that it uses three, rather than two, dimensions. You can think of the planes as protocol suites.

The planes are designated: user, control, and management. The user plane provides user-to-user information transfer and controls required for that transfer, such as flow control and error recovery. The control plane provides call-control and connection-control functions such as signaling. Signaling establishes, supervises, and releases calls and connections.

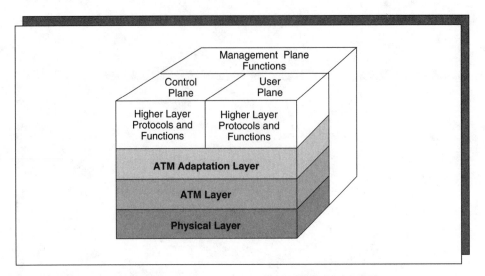

Figure 8–4. B-ISDN Protocol Model *(Courtesy of STACKS, The Network Journal)*

The management plane controls the ATM device, such as a switch or a hub. This plane offers two types of functions: plane management and layer management. Because plane management deals with the system as a whole (management of the other planes and coordination between the planes), it does not have a layered structure. Layer management deals with the resources and parameters residing at each protocol layer, such as OAM information flow.

The layers include: Physical (PHY), ATM, ATM Adaptation (AAL), and Higher. The next section describes these layers in more detail.

8.3.4 ATM layers and sublayers

Figure 8–5 illustrates the ATM layers and sublayers. As you'll see, the Physical layer sends and receives bits on the transmission medium, and it sends and receives cells to and from the next highest layer, the ATM layer. The ATM layer then switches these cells to the appropriate circuit to connect with an end system and its specific application or process. The payload within the cell is generated at, or destined for, the AAL, a layer that interfaces the Higher layer functions and processes with the ATM layer.

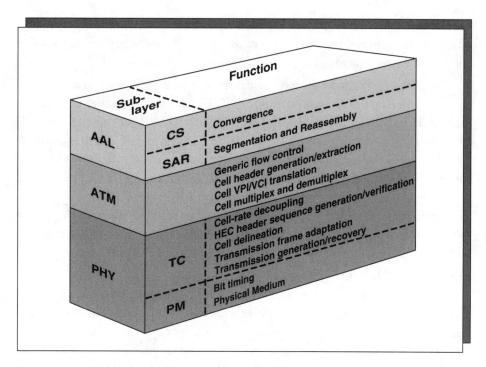

Figure 8–5. ATM layers and sublayers *(Courtesy of* STACKS, The Network Journal*)*

The Physical layer has two sublayers: Physical Medium (PM) and Transmission Convergence (TC). The PM sublayer provides bit-level transmission. Its functions include the electrical or optical interface into the transmission medium, such as a cable, and the timing and recovery of those bits on the transmission medium.

The TC sublayer has five functions: frame generation, frame adaptation, cell delineation, Header Error Correction (HEC) generation, and cell-rate decoupling. Frame generation creates and recovers the data frame sent by the PM sublayer. Next, cells transmitted by the ATM layer must be adapted to the data-frame format required for the PM sublayer. In the receive direction, the frame-adaptation function extracts the cells from the frame. The cell-delineation function identifies the boundaries of cells so the ATM layer can decode them properly. Next, HEC sequence is calculated and added to the ATM header for transmitted frames. For received frames, the cell headers are checked for errors. If errors are found, they are corrected when possible. If they cannot be corrected, the cell is discarded. Finally, cell-rate decoupling inserts or suppresses idle cells, adapting the transmission rate of the valid ATM cells to the payload capacity of the transmission system.

The ATM layer functions independently of the Physical layer, and performs four operations on cells: multiplexing, VPI/VCI translation, header generation, and flow control. In the transmit direction, the ATM layer multiplexes cells from individual virtual paths (VPs) and virtual channels (VCs) into a composite cell flow. In the receive direction, demultiplexing directs cells from the composite cell flow to the appropriate VP or VC. Next, the VPI/VCI fields in the incoming cell may require mapping to new VPI/VCI values. Third, the ATM layer generates an ATM header and adds it to the payload for transmission or extracts the payload from a received cell and passes that payload to the next highest layer. Finally, the ATM layer may generate cells to carry Generic Flow Control (GFC) information.

The AAL maps the higher layers (for example, services that define the signal type used) into the ATM layer (for instance, cells). AAL consists of two sublayers: the Segmentation and Reassembly (SAR) sublayer and the Convergence sublayer (CS). The SAR sublayer segments the variable length higher layer information to be transmitted into fixed-length ATM payloads, and reassembles the received payloads into the higher layer information. The CS performs functions required by the AAL type in use, and is therefore service-dependent. In some cases, CS functions may be subdivided into a Common Part Convergence Sublayer (CPCS), or the lower sublayer; and a Service Specific Convergence Sublayer (SSCS), or the upper sublayer.

8.4 ATM Interfaces

A broadband network may include several interfaces (see Figure 8–6): the UNI, the ATM DXI, the network-node interface (NNI), and the Broadband Inter-Carrier Interface (B-ICI).

The UNI connects the ATM network and premises equipment, which could include an ATM switch. There are two types of UNIs: public and private. A public UNI connects a private ATM switch to a public ATM service provider's network. A private UNI connects ATM users with the ATM switch [8–28].

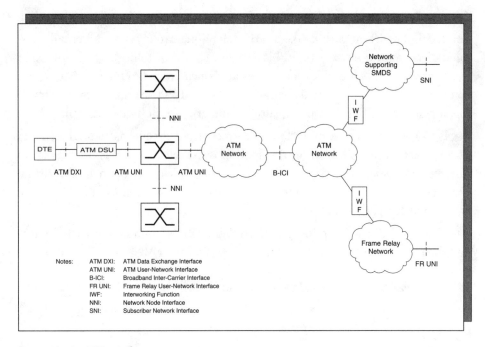

Figure 8–6. ATM interfaces

Some applications divide the ATM protocol functions between the DTE, such as a router, and the hardware interface to the UNI, such as an ATM DSU. The DXI defines the protocol operations between these two devices.

The NNI describes network interconnection within a single carrier's network or between two carrier networks. The ATM Forum calls the NNI that interconnects public ATM carriers the B-ICI.

When an ATM network connects to either a public or private network, such as frame relay or SMDS, conversions between the two network protocols are required. IWF processes, which the ATM Forum's B-ICI specification defines, perform these conversions.

8.5 ATM Connections: VPIs and VCIs

Whether sent at the UNI or the NNI, each ATM cell contains information that identifies its virtual channel. This identification has two parts, which are both used at the ATM layer, a VPI and a VCI (see References [8–29] through [8–31]).

A virtual path is a bundle of virtual channel links, all having the same end-point. So, the virtual path is like a large telephone cable, where all circuits terminate at a central office. The VPI is either assigned or removed to originate or terminate a virtual path link. These links are concatenated to form a virtual path connection (VPC). Each virtual channel link within a VPC maintains the cell transmission sequence, but does not ensure the integrity of an individual cell.

ITU-T Recommendation I.311 defines the virtual channel as "a unidirectional communication capability for the transport of ATM cells." A VCI is either assigned or removed, respectively, to originate or terminate a virtual channel link. Virtual channel links are concatenated to form a virtual channel connection (VCC), an end-to-end cell path at the ATM layer.

The physical transmission path (see Figure 8–7) contains the virtual paths and their VPIs, as well as the virtual channels and their VCIs.

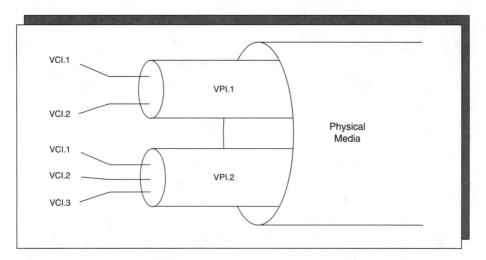

Figure 8–7. The relationship between virtual channels, virtual paths, and physical paths (Source: De Prycker , Peschi and Van Landegem, "B-ISDN and the OSI Protocol Reference Model," IEEE Network Magazine, March 1993, © 1993 IEEE)

The ATM layer provides the logical connection between two AAL processes. The virtual channel link connects a terminal equipment (TE) device with an ATM node (see Figure 8–8). The concatenation of two or more virtual channel links form a VCC. Similarly, VPCs carry bundles of VCCs on an end-to-end basis.

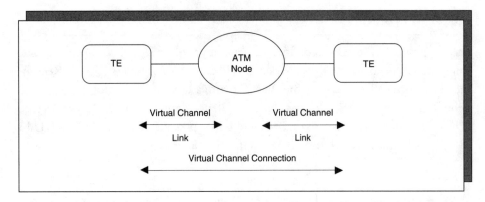

Figure 8–8. Virtual channel link and connection *(Source: De Prycker , Peschi and Van Landegem, "B-ISDN and the OSI Protocol Reference Model," IEEE Network Magazine, March 1993, © 1993 IEEE)*

An ATM node may also simultaneously support multiple end-user services (see Figure 8–9). Each service may require a different data-transfer mechanism, such as variable bit rate or constant bit rate. Thus, different AAL types have been defined. Each end-user service would be addressed by two VCI/VPI pairs: one to transmit and one to receive.

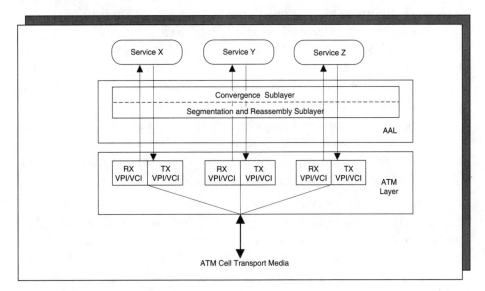

Figure 8–9. Virtual connection end points *(Source: Armitage and Adams, "Packet Reassembly During Cell Loss," IEEE Network Magazine, September 1993, © 1993 IEEE)*

8.6 ATM Protocols

Specific protocols have been defined for each layer of the ATM architecture. The following sections look at the Physical, ATM, and AAL layers. ITU-T Recommendations I.413 and I.432, the ATM Forum's UNI specification [8–28], and Bellcore's TA-NWT-001112 [8–32] are excellent references for the Physical layer. ITU-T Recommendations I.361, I.362, and I.363, plus Bellcore's TA-NWT-001113 [8–33], explain the ATM and ATM Adaptation layers.

8.6.1 The Physical layer: Physical Medium and Transmission Convergence

The ATM PHY layer contains two sublayers: TC and the Physical Medium Dependent (PMD). The PMD sublayer provides the physical interface to the cable and deals with bit timing, connectors, and so on. The TC interfaces with the ATM layer. It extracts cells from the incoming PMD bit stream and passes them to the ATM layer, and vice versa.

ITU-T Recommendation I.432 defines two options for the B-ISDN UNI Physical layer. The first specification operates at 155.520 Mbps over two coaxial cables. The second operates at 622.080 Mbps over two single-mode fiber cables.

The ATM Forum defines a number of options for the Physical layer interface at either public or private UNIs. The SONET STS-3c interface, which operates at 155.520 Mbps, uses multimode or single-mode fiber. An interface for private UNIs operates at 155.520 Mbps with an 8B/10B data-encoding scheme over multimode fiber or shielded twisted-pair cables. Another private UNI option operates at 100 Mbps over multimode fiber. This interface is often called the Transparent Asynchronous Transmitter/Receiver Interface (TAXI®), which was developed by Advanced Micro Devices Inc. TAXI uses 4B/5B encoding, based on the encoding scheme used with FDDI. The DS3 interface is also available, operating at 44.736 Mbps over coaxial cables.

The ATM UNI 3.0 specification also mentions two future interfaces: E3, operating at 34.368 Mbps, and E4, operating at 139.264 Mbps. Both the E3 and E4 interfaces will be based on ITU-T Recommendations G.703 and G.804. Other interfaces under development at the time of this writing include: DS1/E1, STS-1 over unshielded twisted-pair category 3 (UTP-3 cable), STS-3c over unshielded twisted-pair category 5 (UTP-5 cable), and the Universal Test and Operations Physical Interface for ATM (UTOPIA) interface.

8.6.2 The ATM layer

You can loosely compare the ATM layer and its associated Physical layer with the OSI Physical layer. Both architectures require a physical transmission medium, including the cable type, connectors, and so on, as shown in the lower portion of Figure 8–10. But the ATM layer also includes the VPIs and the virtual connection that perform multiplexing (see upper portion of Figure 8–10). These multiplexing functions have been described as a virtual physical service because the VCCs with the VPIs and VCIs act as a "virtual wire" between two end points, as described in Reference [8–27].

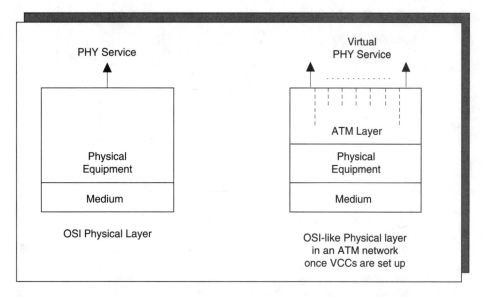

Figure 8–10. OSI and ATM networks: the physical service *(Source: De Prycker , Peschi and Van Landegem, "B-ISDN and the OSI Protocol Reference Model," IEEE Network Magazine, March 1993, © 1993 IEEE)*

8.6.3 ATM Adaptation layer CS and SAR

The AAL translates data from the higher layer into the cell formats carried in the ATM layer. I.362 defines four classes of services that depend on three parameters: the timing relation between source and destination (required or not required), the bit rate (constant or variable), and the connection mode (connection- oriented or connectionless). The use of these four classes, A, B, C, and D, described below, minimizes the number of AAL protocols.

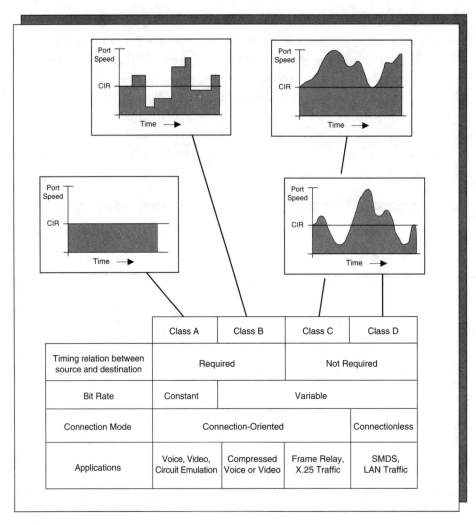

Figure 8–11. AAL service classes *(Courtesy of AT&T)*

Class A: Connection-oriented, constant bit-rate data with a timing relationship between source and destination. Examples include PCM encoded voice, constant bit-rate video, and DS1 circuits.

Class B: Connection-oriented, variable bit-rate data with a timing relationship between source and destination. Examples include compressed audio or video.

Class C: Connection-oriented, variable bit-rate data with no timing relationship between source and destination. Examples include frame relay or X.25 traffic.

Class D: Connectionless, variable bit-rate data with no timing relationship between source and destination. Examples include SMDS or LAN traffic.

Four different types of AALs have been defined to optimize the transmission of these four classes of traffic:

▼ Class A: AAL Type 1

▼ Class B: AAL Type 2 (currently being developed)

▼ Class C: AAL Type 3/4 and AAL Type 5

▼ Class D: AAL Type 3/4.

The associations between the service classes and AAL types are not restrictive, however. Specific implementations may deviate from the list above.

8.6.4 Layer operation and interaction

To see the functions of the Physical, ATM, and AAL layers, follow the transmission of a cell from one ATM layer entity to another (see Figure 8–12).

The originating ATM user, such as the AAL, sends a User PDU to the ATM entity. This User PDU becomes the ATM SDU, or ATM payload at the originating ATM entity. The ATM_SDU is encapsulated with the ATM header, which adds VCI/VPI and other control information.

The resulting ATM cell is multiplexed with other cells, and transmitted on the Physical medium. The logical connection between originating and receiving ATM entities is called the ATM peer-to-peer (APP) connection. Two control functions, Usage Parameter Control (UPC) and Network Parameter Control (NPC), monitor the traffic on that connection to ensure conformance with negotiated parameters. Some ATM entities perform network management, and may copy the payload of a cell and send it to the ATM Management (ATMM) entity for further analysis.

The receiving ATM entity performs the processes described above in the reverse order, first demultiplexing the cells, extracting the ATM_SDU, and finally passing the ATM_SDU as a User PDU to the next higher layer.

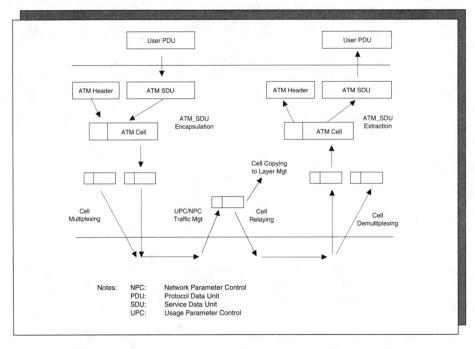

Figure 8–12. ATM_SDU encapsulation and extraction *(Source: TA-NWT-001113, ©1993, Bell Communications Research, Inc., reprinted with permission)*

8.7 The ATM DXI

The ATM DXI lets DTE, such as a router, and DCE, such as an ATM DSU, jointly process the ATM protocol suite. The ATM Forum's DXI specification details the division of protocol responsibilities and the DXI operation [8–34].

The objective for this division of labor is to preserve the protocol functions at the ATM UNI, perform most protocol operations in a specialized DSU (typically referred to as an ATM DSU), and let you change the protocol in the router via a software upgrade.

The DXI Physical layer uses V.35, EIA/TIA 449/530, or EIA/TIA 612/613 (High-Speed Serial Interface—HSSI) interfaces. The DXI Data Link layer protocol is derived from the high-level HDLC protocol. Information from the DTE is encapsulated within the DXI frame, and sent to the DCE. The DCE converts the frame to the appropriate ATM protocol suite.

The mode of operation (1a, 1b, or 2) and the AAL protocol type (3/4 or 5) used determine the protocols implemented within the DCE (see Figure 8–13).

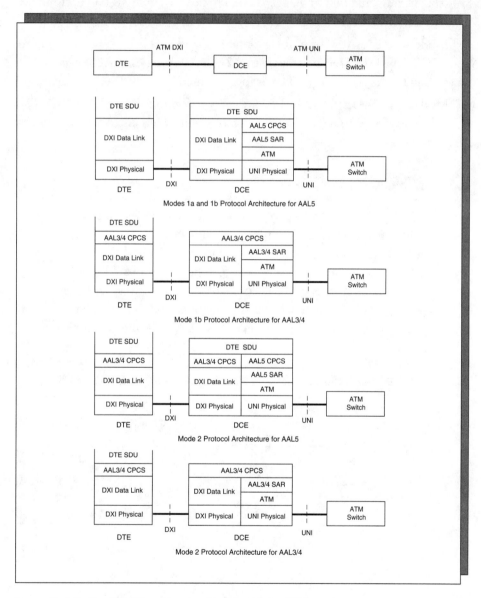

Figure 8–13. The ATM DXI architecture *(Courtesy of the ATM Forum)*

Mode 1a is used with AAL5 only, and can handle up to 1,023 VCs. The DTE SDU may be up to 9,232 octets long. The DCE implements the AAL5 CPCS and SAR sublayers, in addition to the ATM and Physical layers. A 16-bit FCS is implemented between DTE and DCE.

Mode 1b uses AAL3/4 for at least one VC, and AAL5 for other VCs, up to 1,023 VCs. The DTE SDU may be up to 9,224 octets long for AAL3/4 and 9,232 octets long for AAL5. A 16-bit FCS is implemented between DTE and DCE.

Mode 2 uses AAL3/4 and AAL5, one per VC, for up to 16,777,216 VCs. The DTE SDU may be up to 65,535 octets long. A 32-bit FCS is implemented between DTE and DCE.

8.8 ATM Signaling

Because ATM provides a connection-oriented service, it uses signaling to set up and clear the connections. Signaling provides functions such as the ability to establish point-to-multipoint connections, to identify virtual paths and virtual connections, to recover from network errors, to support various ATM address formats, and to communicate end-to-end compatibility parameters (see Figure 8–14). Signaling messages are passed between any combination of three elements: endpoint equipment, such as an ATM switch; a private ATM network; or a public ATM network.

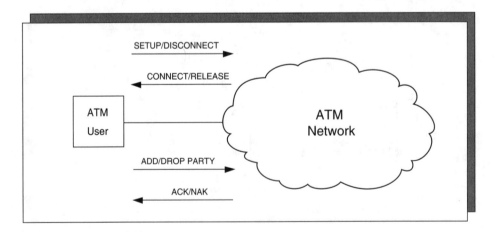

Figure 8–14. ATM signaling

The ATM signaling protocols are based on ITU-T Recommendation Q.2931, formerly called Q.93B. The ATM Forum's UNI 3.0 specification and Bellcore's TA-NWT-001111 [8–35] also address signaling issues.

The ATM Forum UNI 3.0 specification addresses signaling between endpoint equipment and a public network (the Public UNI), as well as signaling between endpoint equipment and a private network (the Private UNI). Private ATM networks may use the private UNI signaling. The ATM Forum's B-ICI specification addresses signaling between public ATM networks.

8.9 Mulitiprotocol Encapsulation over AAL5

The popularity of the TCP/IP suite means that new networking technologies, such as ATM, must support these protocols. RFC 1483, "Multiprotocol Encapsulation over ATM Adaptation Layer 5," defines two methods of support: LLC encapsulation and VC-based multiplexing [8–36]. For both cases, the TCP/IP information is carried in the payload field of the Common Part Convergence Sublayer PDU, and the SSCS of AAL5 is empty.

The LLC encapsulation method, shown in Figure 8–15, is based on techniques developed for use with SMDS. This method allows multiplexing of multiple protocols over a single ATM virtual circuit. The receiver uses information contained within LLC and SNAP headers to identify the protocol carried within that PDU. The LLC encapsulation method is used when it is not feasible to have a separate VC for each protocol or when network charges are based on the number of active VCs.

The VC-based multiplexing technique uses ATM VCs to implicitly provide higher layer protocol multiplexing. In other words, each protocol is carried on a separate VC. This method is used when it is feasible and economical to dynamically create large numbers of virtual circuits.

8.10 Interworking

ATM technology must interoperate with other broadband alternatives. The following sections consider ATM interworking between frame relay and SMDS.

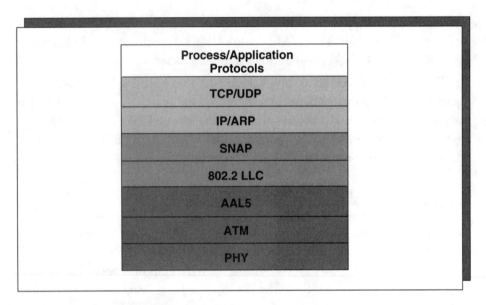

Figure 8–15. Using IP and ARP over AAL5

8.10.1 ATM/frame relay interworking

Frame relay is an established broadband networking protocol, while ATM is emerging as the broadband heir apparent. Therefore, many organizations are concerned with preserving their investment in frame relay networking hardware while migrating to ATM. An architecture that solves this problem was proposed by AT&T, Cisco Systems Inc., and StrataCom Inc., and further developed by the Frame Relay and ATM Forums in the document "Frame Relay/ATM Interworking Implementation Agreement" [8–37].

PVCs between an ATM UNI and a frame relay UNI or NNI provide logical connections between frame relay and ATM. Figure 8–16 illustrates two PVCs. PVC I connects a frame relay user device with an ATM user device. PVC II connects a frame relay network with an ATM user device. Examples of user devices include terminal equipment and a router or a switch.

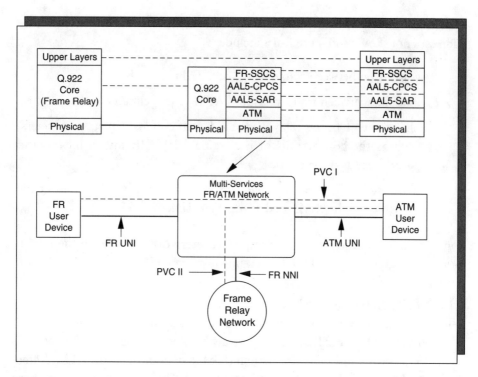

Figure 8–16. ATM/frame relay interworking *(Courtesy of AT&T, Cisco Systems, Inc., and StrataCom Inc.)*

Figure 8–16 illustrates the operations required to convert between the frame relay and ATM protocols. The frame relay user device uses the Q.922 Core protocols while the ATM user device uses ATM, AAL5, and the Frame Relay Service Specific Convergence Sublayer (FR-SSCS). The multiservices FR/ATM network contains both protocol stacks.

The protocol conversion occurs in two steps. First, it makes a correspondence between the two PVC identifiers: the ATM VPI/VCI and the FR DLCI. Second, it maps the protocol data unit between the FR-SSCS protocol and the Q.922 core protocol.

Additional ATM/frame relay interoperability issues that the architecture addresses not shown in Figure 8–16 include:

▼ conversion between frame relay and ATM protocols

▼ mapping between frame relay and ATM virtual circuits

▼ alignment of frame relay and ATM traffic-management parameters, such as the conversions of the frame relay CIR into a meaningful parameter for ATM traffic

▼ mapping of the local management information (the LMI used at the FR-UNI and the ILMI used at the ATM UNI).

For more information on frame relay/ATM interworking, refer to the Implementation Agreement and ITU-T Recommendation I.555.

8.10.2 ATM/SMDS interworking

Bellcore defines SMDS as a connectionless data-transport service. It is provided by a number of LECs and IXCs. The company has documented the design requirements for a broadband switching system (BSS) that would support ATM, frame relay, and SMDS services in TA-NWT-001110. Bellcore has proposed two scenarios for SMDS and ATM interworking (see Figure 8–17). The first (or top) scenario shows an SMDS user accessing the BSS via an SMDS SNI. At the user's end, the SMDS SIP stack is used and protocol conversions occur in the BSS. The second (or lower) scenario shows the SMDS user accessing the network via the ATM UNI. Here, the SMDS CPE uses different protocols: the SIP Connectionless Protocol (SIP_CLS) and AAL3/4. The functions of SIP Level 3 that are not part of AAL3/4 are placed in SIP_CLS. So, the SMDS user receives the equivalent to SIP Level 3.

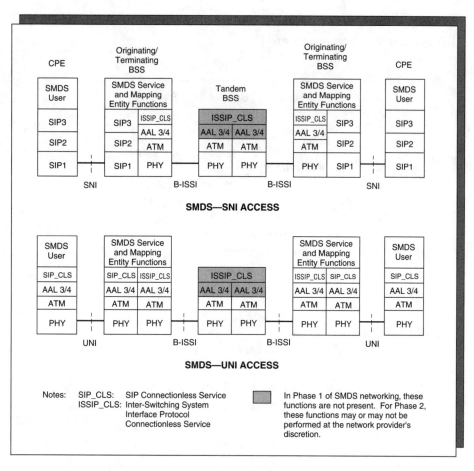

Figure 8–17. ATM/SMDS interworking (Source: TA-NWT-001110, ©1993, Bell Communications Research, Inc., reprinted with permission)

8.11 ATM Network Performance Metrics

ITU-T Recommendation I.350 defines parameters for measuring the quality of service (QOS), or user-oriented end-to-end performance of a B-ISDN. The ATM Forum has furthered this work by defining the QOS parameters and reference configurations for the UNI (see Figure 8–18). The switch manufacturer or network provider state the exact QOS performance objectives, which are based on the terms and parameters defined by the I.350 and ATM UNI documents. The ATM performance parameters are:

$$\text{Cell Error Ratio (CER)} = \frac{\text{Errored Cells}}{\text{Successfully Transferred Cells + Errored Cells}}$$

$$\text{Severely-Errored Cell Block Ratio (SECBR)} = \frac{\text{Severely Errored Cell Blocks}}{\text{Total Transmitted Cell Blocks}}$$

$$\text{Cell Loss Ratio (CLR)} = \frac{\text{Lost Cells}}{\text{Total Transmitted Cells}}$$

$$\text{Cell Misinsertion Rate (CMR)} = \frac{\text{Misinserted Cells}}{\text{Time Interval}}$$

In addition to these parameters, three tests measure the speed of the network. The Cell Transfer Delay (CTD) is the elapsed time between when a cell leaves the originating UNI to when it enters the receiving UNI for a particular connection. The Mean Cell Transfer Delay (MCTD) is the arithmetic average of specified CTDs for one or more connections. The Cell Delay Variation (CDV) measures variability of cell arrival events at different measurement points in the network. The CER, SECBR, and CMR effect network accuracy. CLR effects network dependability, and the CTR, MCTD, and CDV effect network speed.

Network providers should define objective values for service classes A, B, C, and D as applicable:

▼ Specified QOS Class 1 for Service Class A performance, which should be equivalent to digital private lines

▼ Specified QOS Class 2 for Service Class B performance, used for packetized audio and video in teleconferencing and multimedia applications

▼ Specified QOS Class 3 for Service Class C performance, used with connection-oriented protocols, such as frame relay

▼ Specified QOS Class 4 for Service Class D performance, used with connectionless protocols, such as IP or SMDS.

For more information on the ATM QOS parameters, consult ITU-T Recommendation I.350, and Appendix A of the ATM Forum UNI 3.0 specification.

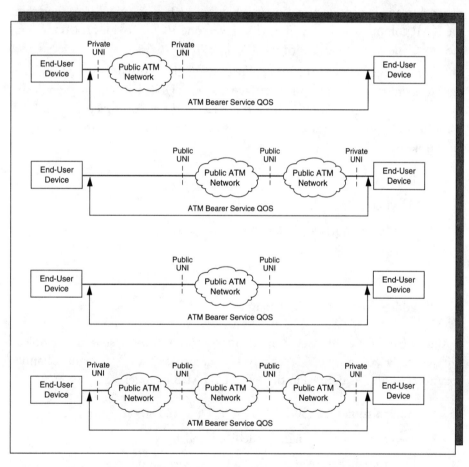

Figure 8–18. ATM QOS reference configuration *(Courtesy of the ATM Forum)*

8.12 The Interim Local Management Interface

As discussed previously, the B-ISDN architecture defines three planes: User plane, Control plane, and Management plane. The ATM Forum has developed the Interim Local Management Interface (ILMI) to address the Management plane functions.

The ILMI assumes that each ATM device supports at least one UNI and has a UNI Management Entity (UME) for each UNI. The UMEs then communicate network management information (see Figure 8–19). The SNMP/AAL performs the ILMI communication. At the ATM layer, one VCC provides ILMI communication. The default value for this VCC is VPI=0, VCI=16.

The management information defined by the ILMI provides status and configuration information from the UME regarding its UNI. This information details the status and configuration of both the ATM and Physical layers at that UNI. This information is organized into a MIB that contains several groups of managed objects:

▼ Physical layer

▼ ATM layer

▼ ATM layer statistics

▼ VPCs

▼ VCCs

▼ address registration information.

Within these groups, managed objects may pertain to the system as a whole, a physical interface, an ATM layer interface, a virtual path or a virtual channel. Examples of objects defined in the ATM UNI MIB include:

▼ transmission type (SONET STS-3c, DS3, and so on)

▼ media type (coax, single-mode fiber, and so on)

▼ operational status (in-service, out-of-service, and loop-back)

▼ maximum number of VCCs

▼ UNI port type (public or private)

▼ ATM cells received

▼ ATM cells dropped

▼ ATM cells transmitted

▼ Transmit QOS class

▼ VPI/VCI value.

For further details on ILMI and the ATM UNI MIB, consult the UNI 3.0 specification published by the ATM Forum.

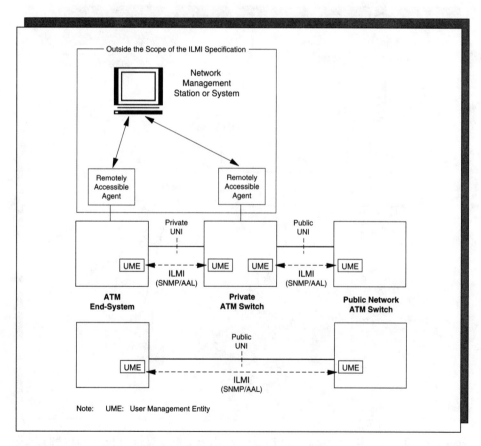

Figure 8–19. Definition and context of ILMI *(Courtesy of ATM Forum)*

8.13 ATM Customer Network Management

Bellcore has defined a CNM Service for use with Exchange PVC Cell Relay Service (CRS) in document TA-TSV-001117 [8–38]. The CRS CNM service provides LEC customers with the ability to manage their access to CRS and ATM UNIs. The LEC provides an SNMP agent within the ATM network, which is accessible by a customer-provided network management station (see Figure 8–20). Because SNMP is used as the communication protocol, CNM may be integrated with other SNMP-based network management platforms, such as the ATM Forum's ILMI.

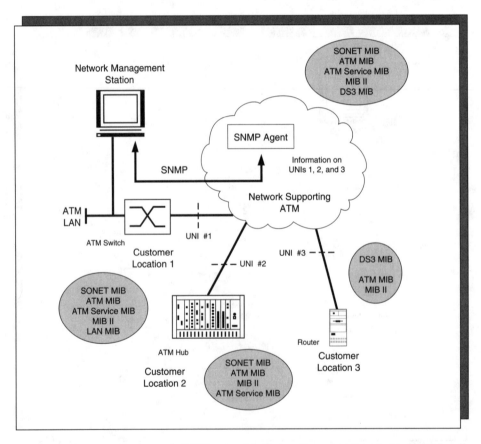

Figure 8–20. ATM CNM agent role (SNMP example) *(Source: Brown and Kostick, "And CNM for all: Customer Network Management Services for Broadband Data Services". Proceedings of the 18th Annual Conference on Local Computer Networks, © 1993 IEEE)*

Two phases of the CRS CNM service have been defined. Phase I, planned for 1995, includes SNMPv1 access; support for MIB II, plus the ATM, DS1, DS3, and SONET MIBs; retrieval of Exchange PVC CRS CNM information and reception of event notifications; and ILMI access-and-layer-management tools.

Plans for Phase II, slated for 1996, will let subscribers modify Exchange PVC CRS CNM information, such as the addition/deletion of a PVC; integrate this CNM architecture with other CNM services, such as ATM-based frame relay or SMDS; support SNMPv2; and access usage information.

This concludes our discussion of ATM architecture, Chapter 9 looks at the ATM protocols in detail.

8.14 References

[8–1] "ATM—Views of the New Frontier." Supplement to *Business Communications Review* (February 1993).

[8–2] Layland, Robin. "Unfinished Business: A Theory of Evolution for ATM Technology." *Data Communications* (March 1993): 89–92.

[8–3] Lunardoni, Mark. "Network Simplification Using ATM." *Telecommunications* (June 1993): 33–36.

[8–4] Robertson, Don. "ATM: Technology for Tomorrow." *STACKS: The Network Journal* (August 1993): 41–48.

[8–5] Feldman, Robert. "Ramping Onto the ATM Superhighway." *LAN Times* (January 24, 1994): 61–72.

[8–6] Kodama, Toshikazu and Takeo Fukuda "Customer Premises Networks of the Future." *IEEE Communications* (February 1994): 96–98.

[8–7] Architecture Technology Corp. "Asynchronous Transfer Mode Report." October 1993.

[8–8] Price, Curtis. "The Reality of ATM." International Data Corp., July 1993.

[8–9] Cisco Systems Inc. Asynchronous Transfer Mode (ATM) Technology Brief, 1993.

[8–10] Leslie, Ian M., et. al. "ATM Everywhere?" *IEEE Network* (March 1993): 40–46.

[8–11] Phillips, Barry. "ATM From Sea to Shining Sea." *Data Communications* (October 1993): 127–128.

[8–12] Wallace, Bob. "The Impact of ATM." *Network World* (November 1, 1993): 44–55.

[8–13] Newman, Peter. "ATM Technology for Corporate Networks." *IEEE Communications* (April 1992): 90–101.

[8–14] Herman, James and Christopher Serjak. "ATM Switches and Hubs Lead the Way to a New Era of Switched Internetworks." *Data Communications* (March 1993): 69–84.

[8–15] Biagoni, Edoardo, et. al. "Designing a Practical ATM LAN." *IEEE Network* (March 1993): 32–39.

[8–16] Spiegel, Leo. "High-Octane ATM Performance." *STACKS: The Network Journal* (June 1993): 24–27.

[8–17] Wittmann, Art. "Local ATM: Is ATM Ready for the Desktop?" *Network Computing* (September 1993): 160–166.

[8–18] Johnson, Johna. "ATM Networking Gear: Welcome to the Real World." *Data Communications* (October 1993): 66–86.

[8–19] Hart, John. "High-Performance Scaleable Networking with Routed ATM." *3TECH, the 3Com Technical Journal* (January 1994): 3–11.

[8–20] McQuillan, John. "Cell Relay." *Data Communications* (September 1991): 58–69.

[8–21] Hewlett-Packard Co. Broadband Testing Technologies, 1993.

[8–22] International Telecommunication Union—Telecommunication Standardization Sector (ITU-T). B-ISDN Asynchronous Transfer Mode Functional Characteristics, I.150, March 1993.

[8–23] Johnson, Johna "The ATM Circus Gets a Ringmaster." *Data Communications* (March 21,1993): 43–47.

[8–24] Bell Communications Research Inc. "Broadband ISDN Switching System Generic Requirements." TA-NWT-001110, August 1993.

[8–25] SynOptics Communications Inc. "The Road to ATM Networking," 1993.

[8–26] Stallings, William. "Components of OSI: Broadband ISDN." *ConneXions* (April 1992): 2–12.

[8–27] De Prycker, M., et. al. "B-ISDN and the OSI Protocol Reference Model." *IEEE Network* (March 1993): 10–18.

[8–28] The ATM Forum. *ATM User-Network Interface Specification*. Prentice-Hall, 1993.

[8–29] De Prycker, Martin. "ATM Switching on Demand." *IEEE Network* (March 1992): 25–28.

[8–30] Crutcher, Laurence A. and A. Gill Waters. "Connection Management for an ATM Network." *IEEE Network* (November 1992): 42–55.

[8–31] Armitage, Grenville J. and Keith M. Adams. "Packet Reassembly During Cell Loss." *IEEE Network* (September 1993): 26–34.

[8–32] Bell Communications Research Inc. "Broadband-ISDN User to Network Interface and Network Node Interface Physical Layer Generic Criteria." TA-NWT-001112, August 1992.

[8–33] Bell Communications Research Inc. "Asynchronous Transfer Mode (ATM) and ATM Adaptation Layer (AAL) Protocols Generic Requirements." TA-NWT-001113, July 1993.

[8–34] The ATM Forum. ATM Data Exchange Interface Specification, version 1.0, August 1993.

[8–35] Bell Communications Research Inc. "B-ISDN Access Signaling Generic Requirements." TA-NWT-001111, August 1993.

[8–36] Heinanen, Juha. "Multiprotocol Encapsulation over ATM Adaptation Layer 5." RFC 1483, July 1993.

[8–37] The Frame Relay Forum. Frame Relay/ATM Network Interworking Implementation Agreement. FRF.5, 1994.

[8–38] Bell Communications Research Inc. "Generic Requirements for Exchange PVC CRS Customer Network Management Service." TA-TSV- 001117, September 1993.

[8–39] Brown, Tracy A. and Deirdre C. Kostick. "And CNM for All: Customer Network Management Services for Broadband Data Services." Proceedings of the IEEE 18th Annual Conference on Local Computer Networks, October 1993.

 **ATM Protocols**

Because current ATM standards and implementations focus on the operation of the ATM Forum's UNI, this chapter focuses on the UNI protocols and the upper layer services that use them. It also discusses ATM network management and interworking.

9.1 ATM Protocols and Network Architecture

To begin the study of the ATM protocols, compare the ATM protocols with the OSI Reference Model. Figure 9–1 illustrates that there is an approximate relationship between the ATM layers (PHY, ATM, and AAL) and the OSI Physical and Data Link layers. Note that ATM-specific signaling and upper layer functions, which may be present for some network configurations, are not shown in the figure.

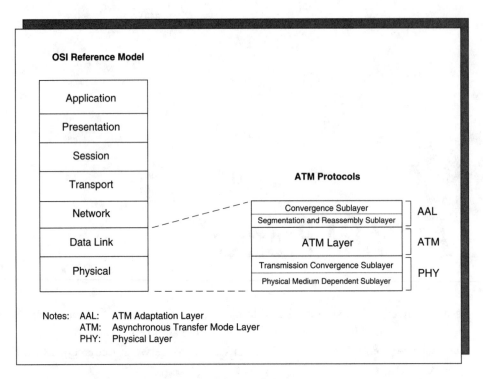

Figure 9–1. Comparing OSI and ATM architectural models

The ATM network architecture includes CPE, BSSes, and the interfaces between them (see Figure 9–2). The CPE includes the User layer, which supplies the information to be transmitted, and the three ATM layers (AAL, ATM, and PHY). Examples of User layers include constant bit rate applications, such as DS1, that use AAL1; connectionless services, such as SMDS, that use AAL3/4; and connection-oriented protocol traffic, such as TCP/IP, that uses AAL5 [9–1].

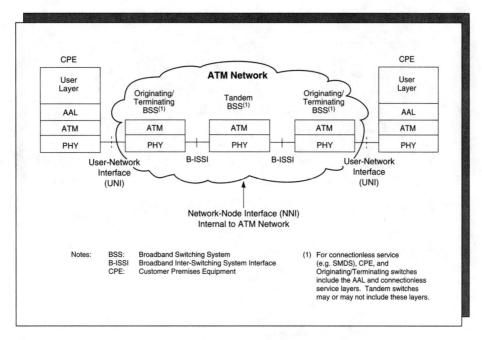

Figure 9–2. ATM network architecture *(Source: TA-NWT-001110, ©1993, Bell Communications Research, Inc., reprinted with permission)*

The CPE uses the UNI to connect to the ATM network [9–2]. The CPE requires no knowledge of the ATM network's internal architecture and operation. Bellcore views the internal ATM network as interconnected BSSes. An originating/terminating BSS connects to the network side of the UNI, and tandem BSSes provide intermediate switching. The BSS functional layers depend on the transmitted applications.

Bellcore has developed a protocol model of the UNI that illustrates the protocols the BSS will support (see Figure 9–3). It has two categories of UNI protocols: core functions that include the PHY and ATM layers and service-specific functions at the AAL and upper layers.

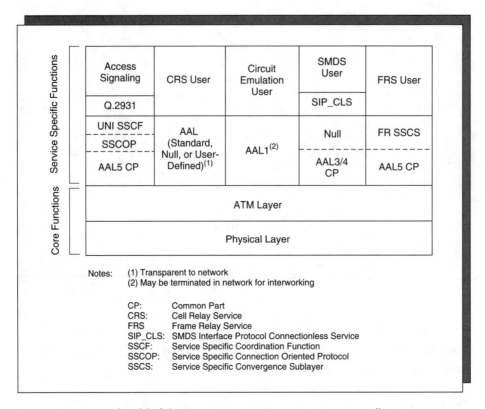

Figure 9–3. Protocol model of the UNI *(Source: TA-NWT-001110, ©1993, Bell Communications Research, Inc., reprinted with permission)*

Access signaling is the exchange of call-control messages that setup, maintain, and disconnect virtual channel connections between end users. ITU-T Q.2931 (formerly Q.93B) defines the signaling messages.

CRS user information is transmitted over standard, null, or user-defined AALs.

Circuit-emulation service, which can carry DS1 traffic, is transmitted over AAL1.

The SMDS Interface Protocol Connectionless Service (SIP_CLS) and AAL3/4 transmit SMDS traffic. To the end user, the combination of SIP_CLS and AAL3/4 is equivalent to SIP level 3 service.

Frame relay traffic is transmitted via a frame relay service-specific convergence sublayer (FR SSCS) over AAL5. These functions are implemented within the device that provides the FR/ATM interworking function. Note that the SMDS and frame relay support are future objectives, which the BSS may not support initially.

9.2 ATM Layer Protocols

Each ATM cell is 53 octets long and consists of a 5-octet header and a 48-octet payload. There are two header formats: one at the UNI and the other at the NNI [9–3].

9.2.1 The User-Network Interface

The ATM header at the UNI consists of six fields (see Figure 9–4):

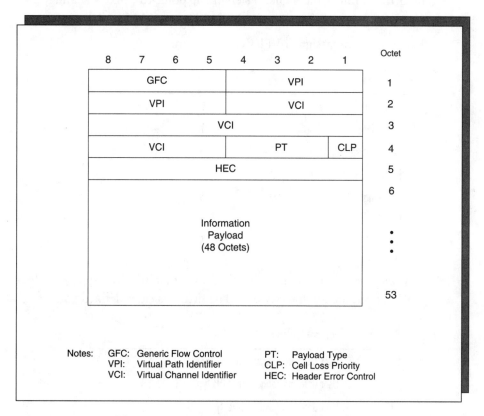

Figure 9–4. ATM cell format (UNI) *(Source: TA-NWT-001113, ©1993, Bell Communications Research, Inc., reprinted with permission)*

▼ *Generic Flow Control (GFC)*, a four-bit field that can provide local functions, such as flow control. This field has local, not end-to-end, significance and is overwritten by intermediate ATM switches. The UNI 3.0 specification states that the transmitting host should fill this field with all zeros.

▼ *Virtual Path Indicator (VPI)*, an eight-bit field that identifies the virtual path across the interface.

▼ *Virtual Channel Indicator (VCI)*, a 16-bit field that identifies the virtual channel across the interface. The UNI 3.0 specification defines some VPI/VCI values for specific functions, such as meta-signaling, used to establish the signaling channel; point-to-point signaling; and Operations Administration and Maintenance (OAM) cells.

Examples of preassigned VPI/VCI values are:

Function	VPI	VCI
Unassigned and Idle	0	0
Meta-signaling	0	1
F4 flow (Segment Data)	0	3
F4 flow (End-to-End Data)	0	4
Signaling	0	5
SMDS	0	15
ILMI	0	16

▼ *Payload Type (PT)*, a three-bit field that identifies the type of information contained in the payload. The field has eight defined values:

PT	Interpretation
000	User data, no congestion, SDU type = 0
001	User data, no congestion, SDU type = 1
010	User data, congestion, SDU type = 0
011	User data, congestion, SDU type = 1
100	OAM segment data, F5, flow related

101	OAM end-to-end data, F5, flow related
110	Reserved, future traffic control and resource management
111	Reserved, future functions

▼ *Cell Loss Priority (CLP)*, a single bit field that the user or network uses to indicate the cell's explicit loss priority. A cell with a CLP = 1 enters the network, it may be discarded under certain network traffic conditions.

▼ *Header Error Control (HEC)*, an eight-bit field that detects and/or corrects bit errors occurring in the header.

9.2.2 The Network-Node Interface

The ATM header at the NNI is 5 octets long, with a format that is almost identical to the UNI format except for the first octet (see Figure 9–5). The NNI, which provides bundles of VCIs between switches, defines an additional 4 bits for the VPI. In other words, the NNI uses 12 bits for the VPI and 16 for the VCI. The UNI uses 8 bits for the VPI and 16 bits for the VCI.

9.2.3 Unassigned Cells

At most interfaces, when there are no user-generated (or assigned) cells to send, filler cells, also called unassigned cells, are sent to occupy the available bandwidth. These cells have the reserved PCI/VCI value of 0/0 and a fixed-payload pattern. Unassigned cells are generated and discarded at the ATM layer and can be replaced by an assigned cell as necessary, for example, by cell-multiplexing functions.

It is worth mentioning that another type of cell also has a VPI/PCI value of 0/0—the physical layer cell. When the VPI/VCI value is 0/0, the 4-bit field normally used for the PT and CLP fields is re-interpreted as follows:

Interpretations	Value	
Unassigned	0000	ATM Layer Cell
Idle	0001	Physical Layer Cell
F1 flow (CBPL)	0011	Physical Layer Cell
F3 flow (CBPL)	1001	Physical Layer Cell

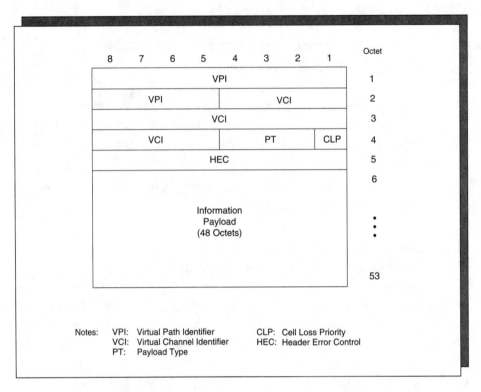

Figure 9–5. ATM cell format (NNI) *(Source: TA-NWT-001113, ©1993, Bell Communications Research, Inc., reprinted with permission)*

Idle cells are used for rate adaptation (cell stuffing) at the physical layer. Unlike unassigned cells, they take precedence over ATM layer cells and, therefore, cannot be replaced by assigned cells. In North America, idle cells are not normally used; rather, the ITU-T has defined a cell-based physical layer (CBPL) in I.432 that comprises only cells without a framing structure, such as SONET, in which to transport them. Because of the absence of a framing structure, the F1 and F3 OAM flows have to be carried in physical layer OAM cells that have a VPI/VCI of 0/0 and PT/CLP field values as shown above. Note that the F2 flow is redundant.

9.2.4 ATM operations and maintenance

The ATM network's ongoing performance is key to the success of a broadband implementation. To support good performance, the ITU-T developed

Recommendation I.610 to define the OAM functions of the Physical and ATM layers and the VP and VC connections. These functions are divided into five phases:

▽ *performance monitoring*, continuous or periodic checks

▽ *defect and failure detection*, malfunction detection and alarms

▽ *system protection*, bypassing a failed component to restore the system

▽ *failure or performance information*, alarms and reports

▽ *fault localization*, testing to determine the failed component.

OAM functions operate on five levels within the Physical and ATM layers. These functions are called OAM flows, designated F1 through F5. The Physical layer contains three OAM levels: the regenerator section (F1), the digital section level (F2), and the transmission path level (F3). The ATM layer contains two OAM levels: the virtual path level (F4) and the virtual channel level (F5) [9–4].

OAM operation is addressed in Bellcore's document TA-NWT-001113 [9–5], the ATM Forum's UNI 3.0 specification, ITU-T Recommendation I.610, ANSI Technical Report T1S1.5/92-029R3, and in Stephen Farkouh's paper about managing ATM networks [9–6]. OAM cells are sent on pre-assigned VCIs. For F4 (virtual path) OAM flows, VCI = 3 identifies a segment OAM flow, while VCI = 4 identifies an end-to-end OAM flow. For F5 (virtual channel) OAM flows, the OAM cell is sent with the same VPI/VCI values as the user data; however, the Payload Type (PT) value within the cell header identifies the type of OAM connection as either segment or end-to-end.

Figure 9–6 shows the ATM Layer Management PDU (or OAM cell). The cell payload consists of five fields:

▽ *OAM Type*, identifies the type of OAM communication (fault management, performance management, or activation/deactivation)

▽ *Function Type*, defines the function performed by this cell

▽ *Function specific field*, the detailed OAM cell contents

▽ *Reserved*, unused bits

▽ *Error Detection Code*, CRC-10.

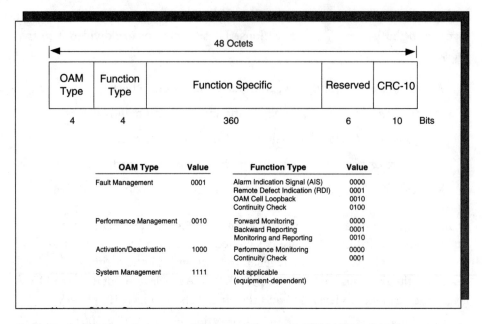

Figure 9–6. ATM Layer Management PDU format *(Source: TA-NWT-001113, ©1993, Bell Communications Research, Inc., reprinted with permission)*

Four function-specific fields perform fault management, performance management, activation/deactivation, and system management functions. Each of these OAM cells contains additional fields to support these functions, which are detailed in ANSI T1S1.5/92-029R3. The fault-management OAM cell performs Alarm Indication Signal (AIS) or Remote Defect Indication (RDI) reporting, continuity checking, OAM cell-loopback testing, and cell-transfer delay measurements. The performance management OAM cell may monitor incoming ATM cell traffic (referred to as inward monitoring) or report on outgoing cell traffic at the distant end (referred to as outward reporting). The activation/deactivation OAM cell enables or disables the performance or continuity check functions. The system management OAM cell is defined by the specific implementation.

9.3 ATM Adaptation Layer Services

Recall from Section 8.6.3 and Figure 8-11 that ATM networks may support different types of data traffic. Each traffic type may use a different AAL protocol, as defined in I.363 [9–7]. The following sections explore each of these protocols individually.

9.3.1 AAL Type 1

AAL Type 1 supports Class A traffic, which is sent at a constant bit rate (CBR); is connection oriented; and has a timing relationship between the source and the destination. Examples of such traffic include pulse code modulation (PCM) encoded voice, or CBR video.

The AAL consists of at least two sublayers: the Convergence Sublayer (CS) and the SAR Sublayer. For AAL1, the CS takes the User Information, provided at a CBR, and divides it into 47-octet protocol data units (AAL1_CS_PDUs), as shown in Figure 9–7. This AAL1_CS_PDU becomes the SAR_PDU payload. Note that no AAL1_CS protocol control information (PCI) is added to the AAL1_CS_PDU. The SAR sublayer adds a header 1 octet long to the AAL1_CS_PDU, forming a 48-octet AAL1_SAR_PDU.

The AAL1_SAR_PDU header consists of two fields: Sequence Number (SN) and Sequence Number Protection (SNP). The SN field contains two subfields: a Convergence Sublayer Indicator (CSI), which is one bit and used by service-specific functions of the AAL1_CS; and a Sequence Count (SC), which is 3 bits and contains a binary encoded sequence counter that is passed between peer AAL1_CS entities. One CSI function is to pass timing information between the sender and receiver. In this method, called the Synchronous Residual Time Stamp (SRTS), the CSI field of successive AAL1_SAR_PDUs carries a 4-bit Residual Time Stamp (RTS). The SC subfield detects lost or misinserted cells. The SNP field contains two subfields: a CRC Control subfield (three bits) and a single Parity bit. These two fields provide error control for the CSI and CS subfields.

The completed AAL1_SAR_PDU is sent to the ATM layer, where the ATM header is added before transmission.

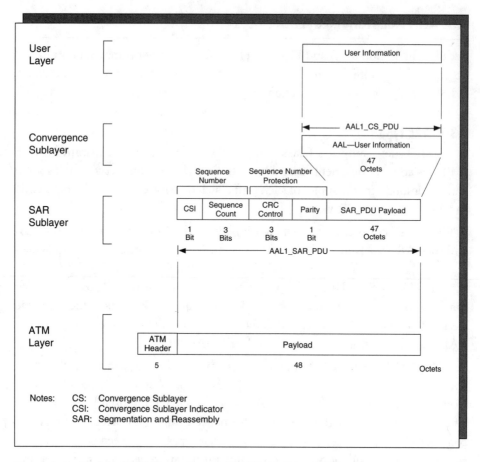

Figure 9–7. AAL Type 1 PDU format *(Source: TA-NWT-001113, ©1993, Bell Communications Research, Inc., reprinted with permission)*

9.3.2 AAL Type 2

AAL Type 2 supports Class B traffic, which is sent at a variable bit rate (VBR); is connection oriented; and has a timing relationship between the source and the destination. Examples include VBR voice and video signals.

The ITU-T is still developing AAL2. However, one suggested format for the AAL2_SAR_PDU is shown in Figure 9–8. The SN field is a binary counter that detects lost or misinserted cells. The Information Type (IT) defines one of three message values: Beginning of Message (BOM), Continuation of Message (COM), or End of Message (EOM). The Length Indicator (LI) states how many octets in the SAR_PDU Payload contain data. Finally, a CRC field provides error detection and correction. Error control is especially important for compressed video signals, which could use AAL2. In this case, single bit errors may affect the encoded data stream, which may produce a more severe effect than a single bit error within a cell carrying CBR audio (Class A and AAL1).

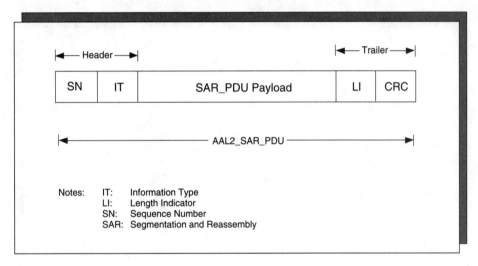

Figure 9–8. AAL Type 2 SAR PDU format

9.3.3 AAL Type 3/4

AAL Type 3/4 supports Class C or D traffic, which is sent at a VBR, with no timing relationship required between the source and destination. At one time, there were two standards: AAL3, which supported connection-oriented traffic, and AAL4, which supported connectionless traffic. These two AALs were later merged into the common AAL3/4. Data traffic that is sensitive to loss but not delay, such as SMDS, would use AAL3/4.

The AAL3/4 Convergence Sublayer is divided into two layers: a SSCS and a CPCS. The SSCS, which may not be present (null), supports the User layer. The AAL3/4 SAR sublayer interacts with the ATM layer.

The CPCS transfers variable-length blocks of data, or AAL3/4_CPCS_SDUs, sequentially between users. Two service modes are defined: Message Mode Service and Streaming Mode Service. Message Mode is used for framed data (see Figure 9–9). It transfers exactly one Interface Data Unit (AAL3/4_IDU) from the user. This IDU may be fixed or variable in length, up to 65,535 octets long. Streaming Mode is used for one or more IDUs, which may be separated in time (see Figure 9–10).

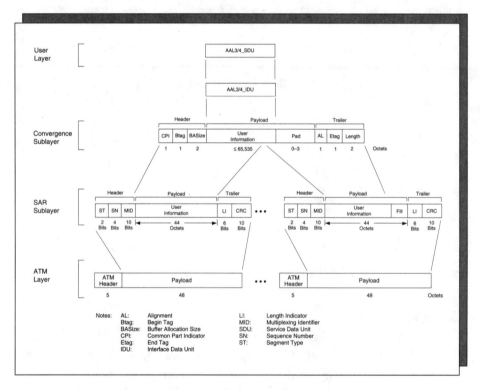

Figure 9–9. AAL Type 3/4 PDU format (Message Mode Service) *(Source: TA-NWT-001113, ©1993, Bell Communications Research, Inc., reprinted with permission)*

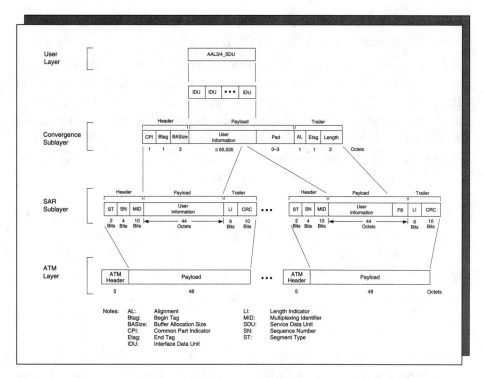

Figure 9–10. AAL Type 3/4 PDU format (Streaming Mode Service) *(Source: TA-NWT-001113, ©1993, Bell Communications Research, Inc., reprinted with permission)*

The AAL3/4 process is initiated when the user information (the AAL3/4_CPCS_SDU) is passed to the CPCS. The CPCS adds a header and trailer, generating the AAL3/4_CPCS_PDU. This unit is then passed to the SAR sublayer, which segments it into 48-octet SAR PDUs to become the ATM cell payload.

The AAL3/4_CPCS_PDU header contains three fields: Common Part Indicator (CPI), Begin Tag (BTag), and Buffer Allocation Size (BAsize). The CPI field (one octet) identifies the message type and the counting units for the BTag and BAsize fields. This field is currently coded as 00H, which indicates that the counting unit is the octet. The BTag field (one octet) is used in conjunction with the End Tag (ETag) in the trailer to associate the beginning and end of the AAL3/4_CPCS_PDU. The same number is placed in the BTag and ETag fields, and incremented for successive AAL3/4_CPCS_PDUs. The BAsize field (two octets) tells the receiving AAL3/4 process the maximum buffer size it must reserve to reassemble the incoming AAL3/4_CPCS_PDU.

The AAL3/4_CPCS_PDU User Information payload is limited to the maximum value of the BAsize field (65,535) times the counting value contained in the CPI field (typically octets). A Pad field may be placed after the Information field. This Pad may contain zero, one, two, or three octets of filler, which forces the AAL3/4_CPCS_PDU to be 32-bit aligned. Note that for SMDS applications, this field is of zero length, because the AAL3/4_CPCS_PDUs are always aligned on 4-octet boundaries.

The AAL3/4_CPCS_PDU trailer contains three fields: Alignment (AL), End Tag (ETag), and Length. The AL field (1 octet) provides 32-bit alignment in the AAL3/4_CPCS_PDU trailer, and is set to 00H. The ETag field (1 octet) is used in conjunction with the BTag, as described above. The Length field (2 octets) indicates the length in counting units of the User Information field.

The SAR process provides the 48-octet payloads carried in the ATM cells. Each AAL3/4_SAR_PDU contains a header (2 octets), User Information (44 octets), and a trailer (2 octets).

The AAL3/4_SAR_PDU header contains three fields: Segment Type (ST), SN, and Multiplexing Identification (MID). The ST field (2 bits) indicates whether the AAL3/4_SAR_PDU is the beginning of a message (BOM, with ST = 10), the continuation of a message (COM, with ST = 00), the end of a message (EOM, with ST = 01), or a single segment message (SSM, with ST = 11). The SN field (4 bits) is a counter that indicates the sequential position of each AAL3/4_SAR_PDU associated with a AAL3/4_CPCS_PDU. The MID (10 bits) identifies the AAL3/4_SAR_PDUs derived from a particular AAL3/4_CPCS_PDU. In other words, several AAL3/4_CPCS_PDUs may be transmitted simultaneously between the same two AAL users. The MID field identifies the AAL3/4_SAR_PDUs from different AAL3/4_CPCS_PDUs, assisting with the interleaving and reassembly process.

The AAL3/4_SAR_PDU payload contains User Information and Fill, and is 44 octets long. The User Information field contains up to 44 octets of a AAL3/4_CPCS_PDU. If the User Information field does not contain 44 octets, the Fill field completes it with zeros.

The AAL3/4_SAR_PDU trailer contains two fields: Length Indicator (LI) and a CRC. The LI field (6 bits) contains the length in octets of the User Information field. The type of segment, as indicated in the ST field, restricts the values of the LI field. The BOM and COM segments may be 44 octets long. The EOM segment must be a multiple of four octets (4, 8, 12, 16, … 44). The SSM must be a multiple of 4 octets, and at least 8 octets long (8, 12, 16, … 44).

When the AAL3/4_SAR processing is complete, it hands the AAL3/4_SAR_PDUs to the ATM layer for transmission.

9.3.4 AAL Type 5

AAL Type 5 supports Class C traffic, which is connection-oriented, sent at a VBR with no timing relationship required between the source and the destination. The AAL5 process is considered much simpler than AAL3/4. It removes some of the overhead at the SAR sublayer and supports only Message Mode service. AAL5 is also known as the Simple and Efficient AAL (SEAL).

The User Layer passes User information 0 to 65,535 octets long to the CPCS, as shown in Figure 9–11. The CPCS generates the AAL5_CPCS_PDU, which consists of a payload and a trailer. At the CPCS, a Pad field 0 to 47 octets long is added to the User Information to align the AAL5_CPCS_PDU on a 48-octet boundary.

The AAL5_CPCS_PDU trailer consists of four fields: User-to-User (UU), Common Part Indicator (CPI), Length, and CRC. The UU field (1 octet) contains information to be transferred transparently between AAL5 users. The CPI field (1 octet) aligns the AAL5_CPCS_PDU trailer on a 64-bit boundary. Other uses are under development, and may include identification of layer-management messages. The Length field (2 octets) indicates the length of the AAL5 CPCS payload. The CRC field contains a CRC-32 calculation that detects bit errors in AAL5_CPCS_PDU, including the payload first 4 octets of the trailer.

When the AAL5_CPCS_PDU is assembled, the SAR sublayer segments it into 48-octet AAL5_SAR_PDUs, which are then passed to the ATM layer. A single bit in the ATM header PTI field indicates the end of the AAL5_CPCS_PDU. This bit is set to zero for the first and intermediate segments, and to one for the last segment.

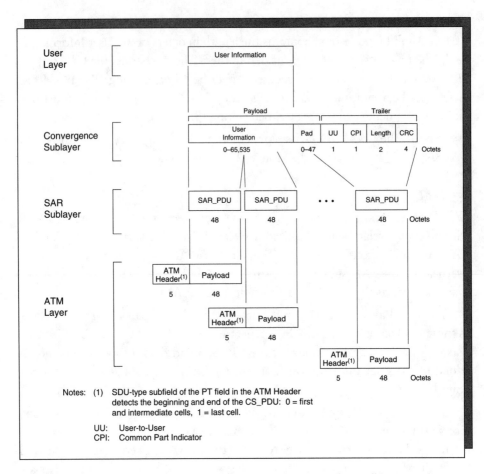

Figure 9–11. AAL Type 5 PDU format *(Source: TA-NWT-001113, ©1993, Bell Communications Research, Inc., reprinted with permission)*

9.4 ATM Physical Layer

The ATM Forum defines several options for the Physical Layer interface at either public or private UNIs. This section concentrates on the two most commonly used interfaces for ATM WANs in North America: SONET STS-3c and DS3. The SONET STS-3c interface, operating at 155.520 Mbps, uses multimode or single-mode fiber. The DS3 interface, operating at 44.736 Mbps, uses coaxial cable for the transmission medium.

9.4.1 SONET

The SONET formats are part of the Synchronous Digital Hierarchy (SDH). The DS3 format is part of the Plesiochronous Digital Hierarchy (PDH). Transmission rates for various signals within these two hierarchies are shown below:

SONET/Synchronous Digital Hierarchy (SDH) Rates

Rate (Mbps)	SONET	SDH
51.840	STS-1	
155.520	STS-3	STM-1
466.560	STS-9	STM-3
622.080	STS-12	STM-4
933.120	STS-18	STM-6
1244.160	STS-24	STM-8
2488.370	STS-48	STM-16

Plesiochronous Digital Hierarchy (PDH) Rates

Rate (Mbps)	North America	Europe
0.064	DS0	
1.544	DS1	
2.048		E1
3.152	DS1C	
6.312	DS2	
8.448		E2
34.368		E3
44.736	DS3	
139.264		E4
274.176	DS4	

The Synchronous Transport Signal-Level 1 (STS-1) frame, transmitted at 51.840 Mbps, is the basis for the higher SONET transmission rates. The STS-1 frame consists of nine rows and 90 columns, for a total of 810 octets. Each frame is transmitted within a period of 125 microseconds, occupying a total bandwidth of 51.840 Mbps (810 octets/frame * 1 frame/125 microseconds * 8 bits/octet). Of the 90 data columns, three (or 27 octets) carry "transport" overhead (TOH), such as framing, error monitoring, management, and payload pointer information. So the STS-1 payload "envelope" (SPE) is 87 columns wide or 783 octets (87 * 9). The SPE is itself a kind of frame that floats inside the available space in the STS-1 frame. The first column of the 87 column SPE is occupied by a 9–octet transmission path overhead (POH) and the start of the SPE is identified by the payload pointer in the TOH. Note that this mechanism exists to let the information carried in the SPE be timed with a bit clock signal that is not locked to the STS-1 clock signal; pointer "movements" let the SPE drift toward the STS-1 frame. Because of the POH, the available capacity per STS-1 frame is further reduced to 774 octets (86 * 9), representing a user payload bandwidth of 49.54 Mbps.

To provide SONET at higher rates (above 51.840 Mbps), multiple STS-1 frames are byte (or octet) interleaved. For example, three STS-1 frames may be combined into one STS-3 frame operating at 155.520 Mbps (the three frames must be frame aligned).The STS-3 frame now has 270 columns and nine rows and a TOH of nine columns. The payload of the STS-3 frame now has 261 columns and nine rows and comprises the three STS-1 SPEs (each 87 columns wide) byte interleaved. Note that these SPEs are independent of each other and can have any phase relationship with each other and the STS-3 frame, as determined by the three individual payload pointers that are byte interleaved in the nine-column TOH. The purpose of this multiplexing exercise is to enable the efficient transportation of three independent STS-1 signals long distance over a single optical fiber. Upon arriving at the far end, the STS-1 signals are demultiplexed to become three STS-1 framed signals again.

A special variant of the STS-3 frame is the STS-3c frame (c is for concatenation), in which the three SPEs of an STS-3 frame are merged (concatenated) together to form one large SPE of 261 columns. Because there is only one SPE, there only needs to be one POH, leaving a payload capacity of 260 columns that represents a usable bandwidth (for cells) of 149.76 Mbps (see Figure 9–12). The same approach can be used to generate an STS-12c signal in which the usable payload capacity is 599.04 Mbps (note that three columns of the STS-12c SPE are not used). When SONET is specified as the UNI, STS-3c is the signal used. SONET is a North American standard. Outside North America, most countries use the SDH equivalent to STS-3c, namely STM-1.

You should also note that when STS-1, STS-3c, or STS-12c are sent through optical fiber, the signals become OC-1, OC-3c, or OC-12c, respectively.

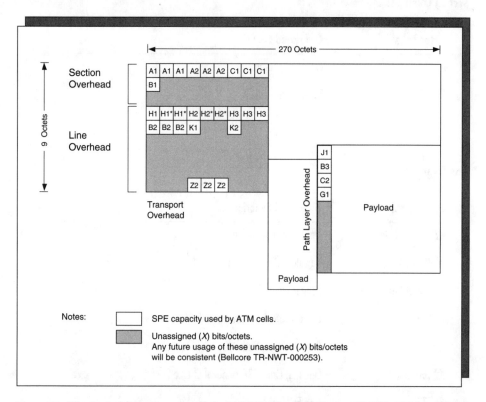

Figure 9–12. Logical frame structure of the 155.520 Mbps UNI *(Source: TA-NWT-001112, ©1992, Bell Communications Research, Inc., reprinted with permission)*

Within the transport overhead, rows one through three contain the SOH, and rows four through nine contain the LOH. The three original STS-1 TOHs are byte interleaved to create the nine rows of the STS-3c TOH. So, we see A1, A1, A1, A2, A2, A2, C1, C1, C1, and so on in the STS-3c TOH. Notice that overhead octets A1, A2, C1, H1, H2, H3, and B2 are replicated, while octets B1, K2, and Z2 are not. The path overhead (POH) carried in STS-3c SWP includes J1, B3, C2, and G1.

Bellcore's TR-NWT-000253 [9–8] is the baseline reference on SONET. The ATM Forum's UNI 3.0 specification defines the overhead octets and their functions for STS-3c implementations with ATM:

Section Overhead

Octet Label	Overhead Function
A1, A2	Frame alignment
C1	STS-1 identification
B1	Section error monitoring

Line Overhead

Octet Label	Overhead Function
B2	Line error monitoring
H1 (bits 1 to 4)	New data flag, Path AIS
H1 and H2 (bits 7 to 16)	Pointer value, Path AIS
H1*, H2*	Concatenation indication, Path AIS
H3	Pointer action, Path AIS
K2 (bits 6 to 8)	Line AIS, Line FERF, removal of Line FERF
3rd Z2	Line FEBE

Path Overhead

Octet Label	Overhead Function
J1	STS path trace
B3	Path error monitoring
C2	Path signal level indicator
G1 (bits 1 to 4)	Path FEBE
G1 (bit 5)	Path RDI (yellow)

AIS: Alarm Indication Signal

FEBE: Far End Block Error

FERF: Far End Receive Failure

RDI: Remote Defect Indicator

STS: Synchronous Transport Signal

ANSI T1.105 [9–9] is an excellent reference about SONET, and References [9–10] through [9–12] provide additional information on SONET implementations for ATM.

9.4.2 DS3

Chapter 6 discussed the DS3 PLCP format used with SMDS. The ATM PLCP is based on that work. The DS3 PLCP frame carries 12 ATM cells, plus overhead information, which is transmitted every 125 microseconds (see Figure 9–13). The overhead functions consist of the following:

▼ *A1 and A2*, framing

▼ *B1*, bit interleaved parity

▼ *C1*, cycle/stuff counter

▼ *G1*, PLCP path status

▼ *P0 to P11*, path overhead identifier

▼ *Z1 to Z6*, growth octets

For details, see Bellcore document TA-NWT-001112 and the ATM Forum UNI 3.0 specification.

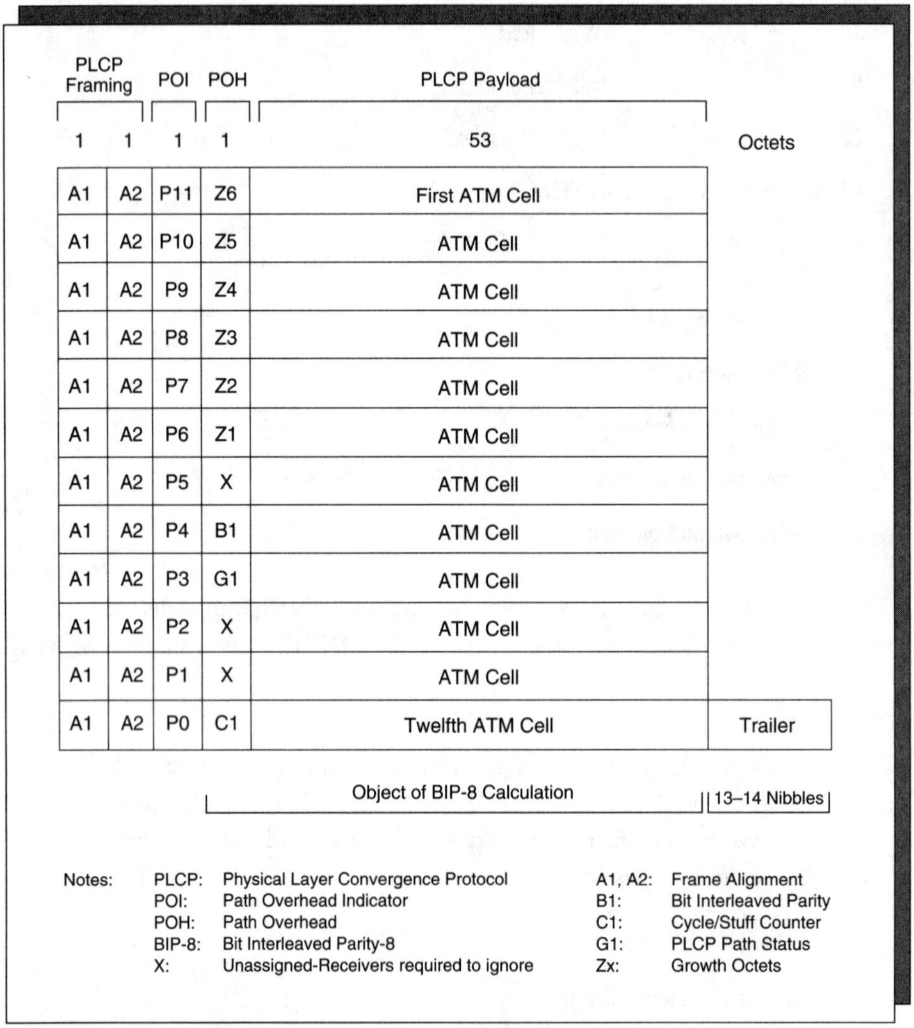

PLCP Framing		POI	POH	PLCP Payload	
1	1	1	1	53	Octets
A1	A2	P11	Z6	First ATM Cell	
A1	A2	P10	Z5	ATM Cell	
A1	A2	P9	Z4	ATM Cell	
A1	A2	P8	Z3	ATM Cell	
A1	A2	P7	Z2	ATM Cell	
A1	A2	P6	Z1	ATM Cell	
A1	A2	P5	X	ATM Cell	
A1	A2	P4	B1	ATM Cell	
A1	A2	P3	G1	ATM Cell	
A1	A2	P2	X	ATM Cell	
A1	A2	P1	X	ATM Cell	
A1	A2	P0	C1	Twelfth ATM Cell	Trailer

Object of BIP-8 Calculation   13–14 Nibbles

Notes:	PLCP:	Physical Layer Convergence Protocol	A1, A2:	Frame Alignment
	POI:	Path Overhead Indicator	B1:	Bit Interleaved Parity
	POH:	Path Overhead	C1:	Cycle/Stuff Counter
	BIP-8:	Bit Interleaved Parity-8	G1:	PLCP Path Status
	X:	Unassigned-Receivers required to ignore	Zx:	Growth Octets

Figure 9–13. DS3 PLCP frame (125μs)
(Source: TA-NWT-001112, ©1992, Bell Communications Research, Inc., reprinted with permission)

9.5 ATM DXI

A number of interfaces and protocols assist with the management of ATM networks (see Figure 9–14), including the DXI [9–13], the ILMI, and the messages that use these interfaces.

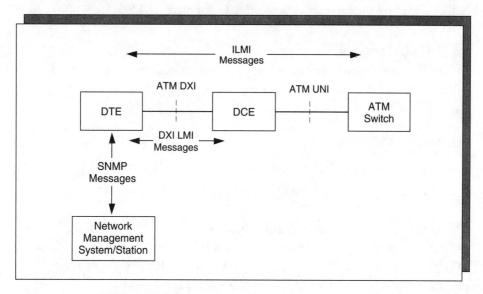

Figure 9–14. ATM DXI LMI *(Courtesy of ATM Forum)*

Assume that the DTE is a router connected to an ATM switch via a DCE, such as a DSU. Also connected to the router is a network management console, running SNMP. Several interfaces are involved: the ATM UNI between the switch and the DSU; the ATM DXI between the DSU and the DTE (router); and some other interfaces, such as a LAN connection, between the router and the network management console.

Several message types may be sent with this configuration. The Network Management System may send SNMP messages to request information contained in the router's MIB. The ATM switch may send ILMI messages to the router requesting information on a virtual path or virtual channel connection. In some cases, such as when the router requests a count of the dropped received cells, the router must consult the DSU. These consultations are referred to the DSU as DXI

LMI messages. Similarly, ATM DXI LMI traps sent from the DSU to the router generate ILMI traps to the switch or SNMP traps to the Network Management Console.

To support these mechanisms, the ATM DXI LMI MIB includes the ATM UNI ILMI MIB, defined in the ATM Forum's UNI 3.0 specification, and the ATM MIB, defined by the Internet Engineering Task Force (IETF).

9.5.1 The DXI protocol

The DXI protocol provides a way for a DTE, such as a router, and a DCE, such as a DSU, to share the processing of the protocols at the ATM UNI. Three modes of operation are defined:

▼ *Mode 1a*, AAL5 only

▼ *Mode 1b*, AAL3/4 for at least one VC, AAL5 for other VCs

▼ *Mode 2*, AAL5 and AAL3/4, one per VC

The DTE transmits the information field of an AAL_PDU, referred to as a DTE_SDU, to a peer process at another DTE. To do so, the DTE sends the DTE_SDU inside a DXI frame to the DCE. The DCE then completes the processing at the AAL sublayers (CPCS and SAR) and the ATM layers.

The format of the transmission frame sent between DTE and DCE varies depending on the AAL type used. For modes 1a or 1b with AAL5, the DTE sends a DTE_SDU, which may be up to 9,232 octets in length, to the DCE in a DXI frame (see upper portion of Figure 9–15). The DCE receives the DTE_SDU, and performs the AAL5 CPCS, AAL5 SAR, and ATM layer functions. The DXI Frame Address (DXA) field maps the VPI/VCI information between the DTE and DCE.

Mode 1b offers the capabilities of mode 1a, plus support for AAL3/4 on individually configurable VCs. The DTE encapsulates a AAL3/4_CPCS_PDU within a DXI frame (see lower portion of Figure 9–15). In this case, the DTE_SDU is reduced in length to 9,224 octets to accommodate the AAL3/4_CPCS header and trailer. The DCE performs the AAL3/4 SAR and ATM layer functions.

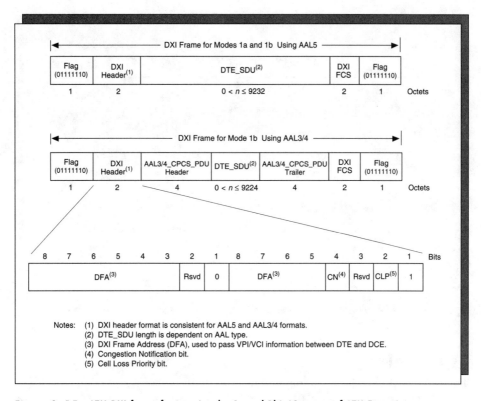

Figure 9–15. ATM DXI frame formats (modes 1a and 1b) *(Courtesy of ATM Forum)*

For Mode 2, the DTE encapsulates a AAL3/4_CPCS_PDU within a DXI frame (see Figure 9–16). In this case, the DTE_SDU may be up to 65,535 octets long. The DCE performs one of the following functions:

▼ For AAL5 VCs, the DCE removes the AAL3/4 CPCS header and trailer, and encapsulates the remainder of the PDU in a AAL5CPCS_PDU. The DCE then performs the AAL5 SAR and ATM layer functions.

▼ For AAL3/4 VCs, the DCE performs the AAL3/4 SAR and ATM layer functions.

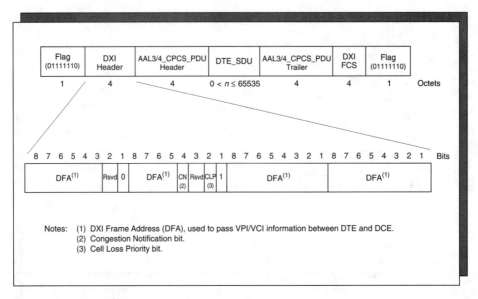

Figure 9–16. ATM DXI frame format (Mode 2) *(Courtesy of ATM Forum)*

9.5.2 The DXI LMI

The DXI LMI exchanges management information across the DXI. The ATM DXI LMI supports network management systems using SNMP and ATM switches running ILMI. The network management system or the ATM switch may request management information. So, the DTE, such as a router, must contain both an SNMP proxy agent and an ILMI proxy agent. If the network management system or the ATM switch sends a request and the DTE does not have the information, it will query the ATM DCE using a DXI LMI PDU (see Figure 9–17).

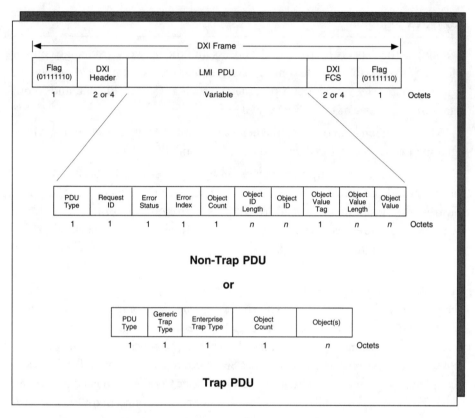

Figure 9–17. ATM DXI LMI PDU formats *(Courtesy of ATM Forum)*

Five LMI messages are defined. The GetRequest, GetNextRequest, and SetRequest originate in the DTE, with a GetResponse returned from the DCE. The Trap message originates in the DCE.

The LMI message formats are similar to those defined for SNMP. The GetRequest, GetNextRequest, SetRequest, and GetResponse messages share a common PDU structure, and the Trap message has a unique PDU format. The ATM Forum's DXI 1.0 specification provides greater details about the PDU formats.

9.6 ATM Signaling

Signaling is the process by which ATM users and the network exchange control information to establish or disconnect VCs, request the use of network resources, or negotiate for the use of circuit parameters, such as QOS, VPI/VCI, and so on. Signaling traffic is sent on VPI = 0, VCI = 5.

Meta-signaling is an optional method of establishing signaling channels. Meta-signaling messages are 1 cell long, and are sent on VPI = 0, VCI = 1.

Meta-signaling sets up three types of signaling channels: point-to-point, general broadcast, and selective broadcast. There are three meta-signaling procedures: the Assignment procedure establishes a new signaling channel, the Removal procedure disconnects a signaling channel, and the Checking procedure verifies a signaling channel.

9.6.1 ATM signaling protocols

The protocols, shown in Figure 9–18, support connection control signaling. ITU-T Recommendation Q.2931 specifies the signaling message format. These messages are sent over the Signaling ATM Adaptation Layer (SAAL), which ensures their reliable delivery. The SAAL is divided into a Service Specific Part and a Common Part. The Service Specific Part is further divided into a Service Specific Coordination Function (SSCF), which interfaces with the SSCF user; and a Service Specific Connection-Oriented Protocol (SSCOP), which assures reliable delivery. These two protocols are specified in ITU-T Recommendations Q.2130 (formerly designated Q.SAAL.2), and Q.2110 (formerly designated Q.SAAL.1), respectively. The common part of SAAL is AAL5.

Bellcore's TA-NWT-001111 [9–14] and the ATM Forum's UNI 3.0 specification provide further details on the signaling architectures.

9.6.2 ATM Address Formats

Before two ATM endpoints can communicate across a private or public UNI, the endpoints must be unambiguously identified. The ATM Forum has defined three Private UNI address formats, each 20 octets long, to provide this identification (see Figure 9–19). The UNI 3.0 specification states that a Private UNI must support all three Private ATM address formats. A Public UNI must support the E.164 address format, the three Private UNI address formats, or all of these. These four formats will be discussed below.

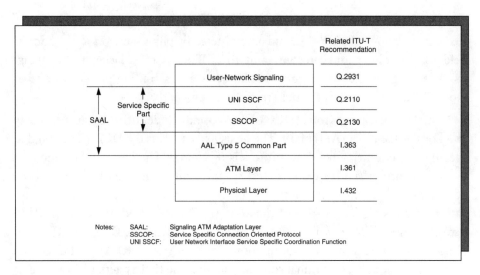

Figure 9–18. SAAL protocol stack at the UNI *(Source: TA-NWT-001111, ©1993, Bell Communications Research, Inc., reprinted with permission)*

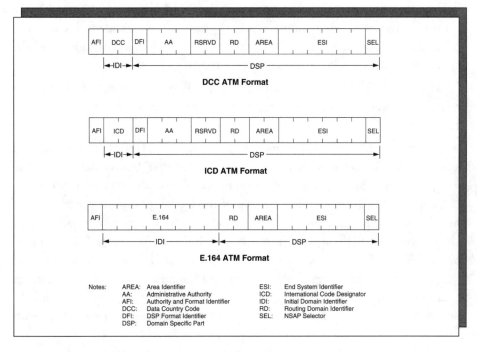

Figure 9–19. ATM address formats *(Courtesy of ATM Forum)*

The E.164 address format (not shown) is an ISDN format defined by ITU-T Recommendation E.164 [9–15], and administered by public networks. The address field is 8 octets long, and can contain up to 15 Binary Coded Decimal (BCD) digits. A leading pattern of a single 0H character and a trailing pattern of one or more FH characters pads the field to the correct length.

The Data Country Code (DCC) ATM format is identified by an Authority and Format Identifier (AFI) of 39. The next field contains the DCC (2 octets) that specifies the country where the address is registered. The Domain Specific Part Format Identifier (DFI) field (1 octet) specifies the structure of the rest of the address. The Administrative Authority (AA) field (3 octets) indicates the organization responsible for the rest of the address. The Reserved (RSRVD) field (2 octets) is reserved for possible field extensions. The Routing Domain (RD) field (2 octets) specifies a unique routing domain. The Area (AREA) field (2 octets) identifies a unique area within a routing domain. The End System Identifier (ESI) field (6 octets) identifies an end system within an area. The Selector (SEL) field (1 octet) is not used for routing, but may be used by end systems.

The International Code Designator (ICD) ATM format is identified by an AFI of 47. The next field contains the ICD (2 octets), which identifies an international organization, and is administered by the British Standards Institute. The remaining address fields are the same as in the DCC ATM format.

The E.164 ATM format is identified by an AFI of 45. The next field contains the E.164 address (8 octets). The rest of the address fields are the same as in the DCC ATM and ICD ATM formats.

Before an ATM connection may be established at a UNI, both the user and network must be aware of the addresses in effect at that UNI. Address-registration procedures, which are an extension to the ILMI, accomplish this. For Private UNI address formats, the user side of the UNI supplies the "user part" of the address: the ESI and SEL fields. The network supplies the network prefix, which consists of all the fields that precede the ESI field. When the E.164 address format is used, the network supplies the entire 8-octet address. The address elements are exchanged using ILMI SetRequest messages, and are stored in tables at either side of the UNI. After the addresses have been registered, they may be used in the Calling Party Number and Called Party Number information elements transmitted in signaling messages.

9.6.3 ATM signaling messages

ATM signaling messages are based on N-ISDN signaling formats specified in Recommendations Q.931 and Q.933. The details of ATM signaling are specified in B-ISDN Recommendation Q.2931, formerly Q.93B [9–16]. In the UNI 3.0 specification, the ATM Forum has defined a subset of Q.2931.

The ATM signaling messages may be grouped according to their function. Messages for ATM call and connection control include:

▼ *CALL PROCEEDING*, sent by the called user to the network or by the network to the calling user to indicate initiation of the requested call

▼ *CONNECT*, sent by the called user to the network and by the network to the calling user to indicate that the called user accepted the call

▼ *CONNECT ACKNOWLEDGE*, sent by the network to the called user to indicate that the call was awarded and by the calling user to the network

▼ *SETUP*, sent by the calling user to the network and by the network to the calling user to initiate a call

▼ *RELEASE*, sent by the user to request that the network clear the connection or sent by the network to indicate that the connection has cleared

▼ *RELEASE COMPLETE*, sent by either the user or the network to indicate that the originator has released the call reference and virtual channel

▼ *RESTART*, sent by the user or the network to restart the indicated virtual channel

▼ *RESTART ACKNOWLEDGE*, sent to acknowledge the receipt of the RESTART message

▼ *STATUS*, sent by the user or network in response to a STATUS ENQUIRY message

▼ *STATUS ENQUIRY*, sent by the user or the network to solicit a STATUS message.

Messages used with ATM Point-to-multipoint call and connection control include:

▼ *ADD PARTY*, adds a party to an existing connection

▼ *ADD PARTY ACKNOWLEDGE*, acknowledges a successful ADD PARTY

▼ *ADD PARTY REJECT*, indicates an unsuccessful ADD PARTY

▼ *DROP PARTY*, drops a party from an existing point-to-multipoint connection

▼ *DROP PARTY ACKNOWLEDGE*, acknowledges a successful DROP PARTY.

ATM signaling messages, as defined in UNI 3.0, use the Q.931 message format (see Figure 9–20a). The message consists of five parts:

▼ *Protocol Discriminator*, distinguishes call-control messages from other traffic

▼ *Call Reference*, associates this message with a call at the UNI, but does not have end-to-end significance

▼ *Message Type*, identifies the message function

▼ *Message Length*, identifies the length of the message contents

▼ *Information Elements*, parameters required by the message.

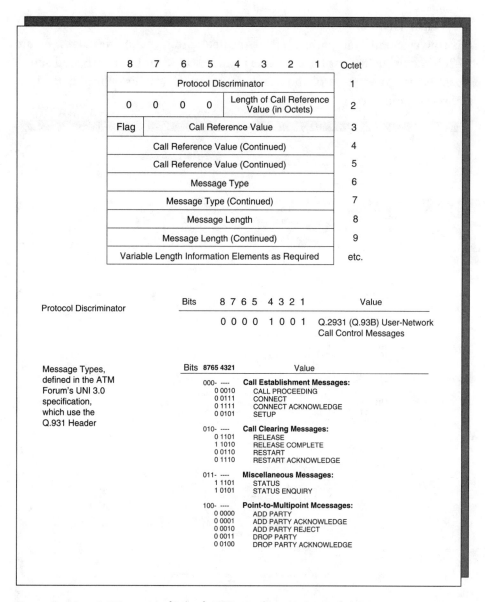

Figure 9–20a. Q.931 message format for ATM signaling *(Courtesy of ATM Forum)*

9.6.4 ATM Information Elements

IEs convey details and parameters associated with signaling messages. Figure 9–20b shows the format for the IEs. The first field identifies the IE, and subsequent fields provide control and length information. The IEs defined in the UNI 3.0 specification are:

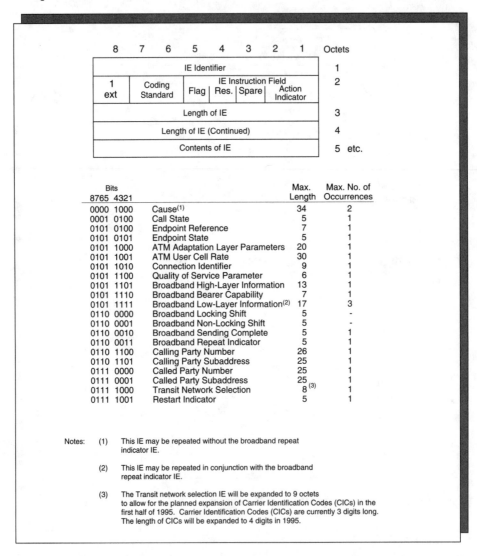

Figure 9–20b. IEs for ATM signaling *(Courtesy of ATM Forum)*

▼ *Cause*, identifies the reason for certain messages and provides diagnostic information

▼ *Call State*, describes the current status of the call, such as call initiated, call present, connect request, or release request

▼ *Endpoint reference*, identifies the individual endpoints in a point-to-multipoint connection

▼ *Endpoint state*, indicates the state of an endpoint in a point-to-multipoint connection, such as add/drop party initiated or received

▼ *ATM Adaptation layer parameters*, indicate the requested AAL end-to-end parameters, such as CPCS_SDU size, CPCS type, or MID size

▼ *ATM user cell rate*, specifies traffic parameters, such as forward or backward peak, sustainable cell rates, or burst sizes

▼ *Connection identifier*, identifies the local ATM connection, including the VPI/VCI values

▼ *Quality of service parameter*, requests or indicates the QoS class (zero to four) for a connection

▼ *Broadband high-layer information*, checks the compatibility of the high-layer information, such as ISO or vendor-specific protocols

▼ *Broadband bearer capability*, requests a connection-oriented bearer service of the network, such as CBR, VBR, point-to-point, or point-to-multipoint

▼ *Broadband low-layer information*, checks the compatibility of the low-layer information type, including the second layer and three protocols, and packet size

▼ *Broadband locking shift*, indicates a new active codeset

▼ *Broadband non-locking shift*, indicates a temporary shift to the specified lower or higher codeset

▼ *Broadband sending complete*, indicates the completion of the called party number

▼ *Broadband repeat indicator*, indicates how repeated IEs should be interpreted

▼ *Calling party number*, identifies the origin of a call

- ▼ *Calling party subaddress*, identifies the calling party subaddress
- ▼ *Called party number*, identifies the called party
- ▼ *Called party subaddress*, identifies the called party subaddress
- ▼ *Transit network selection*, identifies one requested transit network
- ▼ *Restart indicator*, identifies the class of the facility to be restarted, such as one or all, virtual channels.

Figure 9–21 shows the information elements associated with each ATM signaling message. Note that for each message, some of the IEs are mandatory, while others are optional.

Message / Information Element	Protocol Discriminator (5.4.2)	Call Reference (5.4.3)	Message Type (5.4.4.1)	Message Length (5.4.4.2)	Cause (5.4.5.15)	Call State (5.4.5.10)	Endpoint Reference (5.4.8.1)	Endpoint State (5.4.8.2)	ATM Adaptation Layer Parameters (5.4.5.5)	ATM User Cell rate (5.4.5.6)	Connection Identifier (5.4.5.16)	Quality of Service Parameter (5.4.5.18)	Broadband-High Layer Information (5.4.5.8)	Broadband Bearer Capability (5.4.5.7)	Broadband-Low Layer Information (5.4.5.9)	Broadband Locking shift (5.4.5.3)	Broadband Non-Locking Shift (5.4.5.4)	Broadband Sending Complete (5.4.5.21)	Broadband Repeat Indicator (5.4.5.19)	Calling Party Number (5.4.5.13)	Calling Party Subaddress (5.4.5.14)	Called Party Number (5.4.5.11)	Called Party Subaddress (5.4.5.12)	Transit Network Selection (5.4.5.20)	Restart Indicator
Call Establishment Messages																									
CALL PROCEEDING	M	M	M	M			O				O														
CONNECT	M	M	M	M			O		O	O	O			O											
CONNECT ACKNOWLEDGE	M	M	M	M																					
SETUP	M	M	M	M			O		O	M	M	M	O	M	O			O	O	O	O	M	O	O	
Call Clearing Messages																									
RELEASE	M	M	M	M	M																				
RELEASE COMPLETE	M	M	M	M	O																				
RESTART	M	M	M	M							O														M
RESTART ACKNOWLEDGE	M	M	M	M							O														M
Miscellaneous Messages																									
STATUS	M	M	M	M	M	M	O	O																	
STATUS ENQUIRY	M	M	M	M			O																		
Point-to-Multipoint Messages																									
ADD PARTY	M	M	M	M			M		O				O	O	O					O	O	M	O	O	
ADD PARTY ACKNOWLEDGE	M	M	M	M			M																		
ADD PARTY REJECT	M	M	M	M	M		M																		
DROP PARTY	M	M	M	M	M		M																		
DROP PARTY ACKNOWLEDGE	M	M	M	M	O		M																		

M = Mandatory   O = Optional

Figure 9–21. ATM control messages and information elements

9.6.5 Call setup procedures

Before any of the signaling procedures may be invoked, a user-to-network SAAL connection must be established. Call control signaling is then sent over a permanent signaling virtual channel connection, with VPI = 0 and VCI = 5.

To initiate a call, the calling user sends a SETUP message to the network (see Figure 9–22). The SETUP message is one of the most complex messages; it may contain a number of information elements: AAL Parameters, ATM User Cell Rate, Broadband Bearer Capability, Broadband High-Layer Information, Broadband Repeat Indicator, Broadband Low-Layer Information, Called Party Number, Called Party Subaddress, Calling Party Number, Calling Party Subaddress, Connection Identifier, QOS Parameter, Broadband Sending Complete, Transit Network Selection, and Endpoint Reference.

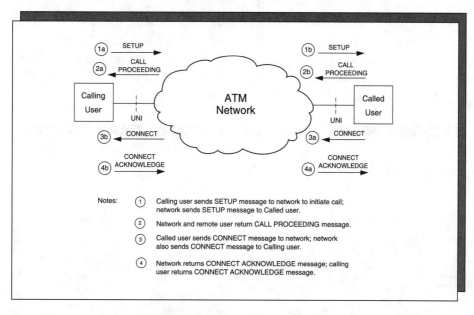

Figure 9–22. ATM call setup procedures

If the network determines that the requested service is authorized and available, it returns a CALL PROCEEDING message to the calling user and a SETUP message to the called user. If the network is unable to accept the call, it initiates call clearing as described in the next section. The CALL PROCEEDING message includes Connection Identifier and Endpoint Reference IEs. If the called user wishes to accept the call, it responds with a CALL PROCEEDING, followed by a CONNECT message. The CONNECT message includes the AAL Parameters, Broadband Low-Layer Information, Connection Identifier, and Endpoint Reference IEs. The network sends a CONNECT ACKNOWLEDGE message to the called user and a CONNECT message to the calling user. The CONNECT ACKNOWLEDGE message conveys no additional parameters. The end-to-end connection is established when the calling user returns a CONNECT ACKNOWLEDGE message to the network.

9.6.6 Call clearing procedures

The user or the network may initiate call and connection clearing. (Figure 9–23 illustrates the procedures when the user initiates the clearing; network-initiated procedures are similar.) The user sends a RELEASE message to the network and disconnects the virtual channel. The RELEASE message includes a Cause IE. The network disconnects the virtual channel, initiates procedures to disconnect the remote user, and responds with a RELEASE COMPLETE message. The RELEASE COMPLETE message also includes a Cause IE.

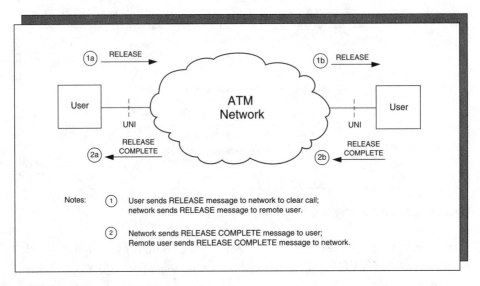

Figure 9–23. ATM call clearing procedures

9.6.7 Point-to-Multipoint Procedures

Point-to-multipoint connections are a superset of point-to-point connections and use the same signaling channel. The calling user is designated the Root, and the called users are designated Leaves. The Root sets up the first connection to one Leaf according to the call setup procedures defined for point-to-point calls (see Figure 9–24).

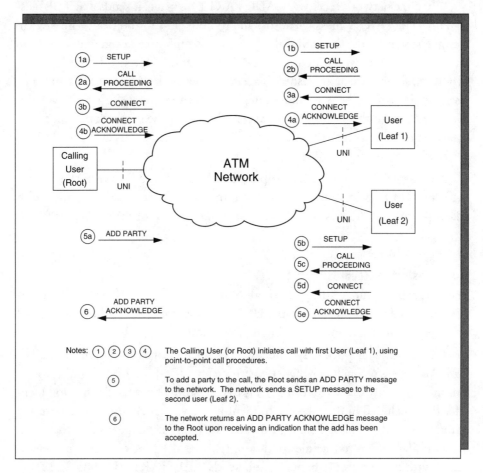

Figure 9–24. ATM point-to-multipoint procedures

The Root adds a second party by sending an ADD PARTY message to a second Leaf. The ADD PARTY message may include the following IEs: AAL Parameters,

Broadband High-Layer Information, Broadband Low-Layer Information, Called Party Number, Called Party Subaddress, Calling Party Number, Calling Party Subaddress, Broadband Sending Complete, Transit Network Selection, and Endpoint Reference. Note that the QOS, Bearer Capability, and ATM User Cell Rate IEs are not included in the ADD PARTY message, as these parameters are the same as the originally established (first Root-to-Leaf) call.

When the network receives an ADD PARTY message, it sends a SETUP message or ADD PARTY message across the remote UNI to the Leaf. The SETUP message is sent across the UNI if the link-state is null or clearing, and it initiates the normal CALL PROCEEDING, CONNECT, and CONNECT ACKNOWL-EDGE sequence if the user wishes to accept the call. The ADD PARTY message is sent if the link is in the Active link-state; it initiates an ADD PARTY ACKNOWL-EDGE message if the user wishes to accept the call. If the network or called user (Leaf) is unable to accept the ADD PARTY message, it returns an ADD PARTY REJECT message to the Root.

A user or the network may drop a party by sending a DROP PARTY message or a RELEASE message across the interface. The recipient responds with a DROP PARTY ACKNOWLEDGE message or a RELEASE COMPLETE message.

9.6.8 Restart Procedures
The restart procedure returns one or all of the virtual channels to the idle condition. It is used when one side of the UNI does not respond to other call-control messages, or after a failure or maintenance action.

A user or the network may send a RESTART message (see Figure 9–25). The RESTART message includes the Restart Indicator IE. If the Restart Indicator IE indicates that only one virtual channel is to be restarted, then a Connection Identifier IE is included in the message to identify the virtual channel to be returned to the idle condition. The recipient of the RESTART message returns the specified virtual channels to the idle condition, releases all of the call references associated with those virtual channels, and sends a RESTART ACKNOWLEDGE message to the originator. The RESTART ACKNOWLEDGE message includes a Restart Indicator IE, and may also include a Connection Identifier IE.

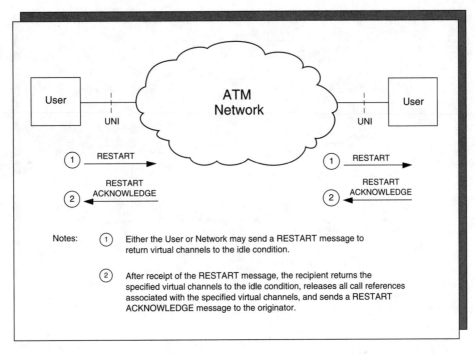

Figure 9–25. ATM restart procedures

9.6.9 Status enquiry procedures

The user or the network may initiate status enquiry procedures to check the status of a call (see Figure 9–26).

The STATUS ENQUIRY message may optionally include an Endpoint Reference IE. The recipient of the STATUS ENQUIRY returns a STATUS message, which reports on the current call state. The STATUS message includes the Call State, Cause, Endpoint Reference, and Endpoint State IEs.

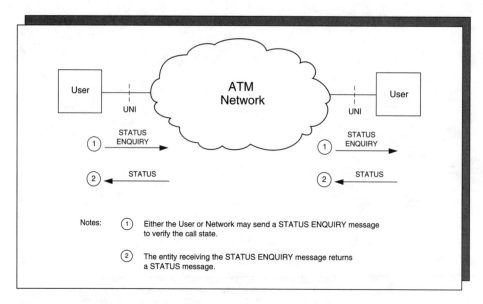

Figure 9–26. ATM status enquiry procedures

9.7 ATM Interworking

Using ATM with other protocols in a collaborative manner is called interworking. The following sections discuss interworking via multiprotocol encapsulation, frame relay, and SMDS.

9.7.1 Multiprotocol encapsulation over AAL5

RFC 1483, "Multiprotocol Encapsulation over ATM Adaptation Layer 5" [9–17] defines a method to carry multiprotocol traffic over AAL5. That document describes two methods of support, LLC encapsulation and VC-based multiplexing. In both cases, the higher layer information, such as TCP/IP or LAN traffic, is carried in the payload field of the Common Part Convergence Sublayer PDU, with the SSCS of AAL5 empty.

The LLC encapsulation method, shown in Figure 9–27, is based on techniques developed for use with SMDS. This method is required when a single ATM virtual circuit carries several protocols. Information contained within IEEE 802.2 LLC header and an IEEE 802.1a SNAP header identifies the protocol carried within that PDU.

350

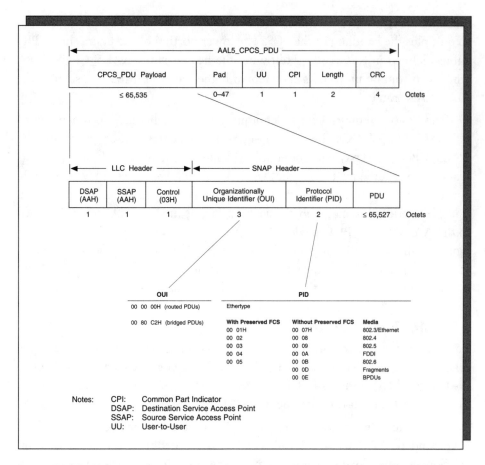

Figure 9–27. Multiprotocol encapsulation over AAL5 (non-ISO routed PDUs or bridged PDUs)

The figure also shows the format used for routed, non-ISO PDUs. (The format for the routed ISO PDUs is slightly different, refer to RFC 1483 for details.) The DSAP address (1 octet) and the Source Service Access Point (SSAP) address (1 octet) both contain a value of AAH, which indicates that a SNAP header follows. The Control field (1 octet) has a value of 03H, indicating an Unnumbered Information (UI) field. The SNAP header (5 octets) contains two fields, a 3-octet Organizationally Unique Identifier, or OUI, and a 2-octet Protocol Identifier, or PID. The OUI has a value of 00 00 00H for routed PDUs, and a value of 00 80 C2H for bridged PDUs. For routed PDUs, the PID is a 2-octet Ethertype, which for IP would have a value of 08 00H. For bridged PDUs, the PID is a 2-octet field that indicates the type of transmission media used (Ethernet/802.3, 802.5, FDDI, and so on), plus the handling of the FCS. The lower portion of the figure shows PID values defined in RFC 1483. Following the header is the AAL5_CPCS_PDU, which can contain up to 65,527 octets of higher layer information, such as the MAC LAN frame.

The VC-based multiplexing technique provides higher layer protocol multiplexing by ATM VCs. Because a separate VC carries each protocol, the AAL5_CPCS_PDU payload does not have to include explicit multiplexing information. For routed protocols, the AAL5_CPCS_PDU payload may be entirely devoted (65,535 octets maximum) to the higher layer information, such as TCP/IP traffic. For bridged frames, only the fields beginning after the PID field are included in the AAL5_CPCS_PDU payload. In other words, the beginning of the PDU would be the MAC Destination Address, followed by the remainder of the MAC frame, any higher layer information, if applicable, and the LAN FCS. RFC 1483 provides further details on these encapsulation formats.

9.7.1 ATM/frame relay

Four organization's documents address interworking between ATM and frame relay: the ITU-T's Recommendation I.555 [9–18], Bellcore's TA-NWT-001115 [9–19], the ATM Forum's B-ICI 1.0 Specification [9–20], and the Frame Relay Forum's Implementation Agreement [9–21].

The logical and physical connection between the frame relay network or device and the ATM network is called an IWF. I.555 defines two functions, encapsulation and protocol mapping, that impact the interworking architectures. Encapsulation occurs when "the conversions in the network or in the terminals are such that the protocols used to provide one service make use of the layer service provided by another protocol." In other words, the protocols are stacked at the interworking point.

In contrast, protocol mapping occurs when "the network performs conversions in such a way that within a common layer service the protocol information of one protocol is extracted and mapped on protocol information of another protocol." In other words, each end of the connect supports different protocols, but a common layer service in the IWF communicates with both end protocols.

Recommendation I.555 defines two scenarios for connecting networks/devices using B-ISDN (or ATM). Scenario 1 connects two networks/devices via an IWF into and out of a B-ISDN network. In this case, the B-ISDN network is not visible to frame relay users. All mapping and encapsulation functions occur transparently to the end users. This scenario is sometimes called frame relay transport over ATM.

Scenario 2 connects a frame relay network/device with a broadband device using a B-ISDN network. This scenario is also transparent to the end user. In this case, the broadband device supports the frame relay Service Specific Convergence Sublayer (FR-SSCS) function on top of the ATM protocols.

The interworking function maps the frame relay functions to the ATM functions and includes both protocol stacks internally. On the frame relay side is the Q.922 Core and Physical layers. The ATM side includes the FR-SSCS, CPCS, and SAR sublayers for AAL5, plus the ATM and PHY layers.

Both the B-ICI 1.0 specification and the FR/ATM IA indicate that the IWF will support the following frame relay service functions: variable length PDU formatting and delimiting, error detection, connection multiplexing, loss priority indication, FECN and BECN indications, and PVC status management.

Figure 9–28 shows the format of the FR-SSCS PDU within AAL5. The B-ICI 1.0 and the FR/ATM IA documents describe details on how the IWF supports each of the above functions.

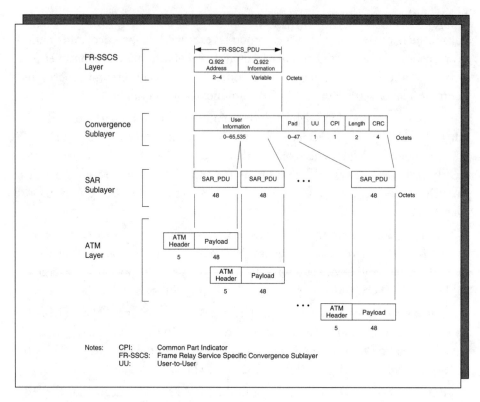

Figure 9–28. FR-SSCS PDU within AAL5

9.7.2 ATM/SMDS

Interworking between ATM and SMDS has been addressed by three organizations: Bellcore in TA-NWT-001110; the SMDS Interest Group (SIG) in a document called "Protocol Interface Specification for Implementation of SMDS over an ATM-based Public UNI" [9–22], and the ATM Forum in the B-ICI 1.0 Specification.

Under normal conditions, an SMDS CPE accesses the SMDS network at the SNI, using the three layers of Bellcore's SIP. Bellcore and the SIG have defined a method that lets an end user connect to an ATM network using a UNI to access an SMDS service offering. In other words, an end user can use the ATM UNI to access SMDS in the same way that other users would use the SNI or DXI/SNI to access SMDS.

The protocol interface defines a new protocol, called SIP Connectionless Service (SIP_CLS). SIP_CLS is a subset of the Connectionless Network Access

Protocol, CLNAP, defined by ITU-T Recommendation I.364. SIP_CLS is transported over AAL3/4 (null SSCS, plus CPCS and SAR), as well as the ATM and PHY layers. The combined functions of SIP_CLS and AAL3/4 result in the equivalent of SIP Level 3 functionality. From the customer's perspective, SMDS and the applications that depend on it require no changes. They continue to support features such as multi-CPE arrangements, access classes, and quality of service.

The SIP_CLS_PDU is a subset of the SMDS L3_PDU. To generate a SIP_CLS_PDU, the first and last octets of the SDMS L3_PDU are removed. The resulting PDU includes the Destination Address (DA) through Header Extension fields (32 octets total), the Information field (up to 9,188 octets) and ends with the CRC-32 field (4 octets), as shown in Figure 9–29. The SIP_CLS_PDU may be 32 to 9,224 octets long.

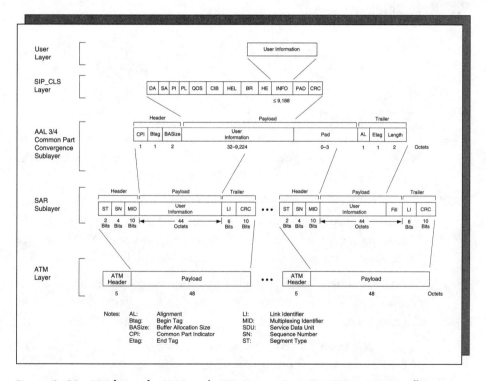

Figure 9–29. PDU format for SMDS on the UNI *(Source: TA-NWT-001110, ©1993, Bell Communications Research, Inc., reprinted with permission)*

The ATM Forum's B-ICI 1.0 specification supports SMDS/ATM interworking. The interworking function differs from the protocol interface in that a SIP L3_PDU is encapsulated inside another protocol, the Inter Carrier Interface Protocol Connectionless Service (ICIP_CLS). The AAL3/4 then transports the ICIP_CLS_PDU. Mapping functions, which include routing, carrier selection, group address resolution, and others, logically connect SIP Level 3 and ICIP_CLS. Mapping between SMDS and ATM QOS occurs, and performance parameters are also performed.

This chapter has discussed the various ATM protocols and their formats and parameters. Chapter 10 provides case studies that illustrate the operation of these protocols.

9.8 References

[9–1]   Bell Communications Research Inc. "Broadband ISDN Switching System Generic Requirements." TA-NWT-001110, August 1993.

[9–2]   The ATM Forum. ATM User-Network Interface Specification. Prentice-Hall, 1993.

[9–3]   Bell Communications Research Inc. "Broadband-ISDN User to Network Interface and Network Node Interface Physical Layer Generic Criteria." TA-NWT-001112, August 1992.

[9–4]   International Telecommunication Union—Telecommunications Standardization Sector. Integrated Services Digital Network (ISDN) Maintenance Principles, B-ISDN Operation and Maintenance Principles and Functions. ITU-T Recommendation I.610, March 1993.

[9–5]   Bell Communications Research Inc. "Asynchronous Transfer Mode (ATM) and ATM Adaptation Layer (AAL) Protocols Generic Requirements." TA-NWT-001113, July 1993.

[9–6]   Farkouh, Stephen C. "Managing ATM-based Broadband Networks." *IEEE Communications Magazine* (May 1993): 82–86.

[9–7]   International Telecommunication Union—Telecommunications
         Standardization Sector. Integrated Services Digital Network (ISDN)
         B-ISDN ATM Adaptation Layer (AAL) Specification. ITU-T
         Recommendation I.363, July 1992.

[9–8]   Bell Communications Research Inc. "Synchronous Optical Network
         (SONET) Transport Systems: Common Generic Criteria." TR-NWT-
         000253, December 1991.

[9–9]   American National Standards Institute. "Digital Hierarchy- Optical
         Interface Rates and Formats Specifications (SONET)." T1.105, 1991.

[9–10]   Stallings, William. "The Role of SONET in the Development of
         Broadband ISDN." *Telecommunications* (April 1992): 21–24.

[9–11]   Giancarlo, Charles. "Making the Transition from T3 to SONET."
         Telecommunications (April 1992): 17–20.

[9–12]   Ching, Yau-Chau and H. Sabit Say "SONET Implementation." *IEEE
         Communications Magazine* (September 1993): 34–40.

[9–13]   The ATM Forum. ATM Data Exchange Interface (DXI) Specification,
         version 1.0, August 1993.

[9–14]   Bell Communications Research Inc. "B-ISDN Access Signaling
         Generic Requirements." TA-NWT-001111, August 1993.

[9–15]   International Telecommunication Union—Telecommunications
         Standardization Sector. Numbering Plan for the ISDN Era. ITU-T
         Recommendation E.164, 1988.

[9–16]   International Telecommunication Union—Telecommunications
         Standardization Sector. Broadband Integrated Services Digital Network
         (B-ISDN) Digital Subscriber Signaling No. 2 (DSS 2), User Network
         Interface Layer 3 Specification for Basic Call/Connection Control.
         ITU-T Recommendation Q.2931, December 1993.

[9–17]   Heinanen, Juha. "Multiprotocol Encapsulation over ATM Adaptation
         Layer 5." RFC 1483, July 1993.

[9–18] International Telecommunication Union—Telecommunications Standardization Sector. Frame Mode Bearer Service (FMBS) Interworking. ITU-T Recommendation I.555, 1993.

[9–19] Bell Communications Research Inc. "BISDN Inter Carrier Interface (B-ICI) Generic Requirements." TA-NWT-001115, September 1993.

[9–20] The ATM Forum. BISDN Inter Carrier Interface (B-ICI) Specification, version 1.0. August 1993.

[9–21] The Frame Relay Forum. Frame Relay/ATM Network Interworking Implementation Agreement. FRF.5, 1994.

[9–22] SMDS Interest Group. Protocol Interface Specification for Implementation of SMDS over an ATM-based Public UNI. TWG-1993/043, March 1994.

10 ATM Analysis

In Chapter 8, I discussed ATM architecture; in Chapter 9, I covered the ATM protocols. This chapter puts that information to use, examining several case studies illustrating the ATM protocols in action.

For this section, I selected the Hewlett-Packard Broadband Series Test System from HP's Telecom Test Division as the network analyzer (see Figure 10-1). This analyzer has a modular architecture, and can be configured with any combination of the following physical interfaces: SONET/SDH (155 Mbps and 622 Mbps), ATM cell-based (155 Mbps), DS3, 4B/5B TAXI, High-Speed Serial Interface (HSSI), and E3 (34 Mbps). It supports a wide range of protocol decodes, including PLCP, ATM, AAL, and SMDS.

If you are not familiar with the HP Test System's display, some explanation is in order. The first line of the display shows the protocol layer being decoded, such as DS3 PLCP, ATM, AAL3/4 SAR, AAL3/4 CPCS, or CLNAP. Subsequent lines show details of the header and payload for those layers. Details for the Header fields include subfield names and values; details for the Payload field are shown in hexadecimal format. Note that the HP analyzer indicates hexadecimal coding by preceding the value with a *0x*. Therefore, a 0xF6 on the analyzer printout would be equivalent to the F6H format for hexadecimal notation used throughout this text.

Figure 10-1. Hewlett-Packard Broadband Test System *(Courtesy Hewlett-Packard Company)*

For all case studies in this chapter, the HP analyzer was connected to a DS3 interface, as shown in Figure 10-2.

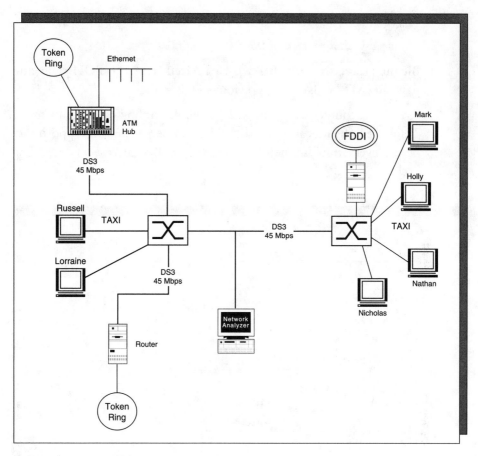

Figure 10-2. Analyzing an ATM network

10.1 The DS3 Physical Layer Convergence Procedure

The PLCP fills the DS3 frame format with data before transmission at 44.736 Mbps. Each frame contains 48 octets of header information, twelve 53-octet ATM cells, and 13 to 14 nibbles of trailer information, and is transmitted in 125 microseconds (see Figure 10-3). With overhead, the maximum throughput for ATM cells is 40.704 Mbps. The overhead octets defined in Bellcore's TA-NWT-001112 are as follows:

A1: Framing, with a pattern of 11110110 (F6H)

A2: Framing, with a pattern of 00101000 (28H)

B1: Bit interleaved parity (BIP-8), calculated over the POH field and payload (ATM cells) of the previous PLCP frame

C1: Cycle/stuff counter, which provides a nibble-stuffing opportunity and a Trailer length indicator for the PLCP frame. A stuffing opportunity occurs every third frame of a 3-frame (or 375-microsecond) stuffing cycle.

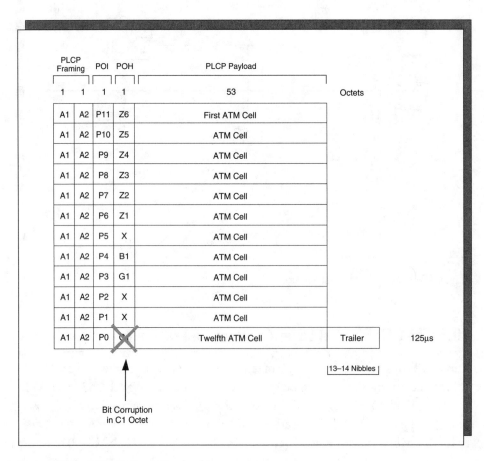

Figure 10-3. DS3 PLCP Frame Overhead Error

C1 values are:

C1 octet	Frame phase	Trailer length
11111111 (FFH)	1	13
00000000 (00H)	2	14
01100110 (66H)	3 (no stuff)	13
10011001 (99H)	3 (stuff)	14

So, the trailer is 13 nibbles long in the first 125-microsecond frame, 14 nibbles long in the second, and 13 or 14 nibbles long in the third frame, depending on whether or not there has been stuffing for frequency adjustment.

G1:   PLCP path status, which conveys the received PLCP status and performance to the transmitter at the other end of the link. The G1 octet has three subfields: one 4-bit Far End Block Error (BEBE), a 1-bit Yellow indication, and three reserved bits.

P0-P11:   Path overhead identifier, which indexes the adjacent POH octet. The coding of the POI octets are:

POI	POI Code	Associated POH
P11	00101100 (2CH)	Z6
P10	00101001 (29H)	Z5
P9	00100101 (25H)	Z4
P8	00100000 (20H)	Z3
P7	00011100 (1CH)	Z2
P6	00011001 (19H)	Z1
P5	00010101 (15H)	X
P4	00010000 (10H)	B1

P3	00001101 (0DH)	G1
P2	00001000 (08H)	X
P1	00000100 (04H)	X
P0	00000001 (01H)	C1

Z1-Z6:   Growth octets, reserved for future use and set to 00000000.

This case study shows the details of a PLCP frame containing 12 ATM cells.

Trace 10-1 shows the contents of each ATM cell. Each cell printout includes 4 header octets, and 48 payload octets. The last line of the trace file shows the contents of the PLCP trailer. In this case, an error occurs on the transmission line, and the C1 octet (the cycle/stuff counter) is invalid. Note that the value of C1 (67H) is identified as an error, and is invalid according to the description above.

Trace 10-1. DS3 PLCP overhead error

HP Broadband Series Tester Capture Data Record

Port 9:1 DS3 PLCP

Header: A1=0xF6 A2=0x28 P11=0x2C Z6=0x00
Payload: 00 00 00 01 52 6A 6A 6A 6A 6A 6A 6A 6A 6A 6A 6A
6A 6A 6A 6A 6A 6A 6A 6A 6A 6A 6A 6A 6A 6A 6A
6A 6A 6A 6A 6A 6A 6A 6A 6A 6A 6A 6A 6A 6A 6A
6A 6A 6A 6A 6A

Header: A1=0xF6 A2=0x28 P10=0x29 Z5=0x00
Payload: 00 A0 03 20 C2 4A 01 00 01 00 54 00 00 00 00 00
  00 00 00 00 00 00 00 00 00 00 00 00 00 00 00 00
  00 00 00 00 00 00 00 00 00 00 00 00 00 00 00 00
  00 00 00 10 29

Header: A1=0xF6 A2=0x28 P9=0x25 Z4=0x00
Payload: 00 A0 03 20 C2 82 01 00 01 00 54 C1 40 35 55 12
   12 FF FF C1 40 34 62 45 45 FF FF 00 0B 00 00 00
   00 00 00 00 00 00 00 00 00 00 00 FF 83 DF 17 32
   09 4E D1 B3 5F

Header: A1=0xF6 A2=0x28 P8=0x20 Z3=0x00
Payload: 00 A0 03 20 C2 06 01 E7 CD 8A 91 C6 D5 C4 C4 40
   21 18 4E 55 86 F4 DC 8A 15 A7 EC 92 DF 93 53 30
   18 CA 34 BF A2 C7 59 67 8F BA 0D 6D D8 2D 7D 36
   C3 E6 5E B0 32

Header: A1=0xF6 A2=0x28 P7=0x1C Z2=0x00
Payload: 00 A0 03 20 C2 4A 01 00 01 00 54 00 00 00 00 00
   00 00 00 00 00 00 00 00 00 00 00 00 00 00 00 00
   00 00 00 00 00 00 00 00 00 00 00 00 00 00 00 00
   00 00 00 10 29

Header: A1=0xF6 A2=0x28 P6=0x19 Z1=0x00
Payload: 00 00 00 01 52 6A 6A 6A 6A 6A 6A 6A 6A 6A 6A 6A
   6A 6A 6A 6A 6A 6A 6A 6A 6A 6A 6A 6A 6A 6A 6A 6A
   6A 6A 6A 6A 6A 6A 6A 6A 6A 6A 6A 6A 6A 6A 6A 6A
   6A 6A 6A 6A 6A

Header: A1=0xF6 A2=0x28 P5=0x15 X=0x00
Payload: 00 A0 03 20 C2 82 01 00 01 00 54 C1 40 35 55 12
   12 FF FF C1 40 34 62 45 45 FF FF 00 0B 00 00 00
   00 00 00 00 00 00 00 00 00 00 00 FF 83 DF 17 32
   09 4E D1 B3 5F

Header: A1=0xF6 A2=0x28 P4=0x10 B1=0x12
Payload: 00 A0 03 20 C2 06 01 E7 CD 8A 91 C6 D5 C4 C4 40
   21 18 4E 55 86 F4 DC 8A 15 A7 EC 92 DF 93 53 30
   18 CA 34 BF A2 C7 59 67 8F BA 0D 6D D8 2D 7D 36
   C3 E6 5E B0 32

Header: A1=0xF6 A2=0x28 P3=0x0D G1=0x00
    FEBE=0 Yellow signal=0 Link status signal=connected

Payload: 00 A0 03 20 C2 4A 01 00 01 00 54 00 00 00 00 00
    00 00 00 00 00 00 00 00 00 00 00 00 00 00 00 00
    00 00 00 00 00 00 00 00 00 00 00 00 00 00 00 00
    00 00 00 10 29

Header: A1=0xF6 A2=0x28 P2=0x08 X=0x00
Payload: 00 A0 03 20 C2 82 01 00 01 00 54 C1 40 35 55 12
    12 FF FF C1 40 34 62 45 45 FF FF 00 0B 00 00 00
    00 00 00 00 00 00 00 00 00 00 00 FF 83 DF 17 32
    09 4E D1 B3 5F

Header: A1=0xF6 A2=0x28 P1=0x04 X=0x00
Payload: 00 00 00 01 52 6A 6A 6A 6A 6A 6A 6A 6A 6A 6A 6A
    6A 6A 6A 6A 6A 6A 6A 6A 6A 6A 6A 6A 6A 6A 6A 6A
    6A 6A 6A 6A 6A 6A 6A 6A 6A 6A 6A 6A 6A 6A 6A 6A
    6A 6A 6A 6A 6A

Header: A1=0xF6 A2=0x28 P0=0x01 C1= 0x67
ERROR: The C1 octet is invalid
Payload: 00 A0 03 20 C2 06 01 E7 CD 8A 91 C6 D5 C4 C4 40
    21 18 4E 55 86 F4 DC 8A 15 A7 EC 92 DF 93 53 30
    18 CA 34 BF A2 C7 59 67 8F BA 0D 6D D8 2D 7D 36
    C3 E6 5E B0 32
Trailer: 0x C C C C C C C C C C C C

10.2 AAL1: Locating a Missing Cell

To verify how the ATM devices being tested will respond to AAL protocol errors, the analyst studies traffic using AAL1, AAL3/4, and AAL5. In this example, test data, consisting of an alternating pattern of ones and zeros, 1010...10, or AAAA...AAH, is sent over AAL1. One of the cells is discovered missing. Let's see how AAL1 identifies this problem.

The transmitted data is divided into eight AAL1_SAR_PDUs, which are passed to the ATM layer for transmission in eight ATM cells (see Figure 10-4). The analyzer output shows each ATM header (5 octets), and the corresponding ATM payload (48 octets). Within each payload, the first octet contains the AAL1_SAR_PDU header, and the remaining 47 octets contain the user data (AAAA...AAH).

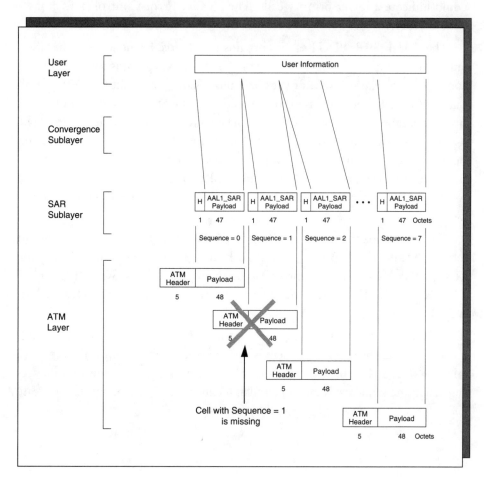

Figure 10-4. Missing AAL1_SAR_PDU

The top of Trace 10-2, just below the time stamp 14:02:40.34404920, shows the ATM header details. The Generic Flow Control (GFC) = 0, the Virtual Path Identifier (VPI) = 1, and the Virtual Channel Identifier (VCI) = 5. The Payload Type (PT) field has a value of 000, indicating a User data cell with no congestion, and an SDU type (or user indication) of zero. The Cell Loss Priority (CLP) field has a value of zero, indicating a higher priority cell (a CLP = 1 would indicate a lower priority cell). The Header Error Control (HEC) has a value of 40H.

The AAL1_SAR_PDU header contains two fields, Sequence Number (SN) and Sequence Number Protection (SNP). The SN field contains two subfields, a Convergence Sublayer Indicator (CSI) = 0 and a Sequence Count (SC) = 0. (Recall that the CSI field could be used for a Residual Time Stamp, or RTS. But not in this case because the values of CSI in each cell have the same value of zero.) The SC field has a value of zero in the first cell, a value of two in the second cell, and then increments from three to seven. Note that the value SC = 1 is not found, indicating a missing cell. The SNP field, a CRC-3, has the value of zero in the first cell, six in the next cell, and so on. The Parity bit is off (P = 0) in the first cell, and on (P = 1) in the next cell.

If you combine the four fields (CSI, SC, CRC, and P) into one octet, you can derive the value of the AAL1_SAR_PDU header, shown as the first octet in the ATM payload. Using the second cell as an example, CSI = 0, SC = 010, CRC-3 = 110, and P = 1. This results in a binary value of 00101101, or 2DH, as shown in the payload.

You could make a similar analysis for the ATM and AAL1_SAR_PDU headers in each cell. The one key element is the Sequence Count field, with respective values of 0, 2, 3, 4, 5, 6, and 7. Because SC = 1 is missing, you know that the second cell in the sequence is missing, which means that 47 bits of constant bit rate (CBR) data from the user layer are also missing.

Trace 10-2. Diagnosing a missing AAL1_SAR_PDU

HP Broadband Series Tester Capture Data Record
14:02:40.34404920 ATM
Header: Generic Flow Control   0
        Virtual Path Identifier   1
        Virtual Channel Identifier   5
        Payload Type   0 (User Data, No Cong, UserInd=0)
        Cell Loss Priority   0 (Higher Priority)
        Header Error Control   0x40
Payload: 00 AA AA AA AA AA AA AA AA AA AA AA AA AA AA AA
         AA AA AA AA AA AA AA AA AA AA AA AA AA AA AA AA
         AA AA AA AA AA AA AA AA AA AA AA AA AA AA AA AA
14:02:40.34404920 AAL-1
Header: Sequence Number
        Convergence Sublayer Ind.   0
        Sequence Count   0
        Sequence Number Protection
        Control Bits (CRC3)   0
        Parity Bit   0
Payload: AA AA AA AA AA AA AA AA AA AA AA ...

14:02:40.34405950 ATM
Header: Generic Flow Contro   0
        Virtual Path Identifier   1
        Virtual Channel Identifier   5
        Payload Type   0 (User Data, No Cong, UserInd=0)
        Cell Loss Priority   0 (Higher Priority)
        Header Error Control   0x40
Payload: 2D AA AA AA AA AA AA AA AA AA AA AA AA AA AA AA
         AA AA AA AA AA AA AA AA AA AA AA AA AA AA AA AA
         AA AA AA AA AA AA AA AA AA AA AA AA AA AA AA AA

```
14:02:40.34405950 AAL-1
  Header: Sequence Number
                  Convergence Sublayer Ind.    0
                  Sequence Count               2
                  Sequence Number Protection
                  Control Bits (CRC3)          6
                  Parity Bit                   1
  Payload: AA AA AA AA AA AA AA AA AA AA ...
14:02:40.34406990 ATM
  Header: Generic Flow Control        0
          Virtual Path Identifier      1
          Virtual Channel Identifier   5
          Payload Type                 0 (User Data, No Cong, UserInd=0)
          Cell Loss Priority           0 (Higher Priority)
          Header Error Control         0x40
  Payload: 3A AA AA AA AA AA AA AA AA AA AA AA AA AA AA AA
           AA AA AA AA AA AA AA AA AA AA AA AA AA AA AA AA
           AA AA AA AA AA AA AA AA AA AA AA AA AA AA AA AA
14:02:40.34406990 AAL-1
  Header: Sequence Number
                  Convergence Sublayer Ind.    0
                  Sequence Count               3
                  Sequence Number Protection
                  Control Bits (CRC3)          5
                  Parity Bit                   0
  Payload: AA AA AA AA AA AA AA AA AA AA ...


14:02:40.34408020 ATM
  Header: Generic Flow Control        0
          Virtual Path Identifier      1
          Virtual Channel Identifier   5
          Payload Type                 0 (User Data, No Cong, UserInd=0)
          Cell Loss Priority           0 (Higher Priority)
          Header Error Control         0x40
  Payload: 4E AA AA AA AA AA AA AA AA AA AA AA AA AA AA AA
           AA AA AA AA AA AA AA AA AA AA AA AA AA AA AA AA
           AA AA AA AA AA AA AA AA AA AA AA AA AA AA AA AA
```

14:02:40.34408020 AAL-1
 Header: Sequence Number
            Convergence Sublayer Ind. 0
            Sequence Count   4
         Sequence Number Protection
            Control Bits (CRC3)   7
            Parity Bit   0
 Payload: AA AA AA AA AA AA AA AA AA AA ...

14:02:40.34409050 ATM
 Header: Generic Flow Control   0
         Virtual Path Identifier   1
         Virtual Channel Identifier 5
         Payload Type   0 (User Data, No Cong, UserInd=0)
         Cell Loss Priority   0 (Higher Priority)
         Header Error Control   0x40
 Payload: 59 AA AA AA AA AA AA AA AA AA AA AA AA AA AA AA
          AA AA AA AA AA AA AA AA AA AA AA AA AA AA AA AA
          AA AA AA AA AA AA AA AA AA AA AA AA AA AA AA AA
14:02:40.34409050 AAL-1
 Header: Sequence Number
            Convergence Sublayer Ind.   0
            Sequence Count   5
         Sequence Number Protection
            Control Bits (CRC3)   4
            Parity Bit   1
 Payload: AA AA AA AA AA AA AA AA AA AA ...

14:02:40.34410080 ATM
 Header: Generic Flow Control   0
         Virtual Path Identifier   1
         Virtual Channel Identifier 5
         Payload Type   0 (User Data, No Cong, UserInd=0)
         Cell Loss Priority   0 (Higher Priority)
    Header Error Control   0x40
 Payload: 63 AA AA AA AA AA AA AA AA AA AA AA AA AA AA AA
          AA AA AA AA AA AA AA AA AA AA AA AA AA AA AA AA
          AA AA AA AA AA AA AA AA AA AA AA AA AA AA AA AA

14:02:40.34410080 AAL-1
Header: Sequence Number
        Convergence Sublayer Ind.   0
        Sequence Count   6
        Sequence Number Protection
        Control Bits (CRC3)   1
        Parity Bit   1
Payload: AA AA AA AA AA AA AA AA AA AA ...

14:02:40.34411110 ATM
Header: Generic Flow Control   0
        Virtual Path Identifier   1
        Virtual Channel Identifier 5
        Payload Type   0 (User Data, No Cong, UserInd=0)
        Cell Loss Priority   0 (Higher Priority)
        Header Error Control   0x40
Payload: 74 AA AA AA AA AA AA AA AA AA AA AA AA AA AA AA
        AA AA AA AA AA AA AA AA AA AA AA AA AA AA AA AA
        AA AA AA AA AA AA AA AA AA AA AA AA AA AA AA AA

14:02:40.34411110 AAL-1
Header: Sequence Number
        Convergence Sublayer Ind.   0
        Sequence Count   7
        Sequence Number Protection
        Control Bits (CRC3)   2
        Parity Bit   0
Payload: AA AA AA AA AA AA AA AA AA AA ...

10.3 AAL3/4: Identifying SAR Sublayer Errors

The next example (see Trace 10-3) looks at the AAL3/4 process, examining the effects that corruption at the Segmentation and Reassembly layer have on the overall data-transfer process. In this case, 168 octets of user information is sent in the payload of one AAL3/4_CPCS_PDU. This results in four AAL3/4_SAR segments, and, therefore, four ATM cells (see Figure 10-5).

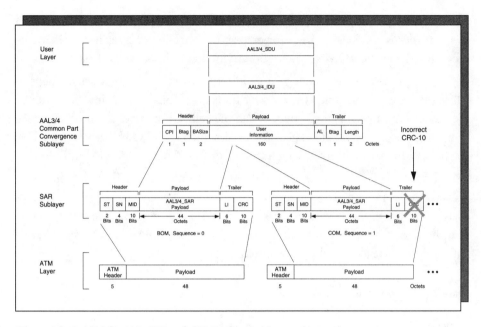

Figure 10-5. AAL3/4_SAR_PDU with SAR Trailer error

The ATM header fields, including the GFC, VPI/VCI, PT, and so on, are identical to those used in the previous case study. But the overhead associated with AAL3/4 is more extensive than that found in AAL1 because AAL3/4 includes more rigorous error control.

The AAL3/4_SAR header (2 octets) includes three fields. The Segment Type (ST) field, 2 bits long, defines one of four segments: the Beginning of Message (BOM) with ST = 10; the COM with ST = 00; the EOM with ST = 01; and a Single Segment Message (SSM) with ST = 11. This amount of user information requires one BOM, two COMs, and one EOM. The SN, zero through three, keeps the AAL3/4_SAR_PDUs in order. The multiplexing identifer (MID), with a value of one, associates all of the AAL3/4_SAR_PDUs from the same message.

The AAL3/4_SAR trailer (2 octets) includes a Length Indicator field (6 bits), which carries the length of the AAL3/4_SAR_PDU. For BOM and COM segments, the length must be 44 octets; and for EOM segments, the length must be a multiple of 4 octets between 4 and 44 octets (4, 8, 12, ..., 44). Note that the

EOM segment has a Length = 36 octets, which is a valid number. The second field in the trailer is a CRC-10, used for error control. The analyzer indicates a correct CRC-10 in the BOM segment, but an incorrect value in the first COM.

You can see the effects of the invalid CRC-10 in the first COM segment in subsequent segments. When the receiver finds the CRC-10 to be invalid, that cell (Sequence Number 1) is discarded. When the cell is discarded, the next sequence number (2) becomes invalid. The fourth cell, which is an EOM, arrives next. This further confuses the receiver, which thinks an EOM occurred before a BOM.

The net result is that corruption of one field within one cell caused the entire message to be invalid. To recover, the receiver would have to request a retransmission of that message from its originator. From this example, we can conclude that the rigorous error control incorporated into AAL3/4 provides a solid verification of the integrity of the transmitted message.

Trace 10-3. Effects of a SAR trailer error

HP Broadband Series Tester Capture Data Record
```
13:24:48.81792030 ATM
   Header: Generic Flow Control        0
           Virtual Path Identifier      1
           Virtual Channel Identifier   5
           Payload Type                 0 (User Data, No Cong, UserInd=0)
           Cell Loss Priority           0 (Higher Priority)
           Header Error Control  0x40
  Payload: 80 01 00 01 00 A0 C1 40 35 55 12 12 FF FF C1 40
           34 62 45 45 FF FF 01 0B 00 00 00 00 00 00 00 00
           00 00 00 00 00 00 00 01 02 03 04 05 06 07 B3 6A
13:24:48.81792030 AAL-3/4 SAR
   Header: Segment Type                 2 (BOM)
           Sequence Number              0
           Multiplexing Identifier      1
  Payload: 00 01 00 A0 C1 40 35 55 12 12 FF FF C1 40 34 62
           45 45 FF FF 01 0B 00 00 00 00 00 00 00 00 00 00
           00 00 00 00 00 01 02 03 04 05 06 07
```

Trailer: Length   44
          CRC10   0x36A

13:24:48.81793170 ATM
  Header: Generic Flow Control   0
          Virtual Path Identifier   1
          Virtual Channel Identifier 5
          Payload Type   0 (User Data, No Cong, UserInd=0)
          Cell Loss Priority   0 (Higher Priority)
          Header Error Control   0x40
  Payload: 04 01 08 09 0A 0B 0C 0D 0E 0F 10 11 12 13 14 15
           16 17 18 19 1A 1B 1C 1D 1E 1F 20 21 22 23 24 25
           26 27 28 29 2A 2B 2C 2D 2E 2F 30 31 32 33 B3 44
13:24:48.81793170 AAL-3/4 SAR
  Header: Segment Type   0 (COM)
          Sequence Number   1
          Multiplexing Identifier   1
  Payload: 08 09 0A 0B 0C 0D 0E 0F 10 11 12 13 14 15 16 17
           18 19 1A 1B 1C 1D 1E 1F 20 21 22 23 24 25 26 27
           28 29 2A 2B 2C 2D 2E 2F 30 31 32 33
  Trailer: Length   44
           CRC10   0x344
  ERROR: CRC10 is incorrect

13:24:48.81794210 ATM
  Header: Generic Flow Control   0
          Virtual Path Identifier   1
          Virtual Channel Identifier 5
          Payload Type   0 (User Data, No Cong, UserInd=0)
          Cell Loss Priority   0 (Higher Priority)
          Header Error Control   0x40
  Payload: 08 01 34 35 36 37 38 39 3A 3B 3C 3D 3E 3F 40 41
           42 43 44 45 46 47 48 49 4A 4B 4C 4D 4E 4F 50 51
           52 53 54 55 56 57 58 59 5A 5B 5C 5D 5E 5F B3 6B

13:24:48.81794210 AAL-3/4 SAR
   Header: Segment Type   0 (COM)
            Sequence Number   2
            Multiplexing Identifier 1
   Payload: 34 35 36 37 38 39 3A 3B 3C 3D 3E 3F 40 41 42 43
            44 45 46 47 48 49 4A 4B 4C 4D 4E 4F 50 51 52 53
            54 55 56 57 58 59 5A 5B 5C 5D 5E 5F
   Trailer: Length   44
            CRC10   0x36B
   PROTOCOL ERROR: Invalid sequence number

13:24:48.81795240 ATM
   Header: Generic Flow Control   0
            Virtual Path Identifier   1
            Virtual Channel Identifier 5
            Payload Type   0 (User Data, No Cong, UserInd=0)
            Cell Loss Priority   0 (Higher Priority)
            Header Error Control   0x40
   Payload: 4C 01 60 61 62 63 64 65 66 67 68 69 6A 6B 6C 6D
            6E 6F 70 71 72 73 74 75 76 77 78 79 7A 00 CD 9A
            E6 DD 00 01 00 A0 00 00 00 00 00 00 00 00 90 79
13:24:48.81795240 AAL-3/4 SAR
   Header: Segment Type   1 (EOM)
            Sequence Number   3
            Multiplexing Identifier 1
   Payload: 60 61 62 63 64 65 66 67 68 69 6A 6B 6C 6D 6E 6F
            70 71 72 73 74 75 76 77 78 79 7A 00 CD 9A E6 DD
            00 01 00 A0 00 00 00 00 00 00 00 00
   Trailer: Length   36
            CRC10   0x079
   PROTOCOL ERROR: EOM before BOM

10.4 AAL3/4: Identifying Higher Layer Errors

The next case study builds on the previous AAL3/4 example, and illustrates the effect that a higher layer protocol problem has on the transmission of user information.

For this example, shown in Trace 10-4, AAL3/4 is sending Connectionless Network Access Protocol (CLNAP) traffic, which is similar to SMDS (see Figure 10-6). This message also requires four AAL3/4_SAR_PDU segments: one BOM, two COMs, and one EOM, with lengths of 44, 44, 44, and 36 octets, respectively. No errors are detected at the SAR layer, as evidenced by the incrementing sequence numbers (zero, one, two, and three) and the correct CRC-10 fields.

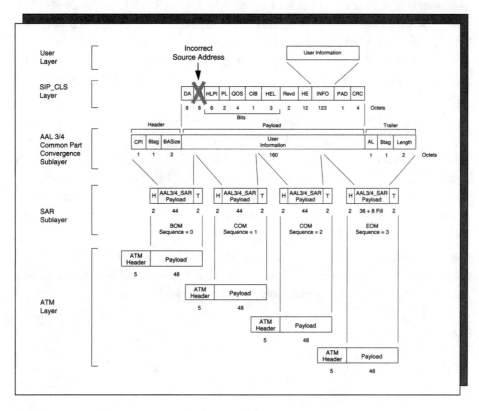

Figure 10-6. AAL3/4_CPCS_PDU with SIP_CLS error

ANALYZING BROADBAND NETWORKS

A decode of the AAL3/4 Common Part Convergence Sublayer (CPCS) header and trailer follows the EOM segment. The AAL3/4_CPCS header (4 octets) includes three fields. The Common Part Indicator (CPI) = 00H indicates that the counting unit is the octet. The BTag field = 01H matches the End Tag (ETag) field in the trailer. The BAsize field = 160 octets indicates the amount of buffer space reserved at the receiver for this message. The values of this header, 00 01 00 A0H, are found in the first line of the BOM payload. Following the CPCS header is the 160 octets of user information, which is distributed between the BOM, COM, and EOM segments.

The AAL3/4_CPCS trailer has an Alignment field (1 octet), filled with 00H; the ETag, as discussed above; and the Length field. Note that the Length field (160 octets) does not equal the sum of the AAL3/4_SAR_PDU payloads (44 + 44 + 44 + 36 = 168 octets). The difference is in the AAL3/4_CPCS header and trailer, which use four octets each. So the Length field measures the length of the AAL3/4_CPCS_PDU payload, not the length of the AAL3/4_CPCS_PDU. The values of the trailer, 00 01 00 A0H, are found at the end of EOM payload, just before the 8 octets of fill.

The CLNAP (SMDS) header begins with the Destination Address field containing the value C14035551212FFFF. This is noted as a valid address, and because it begins with an Address Type of CH (1100 binary), we know that this is an individual address. The other permissible value is EH (1110 binary), which represents a group address. The analyzer flags the Source Address as an invalid address, because it begins with a FFH. The rest of the CLNAP header and trailer do not indicate any errors.

This case study has illustrated that the user information (CLNAP, in this example) is passed transparently by the AAL3/4 processes. Not until the user information reaches the intended receiver is it checked for protocol correctness.

378

Trace 10-4. Effects of a higher layer (CLNAP) error

HP Broadband Series Tester Capture Data Record
13:03:18.11440800 ATM

Header:	Generic Flow Control	0
	Virtual Path Identifier	1
	Virtual Channel Identifier	5
	Payload Type	0 (User Data, No Cong, UserInd=0)
	Cell Loss Priority	0 (Higher Priority)
	Header Error Control	0x40

Payload: 80 01 00 01 00 A0 C1 40 35 55 12 12 FF FF FF 40
34 62 45 45 FF FF 01 0B 00 00 00 00 00 00 00 00
00 00 00 00 00 00 00 01 02 03 04 05 06 07 B1 7D

13:03:18.11440800 AAL-3/4 SAR

Header:	Segment Type	2 (BOM)
	Sequence Number	0
	Multiplexing Identifier	1

Payload: 00 01 00 A0 C1 40 35 55 12 12 FF FF FF 40 34 62
45 45 FF FF 01 0B 00 00 00 00 00 00 00 00 00 00
00 00 00 00 00 01 02 03 04 05 06 07

Trailer:	Length	44
	CRC10	0x17D

13:03:18.11441840 ATM

Header:	Generic Flow Control	0
	Virtual Path Identifier	1
	Virtual Channel Identifier	5
	Payload Type	0 (User Data, No Cong, UserInd=0)
	Cell Loss Priority	0 (Higher Priority)
	Header Error Control	0x40

Payload: 04 01 08 09 0A 0B 0C 0D 0E 0F 10 11 12 13 14 15
16 17 18 19 1A 1B 1C 1D 1E 1F 20 21 22 23 24 25
26 27 28 29 2A 2B 2C 2D 2E 2F 30 31 32 33 B3 16

13:03:18.11441840 AAL-3/4 SAR
  Header: Segment Type   0 (COM)
             Sequence Number   1
             Multiplexing Identifier   1
  Payload: 08 09 0A 0B 0C 0D 0E 0F 10 11 12 13 14 15 16 17
             18 19 1A 1B 1C 1D 1E 1F 20 21 22 23 24 25 26 27
             28 29 2A 2B 2C 2D 2E 2F 30 31 32 33
  Trailer: Length   44
             CRC10   0x316

13:03:18.11442870 ATM
  Header: Generic Flow Control   0
             Virtual Path Identifier   1
             Virtual Channel Identifier 5
             Payload Type   0 (User Data, No Cong, UserInd=0)
             Cell Loss Priority   0 (Higher Priority)
             Header Error Control   0x40
  Payload: 08 01 34 35 36 37 38 39 3A 3B 3C 3D 3E 3F 40 41
             42 43 44 45 46 47 48 49 4A 4B 4C 4D 4E 4F 50 51
             52 53 54 55 56 57 58 59 5A 5B 5C 5D 5E 5F B3 6B
13:03:18.11442870 AAL-3/4 SAR
  Header: Segment Type   0 (COM)
             Sequence Number   2
             Multiplexing Identifier   1
  Payload: 34 35 36 37 38 39 3A 3B 3C 3D 3E 3F 40 41 42 43
             44 45 46 47 48 49 4A 4B 4C 4D 4E 4F 50 51 52 53
             54 55 56 57 58 59 5A 5B 5C 5D 5E 5F
  Trailer: Length   44
             CRC10   0x36B

13:03:18.11443900 ATM

  Header: Generic Flow Control   0
             Virtual Path Identifier   1
             Virtual Channel Identifier   5
             Payload Type   0 (User Data, No Cong, UserInd=0)
             Cell Loss Priority   0 (Higher Priority)
             Header Error Control   0x40
  Payload: 4C 01 60 61 62 63 64 65 66 67 68 69 6A 6B 6C 6D
            6E 6F 70 71 72 73 74 75 76 77 78 79 7A 00 AF 0A
            0F 49 00 01 00 A0 00 00 00 00 00 00 00 00 93 90

13:03:18.11443900 AAL-3/4 SAR

  Header: Segment Type   1 (EOM)
             Sequence Number   3
             Multiplexing Identifier   1
  Payload: 60 61 62 63 64 65 66 67 68 69 6A 6B 6C 6D 6E 6F
            70 71 72 73 74 75 76 77 78 79 7A 00 AF 0A 0F 49
            00 01 00 A0 00 00 00 00 00 00 00 00
  Trailer: Length   36
             CRC10   0x390

13:03:18.11443900 AAL-3/4 CPCS

  Header: Common Part Indicator   0x00 (BAsize,payld len,Length=payld len)
             Beginning Tag   0x01
             Buffer Allocation Size   160
  Payload: C1 40 35 55 12 12 FF FF FF 40 34 62 45 45 FF FF
            01 0B 00 00 00 00 00 00 00 00 00 00 00 00 00 00
            00 01 02 03 04 05 06 07 08 09 0A 0B 0C 0D 0E 0F
            10 11 12 13 14 15 16 17 18 19 1A 1B 1C 1D 1E 1F
            20 21 22 23 24 25 26 27 28 29 2A 2B 2C 2D 2E 2F
            30 31 32 33 34 35 36 37 38 39 3A 3B 3C 3D 3E 3F
            40 41 42 43 44 45 46 47 48 49 4A 4B 4C 4D 4E 4F
            50 51 52 53 54 55 56 57 58 59 5A 5B 5C 5D 5E 5F
            60 61 62 63 64 65 66 67 68 69 6A 6B 6C 6D 6E 6F
            70 71 72 73 74 75 76 77 78 79 7A 00 AF 0A 0F 49
  Pad Characters   not present
  Trailer: Alignment   0x00
             End Tag   0x01
             Length   160

```
13:03:18.11443900 CLNAP
   Header: Destination Address        0xC14035551212FFFF
           Source Address             0xFF4034624545FFFF
    ERROR: Source address type is incorrect
           Higher Layer Protocol Id   0x00
           Pad Length                 1
           Quality Of Service         0x0
           CRC32 Indication Bit       0x1
           Reserved                   0x0000
           Header Extension Length    3 (32 bit words)
           Header Extension           0x00 00 00 00 00 00 00 00 00 00 00 00
  Payload: 00 01 02 03 04 05 06 07 08 09 0A 0B 0C 0D 0E 0F
           10 11 12 13 14 15 16 17 18 19 1A 1B 1C 1D 1E 1F
           20 21 22 23 24 25 26 27 28 29 2A 2B 2C 2D 2E 2F
           30 31 32 33 34 35 36 37 38 39 3A 3B 3C 3D 3E 3F
           40 41 42 43 44 45 46 47 48 49 4A 4B 4C 4D 4E 4F
           50 51 52 53 54 55 56 57 58 59 5A 5B 5C 5D 5E 5F
           60 61 62 63 64 65 66 67 68 69 6A 6B 6C 6D 6E 6F
           70 71 72 73 74 75 76 77 78 79 7A
   Pad Characters                     0x00
   Trailer: CRC32                     0xAF0A0F49
```

10.5 AAL5: Locating Missing Payload Information

The final case study looks at the protocol processes of AAL5, which are considered a subset of AAL3/4. In this example, the user information is divided into five ATM cells (see Figure 10-7). The contents of the user information consist of incrementing hexadecimal numbers: 00, 01, 02, 03, and so on, up to FF, for a total of 256 (16 * 16) octets.

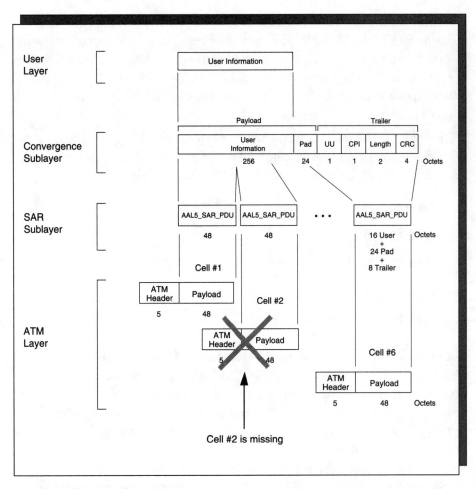

Figure 10-7. Missing AAL5_SAR_PDU

The ATM headers contain the same values for GFC, VPI/VCI, and so on that you have seen in the previous examples. Because AAL5 does not have a header, the payload of the first ATM cell contains 48 octets of user information: 00 01 02 … 2D, 2E, 2F. The second ATM cell contains 60 61 62 … 8D 8E 8F.

Likewise, the third and fourth cells contain 48 octets of data. The fifth cell contains F0 F1 F2 … FD FE FF, 24 octets of zeros, and eight octets containing 00 00 01 00 69 83 2E 15. These last eight octets are the AAL5 trailer, which consists of four fields. The User-User (UU) field = 00. The CPI = 00. The Length field = 0100H, or 256 decimal, which is incorrect. The CRC field is 69 83 2E 15, which is also incorrect.

Knowing that the user information was loaded with 256 octets before transmission, the analyst must determine why the Length and CRC fields were wrong. To find the answer, I looked at the payloads of the five cells:

Cell 1: 00 … 2F

Cell 2: 60 … 8F

Cell 3: 90 … BF

Cell 4: C0 … EF

Cell 5: F0 … FF, plus 24 octets of zeros

The sequence 30 … 5F (or 48 octets), which should have been received between Cell 1 and Cell 2, is missing. Because AAL5 has no cell-sequence number, the problem was only identified by the invalid Length and CRC values. Further analysis of the payload information, and the fact that the missing data (30 … 5F) was easy to identify, lead us to conclude that a cell was missing. Had the missing cell occurred under AAL1, the Sequence Count field in the AAL1 header would have identified the problem; with AAL3/4, the Sequence Number and the Segment Type fields would have assisted. As a result, you can conclude that the error control in AAL5 is not as rigorous as that in AAL3/4.

Trace 10-5. Effects of a missing AAL5_SAR_PDU

HP Broadband Series Tester Capture Data Record

    13:49:18.14378060 ATM

       Header: Generic Flow Control   0

               Virtual Path Identifier   1

               Virtual Channel Identifier   5

               Payload Type   0 (User Data, No Cong, UserInd=0)

               Cell Loss Priority   0 (Higher Priority)

               Header Error Control   0x40

     Payload: 00 01 02 03 04 05 06 07 08 09 0A 0B 0C 0D 0E 0F

              10 11 12 13 14 15 16 17 18 19 1A 1B 1C 1D 1E 1F

              20 21 22 23 24 25 26 27 28 29 2A 2B 2C 2D 2E 2F

    13:49:18.14379090 ATM

       Header: Generic Flow Control   0

               Virtual Path Identifier   1

               Virtual Channel Identifier   5

               Payload Type   0 (User Data, No Cong, UserInd=0)

               Cell Loss Priority   0 (Higher Priority)

               Header Error Control   0x40

     Payload: 60 61 62 63 64 65 66 67 68 69 6A 6B 6C 6D 6E 6F

              70 71 72 73 74 75 76 77 78 79 7A 7B 7C 7D 7E 7F

              80 81 82 83 84 85 86 87 88 89 8A 8B 8C 8D 8E 8F

   13:49:18.14380110 ATM

       Header: Generic Flow Control   0

               Virtual Path Identifier   1

               Virtual Channel Identifier   5

               Payload Type   0 (User Data, No Cong, UserInd=0)

               Cell Loss Priority   0 (Higher Priority)

               Header Error Control   0x40

     Payload: 90 91 92 93 94 95 96 97 98 99 9A 9B 9C 9D 9E 9F

              A0 A1 A2 A3 A4 A5 A6 A7 A8 A9 AA AB AC AD AE AF

              B0 B1 B2 B3 B4 B5 B6 B7 B8 B9 BA BB BC BD BE BF

13:49:18.14381150 ATM

Header: Generic Flow Control   0
        Virtual Path Identifier   1
        Virtual Channel Identifier 5
        Payload Type   0 (User Data, No Cong, UserInd=0)
        Cell Loss Priority   0 (Higher Priority)
        Header Error Control   0x40
Payload: C0 C1 C2 C3 C4 C5 C6 C7 C8 C9 CA CB CC CD CE CF
         D0 D1 D2 D3 D4 D5 D6 D7 D8 D9 DA DB DC DD DE DF
         E0 E1 E2 E3 E4 E5 E6 E7 E8 E9 EA EB EC ED EE EF

13:49:18.14382180 ATM

Header: Generic Flow Control   0
        Virtual Path Identifier   1
        Virtual Channel Identifier 5
        Payload Type   1 (User Data, No Cong, UserInd=1)
        Cell Loss Priority   0 (Higher Priority)
        Header Error Control   0x4E
Payload: F0 F1 F2 F3 F4 F5 F6 F7 F8 F9 FA FB FC FD FE FF
         00 00 00 00 00 00 00 00 00 00 00 00 00 00 00 00
         00 00 00 00 00 00 00 00 00 00 01 00 69 83 2E 15

13:49:18.14382180 AAL-5

Payload: 00 01 02 03 04 05 06 07 08 09 0A 0B 0C 0D 0E 0F
         10 11 12 13 14 15 16 17 18 19 1A 1B 1C 1D 1E 1F
         20 21 22 23 24 25 26 27 28 29 2A 2B 2C 2D 2E 2F
         60 61 62 63 64 65 66 67 68 69 6A 6B 6C 6D 6E 6F
         70 71 72 73 74 75 76 77 78 79 7A 7B 7C 7D 7E 7F
         80 81 82 83 84 85 86 87 88 89 8A 8B 8C 8D 8E 8F
         90 91 92 93 94 95 96 97 98 99 9A 9B 9C 9D 9E 9F
         A0 A1 A2 A3 A4 A5 A6 A7 A8 A9 AA AB AC AD AE AF
         B0 B1 B2 B3 B4 B5 B6 B7 B8 B9 BA BB BC BD BE BF
         C0 C1 C2 C3 C4 C5 C6 C7 C8 C9 CA CB CC CD CE CF
         D0 D1 D2 D3 D4 D5 D6 D7 D8 D9 DA DB DC DD DE DF
         E0 E1 E2 E3 E4 E5 E6 E7 E8 E9 EA EB EC ED EE EF
         F0 F1 F2 F3 F4 F5 F6 F7 F8 F9 FA FB FC FD FE FF
         00 00 00 00 00 00 00 00 00 00 00 00 00 00 00 00
         00 00 00 00 00 00 00 00

```
        Pad Characters   <none>
        Trailer:  User-User Indication      0x00
                  Common Part Indicator     0x00
                  Length                    256
        ERROR:  Length Field is incorrect
                  CRC32                     0x69832E15
        ERROR:  CRC32 is incorrect
```

10.6 Possible ATM Error Conditions

Below are some general guidelines to help you analyze the ATM layer, AAL3/4, and AAL5 protocols [10-1]. Refer to Figures 9-4, 9-7, 9-9, and 9-11, respectively, as you study the following sections.

10.6.1 ATM layer analysis guidelines

If the cell is assigned, check that the VCI on the user side of the UNI is not zero (unassigned cells will have a VCI of zero). Verify that the HEC is correct.

For ATM Layer Management PDUs (OAM cells), look for:

▼ an invalid OAM cell type

▼ an invalid OAM function type

▼ an invalid OAM CRC-10.

10.6.2 AAL3/4 CPCS Analysis Guidelines

1. Verify that the value of the CPI field is not zero.

2. Verify consistency between the BTag and ETag values.

3. Verify that the BAsize field is large enough to contain the PDU.

4. Verify that the size of the PDU is not less than the minimum (8 octets) or larger than the maximum (65,544 octets). Note that the maximum is derived by adding the payload (65,535 octets), the pad (1 octet), the header (4 octets), and the trailer (4 octets), which aligns the PDU to a multiple of 4 octets.

5. Verify that the Pad length is correct.

6. Verify that the value of the Alignment field value is zero.

10.6.3 AAL3/4 SAR analysis guidelines

1. The Segment Type field should not have an unexpected BOM, a COM before a BOM, or an EOM before a BOM.

2. Verify that the Sequence Number is correct.

3. Look for an Abort_SAR_PDU from I.363 Section 4.3.1.2.2, which terminates the reassembly process, but does not start a new reassembly process. The Abort_SAR_PDU is coded with an ST = EOM, Payload = 0, and Length = 63.

4. Some errors are similar to those we discussed in Section 7.5 for SIP Layer 2, and are described in I.363. These include: too many reassemblies, reassembly timeout, and reassembly length overrun. For the "too many reassemblies" error, the number of reassemblies is a negotiated parameter, with a default of one. (Recall that for SIP Layer 2, one or 16 concurrent reassemblies are supported.)

Analysis guidelines for the Length Indication field:

1. The value must be a multiple of 4 octets.

2. The value must be 44 octets for BOM and COMs.

3. The value must be between 4 and 44 octets for EOMs.

4. The value must be between 8 and 44 octets for SSMs.

5. Verify that the CRC-10 value is correct.

10.6.4 AAL5 Analysis Guidelines

1. Verify that the size of the PDU is not less than the minimum (48 octets) or larger than the maximum (65,568 octets). Note that the maximum is derived by adding the payload (65,535 octets), the pad (25 octets), and the trailer (8 octets), which aligns the PDU to a multiple of 48 octets.

2. Verify that the Pad length is correct, so the AAL5_PDU aligns on a 48-octet boundary.

3. The UU is transparent to the protocol, so all codings are valid.

4. The value of the CPI field should be zero, as all other values are for further study, per I.363, Section 6.3.2.1.2d.

5. Verify that the value of the Length field is correct.

6. Verify that the CRC-32 value is correct.

This chapter concludes our study of ATM networks and protocols. The following chapter investigates the management of broadband networks.

10.7 References

[10-1]   Andrew Scott. Personal communication, March 1994.

 # Managing Broadband Networks

This concluding chapter discusses the management of frame relay, SMDS, and ATM networks, as well as the integration of these management schemes into other enterprise-wide network management systems.

11.1 SNMP-Based Network Management

The Simple Network Management Protocol (SNMP) has been used extensively to manage LANs and distributed networks. SNMP is based on an agent/manager paradigm. Agents reside in internetworking devices such as hosts, routers, and servers. These agents keep track of the activity of numerous managed objects within their system. The management system, or network management console, requests information from or sends data to the agents (see Figure 11–1).

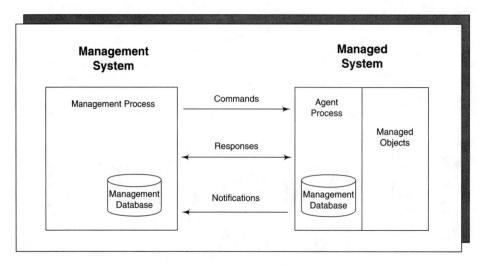

Figure 11–1. Network manager/agent relationships

SNMP is also part of the Internet Network Management Framework (NMF), a four-part solution for managing Internet- connected hosts and systems. The four sections of the NMF are the Structure of Management Information (SMI), Management Information Bases (MIBs), the protocol (SNMP), and administrative and architectural issues. The SMI provides a way to describe and name the managed objects. The MIBs delineate the managed objects and organize them into groups for ease of use. SNMP lets the manager communicate with the agents. This communication involves reading the values of the objects within the MIB and altering these values as appropriate (in other words, managing the objects).

11.1.1 The Structure of Management Information

Internetworks are comprised of numerous elements, such as workstations, servers, network interfaces, wiring hubs, and communications lines. Each has a number of components, such as disk drives or serial ports. Each component, in turn, has parts; for example, a serial port has characteristics that include the size and shape of the connector, the maximum allowable transmission rate, and the electrical characteristics of the attached cable.

The SMI names and organizes these objects to allow easy access from the network management console. For this data transfer to occur, both the agent and the console must agree on syntax for that communication. There are two types of syntax: abstract syntax defines how data is stored in each device and transfer syntax describes the form these messages take during their physical transmission between agent and manager. For SNMP-based internetworks, the SMI is derived from a message-description language known as Abstract Syntax Notation One (ASN.1). The abstract syntax is defined in ISO 8824 [11–1], and the transfer syntax, called the Basic Encoding Rules (BER), is defined in ISO 8825 [11–2].

Each managed object has a name, specified by an object identifier, that uniquely identifies it. The object identifier is a sequence of integers separated by periods.

The numerical sequence is described as a tree having a root with several branches directly attached, which may in turn connect to other branches. The complete structure of roots, branches, sub- branches, and leaves describes the objects within a particular MIB, their relationships, among other things much like a diagram would.

The root does not have (or need) a designation. The three branches immediately underneath are designated with a numeric value. The ISO administers the branch labeled one; the ITU-T (formerly CCITT) is the branch labeled zero. ISO and ITU-T jointly administer the branch labeled two (see Figure 11–2). Starting from the ISO branch, we can derive a path to the Internet-defined MIB objects. That path would consist of the ISO branch, the identified organization (org) branch, the Department of Defense (dod) branch, the management (mgmt) branch, and finally the branch designated for the Internet-standard MIBs (mib), as defined by RFC 1442 [11–3] (previously RFC 1155 for SNMPv1). In shorthand notation, the path to the MIB would be {1.3.6.1.2.1}. Under the Internet standard MIB are a number of groups containing managed objects.

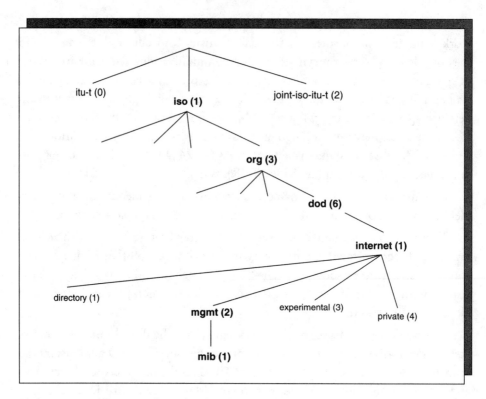

Figure 11–2. The Internet object identifier tree

11.1.2 Management Information Bases

Think of a MIB as an information storehouse containing aisles, shelves, and pigeonholes to organize the managed objects. Objects within this structure can be placed in a MIB. For ease of use, these objects are defined using ASN.1 syntax. A MIB module is a collection of related objects. Many MIB modules are available. Some define standard objects; others are specific to a particular vendor's products or services. For example, MIB modules are available for DS1, SONET, frame relay, and others. RFC 1213 [11–4] specifies the Internet-stand

In relation to this chapter are the objects used to manage broadband networks. These are placed under the transmission subtree, designated {1.3.6.1.2.1.10}. This transmission subtree contains a number of groups supporting various broadband technologies, which the following sections discuss in greater detail.

11.1.3 The Simple Network Management Protocol

SNMP provides communication between the agent and manager by defining the content and structure of messages, or PDUs. SNMP version 1, described by RFC 1157, defined five PDU types for SNMP: GetRequest, GetNextRequest, SetRequest, GetResponse, and Trap. SNMP version 2, described in RFC 1448 [11–5], adds the GetBulkRequest and InformRequest PDUs (see Figure 11–3).

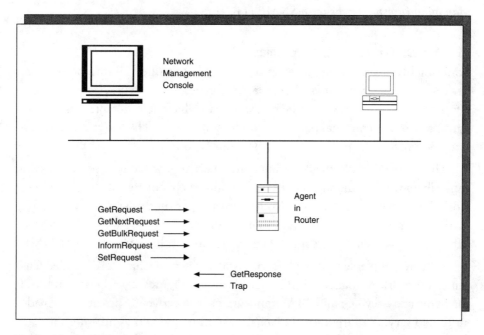

Figure 11–3. SNMP messages

The manager uses the GetRequest PDU to retrieve the value of one or more objects from an agent. The GetNextRequest PDU retrieves the values of one or more objects from an agent, which may be stored in a two-dimensional data structure called a table. The GetBulkRequest PDU allows the retrieval of large amounts of information, such as the entire contents of a routing table. Upon receiving the request, the agent constructs a GetResponse PDU containing the requested information.

The manager transmits the SetRequest PDU to the agent, and uses it to assign a value to a particular object. For example, the manager could define a value for the sysLocation object by setting it to "wire closet—third floor."

The agent uses the Trap PDU to alert the manager that a predefined event has occurred. For example, if a communication link on a router failed, the agent on that router would send a linkDown trap to the management console.

The administrative and architectural aspects of the NMF are described in RFC 1445 [11–6]. For more details on SNMP-based network management, see *Managing Internetworks with SNMP* [11–7].

11.1.4 Customer network management

Traditionally, a single organization owned and controlled all internetworking devices containing the managed objects. In a broadband network, however, a carrier owns and end users subscribe to a service in which objects represent the configuration and operational parameters. The extent to which a carrier lets its subscribers control and manage its network thus becomes an important issue.

The Service Management Architecture, therefore, was developed to provide subscribers with a "management window into their portion of the shared network," as described in Kenneth Rodemann's paper on this subject [11–8]. The carrier uses proprietary methods to manage the network internally, while Service Management lets customers manage their portion of the network using SNMP.

Bellcore's implementation of Service Management Architecture is called Customer Network Management (CNM), shown in Figures 2-16, 5-24, and 8-20 for frame relay, SMDS, and ATM applications, respectively. The carrier provides an IP and service address for the SNMP agent, which allows an external management console to access the SNMP agent within the broadband network (see Figure 11–4).

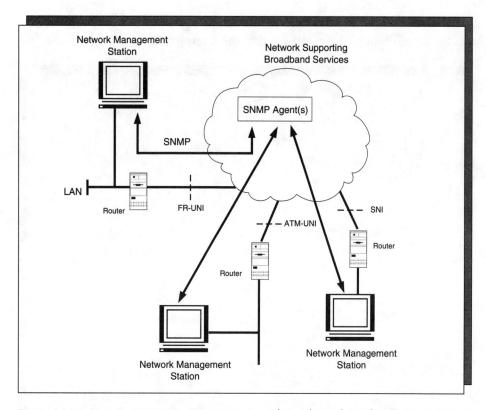

Figure 11–4. Accessing CNM service *(Source: Brown and Kostick, "And CNM for all: Customer Network Management Services for Broadband Data Services". Proceedings of the 18th Annual Conference on Local Computer Networks, © 1993 IEEE)*

MIB modules delineate the broadband service objects for the customer's console to manage. Various MIB modules contain DTE-based objects and network-based objects. For example, the frame relay DTE MIB (RFC 1315) contains a table of parameters for a particular data-link connection-management interface, such as the address field length (2, 3, or 4 octets), the time between successive STATUS ENQUIRY messages (5 to 30 seconds), or the maximum number of virtual circuits that the network allows on this interface. The frame relay service MIB (RFC 1604) contains a table that maintains the committed burst size (Bc), committed information rate (CIR), and maximum frame-size parameters. References [11–12] through [11–18] discuss these in detail. References [11–9], [11–10], and [11–11] give further details on Bellcore's CNM implementations.

The following sections discuss the broadband MIBs individually. Figure 11–5 shows the position of these MIBs within the Internet OID tree.

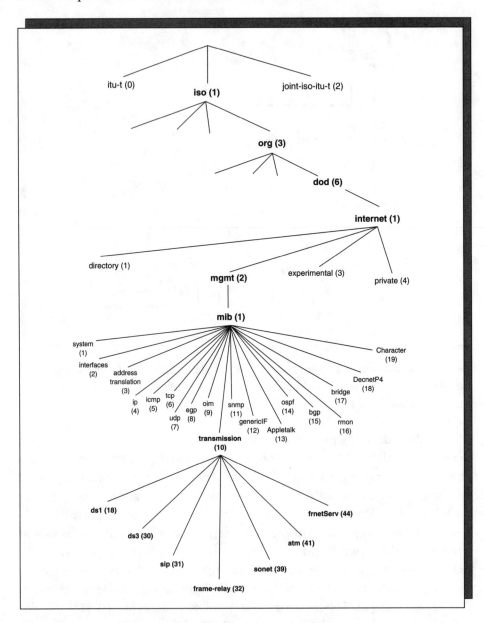

Figure 11–5. Broadband MIBs within the Internet Object Identifier Tree

11.2 The DS1/E1 MIB

DS1 and E1 objects are designated by {transmission 18}, with OID {1.3.6.1.2.1.10.18}, as shown in Figure 11–6. This MIB module consists of three groups: the DS1 Near End group, the DS1 Far End group, and the Fractional Table. The DS1 Near End group consists of four tables that contain configuration information and statistics about the DS1 interface at the near end of the communications link. This group contains four tables: the DS1 Configuration Table, which specifies the line coding, circuit identifier, line status, and other configuration details; the DS1 Current Table, which contains statistics collected over the current 15-minute interval; the DS1 Interval Table, which contains statistics collected over the previous 24 hours, broken into 96 completed 15-minute intervals; and the DS1 Total Table, which contains the cumulative sum of various statistics for the 24-hour period preceding the current interval.

The DS1 Far End group contains statistics from the DS1 interface at the far end of the communications link. This group contains three tables: the DS1 Far End Current Table, which contains statistics collected over the current 15-minute interval; the DS1 Far End Interval Table, which contains statistics collected over the previous 24 hours, broken into 96 complete 15-minute intervals; and the DS1 Far End Total Table, which contains the cumulative sum of various statistics for the 24 hours preceding the current interval.

The Fractional Table contains information regarding channels derived from subdividing DS1, such as a 64 Kbps channel used for voice traffic, or a 384 Kbps channel used for data traffic.

RFC 1406 [11–12] discusses details of the DS1/E1 MIB, as well as DS1 error events, performance defects, performance parameters, and failure states.

11.3 The DS3/E3 MIB

DS3 and E3 objects are designated by {transmission 30}, with OID {1.3.6.1.2.1.10.30}, as shown in Figure 11–7. This MIB module is similar in structure to the DS1 module discussed in Section 11.2. It places DS3 objects in three groups: the DS3/E3 Near End group, the DS3 Far End group, or the DS3 Fractional group. The tables and objects within those groups are similar to those for DS1/E1.

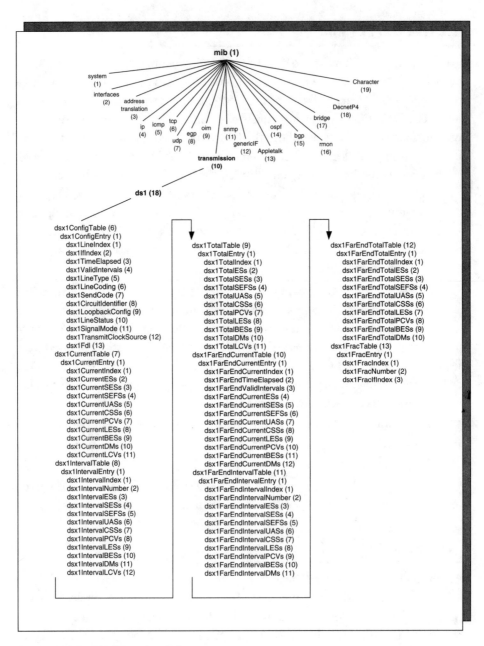

Figure 11–6. DS1/E1 managed objects

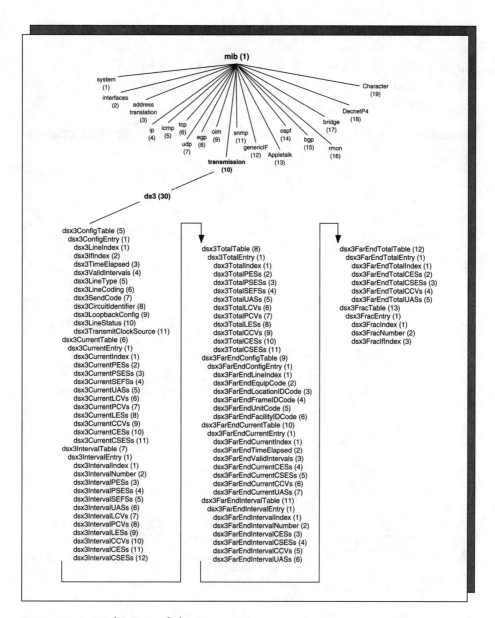

Figure 11–7. DS3/E3 Managed objects

RFC 1407 [11–13] discusses details of the DS3/E3 MIB as well as an explanation of the DS3 error events, performance parameters, and performance defects.

11.4 The SONET/SDH MIB

The SONET/SDH MIB SONET and SDH objects are designated by {transmission 39}, with OID {1.3.6.1.2.1.10.39}, as shown in Figure 11–8. This MIB module contains eight groups.

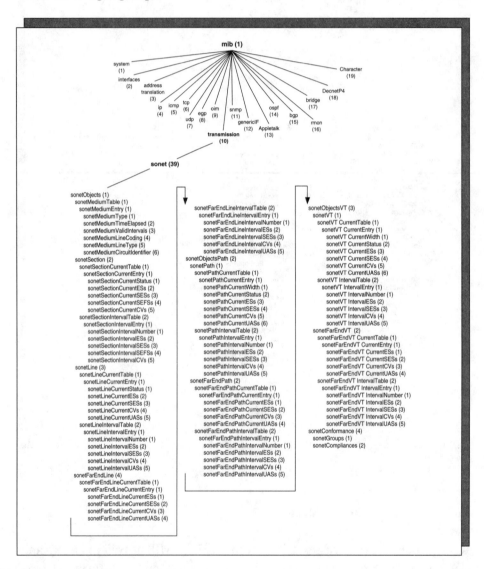

Figure 11–8. SONET managed objects

The SONET/SDH Medium group contains configuration information for optical and electrical SONET/SDH interfaces. The SONET/SDH Section group contains two tables that pertain to the SONET/SDH Section Layer: the SONET Section Current Table, with current statistics collected over a 15-minute interval; and the SONET/SDH Section Interval Table, with statistics collected over the previous 24 hours. The SONET/SDH Line group contains interval and current tables that pertain to the SONET/SDH Line Layer. The SONET/SDH Far End Line group is implemented for systems that provide for FEBE information at the SONET/SDH Line Layer, and contains both current and interval tables. The SONET/SDH Path and SONET/SDH Far End Path groups contain current interval information regarding the SONET/SDH Path Layer. Finally, the SONET/SDH Virtual Tributary (VT) and SONET/SDH Far End VT groups contain current and interval information regarding the SONET/SDH VT Layer.

Details of the SONET/SDH MIB are discussed in RFC 1595 [11–14], which is considered a companion document to the DS1/E1 and DS3/E3 MIBs. The SONET/SDH MIB also includes a listing of applicable terms and error conditions.

11.5 The Frame Relay DTE MIB

Frame relay DTE objects are designated by {transmission 32}, with OID {1.3.6.1.2.1.10.32}, as shown in Figure 11–9. This MIB module contains three principal groups: the Data Link Connection Management Interface (DLCMI) group, the Circuits group, and the Errors group.

The DLCMI group contains variables that configure the DLCMI, such as the Address field length, the interval between T1.617 Annex D STATUS ENQUIRY messages, the maximum number of virtual circuits on this interface, and so on. The Circuit group contains one table with information regarding specific DLCIs and their corresponding virtual circuits. The Error group contains one table that describes errors that have occurred on that frame relay interface. A fourth group, Frame-Relay-Globals, contains trap information. Details of the Frame Relay DTE MIB are discussed in RFC 1315 [11– 15].

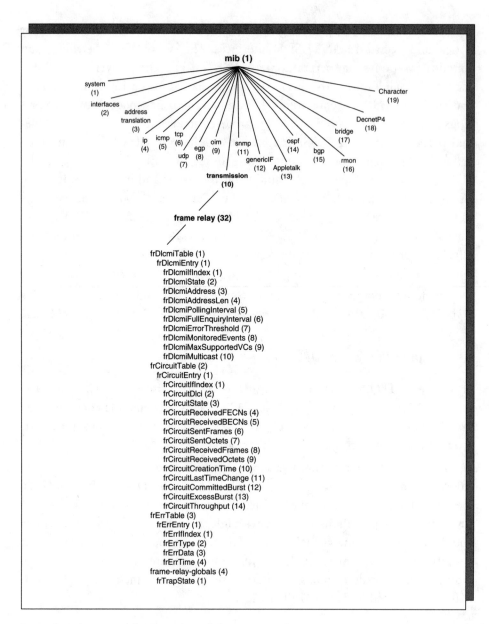

Figure 11–9. Frame relay DTE managed objects

11.6 The Frame Relay Service MIB

Frame relay network service objects are designated by {transmission 44}, with OID {1.3.6.1.2.1.10.44} (as shown in Figure 11–10). This MIB module is intended for CNM of a frame relay network service, and lets customers obtain details of the performance, faults, and configuration about their frame relay network service. The network's SNMP proxy agent obtains those details. A PVC between that agent and the customer constitutes the logical transmission path.

This MIB module consists of seven groups. The Frame Relay Logical Port group is an addendum to the ifTable found in MIB-II (RFC 1213). The Frame Relay Management VC Signaling group contains objects that relate to the T1.617 Annex D signaling channel. The PVC End-Point group identifies traffic parameters and provides statistics for a PVC segment end-point. The Frame Relay PVC Connection group models PVC information flows and connections. The PVC Connection Table contains connection information. The PVC Accounting group contains accounting information for PVC segment end-points. The Accounting on a Frame Relay Logical Port basis group contains additional accounting information. Two additional groups define traps and conformance information. Details of the Frame Relay Service MIB are discussed in RFC 1604 [11–16]. This MIB also includes a listing of applicable frame relay terms and parameters.

11.7 The SIP Interface MIB

SIP objects are designated by {transmission 31} with OID {1.3.6.1.2.1.10.31}, as shown in Figure 11–11. This MIB module consists of six groups. The SIP Level 3 group contains SIP L3 parameters and state variables. The SIP Level 2 group contains SIP L2 parameters and state variables. The SIP PLCP group contains tables with both DS1 and DS3 PLCP parameters and state variables. The SMDS Applications group is used with IP over SMDS (from RFC 1209). The SMDS Carrier Selection group is a place holder for carrier-selection objects. The SIP Error Log group is a table that contains SIP L3 PDU errors. RFC 1304 [11– 17] provides details of the SIP Interface MIB.

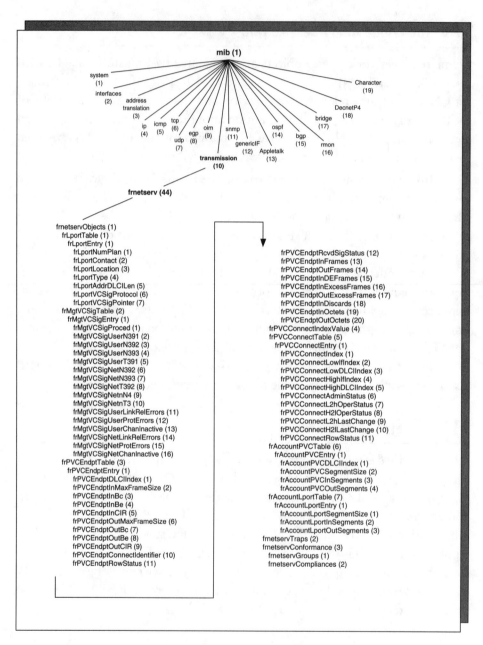

Figure 11-10. Frame relay network service managed objects

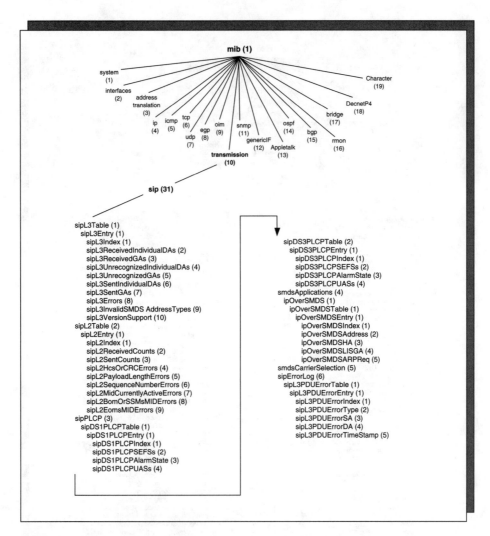

Figure 11–11. SIP managed objects

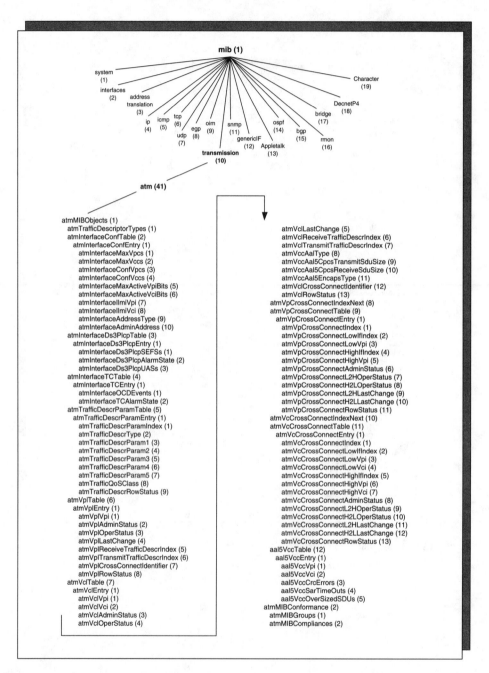

Figure 11-12. ATM managed objects

11.8 The ATM MIB

ATM objects are designated by {transmission 41} with OID {1.3.6.1.2.1.10.41}, as shown in Figure 11–12. This MIB module consists of nine groups.

The ATM Interface Configuration Parameters group contains configuration information associated with an ATM interface, which supplements the information provided in MIB-II. The ATM Interface DS3 PLCP group contains configuration and state parameters for DS3-based ATM interfaces. The ATM Interface TC Sublayer group contains Transmission Convergence configuration information and state parameters. The ATM Traffic Descriptor Parameter group contains traffic parameters such as the QoS class. The ATM Interface Virtual Path Link (VPL) group contains configuration and state information of a bidirectional VPL. The ATM Interfaces Virtual Channel Link (VCL) group contains configuration and state information of a bidirectional VCL. The ATM Virtual Path (VP) Cross Connect group contains configuration and state information of all point-to-point, point-to-multipoint, or multipoint-to-multipoint VP cross connects. The ATM Virtual Channel (VC) Cross Connect group contains configuration and state information of a bidirectional VC cross connect. The AAL5 Virtual Channel Connection (VCC) Performance Statistics group contains AAL5 VCC performance parameters.

11.9 Broadband Technologies: A Double-Edged Sword

Broadband technologies are a double-edged sword. On one hand, they promise virtually unlimited bandwidth, which lets users transmit exciting new technologies, such as multimedia, from desktop to desktop. On the other hand, they present challenges, including new standards, new testing and manufacturing processes, and multivendor interoperability.

When evaluating these technologies, the wise network manager will keep in mind the suitability of the technology for the network application being considered, and he or she will show the wisdom of implementing a technology with unproven elements.

Network managers with the courage to draw this sword deserve our best wishes and utmost respect.

11.10 References

[11–1] International Organization for Standardization, Information Technology Open Systems Interconnection Specification of Abstract Syntax Notation One (ASN.1), ISO/IEC 8824: 1990.

[11–2] International Organization for Standardization, Information Technology—Open Systems Interconnection Specification of Basic Encoding Rules for Abstract Syntax Notation One (ASN.1), ISO/IEC 8825: 1990.

[11–3] Case, J., McCloghrie, K., Rose, M. and S. Waldbusser. Rose, M.T. and K. McCloghrie. "Structure of Management Information for version 2 of the Simple Network Management Protocol (SNMPv2)." RFC 1442, April 1993.

[11–4] McCloghrie, K. and M.T. Rose, editors. "Management Information Base for Network Management of TCP/IP-based Internets: MIB-II." RFC 1213, March 1991.

[11–5] Case, J., McCloghrie, K., Rose, M. and S. Waldbusser. "Protocol Operations for version 2 of the Simple Network Management Protocol (SNMPv2), RFC 1448, April 1993.

[11–6] J.R. Davin, J.M. Galvin, K. McCloghrie, Administrative Model for version 2 of the Simple Network Management Protocol (SNMPv2). RFC 1445, April 1993.

[11–7] Miller, Mark A. *Managing Internetworks with SNMP.* New York, M&T Books Inc., 1993.

[11–8] Rodemann, Kenneth R. "Service Management Architecture." *The Simple Times* (September/October 1993): 1–5.

[11–9] Bell Communications Research Inc. "Generic Requirements for Phase 1 Frame Relay PVC Customer Network Management Service." TA-NWT-001371, 1993.

[11–10] Bell Communications Research Inc. "Generic Service Requirements for Phase 1 SMDS Customer Network Management Service." TR-TSV-001062, March 1993 and Revision 1, December 1993.

[11–11] Bell Communications Research Inc. "Generic Requirements for Exchange PVC CRS Customer Network Management Service." TA-TSV-001117, September 1993.

[11–12] Baker, F. and J. Watt, editors. "Definitions of Managed Objects for the DS1 and E1 Interface Types." RFC 1406, January 1993.

[11–13] Cox, T. and Tesink, K., editors. "Definitions of Managed Objects for the DS3/E3 Interface Type." RFC 1407, January 1993.

[11–14] Brown, T., and K. Tesink, editors. "Definitions of Managed Objects for the SONET/SDH Interface Type." RFC 1595, March 1994.

[11–15] Brown, C., et. al. "Management Information Base for Frame Relay DTEs. RFC 1315, April 1992.

[11–16] Brown, T., editor. "Definitions of Managed Objects for Frame Relay Service." RFC 1604, March 1994.

[11–17] Cox, T., and K. Tesink, editors. "Definitions of Managed Objects for the SIP Interface Type." RFC 1304, February 1992.

 # Addresses of
Standards Organizations

AT&T PUBLICATIONS

AT&T Technologies Commercial Sales
P.O. Box 19901
Indianapolis, IN 46219
Telephone (317) 322-6557 or (800) 432-6600

ATIS STANDARDS

Alliance for Telecommunications Industry Solutions
1200 G St. NW, Suite 500
Washington, DC 20005
Telephone (202) 628-6380

BELLCORE STANDARDS

Bell Communications Research Information Management Services
8 Corporate Place, 3A-184
Piscataway, NJ 08854-4196
Telephone (908) 699-5800 or (800) 521-2673

CSA STANDARDS

Canadian Standards Association
178 Rexdale Boulevard Rexdale, ONT
CANADA   M9W 1R3
Telephone (416) 747-4363

ECMA STANDARDS

European Computer Manufacturers Association
114, Rue de rhone CH-1204
Geneva, Switzerland
Telephone 41 22 735-3634

EIA STANDARDS

Electronic Industries Association
2001 Pennsylvania Ave. NW
Washington, DC 20006
Telephone (202) 457-4966 or (800) 854-7179

IEEE STANDARDS

Institute of Electrical and Electronics Engineers, Inc.
445 Hoes Lane
P.O. Box 1331
Piscataway, NJ 08855-1331
Telephone (908) 981-1393 or (800) 678-4333

INTERNET STANDARDS

InterNIC Information Services Reference Desk
P.O. Box 85608
San Diego, CA 92186-9784
Telephone (619) 455-4600 or (800) 444-4345
(See Appendix D for further information)

ISO AND ANSI STANDARDS

American National Standards Institute
11 West 42nd St., 13th Floor
New York, NY 10036
Telephone (212) 642-4900

ISO STANDARDS

International Organization for Standardization
1, Rue de Varembe CH-1211
Geneva 20, Switzerland
Telephone 41 22 749-0111
Facsimile 41 22 730-5853

ITU-T (CCITT) RECOMMENDATIONS
AND
FEDERAL INFORMATION PROCESSING STANDARDS (FIPS)

U.S. Department of Commerce National Technical Information Service
5285 Port Royal Road
Springfield, VA 22161
Telephone (703) 487-4650

MILITARY STANDARDS SALES

Naval Publications and Forms Center
Commanding Officer
NPFC 43 5801 Tabor Ave.
Philadelphia, PA 19120
Telephone (215) 697-3321

NATIONAL INSTITUTE OF STANDARDS AND TECHNOLOGY

Technology Building 225, Room B-64
Gaithersburg, MD 20899
Telephone (301) 975-2816

Broadband Technology Forums

ATM Forum Worldwide Headquarters

303 Vintage Park Drive
Foster City, CA 94404
Telephone (415) 578-6860
Fax (415) 525-0182
Faxback Service (415) 688-4318
Internet info@atmforum.com

ATM Forum European Offices

10, rue Thierry Le Luron 92593
Levallois-Perret Cedex, France
Telephone 33 1 46 39 56 56
Fax 33 1 46 39 56 99

Frame Relay Forum North America Office

303 Vintage Park Drive
Foster City, CA 94404
Telephone (415) 578-6980
Fax (415) 525-0182
Faxback Service (415) 688-4317
Internet frf@interop.com

Frame Relay Forum Australian Office

c/o Interlink Communications Unit
#4 14 Aquatic Drive Frenchs Forest, NSW
2086 Australia
Telephone 61 2 975 2577
Fax 61 2 452 5397

Frame Relay Forum

c/o OST, BP 158 Z1 Sud Est
rue du bas Village 35510
Cesson Sevigne Cedex, France
Telephone 33 99 51 76 55
Fax 33 99 41 71 75

SMDS Interest Group

303 Vintage Park Drive
Foster City, CA 94404
Telephone (415) 578-6979
Fax (415) 525-0182
Faxback Service (415) 688-4314
Internet smds@interop.com

 # Obtaining Internet Information

The InterNIC is a central repository of Internet information, including the RFC documents. The InterNIC is located at:

InterNIC Information Services Reference Desk

P.O. Box 85608

San Diego, CA 92186-9784

Telephone (619) 455-4600 or (800) 444-4345

Obtaining RFCs

Hard copy RFCs may be obtained from the NIC for a minimal fee or online via the Internet. To obtain an RFC online, use FTP to login to the desired host (see below), with name = anonymous and password = guest. The RFCs are located in a designated subdirectory (see below), filename *rfcnnnn.txt* or *rfcnnnn.ps*. The nnnn represents the RFC number, for example, RFC1175. Both ASCII (*txt* suffix) and PostScript (*ps* suffix) files are available. FYI documents may be obtained in a similar manner. The filenames are *fyinn.txt* or *fyinn.ps*.

The primary repositories of RFCs include:

▼ DS.INTERNIC.NET, directory *ftp/rfc*, filename *rfcnnnn.txt* or *rfcnnnn.ps*

▼ NIS.NSF.NET, directory *internet/documents/rfc*, filename *rfcnnnn.txt*

▼ NISC.SRI.COM, directory *rfc*, filename *RFCnnnn.TXT.v*
(*v* represents the version number of the RFC)

▼ VENERA.ISI.EDU, directory *in-notes*, filename *rfcnnnn.txt*

Note that some systems require leading zeros in the RFC number. In other words, if *rfc868.txt* does not work, try *rfc0868.txt.*

A second method of obtaining RFCs is to use electronic mail. The following is an excerpt from the HELP file, obtained via the Internet using this method.

This automated mail service is provided by the DDN Network Information Center. It allows access to NIC documents and information via ordinary electronic mail. This is especially useful for people who do not have access to the NIC via a direct Internet link, such as BITNET, CSNET, and UUCP sites.

To use the mail service, send a mail message to SERVICE@NIC.DDN.MIL. In the SUBJECT field, request the type of service you wish, followed by any needed arguments. The message body is normally ignored. But if the SUBJECT field is empty, the first line of the message body will be used as the request. Large files will be broken into smaller separate messages. However, a few files are too large to be sent through the mail system. Requests are processed automatically once a day.

The following services are currently available:

▼ HELP   This message lists current services.

▼ HOST *xxx*   Returns information about host *xxx*.

▼ WHOIS *xxx*   This is used to get more details about a host.

▼ IEN *nnn*   *nnn* is the IEN number or the word *INDEX*.

▼ IETF *xxx*   *xxx* is a filename.

▼ INDEX   Returns the master list of available index files.

INTERNET-DRAFTS xxx xxx is a filename; NETINFO xxx xxx is a filename or the word *INDEX*. RFC nnn nnn is the RFC number or the word *INDEX*. RFC nnn.PS to retrieve an available PostScript RFC. Check RFC INDEX for form of RFC. FYI nnn nnn is the FYI number or the word *INDEX*. FYI nnn.PS retrieves PostScript versions of FYI files. SEND xxx xxx is a fully specified filename. WHOIS xxx returns information about xxx from the WHOIS service. Use WHOIS HELP for information on how to use WHOIS.

The following are example SUBJECT lines:

```
HELP
RFC 822
RFC INDEX
RFC 1119.PS
FYI 1
IETF 1IETF-DESCRIPTION.TXT
INTERNET-DRAFTS 1ID-ABSTRACTS.TXT
NETINFO DOMAIN-TEMPLATE.TXT
SEND RFC: RFC-BY-AUTHOR.TXT
SEND IETF/1WG-SUMMARY.TXT
SEND INTERNET-DRAFTS/DRAFT-IETF-NETDATA-NETDATA-00.TXT
HOST DIIS
WHOIS KOSTERS, MARK
```

Send comments or suggestions to SUGGESTIONS@NIC.DDN.MIL. Send questions and bug reports to BUG-SERVICE@NIC.DDN.MIL.

Note that a space is required between the document type and the document number. In other words, RFC 1187 will work; RFC1187 will not.

The RFC-Info Service

A new service to assist users with Internet information was announced in the March 1992 issue of *ConneXions, the Interoperability Report*. The following is text detailing the new service, which was obtained by using *Help:Help*, described below.

RFC-Info is an E–mail-based service to help locate and retrieve RFCs and FYIs. Users can ask for "lists" of all RFCs and FYIs having certain attributes (filters) such as IDs, keywords, title, author, issuing organization, and date. Once an RFC is uniquely identified (for example, by its RFC number), it may also be retrieved.

To use the service, send E-mail to RFC-INFO@ISI.EDU with your requests in the body of the message. You can put anything in the SUBJECT; the system ignores it. (All is case independent, obviously.)

To begin, you may send a message to RFC-INFO@ISI.EDU with requests, as shown in the following examples (without the explanation between []):

Help: Help	[to get this information]
List: FYI	[list the FYI notes]
List: RFC	[list RFCs with window as keyword or in title]
Keywords: window List: FYI	[list FYIs about windows]
Keywords: window List: *	[list both RFCs and FYIs about windows]
Keywords: window List: RFC	[list RFCs about ARPANET, ARPA NETWORK, etc.]
title: ARPA*NET List: RFC	[list RFCs issued by MITRE, dated 7+8/1991]
Organization: MITRE Dated-after: Jul-01-1991	Dated-before: Aug-31-1991
List: RFC	[list RFCs obsoleting a given RFC]
Obsolete: RFC0010 List: RFC	[list RFCs by authors starting with "Bracken"]
Author: Bracken*	[* is a wild card that matches everything]
List: RFC	[list RFCs by both Postel and Gillman]
Authors: J. Postel Gillman	[note, the "filters" are ANDed] Authors: R.
List: RFC	[list RFCs by any Crocker]
Authors: Crocker List: RFC	[list only RFCs by S.D. Crocker]

Authors: S.D. Crocker List: RFC	[list only RFCs by D. Crocker]
Authors: D. Crocker	
Retrieve: RFC	[retrieve RFC-822]
Doc-ID: RFC0822	[note, always four digits in RFC#]
Help: Manual	[to retrieve the long user manual, 30+ pages]
Help: List	[how to use the LIST request]
Help: Retrieve	[how to use the RETRIEVE request]
Help: Topics	[list topics for which help is available]
Help: Dates	["Dates" is such a topic]
List: keywords	[list the keywords in use]
List: organizations	[list the organizations known to the system]

Please try using this service. Report problems to RFC- MANAGER@ISI.EDU. A useful way to test this service is to retrieve the file "Where and how to get new RFCs." Place the following in the message body:

Help: ways_to_get_rfcs

Internet Mailing Lists

A number of mailing lists are maintained on the Internet for the purposes of soliciting information and discussions on specific subjects. In addition, a number of the IETF working groups maintain a list for the exchange of information that is specific to a particular group.

For example, the IETF maintains two lists: the IETF General Discussion list and the IETF Announcement list. To join the IETF Announcement list, send a request to: <ietf-announce-request@cnri.reston.va.us>. To join the IETF General

A number of other mailing lists are available. To join a mailing list, send a message to the associated request list: <listname>-request@<listhost> (see the example for the IETF lists given above). In the table below are some mailing lists and their E-mail addresses:

Mailing List Subject	E-mail Address
ATM General Discussion	atm@hpl.hp.com
IP over ATM Working Group	matmos@hpl.hp.com
AToM MIB Working Group	atommib@thumper.bellcore.com
Bridge MIB Working Group	bridge-mib@decwrl.dec.com
Frame Relay General Discussion	frftc@acc.com
Frame Relay MIB Working Group	frftc@acc.com
Host MIB Working Group	hostmib@andrew.cmu.edu
Remote Monitoring Working Group	rmonmib@jarthur.claremont.edu
SMDS General Discussion	smdstc@thumper.bellcore.com
SNMP General Discussion	snmp@psi.com

ip-atm@request

ip-atm@hpl.hp.com

 # Selected Broadband Networking Standards

Frame Relay

ANSI

T1.602 (1990)	Telecommunications-ISDN-Data Link Layer Signaling Specification for Applications at the User-Network Interface
T1.606 (1990)	Frame Relaying Bearer Service-Architectural Framework and Service Description
T1.617 (1991)	DSS1—Signaling Specification for Frame Relay Bearer Service
T1.617a (1991)	Frame Relay Bearer Service—Architectural Framework and Service Description on Congestion Management Principles
T1.618 (1991)	DSS1—Core Aspects of Frame Protocol for Use with Frame Relay Bearer Service

Bellcore

TA-TSV-001240 (1993)	Generic Requirements for Frame Relay Access to SMDS
TA-NWT-001248 (1993)	Generic Requirements for Operations of Broadband Switching Systems
FA-NWT-001327 (1992)	Framework Generic Requirements for Frame Relay Network Element Operations
TA-NWT-001328 (1992)	ISDN Exchange Termination (ET) to Frame Handler (FH) Interface Framework Generic Criteria
TR-TSV-001369 (1993)	Generic Requirements for Frame Relay PVC Exchange Service
TR-NWT-001370 (1993)	Generic Requirements for Exchange Access Frame Relay PVC Service
TA-NWT-001371 (1993)	Generic Requirements for Phase 1 Frame Relay PVC Customer Network Management Service

IETF

RFC 1315 (1992)	Definition of Managed Objects for Frame Relay DTEs
RFC 1490 (1993)	Multiprotocol Interconnect over Frame Relay
RFC 1573 (1994)	The New Interfaces MIB
RFC 1604 (1994)	Definitions of Managed Objects for Frame Relay Service

ITU-T (CCITT)

I.122 (1988)	Framework for Providing Additional Packet Mode Bearer Services
Q.922 (1992)	ISDN Data Link Layer Specification for Frame Mode Bearer Services
Q.931 (1988)	ISDN Signaling Specification for Frame Mode Bearer Services
I.233 (1992)	Frame Mode Bearer Service (FMBS)
I.370 (1991)	Frame Mode Bearer Service (FMBS) Congestion Management
I.372 (1993)	Frame Mode Bearer Service (FMBS) Network-to-Network Requirements
I.555 (1993)	Frame Mode Bearer Service (FMBS) Interworking

Frame Relay Forum

FRF.1 (1991)	User to Network Interface Implementation Agreement
FRF.2 (1992)	Frame Relay Network-to-Network Interface Implementation Agreement
FRF.3 (1993)	Multiprotocol Interconnect over Frame Relay
FRF.4 (1993)	User-to-Network SVC Implementation Agreement
FRF.5 (1994)	Frame Relay/ATM Network Interworking Implementation Agreement
FRF.6 (1994)	Frame Relay Service Customer Network Management Implementation Agreement

Switched Multimegabit Data Service

Bellcore

TR-TSV-000772 (1991)	Generic System Requirements in Support of Switched Multimegabit Data Services
TR-TSV-000773 (1991) Revision 1 (1993)	Local Access System Generic Requirements Objectives and Interfaces in Support of Switched Multimegabit Data Service
TR-TSV-000774 (1992) Sup.1 (1993)	SMDS Operations Technology Network Element Generic Requirements
TR-TSV-000775 (1991)	Usage Measurement Generic Requirements in Support of Billing for Switched Multimegabit Data Service
TA-TSV-001059 (1992)	Generic Requirements for SMDS Networking
TR-TSV-001060 (1991) Rev.1 (1992) Rev.2 (1993)	Switched Multimegabit Data Services Generic Requirements for Exchange Access and Intercompany Serving Arrangements (SMDS)
TA-TSV-001061 (1991)	Operations Technology Network Element Generic Requirements in Support of Interswitch and Exchange Access SMDS
TR-TSV-001062 (1993)	Generic Requirements for Phase 1 SMDS Customer Network Management Service
TR-TSV-0001063 (1992)	Operations Technology Generic Criteria Rev.1 (1993) in Support of Exchange Access SMDS and Intercompany Serving Arrangements
TR-TSV-001064 (1992)	SMDS Generic Criteria on Operations Interfaces—SMDS Information Model and Usage

TR-TSV-001239 (1993)   Generic Requirements for Low-Speed SMDS Access

TR-TSV-001240 (1993)   Generic Requirements for Frame Relay Access to SMDS

IETF

RFC 1209 (1991)   The Transmission of IP Datagrams over the SMDS Service

RFC 1304 (1992)   Definitions of Managed Objects for the SMDS Interface Type

RFC 1406 (1993)   Definitions of Managed Objects for the DS1 and E1 Interface Types

RFC 1407 (1993)   Definitions of Managed Objects for the DS3/E3 Interface Type

SMDS Interest Group

SIG-TS-001 (1991)   Data Exchange Interface (DXI) Specification

SIG-TS-002 (1992)   Local Management Interface (LMI) Specification

SIG-TS-003 (1992)   DECnet over SMDS Specification

SIG-TS-004 (1993)   Connectionless OSI over SMDS Specification

SIG-TS-005 (1993)   DXI/SNI Specification

SIG-TS-006 (1993)   SIP Relay Interface (SRI) Specification

SIG-IS-002 (1993)   Guiding Principles for Ordering and Provisioning of Intercarrier SMDS

SIG-IS-003 (1993)   Guiding Principles for SMDS Intercarrier Operations Management

Asynchronous Transfer Mode

ANSI

T1.624 (1993)	Broadband ISDN User-Network Interfaces— Rates and Formats Specifications
T1.627 (1993)	Broadband ISDN—ATM Layer Functionality and Specification

ATM Forum

B-ICI 1.0 (1993)	BISDN Inter-Carrier Interface (B-ICI) Specification
DXI 1.0 (1993)	ATM Data Exchange Interface (DXI) Specification
UNI 3.0 (1993)	ATM User-Network Interface (UNI) Specification

Bellcore

TR-NWT-000233 (1993)	Wideband and Broadband Digital Cross-Connect Systems Generic Requirements and Objectives
TR-TSY-000301 (1990)	Public Packet Switched Network Generic Requirements (PPSNGR)
SR-TSY-000857 (1987)	Preliminary Special Report on Broadband ISDN Access
FA-NWT-001109 (1990)	BISDN Transport Network Framework Generic Criteria
TA-NWT-001110 (1993)	Broadband ISDN Switching System Generic Requirements
TA-NWT-001111 (1993)	Broadband ISDN Access Signaling Framework Generic Criteria for Class II Equipment

TA-NWT-001112 (1992)   Broadband ISDN User to Network Interface and Network Node Interface Physical Layer Generic Criteria

TA-NWT-001113 (1993)   Asynchronous Transfer Mode (ATM) and ATM Adaptation Layer (AAL) Protocols Generic Requirements

TA-NWT-001114 (1993)   Generic Requirements for Operations Interfaces Using OSI Tools: Broadband ATM Network Operations

TA-NWT-001115 (1993)   BISDN Inter-Carrier Interface (B-ICI) Requirements

TA-TSV-001117 (1993)   Generic Requirements for Exchange PVC CRS Customer Network Management Service

TA-TSV-001238 (1992)   Generic Requirements for SMDS on the 155.520-Mbps Multi-Services Broadband ISDN Inter-Carrier Interface (B-ICI)

TA-NWT-001248 (1993)   Generic Requirements for Operations of Broadband Switching Systems

SR-NWT-002076 (1991)   Report on the Broadband ISDN Protocols for Providing SMDS and Exchange Access

IETF

RFC 1483 (1993)   Multiprotocol Encapsulation over ATM Adaptation Layer 5

RFC 1577 (1994)   Classical IP and ARM over ATM

RFC 1595 (1994)   Definitions of Managed Objects for the SONET/SDH Interface Type

ITU-T (CCITT)

E.164 (1988)	Numbering Plan for the ISDN Era
F.811 (1992)	Broadband Connection-Oriented Bearer Services
F.812 (1992)	Broadband Connectionless Data Bearer Service
I.113 (1991)	B-ISDN Vocabulary of Terms
I.121 (1991)	Broadband Aspects of ISDN
I.150 (1992)	B-ISDN ATM Functional Characteristics
I.211 (1992)	B-ISDN Service Aspects
I.311 (1992)	B-ISDN General Network Aspects
I.321 (1991)	B-ISDN Protocol Reference Model and Its Applications
I.327 (1993)	B-ISDN Functional Architecture Aspects
I.361 (1992)	B-ISDN ATM Layer Specification
I.362 (1993)	B-ISDN ATM Adaptation Layer Functional Description
I.363 (1992)	B-ISDN ATM Adaptation Layer Specification
I.364 (1992)	Connectionless Network Access Protocol
I.371 (1992)	Traffic Control and Congestion Control in B-ISDN
I.413 (1992)	B-ISDN User-Network Interface
I.432 (1992)	B-ISDN User-Network Interface-Physical Layer Specification
I.555 (1993)	Frame Relay and ATM Interworking
I.610 (1992)	B-ISDN UNI Operations and Maintenance Principles
Q.2931 (1993)	B-ISDN User-Network Interface Signaling for Call/Connection Control

 # Selected Broadband Networking Vendors

Adax Inc.
614 Bancroft Way
Berkeley, CA 94710
(510) 548-7047
Fax: (510) 548-5526

Applitek Corp.
100 Brickstone Square
Andover, MA 01810
(508) 475-4050
(800) 526-2489
Fax: (508) 475-0550

ADC Kentrox
14375 N.W. Science Park Drive
Portland, OR 97210
(503) 643-1681
(800) 733-5511
Fax: (503) 641-3341

Advanced Computer Communications (ACC)
10261 Bubb Road
Cupertino, CA 95014
(408) 864-0600
(800) 444-7854
Fax: (408) 446-5234

Advanced Micro Devices (AMD)
P.O. Box 3453
Sunnyvale, CA 94088
(408) 732-2400
(800) 538-8450
Fax: (408) 982-6585

Alantec
47800 Westinghouse Drive
Fremont, CA 94539
(510) 770-1050
(800) 727-1050
Fax: (510) 770-1054

Alcatel Data Networks
12502 Sunrise Valley Drive
Reston, VA 22096
(703) 689-7400
Fax: (703) 689-5843

Alcatel Network Systems
1225 North Alma Road
Richardson, TX 75081
(214) 996-5000
Fax: (214) 996-5211

Allied Telesis, Inc.
585 E. Middlefield Road
Mountain View, CA 94070
(415) 964-2771
Fax: (415) 964-0944

American Computer and Electronics Corp.
209 Perry Parkway
Gaithersburg, MD 20877
(301) 258-9850
(800) 989-5566
Fax: (301) 921-0434

Amnet Inc.
1881 Worcester Road
Framingham, MA 01701
(508) 879-6306
(800) 846-2001
Fax: (508) 872-8136

AMP
P.O. Box 3608
Harrisburg, PA 17105
(717) 564-0100
(800) 522-6752
Fax: (717) 986-7575

Ando Corp.
7617 Standish Place
Rockville, MD 20855
(301) 294-3365
Fax: (301) 294-3359

Andrew Corp.
10500 W 153rd St.
Orland Park, IL 60462
(708) 349-3300
(800) 255-1479
Fax: (708) 349-5943

Apple Computer Inc.
20525 Mariani Ave.
Cupertino, CA 95014
(408) 996-1010
(800) 776-2333
Fax: (408) 974-6726

Ascom Timeplex Inc.
400 Chestnut Ridge Road
Woodcliff Lake, NJ 07675
(201) 391-1111
Fax: (201) 573-6470

AT&T Computer Systems
Gatehall Drive
Parsippany, NJ 07054
(201) 397-4800
Fax: (201) 397-4918

AT&T Global Information Solutions
1700 S. Patterson Blvd.
Dayton, OH 45479
(513) 445-5000
(800) 225-5627
Fax: (513) 445-1847

Banyan Systems Inc.
115 Flanders Road, #5
Westboro, MA 01581
(508) 898-1000
(800) 828-2404
Fax: (508) 836-1810

BBN Communications Corp.
150 Cambridge Park Drive Cambridge,
MA 02140
(617) 873-2000
Fax: (617) 873-2509

Bell Atlantic Software Systems
14 Washington Road, Bldg. 2
Princeton Junction, NJ 08550
(609) 936-2900
Fax: (609) 936-2859

Bellcore
331 Newman Springs Road
Red Bank, NJ 07701-7030
(908) 758-2032
(800) 521-2673

Brooktree Corp.
9868 Scranton Road
San Diego, CA 92121
(619) 535-3200
Fax (619) 452-2104

Bull HN
Information Systems Technology Park
2 Wall Street
Billerica, MA 01821
(508) 294-6000
Fax: (508) 294-6440

Cabletron Systems Inc.
P.O. Box 5005
Rochester, NH 03867-0505
(603) 332-9400
Fax: (603) 332-4616

Cascade Communications
5 Carlisle Road
Westford, MA 01886
(508) 692-2600
Fax: (508) 692-9214

CBIS Inc.
5875 Peachtree Industrial Blvd., Bldg.
100/170
Norcross, GA 30092
(404) 446-1332
(800) 835-3375
Fax: (404) 446-9164

Chipcom Corp.
118 Turnpike Road
Southborough, MA 01772
(508) 460-8900
(800) 228-9930
Fax: (508) 460-8950

Cisco Systems Inc.
501 East Middlefield Road
Mountain View, CA 94043
(415) 326-1941
(800) 553-6387
Fax: (415) 326-1989

Codex/Motorola
20 Cabot Blvd.
Mansfield, MA 02048
(508) 261-4000
Fax: (508) 261-7105

Computer Network Technology
6500 Wedgwood Road
Maple Grove, MN 55311
(612) 550-8000
Fax: (612) 550-8800

Cray Communications Inc.
9020 Junction Drive
Annapolis Junction, MD 20701
(301) 317-7710
(800) 359-7710
Fax: (301) 317-7220

CrossComm Corp.
450 Donald Lynch Blvd. Marlborough,
MA 01752
(508) 481-4060
(800) 388-1200
Fax: (508) 490-5535

DigiBoard
6400 Flying Cloud Dr.
Eden Prairie, MN 55344
(612) 943-9020
(800) 344-4273
Fax: (612) 943-5331

Digital Communications Associates (DCA)
1000 Alderman Drive
Alpharetta, GA 30201
(404) 442-4000
(800) 348-3221
Fax: (404) 442-4366

Digital Equipment Corporation (DEC)
146 Main Street
Maynard, MA 01754
(508) 493-5111
(800) 344-4825
Fax: (508) 493-8780

Digital Link
217 Humboldt Court
Sunnyvale, CA 94089
(408) 745-6200
(800) 441-1142
Fax: (408) 745-6250

Digital Technology
2300 Edwin C. Moses Blvd.
Dayton, OH 45408
(513) 443-0412
(800) 852-1252
Fax: (513) 226-0511

Digitech Industries

55 Kenosha Ave.
Danbury, CT 06813
(203) 797-2676
Fax: (203) 797-2682

DSC Communications

1000 Coit Road
Plano, TX 75075
(214) 519-3000
(800) 777-6804
Fax: (214) 519-4646

Dynatech Communications Inc.

991 Annapolis Way
Woodbridge, VA 22191
(703) 550-0011
(800) 727-7215
Fax: (703) 550-7560

Eicon Technology Corp.

2196 32nd Ave.
Montreal, QUE Canada H8T 3H7
(514) 631-2592
Fax: (514) 631-3092

FastComm Communications Corp.

45472 Holiday Drive, Suite 3
Sterling, VA 20166
(703) 318-7750
(800) 521-2496
Fax: (787-4625

FiberCom Inc.

3353 Orange Ave. NE
Roanoke, VA 24012
(703) 342-6700
(800) 423-1183
Fax: (703) 342-5961

Fibermux Corp.

21415 Plummer
Chatsworth, CA 91311
(818) 709-6000
(800) 800-4624
Fax: (818) 709-1556

Fore Systems Inc.

174 Thorn Hill Rd.
Warrendale, PA 15086
(412) 772-6600
Fax: (412) 772-6500

Frame Relay Technologies Inc.

3554 Business Park Drive
Costa Mesa, CA
(714) 668-0222
Fax: 668-0350

Frederick Engineering Inc.

10200 Old Columbia Road
Columbia, MD 21046
(410) 290-9000
Fax: (410) 381-7180

FTP Software Inc.

2 High St. N.
Andover, MA 01845
(508) 685-4000
Fax: (508) 794-4477

Fujitsu Business Communications
3190 Miraloma Ave.
Anaheim, CA 92806
(714) 630-7721
Fax: (714) 764-2748

Fujitsu Network Switching
4403 Bland Road
Somerset Park Raleigh, NC 27609
(919) 790-2211
Fax: (919) 790-8376

Gandalf Data Inc.
9 N. Olney Ave.
Cherry Hill, NJ 08083
(609) 424-9400
(800) 426-3253
Fax: (609) 751-4374

General DataCom Inc.
1579 Straits Turnpike
Middlebury, CT 06762-1299
(203) 574-1118
Fax: (203) 758-8507

GTE Government Systems
40 Sylvan Road
Waltham, MA 02254
(617) 890-8460
Fax: (617) 890-9320

Hayes Microcomputer Products Inc.
P.O. Box 105203
Atlanta, GA 30348
(404) 840-9200
Fax: (404) 447-0178

Hewlett-Packard Co.
3000 Hanover St.
Palo Alto, CA 94304
(415) 857-1501
(800) 752-0900

Hewlett-Packard Colorado Telecommunications Division
5070 Centennial Blvd.
Colorado Springs, CO 80919
(719) 531-4000
Fax: (719) 531-4505

Hewlett-Packard Business Computing Systems
19091 Pruneridge Ave.
Cupertino, CA 95014
(800) 752-0900

Hitachi Telecom USA
3617 Parkway Lane
Norcross, GA 30092
(404) 446-8820
Fax: (404) 242-1414

Hughes LAN Systems Inc.
1225 Charleston Road
Mountain View, CA 94043
(415) 966-7300
(800) 395-5267
Fax: (415) 960-3738

IBM
Old Orchard Road
Armonk, NY 10504
(914) 765-1900
(800) 426-2468
Fax: (800) 232-9426

Intel Corp.
2402 W. Beardsley Road
Phoenix, AZ 85027
(602) 869-4647
(800) 538-3373
Fax: (800) 525-3019

Interphase
13800 Senlac
Dallas, TX 75234
(214) 919-9000
Fax: (214) 919-9200

Kalpara Inc.
1154 Argues Ave.
Sunnyvale, CA 95054
(408) 749-1600
Fax: (408) 749-1690

Krone Inc.
5 East Stow Rd., Suite H
Marlton, NJ 08053
(609) 985-9559
(800) 274-6113
Fax: (609) 985-9689

LANNET Data Communications Inc.
7711 Center Avenue, Suite 600
Huntington Beach, CA 92714
(714) 891-5580
Fax: (714) 891-7788

Lanwan Technologies
1566 La Pradera Drive
Campbell, CA 95008
(408) 374-8190
Fax: (408) 741-0152

Larse Corp.
4600 Patrick Henry Drive
P.O. Box 58138
Santa Clara, CA 95052
(408) 988-6600
Fax: (408) 986-8690

Loral Command & Control
9970 Federal Drive
Colorado Springs, CO 80921
(719) 594-1000
Fax: (719) 594-1305

Madge Networks Inc.
2310 North 1st St.
San Jose, CA 95131
(408) 955-0700
(800) 876-2343
Fax: (408) 955-0970

Micom Systems Inc.
4100 Los Angeles Ave.
Simi Valley, CA 93063
(805) 583-8600
(800) 642-6687
Fax: (805) 583-1997

Microcom Inc.
500 River Ridge Drive
Norwood, MA 02062-5028
(617) 551-1000
(800) 822-8224
Fax: (617) 551-1006

Microsoft Corp.
One Microsoft Way
Redmond, WA 98052-6399
(206) 882-8080
(800) 227-4679
Fax: (206) 635-6100

Microtest Inc.
3519 E. Shea Boulevard, Suite 134
Phoenix, AZ 85028
(602) 971-6464
(800) 526-9675
Fax: (602) 971-6963

Mitel Corp.
350 Legget Dr.
Kanata, Ontario
CANADA K2K 1X3
(613) 592-2122
(800) 648-3587
Fax: (613) 592-4784

Mitsubishi Electronics America
5665 Plaza Dr.
Cypress, CA 90630
(714) 220-2500
Fax: (714) 229-6550

MOD-TAP
285 Ayer Rd.
Harvard, MA 01451
(508) 772-5630
Fax: (508) 772-2011

Motorola Codex
20 Cabot Blvd.
Mansfield, MA 02048
(508) 261-4000
(800) 544-0062
Fax: (508) 261-7118

Multi-Access Computing Corp.
5350 Hollister Ave., Suite C
Santa Barbara, CA 93111
(805) 964-2332
Fax: (805) 681-7469

Multi-Tech Systems
2205 Woodale Drive
Mounds View, MN 55112
(612) 785-3500
(800) 328-9717
Fax: (612) 785-9874

National Semiconductor
2900 Semiconductor Drive, 16-195 M/S
Santa Clara, CA 95052
(408) 721-5020
(800) 538-8510
Fax: (408) 721-7662

NEC America
8 Old Sod Farm Rd.
Melville, NY 11747
(516) 753-7000
(800) 626-3349
Fax: (516) 753-7041

NEC Electronics
401 Ellis St.
Mountain View, CA 94039
(408) 960-6000
(800) 366-9782
Fax: (408) 965-6131

Net Express
1953 Gallows Rd., Suite 300
Vienna, VA 22182
(703) 749-2200

Netlink
3214 Spring Forest Road
Raleigh, NC 27604
(919) 878-8612
(800) 638-5465
Fax: (919) 872-2132

Netrix
13595 Dulles Technology Drive
Herndon, VA 22071
(703) 742-6000
Fax: (703) 742-4048

Network Communications
5501 Green Valley Drive
Bloomington, MN 55437
(612) 844-0584
(800) 333-1896
Fax: (612) 844-0487

Network Computing Inc.
1950 Stemmons Freeway, Suite 3016
Dallas, TX 75027
(214) 746-4949
(800) 736-3012
Fax: (214) 746-4955

Network Equipment Technologies Inc.
800 Saginaw Drive
Redwood City, CA 94063
(415) 366-4400
(800) 234-4638
Fax: (415) 366-5675

Network General Corp.
4200 Bohannon Drive
Menlo Park, CA 94025
(415) 688-2700
(800) 395-3151
Fax: (415) 321-0855

Network Peripherals Inc.
1371 McCarthy Blvd.
Milpitas, CA 95035
(408) 321-7300
Fax: (408) 321-9218

Network Systems Corp.
7600 Boone Ave. N.
Minneapolis, MN 55428
(612) 424-4888
(800) 248-8777
Fax: (612) 424-1661

Newbridge Networks
593 Herndon Parkway
Herndon, VA 22070
(703) 834-3600
(800) 332-1080
Fax: (703) 471-7080

Newport Systems Solutions Inc.
4019 Westerly Place, Suite 103
Newport Beach, CA 92660
(714) 752-1511
(800) 368-6533
Fax: (714) 752-8389

Northern Telecom Inc.
200 Athens Way
Nashville, TN 37228
(615) 734-4000

Novell Inc.
122 East 1700
South Provo, UT 84606
(801) 429-7000
(800) 638-9273
Fax: (801) 429-5155

Novell Inc.
2180 Fortune Drive
San Jose, CA 95131
(408) 473-8333
(800) 243-8526
Fax: (408) 435-1706

NTT America Inc.
800 El Camino Real W., Suite 300
Mountain View, CA 94040
(415) 940-1414
Fax: (415) 940-1375

Nynex Information Solutions Group Inc.
Four W. Red Oak Lane
White Plains, NY 10604
(914) 644-6000
Fax: (914) 694-2609

Odetics, Inc.
1515 S. Manchester Ave.
Anaheim, CA 92802
(714) 774-5000
Fax: (714) 774-9432

OKI America
666 Fifth Ave., 12th Floor
New York, NY 10103
(212) 489-8873
Fax: (212) 489-2358

Olicom USA, Inc.
900 East Park Boulevard, Suite 180
Plano, TX 75074
(214) 423-7560
Fax: (214) 423-7261

Optical Data Systems (ODS)
1101 E. Arapaho Road
Richardson, TX 75081
(214) 234-6400
Fax: (214) 234-4059

OST Inc.
14225 Sullyfield Circle
Chantilly, VA 22021
(703) 817-0400
Fax: (703) 817-0402

Pacific Access Computers
3079 Kilgore Road
Rancho Cordova, CA 95670
(916) 635-9300
(800) 648-6161
Fax: (916) 852-3870

Pairgain Technologies Inc.
12921 E. 166th Street
Cerritos, CA 90701
(310) 404-8811
(800) 638-0031
Fax: (310) 404-8939

Penril DataComm Networks
1300 Quince Orchard Blvd.
Gaithersburg, MD 20878
(301) 921-8600
(800) 473-6745
Fax: (301) 921-8376

PMC-Sierra Inc.
8501 Commerce Court
Burnaby, BC Canada V5A 4N3
(604) 668-7300
Fax: (604) 668-7301

Premisys Communications
1032 Elwell CT.
Palo Alto, CA 94303
(415) 940-4764
Fax: (415) 940-7713

Primary Access Corp.
10080 Carroll Canyon Road
San Diego, CA 92131
(619) 536-3000
Fax: (619) 693-8829

Primary Rate Inc.
5 Manor Parkway
Salem, NH 03079
(603) 898-1800
Fax: (603) 898-1199

Process Software Corp.
959 Concord Street
Framingham, MA 01701
(508) 879-6994
Fax: (508) 879-0042

Proteon Inc.
9 Technology Drive
Westborough, MA 01581
(508) 898-2800
(800) 545-7464
Fax: (508) 366-8901

ProTools Inc.
14976 N.W. Greenbrier Pkwy.
Beaverton, OR 97006
(503) 645-5400
(800) 743-4335
Fax: (503) 645-3577

Racal-Datacom Inc.
155 Swanson Road
Boxborough, MA 01719
(508) 263-9929
(800) 526-8255
Fax: (508) 263-8655

Racal Data Communications
1601 N. Harrison Pkwy.
Sunrise, FL 33323-2899
(305) 846-1601
(800) 722-2555
Fax: (305) 846-5510

RAD Data Communications Inc.
900 Corporate Drive
Mahwah, NJ 07430
(201) 529-1100
Fax: (201) 529-5777

RAD Network Devices Inc.
3505 Cadillac Ave., Suite G5
Costa Mesa, CA 92626
(714) 436-9700
Fax: (714) 436-1941

Retix
2401 Colorado Ave., Suite 200
Santa Monica, CA 90404
(310) 828-3400
(800) 255-2333
Fax: (310) 828-2255

Rockwell Network Systems
125 Cremona Drive
Santa Barbara, CA 93117
(805) 968-4262
Fax: (805) 968-6478

Scientific Atlanta
1 Technology Parkway South
Norcross, GA 30092
(404) 903-5000
Fax: (404) 903-2618

Scope Communications
100 Otis Street
Northboro, MA 01532
(508) 393-1236
Fax: (508) 393-2213

Siecor Corporation
489 Siecor Park
Hickory, NC 28603
(704) 327-5000
Fax: (704) 327-5973

Siemens Stromberg-Carlson
900 Broken Sound Pkwy.
Boca Raton, FL 33487
(407) 955-6645
Fax: (407) 955-6538

Silicom Manufacturing Technology Inc.
15321 S. Dixie Highway, Suite 303A
Miami, FL 33157
(305) 378-4722
Fax: (305) 378-4703

Silicon Graphics Inc.
2011 N. Shoreline Blvd.
Mountain View, CA 94043
(415) 960-1980; (800) 326-1020
Fax: (415) 961-0595

Silicon Systems Inc.
14351 Myford Road
Tustin, CA 92680
(714) 573-6773
Fax: (714) 573-6906

SNMP Research
3001 Kimberlin Heights Road
Knoxville, TN 37920
(615) 573-1434
Fax: (615) 573-9197

Sony Corp.
3300 Zanker Road
San Jose, CA 95134
(408) 955-5169
Fax: (408) 432-1874
Fax: 81-3-3448-7461

Standard Microsystems Corp.
80 Arkay Dr.
Hauppauge, NY 11788
(516) 435-6000
(800) 762-4968
Fax: (516) 273-2136

Stentor Resource Center
160 Elgon Street, Suite 1040
Ottawa, ON Canada K1G 3J4
(613) 781-8972
Fax: (613) 234-1442

StrataCom Inc.
1400 Parkmoor Ave.
San Jose, CA 95126
(408) 294-7600
Fax: (408) 999-0115

Sun Microsystems Inc.
2550 Garcia Ave.
Mountain View, CA 94043-1100
(415) 960-1300
(800) 872-4786
Fax: (415) 856-2114

Sync Research Inc.
7 Studebaker
Irvine, CA 92718
(714) 588-2070
Fax: (714) 588-2080

SynOptics Communications Inc.
P.O. Box 58185
4401 Great America Pkwy.
Santa Clara, CA 95052-8185
(408) 988-2400
Fax: (408) 988-5525

Syskonnect Inc.
12930 Saratoga Ave., Suite D-1
Saratoga, CA 95070
(408) 725-4650
(800) 752-3334
Fax: (408) 725-4654

T3plus Networking Inc.
3393 Octavius Drive
Santa Clara, CA 95054
(408) 727-4545
(800) 477-7050
Fax: (408) 727-4545

Tekelec
26580 W. Agoura Rd.
Calabasas, CA 91302
(818) 880-5656
(800) 835-3532
Fax: (818) 880-6993

Tektronix Inc.
625 SE Salmon
Redmond, OR 97756
(503) 923-0333
(800) 833-9200
Fax: (503) 923-4434

Telco Systems Inc./Magnalink Communications
63 Nahatan Street
Norwood, MA 02062
(617) 255-9400
Fax: (617) 255-5885

Telebit Corp.
1315 Chesapeake Terrace
Sunnyvale, CA 94089
(408) 734-4333
(800) 835-3248
Fax: (408) 734-4333

Telecommunications Techniques Corp.
20400 Observation Drive
Germantown, MD 20874
(301) 353-1550
(800) 638-2049
Fax: (301) 353-0731

Telematics International Inc.
1201 Cypress Creek Road
Ft. Lauderdale, FL 33309
(305) 772-3070
Fax: (305) 351-4405

Telenex Corp.
7401 Boston Blvd.
Springfield, VA 22153
(703) 644-9148
Fax: (703) 644-9011

Tellabs Operations, Inc.
1000 Remington Blvd.
Bolingbrook, IL 60440
(708) 969-8800
Fax: (708) 378-5620

Texas Instruments
Peripheral Products Division
5701 Airport Road
Temple, TX 76501
(817) 774-6001
(800) 527-3500
Fax: (817) 774-6501

The Mitre Corp.
7525 Colshire Drive
McLean, VA 22102
(703) 883-6000
Fax: (703) 883-3315

3Com Corp.
5400 Bayfront Plaza
Santa Clara, CA 95052
(408) 562-6400
(800) 638-3266
Fax: (408) 764-5001

Transwitch Corp.
8 Progress Dr.
Shelton, CT 06484
(203) 929-8810
Fax: (203) 926-9453

Triticom
11800 Single Tree Lane, Suite 310
Eden Prairie, MN 55344
(612) 937-0772
Fax: (612) 937-1998

TRW Inc.
1760 Glenn Curtiss Street
Carson, CA 90746
(310) 764-9467
Fax: (213) 764-9491

UDS Motorola Inc.
5000 Bradford Drive
Huntsville, AL 35805-1993
(205) 430-8000
(800) 451-2369
Fax: (205) 430-7265

Ungermann-Bass Inc.
3990 Freedom Circle
Santa Clara, CA 95052-8030
(408) 496-0111
(800) 873-6381
Fax: (408) 727-4456

Unisys
Township Line and Union Mtg. Rd.
Blue Bell, PA 19422
(215) 986-4011
Fax: (215) 986-6850

Verilink Corp.
145 Baytech Drive
San Jose, CA 95134
(408) 945-1199
(800) 543-1008
Fax: (408) 946-5124

Vitalink Communications Corp.
48761 Kato Road
Fremont, CA 94538
(510) 226-6500
(800) 443-5740
Fax: (510) 440-2380

VLSI Technology
11098 McKay Drive
San Jose, CA 95131
(408) 434-3000
Fax: (408) 434-7937

Wandel and Goltermann
1030 Swabia Court
Research Triangle Park, NC 27709
(919) 941-5730
Fax: (919) 941-5751

WellFleet Communications Corp.
8 Federal Street
Billerica, MA 01821
(508) 670-8888
Fax: (508) 436-3658

Wollongong Group Inc.
1129 San Antonio Road
Palo Alto, CA 94303
(415) 962-7100
(800) 872-8649
Fax: (415) 969-5547

XLNT Designs Inc.
15050 AVenue of Science, Suite 106
San Diego, CA 92128
(619) 487-9320
Fax: (619) 487-9768

Xyplex Inc.
330 Codman Hill Rd.
Boxboro, MA 01719
(508) 264-9900
Fax: (508) 952-5303

 Selected Carriers Providing
Broadband Services

Ameritech Corp.
2000 W. Ameritech Center Drive
Hoffman Estates, IL 60196
(708) 248-2000

AT&T
32 Avenue of the Americas
New York, NY 10013
(212) 387-5400

Bell Atlantic Corp.
540 Broad Street
Newark, NJ 07102
(201) 649-9900

Bellsouth Corp.
1155 Peachtree Street NE
Atlanta, GA 30309
(404) 249-2000

Cable & Wireless Inc.
1919 Gallows Road
Vienna, VA 22182
(703) 790-5300

Compuserve Inc.
5000 Arlington Center
Boulevard Columbus, OH 43220
(614) 457-8600

EMI Communications Corp.
5015 Compuswood Drive
East Syracuse, NY 13057
(315) 433-0022

GTE Corp.
600 Hidden Ridge
Irving, TX 75038
(214) 718-5000

Infonet Inc.
2100 E. Grand Ave.
El Segundo, CA 90245
(310) 335-2600

MCI Communications Corp.
1801 Pennsylvania Ave. NW
Washington DC 20006
(202) 872-1600

MFS Communications Company
1 Tower Lane, Suite 1600
Oakbrook, IL 60181
(708) 218-7200

Nynex Corp.
1113 Westchester Ave.
White Plains, NY 10604
(914) 644-7600

Pacific Bell
140 New Montgomery Street
San Francisco, CA 94105
(415) 542-9000

PacNet, Inc.
7525 SE 24th Street
Mercer Island, WA 98040
(206) 232-9900

Southern New England Telephone Co.
227 Church Street
New Haven, CT 06510
(203) 771-5200

Southwestern Bell Corp.
One Bell Center
St. Louis, MO 63101
(314) 235-0299

Sprint International
12524 Sunrise Valley Drive
Reston, VA 22091
(703) 689-6000

US West Inc.
7800 E. Orchard Road
Englewood, CO 80111
(303) 793-6500

WilTel
One Williams Center
Tulsa, OK 74172
(918) 588-3210

 # Acronyms and Abbreviations

A	Ampere
AA	Administrative Authority
AAL	ATM Adaptation Layer
AARP	AppleTalk Address Resolution Protocol
ABM	Asynchronous Balanced Mode (of HDLC)
ABP	Alternate Bipolar
ABR	Available Bit Rate
ACF	Access Control Field
ACK	Acknowledgment
ACS	Asynchronous Communication Server
ACTLU	Activate Logical Unit
ACTPU	Activate Physical Unit
ADPCM	Adaptive Differential Pulse Code Modulation
ADSP	AppleTalk Data Stream Protocol

AEP	AppleTalk Echo Protocol
AFI	Authority and Format Identifier
AFP	AppleTalk Filing Protocol
AFRP	ARCNET Fragmentation Protocol
AGS	Asynchronous Gateway Server
AI	Artificial Intelligence
AIN	Advanced Intelligent Network
AIS	Alarm Indication Signal
AL	Alignment
AMI	Alternate Mark Inversion
AMT	Address Mapping Table
ANSI	American National Standards Institute
API	Applications Program Interface
APPC	Advanced Program-to-Program Communication
ARE	All Routes Explorer
AREA	Area Identifier
ARI	Address Recognized Indicator Bit
ARM	Asynchronous Response Mode
ARP	Address Resolution Protocol
ARPA	Advanced Research Projects Agency
ARPANET	Advanced Research Projects Agency Network
ACCE	Association Control Service Element
ASCII	American Standard Code for Information Interchange
ASN.1	Abstract Syntax Notation One

ASP	AppleTalk Session Protocol
ATIS	Alliance for Telecommunications Industry Solutions
ATM	Asynchronous Transfer Mode
ATM DXI	ATM Data Exchange Interface
ATM UNI	ATM User-Network Interface
ATP	AppleTalk Transaction Protocol
AU	Access Unit
B	B Channel
B	Broadband
B8ZS	Bipolar with 8 ZERO Substitution
BAsize	Buffer Allocation size
BC	Block Check
BC	Bearer Capability
Bc	Committed Burst
BCD	Binary Coded Decimal
BCN	Backward Congestion Notification
Be	Excess Burst
BECN	Backward Explicit Congestion Notification
BER	Basic Encoding Rules
BER	Bit Error Rate
BEtag	Beginning-End tag
B-ICI	Broadband Inter-Carrier Interface
BIF	Bus Identification Field
BIOS	Basic Input/Output System

BIP	Bit Interleaved Parity
BIP-n	Bit Interleaved Parity-n
B-ISDN	Broadband Integrated Services Digital Network
B-ISSI	Broadband Inter-Switching System Interface
B-ISUP	Broadband ISDN User Part
BITNET	Because It's Time NETwork
BIU	Basic Information Unit
B-NT1	Network Termination 1 for B-ISDN
B-NT2	Network Termination 2 for B-ISDN
BOC	Bell Operating Company
BOM	Beginning of Message
BOOTP	Bootstrap Protocol
BPDU	Bridge Protocol Data Unit
bps	Bits Per Second
BPV	Bipolar Violations
BRI	Basic Rate Interface
BSC	Binary Synchronous Communication
BSD	Berkeley Software Distribution
BSS	Broadband Switching System
B-TE	B-ISDN Terminal Equipment
B-TE1	Terminal Equipment 1 for B-ISDN
B-TE2	Terminal Equipment 2 for B-ISDN
B-TA	Terminal Adapter for B-ISDN
Btag	Begin Tag

BTU	Basic Transmission Unit
BW	Bandwitdth
CAD/CAM	Computer-Aided Design and Manufacturing
CBR	Constant Bit Rate
CC	Configuration Control
CCITT	International Telegraph and Telephone Consultative Committee
CDV	Cell Delay Variance
CI	Congestion Indication
CIR	Committed Information Rate
CIR	Cell Insertion Ratio
CLNAP	Connectionless Network Access Protocol
CLP	Cell Loss Priority
CLR	Cell Loss Ratio
CLS	Connectionless Service
COM	Continuation of Message
CP	Common Part
CPE	Customer Premises Equipment
CS	Convergence Sublayer
CPCS	Common Part Convergence Sublayer
CPI	Common Part Indicator
CRC	Cyclic Redundancy Check
C/R	Command/Response bit
CRS	Cell Relay Service
CSI	Convergence Sublayer Indicator

CSMA/CD	Carrier Sense Multiple Access with Collision Detection
CSNET	Computer+Science Network
CSPDN	Circuit Switched Public Data Network
CSU	Channel Service Unit
CTERM	Command Terminal Protocol
D	D Channel
DA	Destination Address
DAP	Data Access Protocol
DARPA	Defense Advanced Research Projects Agency
DAT	Duplicate Address Test
DCA	Defense Communications Agency
DCC	Data Country Code
DCE	Data Circuit-Terminating Equipment
DCN	Data Communications Network
DCS-n	Digital Cross Connect System at Level n
DDCMP	Digital Data Communications Message Protocol
DDI	Direct Dialing In
DDN	Defense Data Network
DDP	Datagram Delivery Protocol
DDS	Digital Data Service
DE	Discard Eligible
DECmcc	DEC Management Control Center
DEMPR	DEC Multiport Repeater
DFA	DXI Frame Address

DFI	DSP Format Identifier
DH	DMPDU Header
DIX	DEC, Intel, and Xerox
DL	Data Link
DLC	Data Link Control
DLCI	Data Link Connection Identifier
DMA	Direct Memory Access
DMDD	Distributed Multiplexing Distributed Demultiplexing
DMPDU	Derived MAC Protocol Data Unit
DNIC	Data Network Identification Code
DNS	Domain Name System
DOD	Department of Defense
DPA	Demand Protocol Architecture
DQDB	Distributed Queue Dual Bus
DQSM	Distributed Queue State Machine
DRP	DECnet Routing Protocol
DSAP	Destination Service Access Point
DSG	Default Slot Generator
DSGS	Default Slot Generator Subfield
DS0	Digital Signal, Level 0 (64 Kbps)
DS1	Digital Signal, Level 1 (1.544 Mbps)
DS3	Digital Signal, Level 3 (44.736 Mbps)
DSP	Domain Specific Part
DSU	Data Service Unit

DSU/CSU	Data Service Unit/Channel Service Unit
DSX-n	Digital Signal Cross Connect Level n
DT	DMPDU Trailer
DTE	Data Terminal Equipment
DTR	Data Terminal Ready
DXC	Digital Cross-Connect
DXI	Data Exchange Interface
EA	Extended Address
EBCDIC	Extended Binary Coded Decimal Interchange Code
ECL	End Communication Layer
ECSA	Exchange Carriers Standards Association
ED	End Delimiter
EDI	Electronic Data Interchange
EFCN	Explicit Forward Congestion Notification
EFI	Errored Frame Indicator
EGA	Enhanced Graphics Array
EGP	Exterior Gateway Protocol
EIA	Electronic Industries Association
ELAP	EtherTalk Link Access Protocol
EOM	End of Message
EOT	End of Transmission
ES	Errored Second
ESF	Extended Superframe Format
ESI	End System Identifier

ESIG	European SMDS Interest Group
ES-IS	End System to Intermediate System Protocol
ET	Exchange Termination
ETS	External Timing Source
Etag	End Tag
ETSS	External Timing Source Subfield
ETSI	European Telecommunications Standards Institute
Ext	Extension
FAL	File Access Listener
FAS	Frame Alignment Signal
FAT	File Access Table
FCC	Federal Communications Commission
FCI	Frame Copied Indicator Bit
FCN	Forward Congestion Notification
FCS	Frame Check Sequence
FDDI	Fiber Data Distributed Interface
FDM	Frequency Division Multiplexing
FEBE	Far-End Block Error
FEC	Forward Error Correction
FECN	Forward Error Congestion Notification
FERF	Far-End Receive Failure
FFS	For Further Study
FH	Frame Handler
FID	Format Identifier

FIFO	First In, First out
FIPS	Federal Information Processing Standard
FM	Function Management
FMD	Function Management Data
FMIF	Frame Mode Information Field
FOTS	Fiber-Optic Transport System
FR	Frame Relay
FRAD	Frame Relay Access Device
FRS	Frame Relay Service
FR-UNI	Frame Relay User-Network Interface
FRAD	Frame Relay Assembler/Disassembler
FRND	Frame Relay Network Device
FR-SSCS	Frame Relay Service Specific Convergence Sublayer
FT1	Fractional T1
FTAM	File Transfer Access and Management
FTP	File Transfer Protocol
G	Giga-
GB	Gigabyte
GFC	Generic Flow Control
GHz	Gigahertz
GOSIP	Government OSI Profile
GUI	Graphical User Interface
HA	Hardware Address
HCS	Header Check Sequence

HDLC	High-Level Data-Link Control
Hdr	Header
HEC	Header Error Control
HEL	Header Extension Length
HEMS	High-Level Entity Management System
HLC	High-Layer Compatibility
HLLAPI	High-Level Language API
HLPI	Higher Layer Protocol Identifier
HOB	Head-of-Bus
HOB_A	Head of Bus A
HOB_B	Head of Bus B
HOBS	Head of Bus Subfield
HSSI	High-Speed Serial Interface
Hz	Hertz
I	Information
IA5	International Alphabet No. 5
IAB	Internet Architecture Board
IANA	Internet Assigned Numbers Authority
ICD	International Code Designator
ICF	Isochronous Convergence Function <<Mark: verify spelling of Isochronous.>>
ICI	Interexchange Carrier Interface
ICIP	Inter-Carrier Interface Protocol
ICIP_CLS	ICIP Connectionless Service
ICMP	Internet Control Message Protocol

ICP	Internet Control Protocol
IDI	Initial Domain Identifier
IDP	Internetwork Datagram Protocol
IDU	Interface Data Unit
IE	Information Element
IEC	International Electrotechnical Commission
IEEE	Institute of Electrical and Electronics Engineers, Inc.
IETF	Internet Engineering Task Force
I/G	Individual/Group
IGP	Interior Gateway Protocol
IGRP	Internet Gateway Routing Protocol
ILMI	Interim Local Management Interface
IMPDU	Initial MAC Protocol Data Unit
IMPS	Interface Message Processors
I/O	Input/Output
IOC	Inter-Office Channel
IP	Internet Protocol
IPC	Interprocess Communications Protocol
IPX	Internetwork Packet Exchange
IR	Internet Router
IRTF	Internet Research Task Force
ISA	Industry Standard Architecture
ISDN	Integrated Services Digital Network
ISDU	Isochronous Service Data Unit

IS-IS	Intermediate System to Intermediate System Protocol
ISO	International Organization for Standardization
ISODE	ISO Development Environment
ISSI	Inter-Switching System Interface
ISSIP_CLS	Inter-Switching System Interface Protocol Connectionless Service
ISU	Isochronous Service User
IT	Information Type
ITU	International Telecommunication Union
ITU-T	ITU Telecommunication Standardization Sector (formerly CCITT)
IVDLAN	Integrated Voice/Data Local Area Network
IWF	Interworking Function
IWU	Interworking Unit
IXC	Inter-Exchange Carrier
Kbps	Kilo Bits per Second
KHz	Kilohertz
LAA	Locally Administered Address
LAN	Local Area Network
LAP	Link Access Procedure
LAPB	Link Access Procedure Balanced
LAPD	Link Access Procedure D Channel
LAPF	Link Access Procedures to Frame Mode Bearer Services
LAT	Local Area Transport

LATA	Local Access Transport Area
LAVC	Local Area VAX Cluster
LE	Local Exchange
LEC	Local Exchange Carrier
LEN	Length
LF	Largest Frame
LFC	Local Function Capabilities
LI	Link Identifier
LI	Length Indicator
LIF	Line Interface
LL	Logical Link
LLAP	LocalTalk Link Access Protocol
LLC	Logical Link Control
LLI	Logical Link Identifier
LME	Layer Management Entity
LMI	Local Management Interface
LMI	Layer Management Interface
LMMP	LAN/MAN Management Protocol
LMMPE	LAN/MAN Management Protocol Entity
LMMS	LAN/MAN Management Service
LMMU	LAN/MAN Management User
LMM	LAN WAN Management User
LOC	Loss of Cell delineation
LOF	Loss of Frame
LOH	Line Overhead

LOP	Loss of Pointer
LOS	Loss of Signal
LPP	Lightweight Presentation Protocol
LSB	Least Significant Bit
LSL	Link Support Layer
LSS	Link Status Signal
LT	Line Termination
LTE	Line Terminating Equipment
MAC	Medium Access Control
MAN	Metropolitan Area Network
MAP	Management Application Protocol
Mbps	Megabits Per Second
MCF	MAC Convergence Function
MCP	MAC Convergence Protocol
MHS	Message Handling Service
MHz	Megahertz
MIB	Management Information Base
MID	Message Identifier
MID	Multiplexing Identifier
MILNET	MILitary NETwork
MIPS	Millions Instructions Per Second
MIS	Management Information Systems
MLID	Multiple Link Interface Driver
MM	Multi-Mode
MMF	Multi-Mode Fiber

MNP	Microcom Networking Protocol
M/O	Mandatory/Optional
MOP	Maintenance Operations Protocol
MPA	MID Page Allocation
MPAF	MID Page Allocation Field
MPEG	Motion Picture Expert Group
ms	Milliseconds
MSAP	MAC Service Access Point
MSAU	Multistation Access Unit
MSB	Most Significant Bit
MSDU	MAC Service Data Unit
MSN	Monitoring Cell Sequence Number
MSS	MAN Switching System
MTA	Message Transfer Agent
MTBF	Mean Time Between Failure
MTTR	Mean Time To Repair
MTU	Maximum Transmission Unit
MUX	Multiplex, Multiplexor
NACS	NetWare Asynchronous Communications Server
NAK	Negative Acknowledgment
NANP	North American Numbering Plan
NASI	NetWare Asynchronous Service Interface
NAU	Network Addressable Unit
NAUN	Nearest Active Upstream Neighbor

NBP	Name Binding Protocol
NCP	Network Control Program
NCP	NetWare Core Protocol
NCSI	Network Communications Services Interface
NDIS	Network Driver Interface Standard
NetBEUI	NetBIOS Extended User Interface
NetBIOS	Network Basic Input/Output System
NFS	Network File System
NIC	Network Information Center
NIC	Network Interface Card
NIC	Network Independent Clock
NICE	Network Information and Control Exchange
NIS	Names Information Socket
N-ISNDN	Narrowband Integrated Services Digital Network
NIST	National Institute of Standards and Technology
NLM	NetWare Loadable Module
NMP	Network Management Process
NMS	Network Management Station
NNI	Network-Network Interface
NNI	Network-Node Interface
NOC	Network Operations Center
NOS	Network Operating System
NPC	Network Parameter Control
NRM	Normal Response Mode

NRZ	Non-Return to Zero
NSF	National Science Foundation
NSAP	Network Service Access Point
NSP	Network Services Protocol
NT	Network Termination
NT1	Network Termination of type 1
NT2	Network Termination of type 2
OAM	Operations, Administration and Maintenance
OC-1	Optical Carrier, Level 1 (51.840 Mbps)
OC-3	Optical Carrier, Level 3 (155.520 Mbps)
OC-n	Optical Carrier, Level n
ODI	Open Data-Link Interface
OID	Object Identifier
OIM	OSI Internet Management
OOF	Out of Frame
OS	Operating System
OSF	Open Software Foundation
OSI	Open Systems Interconnection
OSI-RM	Open Systems Interconnection Reference Model
OSPF	Open Shortest Path First
OUI	Organizationally Unique Identifier
PA	Pre-Arbitrated Functions
PA	Protocol Address
PABX	Private Automatic Branch Exchange

PAD	Packet Assembler and Disassembler
PAD	Padding
PAP	Printer Access Protocol
PBX	Private Branch Exchange
PC	Personal Computer
PCI	Protocol Control Information
PCM	Pulse Code Modulation
PCSM	Page Counter State Machine
PDH	Plesiochronous Digital Hierarchy
PDN	Public Data Network
PDU	Protocol Data Unit
PEP	Packet Exchange Protocol
PH	Packet Handler
Ph-SAP	Physical layer Service Access Point
PHY	Physical Layer Protocol
PI	Protocol Identification
PID	Protocol Identifier
PL	PAD Length
PL	Physical Layer
PLEN	Protocol Length
PLCP	Physical Layer Convergence Procedure
PLCSM	Physical Layer Connection State Machine
PLP	Packet Layer Protocol
PM	Physical Medium
PMD	Physical Medium Dependent

P-NNI	Private Network to Network Interface
POH	Path Overhead
POI	Path Overhead Identifier
POP	Point of Presence
POSIX	Portable Operating System Interface—UNIX
POTS	Plain Old Telephone Service
PPP	Point-to-Point Protocol
PRSIG	Pacific Rim SMDS Interest Group
PSN	Packet Switch Node
PSP	Presentation Services Process
PSPDN	Packet Switched Public Data Network
PSR	Previous Segment Received
PSTN	Public Switched Telephone Network
PT	Payload Type
PTN	Personal Telecommunications Number
PTP	Point-to-Point
PTT	Postal, Telegraph and Telephone
PUC	Public Utility Commission
PVC	Permanent Virtual Circuit
PVC	Permanent Virtual Connection
QA	Queued Arbitrated
QOS	Quality of Service
RARP	Reverse Address Resolution Protocol
RBOC	Regional Bell Operating Company
RC	Routing Control

RD	Route Descriptor
RD	Routing Domain Identifier
RDI	Remote Defect Indication
RDT	Remote Digital Terminal
RDTD	Restricted Differential Time Delay
REQ	Request
RFC	Request for Comments
RFH	Remote Frame Handler
RFS	Remote File System
RH	Request/Response Header
RI	Routing Information
RII	Route Information Indicator
RIP	Routing Information Protocol
RJE	Remote Job Entry
ROSE	Remote Operations Service Element
RMON	Remote Monitoring
RPC	Remote Procedure Call
RPS	Ring Parameter Service
RQ	Request Counter
RQM	Request Queue Machine
RSM	Reassembly State Machine
RSX	Real time resource-Sharing eXecutive
RT	Routing Type
RU	Request/Response Unit
RX	Receive

SA	Source Address
SAAL	Signaling ATM Adaptation Layer
SABME	Set Asynchronous Balanced Mode Extended
SAP	Service Access Point
SAP	Service Advertising Protocol
SAPI	Service Access Point Identifier
SAR	Segmentation and Reassembly
SAT	Subscriber Access Termination
SCS	System Communication Services
SDH	Synchronous Digital Hierarchy
SDLC	Synchronous Data Link Control
SDN	Software Defined Network
SDSU	SMDS Data Service Unit
SDU	Service Data Unit
SEL	NSAP Selector
SEQ	Sequence
SET	Switching System Exchange Termination
SGMP	Simple Gateway Management Protocol
SIG	SMDS Interest Group
SIP	SMDS Interface Protocol
SIP_CLS	SIP Connectionless Service
SIR	Sustained Information Rate
SIU	Subscriber Interface Unit
SLIP	Serial Line IP
SM	Single-Mode

SMAE	System Management Application Entity
SMB	Server Message Block
SMDS	Switched Multimegabit Data Service
SMF	Single Mode Fiber
SMI	Structure of Management Information
SMT	Station Management
SMTP	Simple Mail Transfer Protocol
SN	Sequence Number
SNA	System Network Architecture
SNADS	Systems Network Architecture Distribution Services
SNAP	Sub-Network Access Protocol
SNCF	SubNetwork Configuration Field
SNI	Subscriber-Network Interface
SNMP	Simple Network Management Protocol
SOH	Start of Header
SOH	Section Overhead
SONET	Synchronous Optical Network
SPE	Synchronous Payload Envelope
SPN	Subscriber Premises Network
SPP	Sequenced Packet Protocol
SPX	Sequenced Packet Exchange
SR	Source Routing
SRF	Specifically Routed Frame
SRI	Stanford Research Institute

SRI	SIP Relay Interface
SRT	Source Routing Transparent
SRTS	Synchronous Residual Time Stamp
SS	Switching System
SSAP	Source Service Access Point
SSCS	Service-Specific Convergence Sublayer
SSCF	Service-Specific Coordination Function
SSCOP	Service-Specific Connection-Oriented Protocol
SSM	Single Segment Message
SS7	Common Channel Signaling System No. 7
ST	Segment Type
STE	Spanning Tree Explorer
STE	Section Terminating Equipment
STM	Synchronous Transfer Mode
STP	Shielded Twisted Pair
STS-1	Synchronous Transport Signal, Level-1
STS-3	Synchronous Transport Signal, Level-3
STS-3c	Synchronous Transport Signal, Level-3, concatenated
STS-n	Synchronous Transport Signal, level-n
SUA	Stored Upstream Address
SVC	Switched Virtual Connection
SVC	Switched Virtual Circuit
TA	Technical Advisory
TA	Terminal Adapter

TAG	Technology Advisory Group
TB	Terabyte
TC	Transmission Convergence
TCP	Transmission Control Protocol
TDM	Time Division Multiplexing
TE	Terminal Equipment
TE1	Terminal Equipment of type 1
TE2	Terminal Equipment of type 2
TEI	Terminal Endpoint Identifier
TID	Terminal Identifier
TR	Technical Reference
TCP	Transmission Control Protocol
TCP/IP	Transmission Control Protocol/Internet Protocol
TDM	Time Division Multiplexing
TELNET	Telecommunications Network
TFTP	Trivial File Transfer Protocol
TH	Transmission Header
TLAP	TokenTalk Link Access Protocol
TLI	Transport Layer Interface
TLV	Type-Length-Value Encoding
TP	Transport Protocol
TR	Technical Reference
Trlr	Trailer
TS	Time Stamp

TSR	Terminate-and-Stay Resident
TUC	Total User Cell Number
TX	Transmit
UA	Unnumbered Acknowledgment
UA	User Agent
UAS	Unavailable Seconds
UDI	Unrestricted Digital Information
UDI-TA	Unrestricted Digital Information with Tones/Announcements
UDP	User Datagram Protocol
UI	Unnumbered Information Frame
U/L	Universal/Local
ULP	Upper Layer Protocols
UME	User Management Entity
UNI	User-Network Interface
UNMA	Unified Network Management Architecture
UPC	Usage Parameter Control
USID	User Service Identificator
UT	Universal Time
UTP	Unshielded Twisted Pair
UTP-3	Unshielded Twisted Pair, category 3
UTP-5	Unshielded Twisted Pair, category 5
UU	User-to-User
UUCP	UNIX-to-UNIX Copy Program
V	Volt

VAN	Value Added Network
VAP	Value Added Process
VARP	VINES Address Resolution Protocol
VBR	Variable Bit Rate
VC	Virtual Channel
VCC	Virtual Channel Connection
VCI	Virtual Channel Identifier
VF	Voice Frequency Services
VFRP	VINES Fragmentation Protocol
VGA	Video Graphics Array
VICP	VINES Internet Control Protocol
VINES	Virtual Networking System
VIP	VINES Internet Protocol
VIPC	VINES Interprocess Communications
VLSI	Very Large-Scale Integration
VMS	Virtual Memory System
VP	Virtual Path
VPC	Virtual Path Connection
VPI	Virtual Path Identifier
VRTP	VINES Routing Update Protocol
VSPP	VINES Sequenced Packet Protocol
VT	Virtual Terminal
VT	Virtual Tributary
WAN	Wide Area Network
WDM	Wavelength Division Multiplexing

WIN	Window
X	Unassigned Bit
XA-SMDS	Exchange Access SMDS
XDR	External Data Representation
XID	Exchange Identification
XMP	X/Open Management Protocol
XNS	Xerox Network System
ZIP	Zone Information Protocol
ZIS	Zone Information Socket
ZIT	Zone Information Table

 # Data Link Layer Frame Formats

Alert Burst | EOT | DID | DID

Invitation to transmit: The token to pass line control

Alert Burst | ENQ | DID | DID

Free Buffer Enquiry: Can the destination node accept a packet?

Alert Burst | SOH | SID | DID | DID | Count | Data | CRC | CRC

Count: 1–2 Octets
Data: 1–508 Octets

Packet: The Data or Message

Alert Burst | ACK

ACK: Positive response to Packets or Free Buffer Enquiry

Alert Burst | NAK

NAK: Negative response to Free Buffer Enquiry

Alert Burst: 111111
ACK: ASCII ACK
CRC: Cyclic Redundancy Check
DID: Destination Node ID
ENQ: ASCII ENQ

EOT: ASCII EOT
NAK: ASCII NAK
SID: Source Node ID
SOH: ASCII SOH

Figure H–1. ARCNET Frame Formats

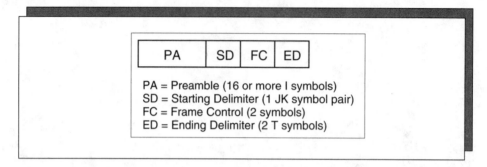

Figure H–2a. FDDI Token Format.

This material is reproduced with permission from American National Standard Fiber Distributed Data Interface (FDDI)—Token Ring Media Access Control (MAC), ANSI X3.139-1987, ©1987 by the American National Standards Institute. Copies of this standard may be purchased from the American National Standards Institute at 11 West 42nd Street, New York, NY 10036.

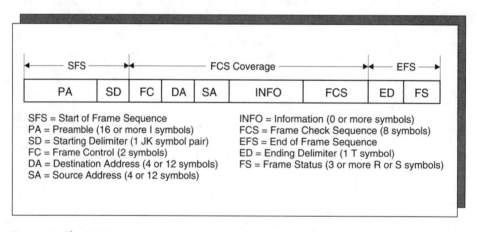

Figure H–2b. FDDI Frame Format.

This material is reproduced with permission from American National Standard Fiber Distributed Data Interface (FDDI)—Token Ring Media Access Control (MAC), ANSI X3.139-1987, ©1987 by the American National Standards Institute. copies of this standard may be purchased from the American National Standards Institute at 11 West 42nd Street, New York, NY 10036.

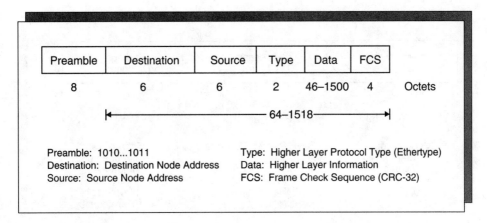

Figure H-3. Ethernet Frame Format.

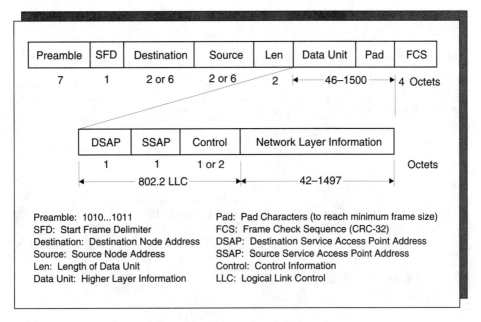

Figure H-4. IEEE 802.3 Frame Format including 802.2 LLC Header *(Courtesy IEEE)*

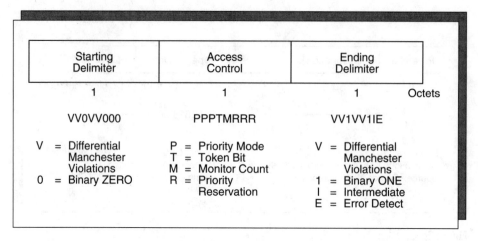

Figure H-5a. IEEE 802.5 Token Format *(Courtesy IEEE)*

Starting Delimiter	Access Control	Frame Control	Dest Addr	Source Addr	Route Info	Information Field	FCS	Ending Delimiter	Frame Status
1	1	1	2 or 6	2 or 6	0–30	Variable	4	1	1

Octets

Starting Delimiter: Beginning of Frame
Access Control: Transmission Parameters
Frame Control: Frame Type
Dest Addr: Destination Node Address
Source Addr: Source Node Address

Route Info: Routing Information Field
Information: Higher Layer Information
FCS: Frame Check Sequence (CRC-32)
Ending Delimiter: End of Frame
Frame Status: Receiver-Provided Feedback

Figure H-5b. IEEE 802.5 Frame Format *(Courtesy IEEE)*

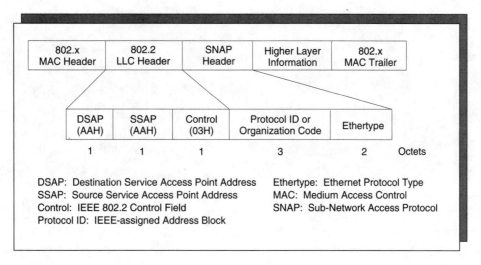

Figure H–6. Sub-Network Access Protocol (SNAP) header encapsulated within an IEEE 802.x frame *(Courtesy IEEE)*

Physical Layer Connector Pinouts

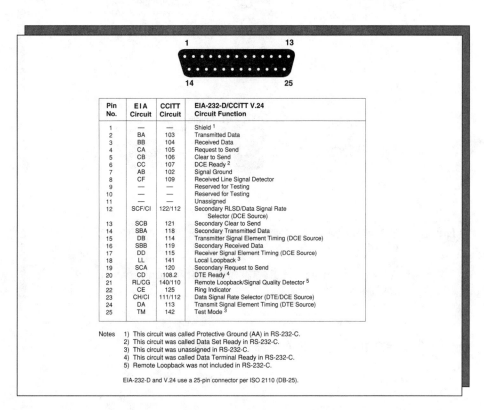

Pin No.	EIA Circuit	CCITT Circuit	EIA-232-D/CCITT V.24 Circuit Function
1	—	—	Shield [1]
2	BA	103	Transmitted Data
3	BB	104	Received Data
4	CA	105	Request to Send
5	CB	106	Clear to Send
6	CC	107	DCE Ready [2]
7	AB	102	Signal Ground
8	CF	109	Received Line Signal Detector
9	—	—	Reserved for Testing
10	—	—	Reserved for Testing
11	—	—	Unassigned
12	SCF/CI	122/112	Secondary RLSD/Data Signal Rate Selector (DCE Source)
13	SCB	121	Secondary Clear to Send
14	SBA	118	Secondary Transmitted Data
15	DB	114	Transmitter Signal Element Timing (DCE Source)
16	SBB	119	Secondary Received Data
17	DD	115	Receiver Signal Element Timing (DCE Source)
18	LL	141	Local Loopback [3]
19	SCA	120	Secondary Request to Send
20	CD	108.2	DTE Ready [4]
21	RL/CG	140/110	Remote Loopback/Signal Quality Detector [5]
22	CE	125	Ring Indicator
23	CH/CI	111/112	Data Signal Rate Selector (DTE/DCE Source)
24	DA	113	Transmit Signal Element Timing (DTE Source)
25	TM	142	Test Mode [3]

Notes
1) This circuit was called Protective Ground (AA) in RS-232-C.
2) This circuit was called Data Set Ready in RS-232-C.
3) This circuit was unassigned in RS-232-C.
4) This circuit was called Data Terminal Ready in RS-232-C.
5) Remote Loopback was not included in RS-232-C.

EIA-232-D and V.24 use a 25-pin connector per ISO 2110 (DB-25).

Figure I–1. EIA-232-D/ITU-T Recommendation V.24 *(Courtesy of Hill Associates Inc., © 1992)*

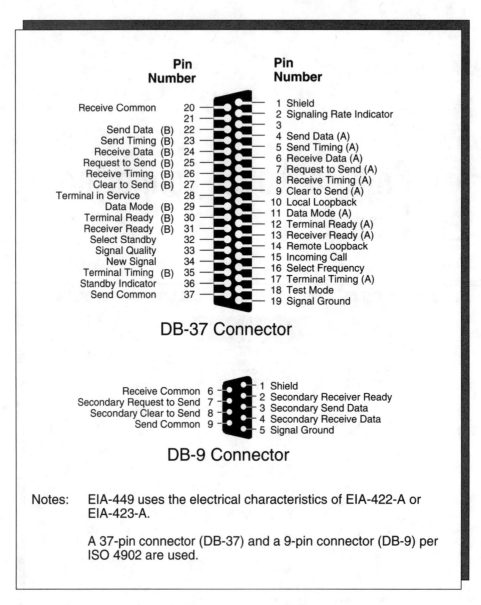

Pin Number

Receive Common 20

21

Send Data (B) 22
Send Timing (B) 23
Receive Data (B) 24
Request to Send (B) 25
Receive Timing (B) 26
Clear to Send (B) 27
Terminal in Service 28
Data Mode (B) 29
Terminal Ready (B) 30
Receiver Ready (B) 31
Select Standby 32
Signal Quality 33
New Signal 34
Terminal Timing (B) 35
Standby Indicator 36
Send Common 37

Pin Number

1 Shield
2 Signaling Rate Indicator
3
4 Send Data (A)
5 Send Timing (A)
6 Receive Data (A)
7 Request to Send (A)
8 Receive Timing (A)
9 Clear to Send (A)
10 Local Loopback
11 Data Mode (A)
12 Terminal Ready (A)
13 Receiver Ready (A)
14 Remote Loopback
15 Incoming Call
16 Select Frequency
17 Terminal Timing (A)
18 Test Mode
19 Signal Ground

DB-37 Connector

Receive Common 6
Secondary Request to Send 7
Secondary Clear to Send 8
Send Common 9

1 Shield
2 Secondary Receiver Ready
3 Secondary Send Data
4 Secondary Receive Data
5 Signal Ground

DB-9 Connector

Notes: EIA-449 uses the electrical characteristics of EIA-422-A or EIA-423-A.

A 37-pin connector (DB-37) and a 9-pin connector (DB-9) per ISO 4902 are used.

Figure I–2. EIA-449 *(Courtesy of Hill Associates Inc., © 1992)*

Pin No.	EIA Circuit	EIA-530 Circuit Name
1	—	Shield
2	BA (A)	Transmitted Data (A)
3	BB (A)	Received Data (A)
4	CA (A)	Request to Send (A)
5	CB (A)	Clear to Send (A)
6	CC (A)	DCE Ready (A)
7	AB	Signal Ground
8	CF (A)	Received Line Signal Detector (A)
9	DD (B)	Receiver Signal Element Timing, DCE Source (B)
10	CF (B)	Received Line Signal Detector (B)
11	DA (B)	Transmit Signal Element Timing, DTE Source (B)
12	DB (B)	Transmit Signal Element Timing, DCE Source (B)
13	CB (B)	Clear to Send (B)
14	BA (B)	Transmitted Data (B)
15	DB (A)	Transmit Signal Element Timing, DCE Source (A)
16	BB (B)	Received Data (B)
17	DD (A)	Receiver Signal Element Timing, DCE Source (A)
18	LL	Local Loopback
19	CA (B)	Request to Send (B)
20	CD (A)	DTE Ready (B)
21	RL	Remote Loopback
22	CC (B)	DCE Ready (B)
23	CD (B)	DTE Ready (B)
24	DA (A)	Transmit Signal Element Timing, DTE Source (A)
25	TM	Test Mode

Notes: EIA-530 uses electrical characteristics of
EIA-422-A or EIA-423-A.

A 25-pin connector per ISO 2110 (DB-25) is used.

Figure I–3. EIA-530 *(Courtesy of Hill Associates Inc., © 1992)*

EIA 530			EIA-449	
Circuit, Name, and Mnemonic		Con-tact	Con-tact	Circuit, Name, and Mnemonic
Shield	---	1	1	Shield
Transmitted Data	BA (A)	2	4	SD (A) Send Data
	BA (B)	14	22	SD (B)
Received Data	BB (A)	3	6	RD (A) Receive Data
	BB (B)	16	24	RD (B)
Request to Send	CA (A)	4	7	RS (A) Request to Send
	CA (B)	19	25	RS (B)
Clear to Send	CB (A)	5	9	CS (A) Clear to Send
	CB (B)	13	27	CS (B)
DCE Ready	CC (A)	6	11	DM (A) Data Mode
	CC (B)	22	29	DM (B)
DTE Ready	CD (A)	20	12	TR (A) Terminal Ready
	CD (B)	23	30	TR (B)
Signal Ground	AB	7	19	SG Signal Ground
Received Line	CF (A)	8	13	RR (A) Receiver Ready
Signal Detector	CF (B)	10	31	RR (B)
Transmit Signal	DB (A)	15	5	ST (A) Send Timing
Element Timing (DCE Source)	DB (B)	12	23	ST (B)
Receiver Signal	DD (A)	17	8	RT (A) Receive Timing
Element Timing (DTE Source)	DD (B)	9	26	RT (B)
Local Loopback	LL	18	10	LL Local Loopback
Remote Loopback	RL	21	14	RL Remote Loopback
Transmit Signal	DA (A)	24	17	TT (A) Terminal Timing
Element Timing (DTE Source)	DA (B)	11	35	TT (B)
Test Mode	TM	25	18	TM Test Mode

Figure I–4. Interconnecting EIA-530 with EIA-449 *(Courtesy of Hill Associates Inc., © 1992)*

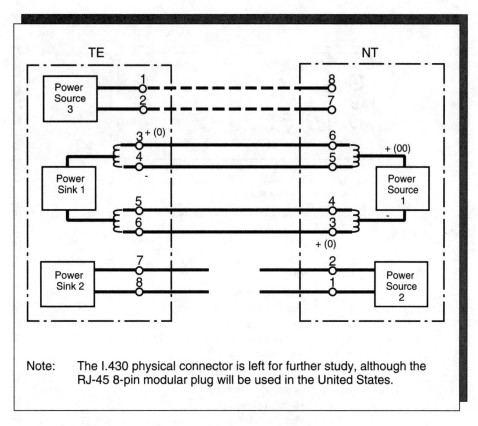

Note: The I.430 physical connector is left for further study, although the RJ-45 8-pin modular plug will be used in the United States.

Figure I–5. ITU-T Recommendation I.430 (ISDN Basic Rate Interface)
(Courtesy of Hill Associates Inc., © 1992)

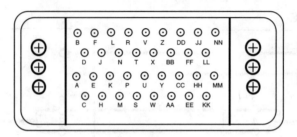

Pin	Circuit Name
A	Chassis Ground
B	Signal Ground
C	Request to Send
D	Clear to Send
E	Data Set Ready
F	Receive Line Signal Detect
P	Transmit Data (A)
R	Received Data (A)
S	Transmit Data (B)
T	Received Data (B)
U	Terminal Timing (A)
V	Receive Timing (A)
W	Terminal Timing (B)
X	Receive Timing (B)
Y	Transmit Timing (A)
AA	Transmit Timing (B)

Notes:

Control signals conform to CCITT Recommendation V.28
A 34-pin connector per ISO 2593 is utilized.

Figure I–6. ITU-T Recommendation V.35 *(Courtesy of Hill Associates Inc., © 1992)*

Circuit	Name
G	Signal Ground or Common Return
Ga	DTE Common Return
T	Transmit
R	Receive
C	Control
I	Indication
S	Signal Element Timing
B	Byte Timing

Notes: X.21 uses electrical characteristics from X.26 (V.10)
          or X.27 (V.11)
        A 15-pin connector per ISO 4903 (DB-15) is used.

Figure I-7. ITU-T Recommendation X.21 *(Courtesy of Hill Associates Inc., © 1992)*

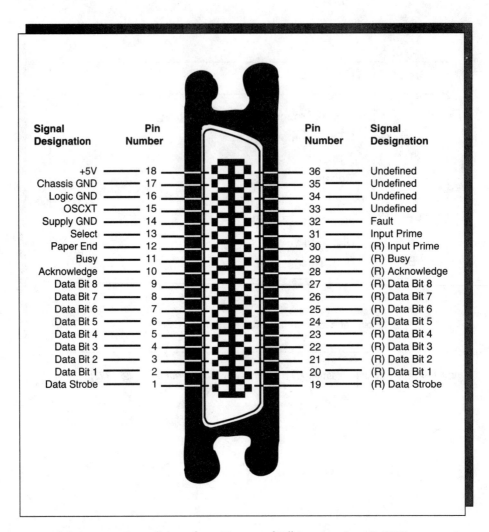

Signal Designation	Pin Number		Pin Number	Signal Designation
+5V	18		36	Undefined
Chassis GND	17		35	Undefined
Logic GND	16		34	Undefined
OSCXT	15		33	Undefined
Supply GND	14		32	Fault
Select	13		31	Input Prime
Paper End	12		30	(R) Input Prime
Busy	11		29	(R) Busy
Acknowledge	10		28	(R) Acknowledge
Data Bit 8	9		27	(R) Data Bit 8
Data Bit 7	8		26	(R) Data Bit 7
Data Bit 6	7		25	(R) Data Bit 6
Data Bit 5	6		24	(R) Data Bit 5
Data Bit 4	5		23	(R) Data Bit 4
Data Bit 3	4		22	(R) Data Bit 3
Data Bit 2	3		21	(R) Data Bit 2
Data Bit 1	2		20	(R) Data Bit 1
Data Strobe	1		19	(R) Data Strobe

Figure I–8. Centronics® parallel interface *(Courtesy of Hill Associates Inc., © 1992)*

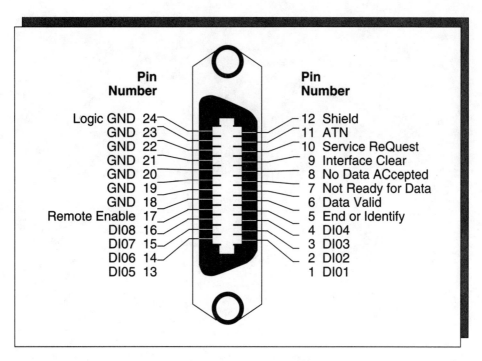

Figure I–9. IEEE-488 Digital Interface for Programmable Instrumentation
(Courtesy of Hill Associates Inc., © 1992)

Trademarks

TAXI and TAXIchip are trademarks of Advanced Micro Devices, Inc.

Apple, the Apple logo and AppleTalk are registered trademarks of Apple Computer, Inc.

ARCNET is a trademark of Datapoint Corporation.

Banyan, the Banyan logo, and VINES are registered trademarks of Banyan Systems Inc.

DEC and DECnet are trademarks, and Ethernet is a registered trademark of Digital Equipment Corporation.

HP is a trademark of Hewlett-Packard Company.

Ethernet is a registered trademark of Intel Corporation.

NetBIOS is a trademark of International Business Machines Corporation; and IBM is a registered trademark of International Business Machines Corporation.

X and X Window System are trademarks of the Massachusetts Institute of Technology.

Microsoft and Windows are registered trademarks of Microsoft Corporation.

Network General and Sniffer Analyzer are trademarks of Network General Corporation.

IPX, NetWare, Novell, and SPX are trademarks, and Novell is a registered trademark of Novell, Inc.

Motif is a trademark of the Open Software Foundation, Inc.

BSD is a trademark of the Regents of the University of California.

UNIX is a registered trademark of UNIX System Laboratories Inc.

Xerox and XNS are trademarks, and Ethernet and Xerox are registered trademarks of Xerox Corporation.

All other trademarks are the property of their respective owners.

Index

A

AAL1, 289, 317, 366

AAL1 Segmentation and Reassembly Sublayer, 317

AAL2, 289, 318, 319

AAL3/4, 289, 319, 372, 377

AAL3/4 Convergence Sublayer (SSCS), 320

AAL3/4 Segmentation and Reassembly (SAR) Sublayer, 322, 388

AAL5, 293, 323, 324, 382, 389

AAL5 Common Part Convergence Sublayer, 350

Abstract Syntax, 393

Abstract Syntax Notation 1 (ASN.1), 393

Access

    Connection, 40

    Control Field (SIP), 185, 215

    DQDB, 171, 196

    Rate, 48

    Unit, 180, 181, 186

Address

    ATM Formats, 336, 337

    E.164, 338, 357

    Extended, 166

    Extension bit, 231

    Field, 44, 63, 122, 142, 212, 231

    Field Extension, 44

    Group Address, 207

    Individual address, 207

    Multicast address, 207

    Resolution Protocol (ARP), 239

    Screens, 208

    SMDS, 207, 208

    Source Service Access Point, 351

    Subfield (SIP), 213

    Type field, 208

    Type Subfield (SIP), 212

ADD PARTY ACKNOWLEDGE Message, 340, 348

ADD PARTY Message, 340, 347, 348

ADD PARTY REJECT Message, 340, 348

Administrative Authority (AA) field (ATM), 338

Advanced Micro Devices Inc., 286

AIS, 223, 229, 326, 329

AISS, 222, 228

Alarm Indication Signal (AIS), 223, 229, 316, 329

Alarm Indication Signal Second (AISS), 222, 228

Alignment field (ATM), 322, 378

American National Standards Institute (ANSI), 7

Ameritech, 31, 171

Analysis

    AAL1, 366

    AAL3/4, 372, 377, 387, 388

    AAL5, 382, 389

    ATM, 359, 387

    Bandwidth Requirements, 126

    Data Exchange Interface with SIP_L3 PDUs, 259

    DS3 PLCP, 364

    Encapsulating LAN Data Within T1.618 Frames, 113

    Encapsulating LAN Traffic over SMDS, 252

T

521

majordomo @
matmos.hpl.hp.com

subscribe ip-atm